THE CREATIVE CURRICULUM® FOR PRESCHOOL

COLLEGE EDITION

Diane Trister Dodge

Laura J. Colker

Cate Heroman

Toni S. Bickart, Contributing Author

Teaching Strategies® Inc.
Washington, DC

Editor: Sybil Wolin
Cover: Based on an original design by Kathi Dunn
Book design and computer illustrations: Carla Uriona
Illustrations: Jennifer Barrett O'Connell

Teaching Strategies, Inc.
P.O. Box 42243
Washington, DC 20015
www.TeachingStrategies.com
ISBN: 978-1-933021-67-6

Teaching Strategies and *The Creative Curriculum* names and logos are
registered trademarks of Teaching Strategies, Inc., Washington, DC.

Library of Congress Cataloging-in-Publication Data

Dodge, Diane Trister.
   The creative curriculum for preschool / Diane Trister
Dodge, Laura J. Colker, Cate Heroman ; Toni S. Bickart,
contributing author. -- College ed.
   p. cm.
   Includes bibliographical references and index.
   ISBN 978-1-933021-67-6

   1. Education, Preschool--Curricula--Textbooks.
2. Education, Preschool--Activity programs--Textbooks.
I. Colker, Laura J. (Laura Jean) II. Heroman, Cate.
III. Bickart, Toni S. IV. Title.

   LB1140.4.D633 2008
   372.11--dc22
                              2007051234

Printed and bound in the United States of America
2012 2011 2010   2 3 4 5

Dedication

to Helen Hollingshed Taylor

This edition of *The Creative Curriculum* is dedicated to Helen H. Taylor, a dear friend, colleague, and mentor who in so many ways helped to shape and inspire my work and vision. It was under Helen's leadership of the Washington, D.C., Model Cities Centers in the early 1970s that *The Creative Curriculum*'s environmental approach first began taking shape. Helen, who later became Executive Director of the National Child Day Care Association, was always open to any innovative idea that promised to improve the quality of her program and, thus, the lives of children and families. She supported my interest in demonstrating the impact of room arrangement on children's behavior; collaborated with Laura Colker and me on an innovative grant to adapt *The Creative Curriculum* to family child care settings; and involved us in working with the District of Columbia Public Schools to extend developmentally appropriate practice into the primary grades.

We have chosen to honor Helen because she honored all of us with her unswerving support for children and families. Helen devoted her entire career to public service and was committed to the early childhood profession. Her dedication to improving the lives of low-income families and children went far beyond Washington, D.C. From 1994, until her death in 2000, Helen served as Associate Commissioner of the Head Start Bureau (DHHS). She worked tirelessly to extend the reach of Head Start to serve more children and families while also improving the quality and impact of the program's services. Helen understood the difference a quality program can make, and she never ceased in her efforts to ensure that early childhood programs lived up to these standards.

Both professionally and personally, Helen personified the ideals that my co-authors and I have sought to reflect in our writing. I am eternally grateful to Helen.

Diane Trister Dodge

Acknowledgments

When we began the process of updating *The Creative Curriculum*, we never anticipated what a challenging and exciting journey it would become. Along the way, we worked with many supportive and wise colleagues who added to our ideas, enriched our understanding, and helped us to shape our message. If this new edition contributes to improving the quality of early childhood programs, we must share the credit with many special people.

We probably wouldn't have begun this task were it not for our readers—the teachers and administrators in programs across the country. They used our book, shared their successes and frustrations, and helped us to better understand the real world of teaching today. The Teaching Strategies staff development specialists—our voices in the field—regularly gave us their best thinking on what was working and what more was needed.

We would like to thank the following people for their very thoughtful and insightful reviews of the first draft: Mindy Brookshire, Geralyn Jacobs, Candy Jones, Jean Monroe, Peter Pizzolongo, Mia Plehn, Michele Plutro, Charlotte Stetson, Monica Vacca, and Jan Whitney. Thanks also to Karen Kirk for providing specific strategies to include children with special needs, Elaisa Sanchez-Gosnell and Sharon Yandian for helping us with issues related to English Language Learners, Bonnie Blagojevic, for sharing her expertise with us on the chapter on computers, and Whit Hayslip, for articulating so passionately what best practice looks like for all children.

Books are written by authors and refined by editors. Our deepest appreciation goes to Sybil Wolin, a developmental psychologist and educator who became so convinced of the value of the work we were doing that she put aside her own work to become our content editor. Sybil challenged us when we weren't clear in our writing, instructed us to rewrite and reorganize chapters, and gave us advice from her own years of experience. She is an exceptional editor and we are deeply grateful for her commitment to improving our book. We are equally indebted to Toni Bickart, editor in chief at Teaching Strategies, who managed the entire editing process. She ultimately made so many substantial contributions that we have listed her as a contributing author. We also thank the following people who assisted us in the editing process: Jean Bernard, Emily Kohn, Rachel Friedlander Tickner, and Judy Wohlberg.

The beautiful illustrations of Jennifer Barrett O'Connell and graphic design by Carla Uriona, production coordinator, make the book engaging and our words more accessible. We are grateful to Terri Rue-Woods and Kylie Breedlove for their help with production. We thank Larry Bram, marketing director, and Fran Simon, marketing/communications manager, for keeping us focused and getting the word out about this book.

Finally, we thank our families, our friends, and every staff member of Teaching Strategies who put up with our preoccupation with this work, which kept us busy for many late nights and weekends. They understood how important this work was to us and gave us their full support. We know they share our joy in getting *The Creative Curriculum for Preschool* into the hands of the people who will bring it to life in their classrooms.

Table of Contents

PART 1

Introduction xiii

Foundation 1

Chapter 1–How Children Develop and Learn 17

What Preschool Children Are Like 18
Areas of Development 18
Ages and Stages of Development 23

Individual Differences 27
Gender 27
Temperament 28
Interests 30
Learning Styles 31
Life Experiences 33
Culture 34
Special Needs 35
English Language Learners 38

The Developmental Continuum 42
What the *Developmental Continuum* Looks Like 43

Conclusion and References 59

Chapter 2–The Learning Environment 61

Setting Up and Maintaining the Classroom 62
Establishing Interest Areas 62
Other Aspects of the Physical Setting 67
Caring for the Classroom and Children's Work 73
Evaluating the Effectiveness of the Physical Environment 76

Establishing a Structure for Each Day 82
Daily Events 82
The Daily Schedule 92
Weekly Planning 97
Preparing for the First Few Days 100

Creating a Classroom Community 102
Promoting Positive Relationships in the Classroom 102
Developing Rules for a Classroom Community 108
Teaching Social Problem-Solving Skills 110
Responding to Challenging Behavior 116

Conclusion and References 123

Chapter 3–What Children Learn 125

Literacy 126
Components of Literacy 126
Connecting Literacy Content, Teaching, and Learning 132

Mathematics 134
Components of Mathematics 134
Connecting Math Content, Teaching, and Learning 140

Science 142
Components of Science 142
Connecting Science Content, Teaching, and Learning 144

Social Studies... 146
Components of Social Studies..................................... 146
Connecting Social Studies Content, Teaching, and Learning........... 150

The Arts... 152
Components of the Arts 152
Connecting Content in the Arts, Teaching, and Learning................. 154

Technology.. 156
Components of Technology 156
Connecting Technology Content, Teaching, and Learning............... 159

Process Skills.. 161

Conclusion and References.. 163

Chapter 4–The Teacher's Role   165

Observing Children.. 166
How, When, What to Observe..................................... 166
Being Objective... 167
Using the *Developmental Continuum*...................... 169

Guiding Children's Learning... 173
Using a Range of Teaching Approaches 173
Adapting Instruction to Include All Children........... 179
Working With Groups of Children 183
Promoting Learning in Interest Areas....................... 187
Exploring Content in Interest Areas 188
Integrating Learning Through Studies 190

Assessing Children's Learning...................................... 199
Collecting Facts 199
Analyzing and Evaluating the Collected Facts 204
Using What You've Learned to Plan........................... 206

Conclusion and References.. 209

Chapter 5–The Family's Role   211

Getting to Know Families 212
Appreciating Differences... 212
Using Initial Contacts to Learn About Families 214

Making Families Feel Welcome 218
Creating a Welcoming Environment 218
Introducing Your Program... 220
Building Trust 221
Reaching Out to All Family Members 222

Communicating With Families...................................... 223
Daily Exchanges 223
Formal Communications 224

Partnering With Families on Children's Learning 225
Offering a Variety of Ways to Be Involved 225
Making Classroom Participation Meaningful 228
Meeting With Families to Share Information and Plan.............. 231

Responding to Challenging Situations....................... 235
Families Under Stress 235
Dealing With Misunderstandings.............................. 236
Addressing Differences Constructively 239

Conclusion and References.. 241

Chapter 6–Blocks   243

How Block Play Promotes Development 243
Connecting Block Play With Curriculum Objectives........................... 244

Creating an Environment for Block Play 246
Selecting Materials.. 247
Displaying Blocks and Props 251
Cleanup—A Special Challenge 252

What Children Learn in the Block Area....................................... 253

The Teacher's Role 255
Observing and Responding to Individual Children............................ 255
Interacting With Children in the Block Area 261
Frequently Asked Questions About Blocks.. 267

A Letter to Families About Block Play 269

Chapter 7–Dramatic Play   271

How Dramatic Play Promotes Development......................... 271
Connecting Dramatic Play With Curriculum Objectives 272

Creating an Environment for Dramatic Play 274
Selecting and Displaying Materials 275
Creating New Settings for Dramatic Play 276

What Children Learn in the Dramatic Play Area 280

The Teacher's Role... 282
Observing and Responding to Individual Children............................ 282
Interacting With Children During Dramatic Play 287
Frequently Asked Questions About Dramatic Play............................. 291

A Letter to Families About Dramatic Play............................... 293

Chapter 8–Toys and Games   295

How Playing With Toys and Games Promotes Development........ 295
Connecting Toys and Games With Curriculum Objectives 296

Creating an Environment for Toys and Games..................... 298
Selecting Materials.. 299
Displaying and Caring for Toys and Games 303

What Children Learn in the Toys and Games Area............. 304

The Teacher's Role... 306
Observing and Responding to Individual Children............................ 306
Interacting With Children in the Toys and Games Area 310
Frequently Asked Questions About Toys and Games......................... 313

A Letter to Families About Toys and Games 315

Chapter 9–Art   317

How Art Promotes Development..317
Connecting Art With Curriculum Objectives..318

Creating an Environment for Art...320
Selecting Materials..322
Displaying and Storing Art Materials 332

What Children Learn in the Art Area..334

The Teacher's Role..336
Observing and Responding to Individual Children.............................337
Interacting With Children in the Art Area..341
Frequently Asked Questions About Art 347

A Letter to Families About Art..349

Chapter 10–Library   351

How the Library Area Promotes Development....................................351
Connecting Play in the Library Area With Curriculum Objectives ..352

Creating an Environment for the Library Area...................................354
Selecting Materials..355
Displaying and Caring for Materials 360

What Children Learn in the Library Area 362

The Teacher's Role..365
Observing and Responding to Individual Children.............................365
Interacting With Children in the Library Area...370
Frequently Asked Questions About the Library Area 376

A Letter to Families About the Library Area...379

Chapter 11–Discovery   381

How the Discovery Area Promotes Development 381
Connecting the Discovery Area With Curriculum Objectives...........382

Creating an Environment for Discovery...384
Selecting Materials..385
Displaying Materials 387

What Children Learn in the Discovery Area...391

The Teacher's Role 394
Observing and Responding to Individual Children.............................394
Interacting With Children in the Discovery Area 397
Frequently Asked Questions About the Discovery Area....................400

A Letter to Families About the Discovery Area...................................401

PART

Chapter 12–Sand and Water — 403

How Sand and Water Play Promote Development............................403
Connecting Sand and Water Play With Curriculum Objectives........404

Creating an Environment for Sand and Water Play..........................406
Selecting Equipment and Materials..407
Displaying Materials...410

What Children Learn in the Sand and Water Area...........................411

The Teacher's Role..413
Observing and Responding to Individual Children............................413
Interacting With Children in the Sand and Water Area....................416
Frequently Asked Questions About Sand and Water Play................419

A Letter to Families About Sand and Water Play.............................421

Chapter 13–Music and Movement — 423

How Music and Movement Promote Development.........................423
Connecting Music and Movement With Curriculum Objectives.....424

Creating an Environment for Music and Movement.......................426
Selecting and Displaying Materials..427

What Children Learn From Music and Movement............................428

The Teacher's Role..430
Observing and Responding to Individual Children............................430
Interacting With Children During Music and Movement Activities...434
Frequently Asked Questions About Music and Movement................440

A Letter to Families About Music and Movement............................441

Chapter 14–Cooking — 443

How Cooking Experiences Promote Development...........................443
Connecting Cooking With Curriculum Objectives...............................444

Creating an Environment for Cooking..446
Selecting Materials..447
Displaying Cooking Equipment and Tools..449
Special Health and Safety Considerations...450

What Children Learn in the Cooking Area...453

The Teacher's Role..456
Observing and Responding to Individual Children............................456
Interacting With Children in the Cooking Area....................................459
Frequently Asked Questions About Cooking...468

A Letter to Families About Cooking..469

Chapter 15–Computers   471

How Computer Play Promotes Development................................ 471
Connecting Computer Play With Curriculum Objectives 472

Creating an Environment for Using Computers............................ 474
Selecting Materials.. 475

What Children Learn From Using Computers 482

The Teacher's Role... 484
Observing and Responding to Individual Children............................ 484
Interacting With Children in the Computer Area 487
Frequently Asked Questions About Computers 489

A Letter to Families About Computers.. 491

Chapter 16–Outdoors   493

How Outdoor Play Promotes Development.................................. 493
Connecting Outdoor Play With Curriculum Objectives 494

Creating and Using the Outdoor Environment............................ 496
Basic Outdoor Spaces and Equipment... 496
Playground Structures 505
Special Considerations 509

What Children Learn Outdoors 511

The Teacher's Role... 514
Observing and Responding to Individual Children............................ 514
Interacting With Children Outdoors.. 517
Frequently Asked Questions About Outdoor Play............................. 521

A Letter to Families About Outdoor Play....................................... 522

References

Part 2 References.. 523

Appendix

Weekly Planning Form (Blank) 526

Weekly Planning Form (Filled In)... 528

Goals & Objectives... 530

Index   531

Introduction

Early childhood education is an exciting and rewarding profession. By working with young children before they enter kindergarten, you have an opportunity to help build a solid foundation for their success in school and in life. Children who attend high-quality preschool programs are more likely to develop the skills and characteristics that are essential to school readiness. What happens every day in a preschool program is so important that it cannot be left to chance. *The Creative Curriculum®️ for Preschool* provides all of the information teachers need to provide a high-quality program for children ages 3–5.

The Creative Curriculum has a long history. First published in 1978, subsequent editions have responded to new research, mandates, and what we believe teachers need to provide an exciting and appropriate program for preschool children. We have learned so much in recent years, in part due to the publication of scholarly research and reports such as *Eager to Learn* (Bowman, Donovan, & Burns, 2001), *From Neurons to Neighborhoods* (Shonkoff & Phillips, 2000), *A Good Beginning: Sending America's Children to School With the Social and Emotional Competence They Need to Succeed* (Peth-Pierce, 2000), *Preventing Reading Difficulties in Young Children* (Snow, Burns, & Griffin, 1998), and the *National Reading Panel Report* (National Institute of Child Health and Human Development, 2000). These reports have expanded our understanding of how children develop and learn. They outline teaching approaches that are most likely to ensure children's success and ways to address academic content appropriately with preschool children. We also recognize that programs are being held accountable for demonstrating positive outcomes and that teachers are being asked to make sure that children are learning important content and skills.

Along with these new developments in the field, our own work with programs across the country led us to focus on helping teachers to observe children more purposefully and to use their observations to plan for each child and the whole group. We realized that we needed to show more clearly how teachers could use a variety of teaching strategies and be intentional about children's learning. And finally, we knew that early learning standards offered us an opportunity to enrich the curriculum if we could demonstrate how to integrate content learning into everyday experiences.

The Creative Curriculum for Preschool is a comprehensive curriculum that addresses all aspects of teaching 3- to 5-year-old children. The curriculum defines *what* to teach; *why* the content and skills are appropriate learning expectations for young children; and *where*, *when*, and *how* to teach effectively. It is linked to an assessment system so that teachers can use what they learn from assessment to plan and guide instruction. The following diagram illustrates the five components of *The Creative Curriculum*, how they rest on a solid foundation of theory and research, and the curriculum's focus on interest areas.

How the Book Is Organized

We start with the Foundation—the theory and research behind *The Creative Curriculum*. Our approach is based on the work of Piaget, Maslow, Erikson, Smilansky, Vygotsky, and Gardner, as well as new information about learning and the brain and resiliency. We explain the influence of research and theory on *The Creative Curriculum*, our view of children, and the recommendations we make to teachers. The book is organized in two parts.

Part 1: The Organizational Structure of *The Creative Curriculum* (chapters 1–5) presents the five components of *The Creative Curriculum* and gives you the information you need to set up your program.

- **How Children Develop and Learn:** what preschool children are like in terms of their social/emotional, physical, cognitive, and language development, and the characteristics and experiences that make each child unique. We present our goals and objectives for children and *The Creative Curriculum Developmental Continuum for Ages 3–5*, a tool for observing children's development and tracking their progress in relation to *The Creative Curriculum* objectives.

- **The Learning Environment:** the classroom structure that makes it possible for teachers to teach and children to learn. This includes how teachers set up and maintain interest areas in the classroom, establish schedules and routines, organize choice times and small- and large-group times, and create a classroom community in which children learn to get along with others and solve problems peacefully.

- **What Children Learn:** the body of knowledge included in national and state standards and research reports for six content areas—literacy, math, science, social studies, the arts, and technology—and the process skills children use to learn that content. We show how children learn content and skills through daily experiences.

- **The Teacher's Role:** how careful observations of children lead to a variety of instructional strategies to guide children's learning. We explain how teachers interact with children in interest areas, during small- and large-group instruction times, and as part of in-depth studies. We describe a systematic approach to assessment that enables teachers to learn about and plan for each child and the group.

- **The Family's Role:** the benefits of developing a partnership with every family and working together to support children's optimal development and learning. This last component includes getting to know families, welcoming them and communicating with them regularly, partnering on their children's learning, and responding to challenging situations.

Part 2: Interest Areas (chapters 6–16) applies the five components of the organizational structure of *The Creative Curriculum* to 11 areas—Blocks, Dramatic Play, Toys and Games, Art, Library, Discovery, Sand and Water, Music and Movement, Cooking, Computers, and Outdoors. We describe the various materials that meet the developmental needs of young children and enhance learning and teaching in each of these interest areas. We make connections between *The Creative Curriculum*'s 50 objectives and academic content and show how teachers guide and assess children's learning. Each chapter ends with a letter to families on ways they can support children's learning at school and at home.

Throughout the book you will find examples of how two teachers, Ms. Tory and Mr. Alvarez, work with a group of 18 preschool children. We made up this group, which we call "our class," to bring to life the teaching strategies we describe and to personalize the approach.

Using *The Creative Curriculum for Preschool in Action* DVD

Teachers and administrators often ask, "Where can I see a classroom in which the teachers implement *The Creative Curriculum* well?" *The Creative Curriculum for Preschool in Action* DVD responds to this question. This special college edition of *The Creative Curriculum for Preschool* includes a copy of the DVD. Its nine sections show implementation in a variety of settings, including public school, Head Start, child care, and teacher-training programs.

We are fortunate that six teachers and their assistants from different programs allowed us into their classrooms to document their experience, expertise, and insights. Each classroom has between 15 and 20 children from diverse backgrounds and with a range of learning needs. You will see children who are learning English as their second language, children with disabilities, children with a wide range of abilities, and children with various socioeconomic and cultural backgrounds. The diversity of the teachers, children, and programs shown in this DVD will help you understand how *The Creative Curriculum* can be used to meet the specific needs of the children in your program. We hope it also will inspire you to explore the curriculum further to continually enhance your work with young children and their families.

References

Bowman, B. T., Donovan, M. S., & Burns, M. S. (Eds.). (2000). *Eager to learn: Educating our preschoolers.* (Committee on Early Childhood Pedagogy, Commission on Behavioral and Social Sciences and Education, National Research Council) Washington, DC: National Academy Press.

National Institute of Child Health and Human Development. (2000). *Report of the National Reading Panel. Teaching children to read: An evidence-based assessment of the scientific research literature on reading and its implications for reading instruction: Reports of the subgroups* (NIH Publication No. 00-4754). Washington, DC: U.S. Government Printing Office.

Peth-Pierce, R. (2000). *A good beginning: Sending America's children to school with the social and emotional competence they need to succeed.* Bethesda, MD: Children's Mental Health Foundations and Agencies Network.

Shonkoff, J. P., & Phillips, D. A. (Eds.). (2000). *From neurons to neighborhoods: The science of early childhood development.* (Committee on Integrating the Science of Early Childhood Development, Board on Children, Youth, and Families) Washington, DC: National Academy Press.

Snow, C. E., Burns, M. S., & Griffin, P. (Eds.). (1998). *Preventing reading difficulties in young children.* (Committee on the Prevention of Reading Difficulties in Young Children, Commission on Behavioral and Social Sciences and Education, National Research Council) Washington, DC: National Academy Press.

Foundation

Theory and Research Behind
The Creative Curriculum

Maslow

Erikson

Learning and the Brain

Piaget

Vygotsky

Gardner

Smilansky

Learning and Resiliency

Until the 20th century, little scientific attention was given to studying how children grow and develop. In the past 75 years, however, research has provided a great deal of information about childhood as a separate and distinct stage of life with its own characteristics. The application of this body of knowledge to teaching is called developmentally appropriate practice. *The Creative Curriculum* shows you how to implement developmentally appropriate practice in your preschool classroom.

Put simply, developmentally appropriate practice means teaching in ways that match the way children develop and learn. A definition of developmentally appropriate practice was first advanced in a position paper issued by the National Association for the Education of Young Children (NAEYC) in 1987 and updated and revised in 1997. The definition is based on an extensive review of the literature about child development and learning with input from knowledgeable practitioners.

According to NAEYC, developmentally appropriate practice provides children with opportunities to learn and practice newly acquired skills. It offers challenges just beyond the level of their present mastery and it takes place "in the context of a community where children are safe and valued, where their physical needs are met, and where they feel psychologically secure" (Bredekamp & Copple 1997, pp. 14–15).

In our application of developmentally appropriate practice, we have sought to highlight the important balance between applying a general knowledge of child development with the particular knowledge a teacher gains by forming a relationship with each child and family. We have also incorporated new information about the content in literacy, math, science, social studies, the arts, and technology that preschool children can and should learn. The Curriculum describes each subject area and shows how to teach it in ways that support children's academic progress while respecting the way they grow and develop.

In the following pages, we summarize the major theories behind developmentally appropriate practice and *The Creative Curriculum*. We tell how each influences the design of the Curriculum, our view of children, and the recommendations we make to teachers.

Maslow: Basic Needs and Learning

Abraham Maslow described a hierarchy of needs common to all human beings. The hierarchy demonstrates that basic needs must be met before children are able to focus on learning.

Physiological needs are hunger, thirst, and bodily comfort. Because a hungry child has difficulty focusing on learning, many early childhood programs provide breakfast, snacks, and lunches. Similarly, children with medical concerns or physical disabilities may require physical supports or special care to function successfully in school.

Safety is security and freedom from danger. When children know they are protected and that no harm will come to them, they feel free to reach out to others and explore their environment. Children with disabilities may require extra attention to meet their needs and feel safe. For example, a child with a visual impairment may require help orienting to the setting of the classroom, and one with physical impairments may require environmental adaptations.

Belongingness is the sense of being comfortable with and connected to others that results from receiving acceptance, respect, and love. Connectedness or belongingness, in turn, promotes learning. However, for some young children feeling that they belong is not easy. Often they have trouble believing that they are worthy of being loved. As a result, they may exhibit behavior that tests acceptance, or they act out, attack others, or behave in ways that show they deserve to be rejected. These children benefit from being around adults who are consistent and caring, not harsh and judgmental.

Esteem is self-respect and respect from others. Esteem emerges from daily experiences that give children the opportunity to discover they are competent and capable learners. If children's experiences are predominantly successful and positive, their sense of self grows. If they are predominantly unsuccessful, their sense of self suffers. A supportive environment that offers children new tasks they can master, and that recognizes their efforts, helps children see themselves as respectable, capable individuals.

In keeping with Maslow's theory, the first priority of *The Creative Curriculum* is to meet the basic needs of children. While the Curriculum recognizes that teachers can do little to change the circumstances of children whose basic needs are not met outside the classroom, it does accept the challenges these children pose when they are in school.

Maslow:
There is a hierarchy of needs common to all human beings.

Inside the classroom, the *Creative Curriculum* teacher creates an atmosphere in which children are safe, feel emotionally secure, and have a sense of belonging. It describes activities and teaching strategies that are challenging but within children's reach. It also suggests giving children choices and a role in determining how they will learn. These practices—which are core to the Curriculum—help children to feel competent, make decisions, and direct their own learning.

Erikson: The Emotions and Learning

Erik Erikson's theory of the "Eight Stages of Man" identifies a sequence of issues that need to be resolved for healthy development to occur. According to Erikson, each stage builds on the success of earlier stages. The stages children pass through before and during preschool are: trust vs. mistrust (infancy), autonomy vs. shame and doubt (ages 1–3), and initiative vs. guilt (ages 3–5). For each, Erikson describes what adults need to provide in order to help children meet the challenges facing them.

Trust vs. Mistrust. Trust involves believing that the world around you is safe, reliable, and responsive to your needs. Infants who receive consistent and loving care learn trust. Infants who cry and get no response, who are not fed when they are hungry, and who are not comforted when they are hurt, develop mistrust. In a *Creative Curriculum* classroom teachers establish a reliable, safe atmosphere that reinforces the trust children learn at home and helps children who mistrust because of difficult experiences.

The Creative Curriculum shows teachers how to

- know and develop a positive relationship with each child

- follow a consistent schedule

- carry through on announced plans and promises

Autonomy vs. Shame and Doubt. Autonomy, or independence, is acting with will and control. It involves a sense of one's power that is built on the foundation of trust described in Erikson's first stage of development. Children develop autonomy when adults give them a chance to do things on their own. When adults make excessive demands or level criticism that devalues children's efforts, they develop shame and doubt. In *The Creative Curriculum*, teachers take care to help children become autonomous by providing structure while allowing them to regulate their own behavior. Teachers honor children's efforts to become independent and foster their sense of competence.

Erikson:
A sequence of issues need to be resolved for healthy development to occur.

The Curriculum shows teachers how to

- set up an environment where children can find and return materials on their own

- provide appropriate play materials that support and challenge children's abilities

- help children express their feelings and resolve conflicts in constructive ways

- provide appropriate real-world responsibilities and jobs

- encourage children to see tasks through to completion

Initiative vs. Guilt. Developing initiative means responding positively to challenges, taking on responsibilities, enjoying accomplishments, and becoming purposeful. In this stage, children direct their energy toward tasks and begin to develop a sense of future possibilities. Children with initiative are eager to try out new materials and ideas. When adults belittle children's work, guilt sets in. Because resolving initiative vs. guilt is the primary achievement of the preschool years, *The Creative Curriculum* places a high priority on creating a classroom environment that encourages children to experiment, explore, and pursue their own interests.

The Creative Curriculum encourages children to experiment, explore, and pursue their own interests.

The Curriculum shows teachers how to

- offer children choices

- give children ample opportunities for creative expression

- allow children freedom to explore the environment

- permit children to get messy during play

- encourage children to work independently

- value children's ideas

- promote problem solving and appropriate risk taking

By taking into account the first two stages of development in Erikson's scheme, which children typically negotiate before entering preschool, *The Creative Curriculum* can reinforce early positive growth. At the same time, it also can remediate the difficulties of children whose earliest years were less supportive of positive growth. The focus in the Curriculum on the third stage, initiative, opens the door to lifelong learning.

Learning and the Brain

Findings from research on learning and the brain provide concrete evidence of how and when children learn best. Recent innovations in medical technology have led to new insights. Here are some of the elements of brain research that have informed *The Creative Curriculum*.

What We Know From Brain Research	Implications for Teachers
Learning is not a matter of nature vs. nurture; it is both. We used to think that heredity (what a person is born with) was more important than environment (what he or she is exposed to) in determining how much a person learns. In fact, both have a major role to play.	IQ is not as fixed as we once thought. All children benefit from rich experiences in early childhood. *Creative Curriculum* teachers can have a profound influence on all children's learning.
The human brain grows as a result of learning and experience. Learning changes the physical structure of the brain. When a new skill or concept is learned, a brain connection (known as a synapse) is formed.	During the first five years, trillions upon trillions of synapses are formed in response to learning experiences. In *The Creative Curriculum*, teachers provide many experiences for children, so more connections are made.
Learning needs to be reinforced. For a connection to become permanent, it must be used repeatedly. Connections that are not used eventually disappear.	Children need many different opportunities to practice new skills. Rather than jumping from one topic to another each week, *Creative Curriculum* teachers allow children to explore concepts over time.
Emotions play a significant role in learning. In order to learn, children need to feel safe and confident. Stress, on the other hand, can destroy brain cells and make learning more difficult.	Secure relationships with family members, teachers, and other significant people in a child's life are essential to learning. How *Creative Curriculum* teachers treat children is as important to learning as what they teach.
Nutrition, health, and physical activity affect learning. Movement stimulates connections in the brain. A well-balanced diet, sufficient sleep, and plenty of exercise support healthy brain growth.	Children are active learners. Daily exercise and time outdoors are essential for health and well-being. Many programs provide health screenings as well as meals and snacks.
The brain is very receptive to certain kinds of learning in the preschool years. Children learn emotional control, form attachments to others, and acquire language skills. Appropriate intervention can promote learning.	*Creative Curriculum* teachers focus on skills that are the foundation for all learning. The development of social/emotional competence and language skills is emphasized in *The Creative Curriculum*.

In all, brain research has found physical evidence to support what Maslow, Erikson, and other prominent theorists have taught us. It shows that the wiring in children's brains is positively affected when they are healthy and well fed, feel safe from threats, and have nurturing, stable relationships. The central role assigned to teachers' relationships with children in *The Creative Curriculum* is a direct outgrowth of this understanding.

Piaget: Logical Thinking and Reasoning

Jean Piaget observed how logical thinking unfolds. Like Erikson, Piaget divided development into stages. He showed that young children think differently from older children and that older children think differently from adults. For instance, take the concept of quantity. If you show young children two lumps of clay that are identical and ask if each lump has the same or different amount (quantity) of clay, they will say, "The same." If you then flatten out one lump like a pancake and ask the same question, they answer, "Different." Only as they grow do they learn conservation of matter, that a given amount of material stays the same no matter how it is reshaped or how many times it is divided.

Piaget taught that children refine their logic and construct an accurate understanding of the world by manipulating concrete objects. Working with objects of different sizes, shapes, and colors, they learn to sort, classify, compare, and sequence. Their knowledge grows as they experiment, make discoveries, and modify their earlier way of thinking to incorporate new insights. Piaget calls the process accommodation and assimilation. Accommodation is making observations that unseat early misconceptions in logic. Assimilation is establishing more sophisticated ways of thinking. Accommodation and assimilation create a positive growth cycle.

Piaget's theory identifies four stages of cognitive development: sensorimotor, preoperational, concrete operations, and formal operations. The sensorimotor stage and the preoperational stage are relevant to *The Creative Curriculum*. The concrete and formal operations stages typically apply to older children.

Piaget:
Logical thinking unfolds
in stages.

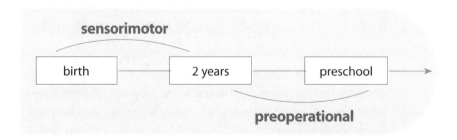

Sensorimotor. In the sensorimotor stage, which begins at birth and lasts until about age 2, babies learn by reacting to what they experience through their senses. They put a book in their mouth, kick a mobile with their feet, and pull at the string on a wheeled toy to discover what these objects can do. Eventually they learn that the book has a cover and pages, that kicking the mobile will cause it to spin, and that pulling on a string toy will bring it to them. They learn that mother from the back and mother from the front are the same mother, and that when a ball rolls under a chair and is out of view, it still exists.

Preoperational. At about age 2, children enter a stage that Piaget calls the preoperational period. During this stage, which lasts throughout the preschool years, children begin to notice properties in the objects they explore. However, their observations are limited to only one attribute of an object at a time. They focus on how things look rather than on using logic.

Returning to the clay example above, the child does not use logic to determine the amount of clay in each lump. He goes by what he sees and does not consider that making a pancake does not involve adding more clay. Rather, he responds to the increased surface of the pancake-shaped lump of clay, and concludes that an object that takes up more space on the table is greater in quantity than an object that is more compact. His learning task is to focus on two attributes, length and thickness, at the same time, and to keep in mind the original equality in the two lumps of clay before one was manipulated to change its shape.

In addition to their concreteness, preoperational children tend to see the world from their own point of view. They believe everyone thinks and feels as they do. Piaget calls this quality egocentrism. "Jonelle's not here today. She must be at her grandmother's house." When asked how she knows, the child responded, "I just went to see my Granny." Children even attribute their own feelings to objects: "The tire in our car went flat because it got sick." Here the child is not yet able to do what Piaget calls decentering—understanding perspectives different from his or her own.

Recent research has shown that Piaget's stages are more fluid and more tied to specific content knowledge than he had suggested originally. For instance, the same child who makes an error in logic based upon the changed appearance of a lump of clay might think logically and conclude that five pencils spread across a table and five pencils held close together by a rubber band are the same quantity. Nevertheless the sequential development of logic that Piaget identified still holds.

Babies learn by reacting to what they experience through their senses.

Children begin to notice properties in the objects they explore.

Although children go through the sequence at different rates, Piaget's descriptions of how children construct understanding are the foundation of the teaching techniques, selection of materials, and suggested activities in *The Creative Curriculum*.

Using what we have learned from Piaget, *The Creative Curriculum* structures the environment and activities based on children's cognitive development. By varying the complexity and levels of prompts, choices, comments, and questions for individual children, *Creative Curriculum* teachers invite children into a world of learning that they can manage. The Curriculum shows you how to help children

- create graphs showing the characteristics of objects according to their color, size, or type of closure

- look at objects and experiences from multiple perspectives

- arrange objects in order according to their length

- describe objects in terms of their features (e.g., cars are big and little, wide and narrow; papers are rough and smooth, light and heavy)

Teachers give children many opportunities to work with concrete objects and to discover the logic of how these objects behave.

In *The Creative Curriculum*, teachers give children many opportunities to work with concrete objects and to discover the logic of how these objects behave. They process children's experiences and encourage them to interact with one another and to learn about each other's perspectives. Respecting that most preschoolers are in the preoperational stage of development, teachers give children the time they need to master the world of concrete things and situations, and they open the door to the wider world of abstract thinking.

Vygotsky: Social Interaction and Learning

The work of Lev Vygotsky focuses on the social component in children's cognitive development. According to Vygotsky, children grow cognitively not only by acting on objects but also by interacting with adults and more knowledgeable peers. Teachers' verbal directions, physical assistance, and probing questioning help children improve skills and acquire knowledge. Peers who have advanced skills also can help other children grow and learn by modeling or providing verbal guidance.

According to Vygotsky, what children can do with the assistance of others gives a more accurate picture of their abilities than what they can do alone. Working with others gives children the chance to respond to someone else's examples, suggestions, comments, questions, and actions.

Vygotsky uses the term, Zone of Proximal Development (ZPD), to describe the range of a child's learning in a given situation. The lower limit of the Zone represents what a child can learn when working independently. The upper limit of the Zone represents what a child can learn by watching and talking to peers and teachers. With the support of others, the child organizes new information to fit with what he already knows. As a result, he can perform skills at a higher level than he could working on his own. This process of building knowledge and understandings is called scaffolding. A scaffold is a cognitive structure on which children climb from one ZPD to the next.

To facilitate scaffolding experiences, Vygotsky, like Piaget, believed that teachers need to become expert observers of children, understand their level of learning, and consider what next steps to take given children's individual needs. The teacher's most powerful tool in this process is asking questions and talking with children. This give-and-take fosters children's awareness of what they are doing, and it promotes their growth by opening new and different possibilities for approaching a task.

The Creative Curriculum is based on Vygotsky's theories that social interaction is key to children's learning. The *Creative Curriculum* classroom is a community—a place where learning takes place through positive relationships between and among children and adults. Children are taught the skills they need for making friends, solving social problems, and sharing. In this environment, each member is a learner and a teacher.

Furthermore, in the *Creative Curriculum* classroom, instruction is based on observing and documenting what children do and say—in Vygotsky's terms, determining their ZPD. With this information in hand, teachers can provide learning experiences that are challenging enough to move children to a higher level of learning, but not so challenging as to frustrate them. In this way, *Creative Curriculum* teachers facilitate the growth and development of all children in the class and create a classroom environment in which their own effectiveness can be affirmed.

Gardner: Multiple Intelligences

Howard Gardner pioneered the theory of multiple intelligences. His work has shown that thinking of intelligence only in terms of standard "IQ" (intelligence quotient) scores is not always useful because traditional IQ tests measure a narrow range of skills. For instance, the most commonly used IQ test, the Wechsler Intelligence Scale for Children, is limited to verbal, math, and perceptual skills. It will yield only a low score for children who are weak in these areas but who are gifted artistically or musically, or those who have exceptional social and emotional skills.

Gardner began researching different kinds of intelligences in the early 1970s. Realizing that the arts, in particular, had been neglected in our traditional concept of intelligence, he redefined intelligence as "the capacity to solve problems or to fashion products that are valued in one or more cultural settings" (Brualdi, 2000, p. 1). Gardner suggests that rather than having one fixed intelligence, people can be intelligent in many different ways. He has identified at least eight such ways. Below are the characteristics of each of the eight intelligences that Gardner has named. As you read them, keep in mind that children who show evidence of intelligence in a particular area are likely to show some (but not necessarily all) of these associated characteristics.

Linguistic/Verbal Intelligence. Children who are strong in this area may like to play with words and the sounds of language; are good at telling stories; love looking at and hearing books read; and experiment with writing.

Logical/Mathematical Intelligence. Children who show talent in this area may like to reason and solve problems; explore patterns and categorize objects; ask questions and experiment; and count and understand one-to-one correspondence.

Musical/Rhythmic Intelligence. Children with this intelligence may sing, hum, or whistle to themselves; see patterns in music and nature; be sensitive to environmental sounds and the human voice; and respond to music emotionally.

Spatial/Visual Intelligence. Children who are strong in this area may think in images; know where everything in the classroom is located; be fascinated with the way things work; and take toys apart to see how they work.

Bodily/Kinesthetic Intelligence. Children with talent in this area may have good fine motor skills and coordination; learn by moving, not by sitting still; feel things in their "gut"; be athletic or good dancers; and physically mimic others.

Interpersonal Intelligence. Children who are strong in this area may have several best friends; be good at resolving conflicts; be leaders and group organizers; and "read" other peoples' feelings and behavior accurately.

Intrapersonal Intelligence. Children with this intelligence may be aware of their emotions; express their feelings well; require private space and time; and have realistic knowledge of their own strengths and challenges.

Naturalist Intelligence. Children who are strong in this area may observe nature; notice changes in the environment; enjoy conducting experiments; sort and categorize objects; like using magnifying glasses, microscopes, binoculars, and telescopes to study nature; like to care for pets; and enjoy gardening.

While people all possess, to some extent, intelligence in all of these areas, most exhibit higher levels in one or more areas. Moreover, no one intelligence exists by itself, so there is interaction between and among intelligences. Gardner explains that people have the capacity to develop all of their intelligences if given appropriate encouragement, enrichment, and support.

The Creative Curriculum applies Gardner's theory by showing teachers how to provide opportunities for every child to pursue his or her special talents and to demonstrate areas of strength. The use of interest areas— each with different materials—gives children opportunities to learn using their particular kind of intelligence rather than forcing them into a mold. In keeping with Gardner's notion of interpersonal and intrapersonal intelligences, the Curriculum gives learning social skills the same level of importance as learning content. It includes plenty of physical activity and chances to explore nature, along with traditional academics such as literacy, math, science, and social studies.

> *The Creative Curriculum* shows teachers how to provide opportunities for every child to pursue his or her special talents and to demonstrate areas of strength.

Smilansky: The Role of Children's Play in Learning

Sara Smilansky's research focuses on how children learn through play and the relationship of play to future academic success. Smilansky distinguishes four types of play: functional, constructive, dramatic or pretend, and games with rules.

Functional play. Functional play is a form of play in which children use their senses and muscles to experiment with materials and learn how things go together. It satisfies children's need to be active and to explore. Typically, in functional play, children repeat their actions over and over while talking to themselves about what they are doing. Functional play is the earliest to appear and continues throughout childhood whenever there are new objects to explore.

> Smilansky:
> There are four types of play.

The Creative Curriculum shows teachers how to create an environment that allows for functional play experiences by including new materials in each interest area. As children play with these materials they learn about their world. The *Creative Curriculum* teacher facilitates this learning by making descriptive statements that convey information or asking questions that get children to think about what they are doing.

Constructive play. Constructive play also involves handling materials, but with an important new dimension. In constructive play, children learn the different uses of play materials. They start putting things together based on a plan, becoming a creator and organizing their materials and sustaining their attention for longer periods of time than in functional play. At this stage children's actions are purposeful and directed toward a goal. They make constructions, such as roads or houses, and delight in seeing that what they have made will last even when they are finished playing.

The Creative Curriculum shows teachers how to validate and reinforce children's constructive play, to prompt children to extend their ideas, and to interact with children so that they learn from their play.

Dramatic or pretend play. Dramatic or pretend play can develop alongside functional and constructive play and is often seen in toddlers. When one child pretends alone, his behavior is referred to as dramatic play; when two or more children are involved in a sustained make-believe play episode, their activity is called sociodramatic play. The major difference between dramatic play and other types of play is that it is "person-oriented and not material and/or object oriented" (Smilansky & Shefatya 1990, p. 3).

In dramatic play children typically take on a role, pretend to be someone else, and use real or pretend objects to play out the role. Children often re-enact something they have experienced or watched, a cognitive task that requires them to remember what happened, select the aspects that are relevant, and use gestures and words that clearly demonstrate the role they are playing.

Sociodramatic play is often guided by rules children have learned through their own experiences and requires children to adapt to their peers. For example, if a child is pretending to iron and her playmates say that little children aren't allowed to handle irons, the child may have to modify her role and become a grown-up in the play scenario. Sociodramatic play is a high-level cognitive and social task, requiring feats of imagination, reasoning, and negotiations with other children.

According to Smilansky and her associate, Leah Shefatya, studies have shown a connection between high levels of sociodramatic play in preschool and cognitive, verbal, and social ability measures in the early elementary grades (1990). With these findings in mind, we have placed a high priority in *The Creative Curriculum* on promoting this kind of play. The Curriculum shows teachers how to create an environment for frequent and varied sociodramatic play. In addition, the Curriculum shows teachers how to interact with children to expand and learn from their sociodramatic play.

In constructive play, children's actions are purposeful and directed toward a goal.

In dramatic play children typically take on a role, pretend to be someone else, and use real or pretend objects to play out the role.

Games with rules. Games with rules—like sociodramatic play—involve planning. There are two broad types of games with rules—table games and physical or movement games. Both require children to control their behavior, both physically and verbally, to conform to a structure of preset rules. While Smilansky acknowledges the appropriateness and value of games with rules, she does suggest that, unlike sociodramatic play, they are usually very specific and allow for little flexibility. Thus, children may learn to control their behavior by playing games with rules, but they don't engage in complex thinking or interaction.

Based on Smilansky's thinking, *The Creative Curriculum* suggests outdoor games with rules, such as "Red Light, Green Light" that involve physical activity. Some board or card games are also recommended. In addition, *Creative Curriculum* teachers encourage children to make up their own rules for games. They focus attention on playing for enjoyment rather than on winning or losing and on cooperative or collaborative games in which children play with each other rather than against each other. In all play—whether it is functional, constructive, dramatic, or rule governed—the *Creative Curriculum* teacher watches for opportunities to help children learn, expand their world, and master challenges.

Learning and Resiliency

Resilience research, which began in the 1970s, has focused on children who develop well despite the burden of hardship. Perhaps the most significant result of this work has been to reverse the impression that children growing up under the threat of disadvantage and hardship are doomed to a life of problems. To the contrary, resilience research has shown that the negative effects of hardship can be alleviated and that children can develop the strength and skills necessary to deal with adversity (Wolin, in press). As one observer has put it, "Risk is not destiny" (Shore, 1997, p. 61).

In addition to creating a more optimistic picture of children of hardship than was painted in the past, resilience research has begun to shed light on the kind of help children threatened by harmful conditions need to thrive. Not surprising, the research consistently notes the importance of teachers (Wolin, in press). For instance, Emmy Werner (1999), who has been studying the development of resilience for over 40 years, has this to say:

> One of the wonderful things we see now in adulthood is that . . . children really remember one or two teachers who made the difference. [Each]. . . was a person who looked beyond [children's] outward experience, their behavior, and their oftentimes unkempt appearance, and saw the promise. (p. 17)

Games with rules require children to control their behavior, both physically and verbally in order to conform to a set of rules.

Resilience research: The negative effects of hardship can be alleviated and children can develop the strength and skills necessary to deal with adversity.

Anne Masten (2001), in her review of current research on resiliency entitled "Ordinary Magic," concludes that resilience is not a rare quality; all children can be reached by adults who protect their normal development. To date the literature has shown that children develop resilience when they

- spend time in a safe, supportive, and stimulating environment

- have access to caring, supportive adults who believe in them

- have opportunities to develop self-control

- can get a sense of their own competence

- are exposed to teaching strategies that help them become successful learners

These findings are behind the core belief in *The Creative Curriculum*—all children can learn and benefit from developmentally appropriate practice. They also shape the suggestions the Curriculum makes to teachers. We do not ask you to add another duty to your already demanding job. Nor do we tell you to fit resiliency time into the daily schedule or design special resiliency activities. Rather, *The Creative Curriculum* fosters resilience by showing you how to structure your classroom and to have positive, respectful interactions with children. The techniques the Curriculum describes will enable you to make a difference even if you can't change the unfortunate circumstances that children are sometimes dealt (Bickart and Wolin, 1997).

The Creative Curriculum shows you how to structure your classroom and to have positive respectful interactions with children.

Many children come to preschool eager to learn. They are well cared for at home and do not raise complicated questions about your role. Unfortunately, every year in the classroom, teachers see children who fill them with concern and make them feel helpless. Their basic needs have not been met. They haven't been given the emotional support required for learning, the kind of stimulation needed for their brains to develop, or the opportunities to interact socially. They've lacked play materials that promote logical thinking, imagination, and multiple intelligences. Working with children like these can be intensely challenging, and we do not want to minimize the difficulties. You cannot undo their hurt or reverse the situations that have deprived or harmed them, but, you can make a difference. *The Creative Curriculum*, which is based on the research and theory described in these pages, will show you how.

references

Bickart, T., & Wolin, S. (1997). Practicing resilience in the elementary classroom. *Principal, 77*(2): 21–24.

Bredekamp, S., & Copple, C. (Eds.). (1997). *Developmentally appropriate practice in early childhood programs* (Rev. ed.). Washington, DC: National Association for the Education of Young Children.

Brualdi, A. C. (1996, rev. 1999). Multiple intelligences: Gardner's theory. *Practical Assessment, Research & Evaluation, 5*. Article written 1996, revised 1999 by *PARE* editors to include Gardner's eighth intelligence. Retrieved April 14, 2003 from http://ericae.net/pare/getvn.asp?v=5&n=10

Erikson, E. H. (1994). *Identity and the life cycle.* New York: W.W. Norton and Company.

Maslow, A. H. (1999). *Toward a psychology of being* (3rd ed.). New York: J. Wiley & Sons.

Masten, A. S. (2001). Ordinary magic: resilience processes in development. *American Psychologist, 56,* 227–238.

Piaget, J., Inhelder, B., & Weaver, H. (Trans.). (2000). *The psychology of the child.* New York: Basic Books.

Shore, R. (1997). *Rethinking the brain: New insights into early development.* New York: Families and Work Institute.

Smilansky, S., & Shefatya, L. (1990). *Facilitating play: A medium for promoting cognitive, socio-emotional, and academic development in young children.* Gaithersburg, MD: Psychosocial & Educational Publications.

Vygotsky, L. S., Robert W. Rieber (Ed.), & Marie J. Hall (Trans.) (1999). *The collected works of L.S. Vygotsky: Scientific legacy* (Cognition and language: A series in psycholinguistics, Volume 6). London: Kluwer Academic/Plenum Publishers.

Werner, E. (1999). How children become resilient: observations and cautions. In N. Henderson, B. Benard & N. Sharp-Light (Eds.), *Resiliency in action: Practical ideas for overcoming risks and building strengths in youth, families & communities.* Gorham, ME: Resiliency in Action Inc.

Wolin, S. (in press). *Overview of resilience: Research and practice.* Washington, DC: Project Resilience.

inside this chapter

18   What Preschool Children Are Like

18   Areas of Development

23   Ages and Stages of Development

27   Individual Differences

27   Gender

28   Temperament

30   Interests

31   Learning Styles

33   Life Experiences

34   Culture

35   Special Needs

38   English Language Learners

42   The Developmental Continuum

43   What the *Developmental Continuum* Looks Like

59   Conclusion and References

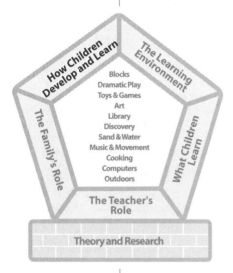

How Children Develop and Learn

Research on child development that has accumulated over the past 75 years has provided a deep knowledge and understanding of children. *The Creative Curriculum*, which is based on this research, will show you how to apply what has been learned about children to everyday practices in the classroom.

This chapter explains the first component of the organizational structure of *The Creative Curriculum*—how children develop and learn. Knowing how children grow and develop is the basis for planning your program, selecting materials, and guiding children's learning. By knowing, we mean appreciating general patterns of growth in all children as well as the differences you will certainly encounter in individual children.

This chapter is divided into three sections.

> **What preschool children are like**—social/emotional, physical, cognitive, and language development and typical qualities of 3-, 4-, and 5-year-olds
>
> **Individual differences**—variations in gender, temperament, interests, learning styles, life experiences, culture, and special needs
>
> **The *Developmental Continuum***—a tool that maps children's development and guides teachers' planning

What Preschool Children Are Like

The preschool years—ages 3–5—are a special time in the life of young children. During this period, they begin to trust others outside the family. They gain independence and self-control, and learn to take initiative and assert themselves in socially acceptable ways. At the same time, they become keen observers of their world and experiment with their surroundings to find out what happens when they interact with other people and handle and maneuver objects and materials. Their language surpasses the limited vocabulary and sentence structure of toddlers.

Preschoolers use thousands of words and complex phrases and sentences to communicate. As they learn to understand others and express their ideas more effectively, their environment becomes larger and richer. In addition, preschoolers are changing physically—growing and gaining strength, agility, and coordination.

Areas of Development

For the sake of discussion and clarity, child development may be divided into four areas—social/emotional, physical, cognitive, and language. While the division is both necessary and useful, it is somewhat artificial. In reality, development does not divide neatly into categories. Rather, the four categories are closely related and often overlap. Development in one area affects and is influenced by development in all other areas. This reality requires teachers to pay attention to every area when guiding children's learning.

Take, for instance, reading and writing. You are working in language development when you talk to children and help them realize that print conveys a message. Social/emotional development comes into play when you expect children to handle books independently or to work cooperatively to use magnetic letters. Physical development is required for using writing tools (chalk, pencils, markers) and cognitive development, when children act out the parts of a story in correct sequence.

- social/emotional
- physical
- cognitive
- language

Below, we describe the four areas of development. The purpose of the description is to give you a framework that will help you focus on particular areas and, at the same time, keep the whole child and the interplay of development in mind.

Social/Emotional Development

Social/emotional development during the preschool years is about socialization—the process by which children learn the values and behaviors accepted by society. It is also about becoming a competent and confident person.

There are three goals for social/emotional development.

Achieving a sense of self: knowing oneself and relating to other people—both children and adults.

Taking responsibility for self and others: following rules and routines, respecting others, and taking initiative.

Behaving in a prosocial way: showing empathy and getting along in the world, for example, by sharing and taking turns.

Social and emotional competence are essential to children's well-being and success, in school and in life. With the current focus on readiness, accountability, and high standards, there is always a danger that programs will focus only on academic content and ignore aspects of development that are equally important for achieving long lasting and positive results.

A Good Beginning: Sending America's Children to School with the Social and Emotional Competence They Need to Succeed (The Child Mental Health Foundations and Agencies Network, 2000, p. 7) provides evidence that social/emotional readiness is critical to a successful kindergarten transition, early school success, and even later accomplishments in the workplace. The report describes a child who is socially and emotionally ready for school. This child is

- confident, friendly, able to develop good relationships with peers

- able to concentrate on and persist at challenging tasks

- able to communicate frustrations, anger, and joy effectively

- able to listen to instructions and be attentive

Social and emotional readiness can be taught and nurtured most effectively when children are young. Because preschool is a prime setting for gaining social and emotional competence, social/emotional development is an important focus for teachers.

Physical Development

Physical development includes children's gross (large muscle) and fine (small muscle) motor skills. Physical development is sometimes taken for granted in the early childhood classroom because it is often assumed that it happens automatically. Not only is this assumption untrue, but teachers need to remember that physical development is just as important to learning as every other area of development.

With more advanced physical development, children master increasingly sophisticated tasks and gain personal responsibility for their own physical needs, such as dressing themselves. In addition, physical development, in many ways, promotes social/emotional development. As children learn what their bodies can do, they gain self-confidence. In turn, the more they can do, the more willing they are to try new and challenging tasks. Thus, a positive cycle, which effects learning overall, is established.

Physical activity contributes significantly to personal health and well-being.

The benefits of promoting physical development are well documented. The Surgeon General's Report on *Physical Activity and Health* (1996) states that physical activity contributes significantly to personal health and well-being. Physical education in the early grades supports children's academic achievement, general health, self-esteem, stress management, and social development. And we know from brain research that moving the body literally wakes up the brain.

There are two goals for physical development.

Achieving gross motor control: moving the large muscles in the body, especially the arms and legs, consciously and deliberately. Gross motor control includes balance and stability; movements such as running, jumping, hopping, galloping, and skipping; and physical manipulations such as throwing, kicking, and catching.

Achieving fine motor control: using and coordinating the small muscles in the hands and wrists with dexterity. As these fine muscles develop, children are able to perform self-help skills and manipulate small objects such as scissors and writing tools. The achievement of fine motor skills generally lags behind gross motor development.

Cognitive Development

Cognitive development refers to the mind and how it works. It involves how children think, how they see their world, and how they use what they learn.

There are three goals for cognitive development.

Learning and problem solving: being purposeful about acquiring and using information, resources, and materials. As children observe events around them, ask questions, make predictions, and test possible solutions, learning reaches beyond just acquiring facts. Persistence and knowing how to apply knowledge expands their learning even further.

Thinking logically: gathering and making sense of the information by comparing, contrasting, sorting, classifying, counting, measuring, and recognizing patterns. As children use logical thinking, they organize their world conceptually and gain a better understanding of how it works.

Representing and thinking symbolically: using objects in a unique way, for instance, a cup to represent a telephone, or a broom to represent a horse; pretending, for instance, to be mommy or a firefighter; portraying the world through charts or pictures, for instance, making a graph to show changes in the weather over time or a drawing to show what happened to a character in a story. Representations and symbols free children from the world of literal meanings and allow them to use materials and their imagination to explore abstract ideas.

One of the joys of observing children's cognitive development is seeing their minds expand. Preschoolers use their imaginations and are creative in their thinking. They can be an astronaut one minute and pretend to be a baby the next, trying out the roles and tasks associated with each. The ability to take on another's perspective leads them into friendships where they can share feelings and experiences. They can also capture their feelings in a clay sculpture or recreate a visit to the fire station with puppets or paints. Cognitive growth in preschool children is remarkable to witness.

Language Development

Language development includes understanding and communicating through words, spoken and written. Children are born with the capacity to communicate with others—verbally and non-verbally. By the time they reach preschool, their ability to communicate thoughts and feelings through spoken language takes on new importance. Language becomes the principal tool for establishing and maintaining relationships with adults and other children.

Because words represent objects and ideas, language development is closely related to cognitive development. With frequent language experiences between the ages of 3 and 5, children's vocabulary can grow dramatically. The richer a child's vocabulary, the more likely that the child will become a good reader. Language and literacy skills go hand in hand. Listening, speaking, reading, and writing develop interdependently in children.

Language becomes the principal tool for establishing and maintaining relationships with adults and other children.

There are two goals for language development.

Listening and speaking: using spoken language to communicate with others, enlarging one's vocabulary, expressing oneself, understanding the oral speech of others, participating in a conversation, and using language to solve problems.

As children learn to listen and speak, they gain control of themselves and their world, relate effectively to others, and gather and store more and more information.

Reading and writing: making sense of written language, understanding the purpose of print and how it works, gaining knowledge of the alphabet, writing letters and words.

When children begin to read they gain access to new worlds of information and faraway places, including the world of imagination. Writing things down expands memory, communication, and understanding.

Ages and Stages of Development

In addition to viewing the four developmental areas (social/emotional, physical, cognitive, and language) one at a time, teachers may find it useful to look at development in another way. Here we look at development in 3-, 4-, and 5-year-olds, the preschool years. Children at each age demonstrate some very predictable behavior. You can anticipate, for example, that 3-year-olds often find sharing difficult. Rather than trying to force 3s to give another child a turn with a favorite toy, it makes more sense to have duplicates of popular toys available. As children learn to trust you and their school environment, you can set up systems for taking turns. Once children know there are sufficient toys for everyone, and that they will get a turn even if they have to wait, sharing becomes less of an issue for them.

Three-Year-Olds

Threes are often described as being in transition. They more closely resemble 4- and 5-year-old preschoolers than 2-year-old toddlers. What sets them apart from toddlers more than anything else is their newfound ability to express themselves in words and ideas. This ability opens up a whole social world.

> What sets 3s apart from toddlers more than anything else is their newfound ability to express themselves in words and ideas.

Social/Emotional Development: Three-year-olds are learning to trust that their parents, teachers, and other important people in their lives will take good care of them. Trust gives them the confidence to become independent and, in turn, to feel pride at being able to brush their teeth and dress themselves—just as their parents do. Threes want you to notice their newly acquired skills, for instance, being able to set the table or pedal a tricycle. While social competence is beginning to emerge at this time, it does not develop fully. The very social 3-year-old can turn egocentric and "me" oriented quickly.

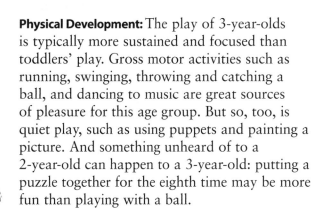

Physical Development: The play of 3-year-olds is typically more sustained and focused than toddlers' play. Gross motor activities such as running, swinging, throwing and catching a ball, and dancing to music are great sources of pleasure for this age group. But so, too, is quiet play, such as using puppets and painting a picture. And something unheard of to a 2-year-old can happen to a 3-year-old: putting a puzzle together for the eighth time may be more fun than playing with a ball.

Cognitive Development: Three-year-olds are exploding with thoughts and ideas. They use all of their senses to make sense of the world around them. However, the ability of 3s to classify and understand their world is only at a beginning level. They can sort objects but usually by only one characteristic at a time. Their egocentric nature generally keeps them from seeing another person's point of view, though this limitation may be affected by circumstances. Many are able to show empathy, and you may see a 3-year-old bringing a special toy to a child who is upset.

Language Development: In this area, 3-year-olds take off. While most 2-year-olds utter only the basic language sounds, most 3s have mastered all sounds, perhaps with the exception of "f," "l," "r," "s," "sk," and "th." Most 3s can use plural terms, talk in sentences, recite simple rhymes, and ask questions. They can tell you their first and last names. They love to share their thoughts with you and participate in conversations.

Four-Year-Olds

Fours are working on many of the same developmental tasks as 3s, but at a higher level. Because their language can be so fluent, you may assume they understand more than they actually do. For instance, they use the word, "why," frequently, creating the impression that they want an explanation. Yet, often, your explanation of "why" is not nearly as important to a 4-year-old as the fact that you are giving her your full attention.

Social/Emotional Development: Fours are a wonderful mix of independence and sociability. They like doing things on their own. They take great pride in imitating adult behaviors, but also love playing with others, especially in groups of two and three. Making friends makes sharing easier. Whether playing alone or in a group, 4s tend to be very expressive, using actions and facial expressions as well as words to get their points across.

Physical Development: Fours are increasingly able to control their muscles. Whereas most 3s go down steps putting both feet on the same step before climbing down, most 4s speed down steps, alternating their feet. The leg muscles of 4s allow them to maintain a rhythmic stride in running. They play enthusiastically on slides, swings, and all outdoor play equipment. Their fine motor coordination improves dramatically as well. On their own, they can wash their hands, button their coats, and use Velcro straps. Some are coordinated enough to cut intricate lines with scissors, zip their coats, and make an attempt at tying their shoes.

Cognitive Development: Four-year-olds act like budding scientists. They are enchanted by principles of cause and effect and always want to know why things happen. They approach the world with great curiosity and use their imaginations to understand it. However, because separating reality from fantasy is hard for them, they can have irrational fears. All of a sudden, the closet may be home to an unwelcome monster. They also might also do what many might describe as "lying." For example, after knocking over a glass of milk they might insist that they didn't do it, truly believing that what just happened was beyond their control. Developmentally, they are struggling with the differences between truth and fiction. In the attempt to discover the boundaries, the truth often is stretched.

Language Development: The language of 4-year-olds progresses rapidly. They usually can understand and use words such as "in," "by," "with," "to," "over," and "under." They love to talk, be spoken to, and listen to books. Trying out new words—including bathroom (potty) language—delights 4s. They like to use big words and deeply enjoy their ability to communicate.

Five-Year-Olds

By the time children turn five, they have gained security about who they are and their place in the world. This is a fascinating age group.

Social/Emotional Development: Fives are increasingly independent, self-sufficient individuals. They are dependable and responsible and enjoy having praise lavished on them for their reliability. In many ways, they are model citizens: obedient, eager to tend to their own personal needs, protective of others, proud to go to school, and usually polite and even tactful. Fives are also exceedingly social. They seek out friends, typically having one or two special playmates. Overwhelmingly, 5s prefer cooperative play to solitary or parallel play. Because the outside world holds great appeal, 5s like taking trips and exploring their environment.

Physical Development: Five-year-olds show more agility, balance, and coordination than 4s in both gross motor and fine motor movements. They can jump rope, ride a bike with training wheels, and stand on their tippy toes. Fives can control a paintbrush, weave ribbons, and write letters and numbers with increasing accuracy.

Fours approach the world with great curiosity and use their imaginations to understand it.

Fives have gained security about who they are and their place in the world.

Cognitive Development: Fives learn new concepts through experimentation and discovery. They solve problems and make predictions by observing the objects and people in the world around them and by making connections to what they already know. They are able to think in complex ways, relating new information that they collect and process to things they knew previously. They can understand concepts of color, size, and shape. They also can categorize by two features, such as color and shape.

Language Development: Five-year-olds show significant growth in their communication skills. They produce sentences that have adult-like word order, using pronunciation like a grown-up. They speak not just in sentences, but in paragraphs. For the most part, their grammar is correct. They ask relevant questions. In short, communicating with a 5-year-old is like communicating with anyone who speaks your language. Five-year-olds also begin to extend their oral language skills to reading and writing.

Your knowledge of the predictable aspects of child development and the typical behaviors of 3-, 4-, and 5-year-old children give you a general basis for planning your program. However, it is important to remember that each child develops on an individual timetable and may respond to your program in different ways. Therefore, you should take the time to get to know each child and to appreciate each child's special characteristics. What works for one child may not work for another.

Individual Differences

A second aspect of knowing the children you teach is learning what makes each one unique. No matter how much children may resemble each other in their patterns of development, every child brings specific interests, experiences, and learning styles to your classroom. Therefore, you will need different strategies to help all children succeed as learners.

Think about the children in your classroom. Perhaps you have a child who loves to experiment. His curiosity frequently gets him into trouble, though, because he never seems to stop exploring—even during naptime. Or, perhaps you have a child who is artistic and loves to dance. In fact, it seems that she can only learn something if she is twirling while she listens.

Your understanding of individual differences will help you respond to children in ways that make every child feel comfortable and ready to learn. Perhaps the most obvious difference in children is gender. Children also have different temperaments, interests, learning styles, and life experiences. They also are strongly influenced by their cultural backgrounds. And some children have special needs or are learning English as a second language.

Gender

As adults, each of us has personal beliefs about what it means to be male or female. Children, however, are still learning what it means to be a girl or a boy. Therefore, teachers need to create a classroom environment where children feel safe in exploring gender-related roles and taking part in activities that are related to these roles.

Making assumptions about children based on gender is easy. It's also easy to back up these assumptions with research and one's own observations. For example, boys tend to like gross motor play, while girls are quite content playing with little people figures and can do so for extended periods of time. Boys engage in parallel play quite happily, while girls tend to like to play cooperatively together. Girls are more likely to make representational drawings and write their names at an earlier age than boys.

But biology is not destiny. Learning and the way we treat children also play a role in how boys and girls behave. As Katherine Hanson (1992) notes:

> In child care settings, with infants and children between 13 months and two years, research shows that child care providers respond to the children based on their own sex role beliefs, and they use the child's gender to guide their responses. . . . Adults were more likely to respond when girls used gestures or gentle touches or talked, and when boys forced attention through physical means or cried, whined, or screamed. . . . (p. 1)

> Create a classroom environment where children feel safe in exploring gender-related roles and taking part in activities that are related to these roles.

Because personality as well as biology plays a role, teachers should ensure that both boys and girls receive positive messages about who they are and what they are capable of doing. You need to be aware consciously of your own beliefs and assumptions that affect the way you teach. Think about your own experiences growing up. What messages did you receive about how boys and girls were expected to behave? Do you expect boys' play to be of the "rough-and-tumble" type and girls to be "well-behaved"? What are the implications of these attitudes, and do you want to pass them along to the children you teach? You may hear children tell each other, "Girls can't build with blocks" or "Boys don't dress up." They are repeating messages they have heard from others or listened to in the media.

> Do you expect boys' play to be of the "rough-and-tumble" type and girls to be "well-behaved"?

Remember that during the early childhood years, children will take the opportunity to learn and explore new ideas if they are given the benefit of a safe place. Play is one of the vehicles they use to work out new understandings. Teachers should capitalize on their play to have them test their ideas about gender and to think more flexibly about what girls and boys can and cannot do.

Teachers can help children to challenge their expectations. You can create an environment that allows children to explore assumptions and feel comfortable. Think about the pictures you display and the books you read to children. Are there strong female role models? Do they include men in nurturing roles?

As you get to know the children in your classroom, take note of how gender differences influence children's behavior and your own expectations. Help children to see that your classroom is a place where they can explore freely and feel comfortable in the process.

Temperament

Temperament is best defined as behavioral style. For example, some children are slow to warm up. They approach new situations cautiously, without a fuss and adapt slowly. Others have an immediate positive response to new situations and are generally cheerful and have regular patterns of behavior. Still others withdraw or protest in new situations, and their behavior is fussy.

Research suggests that temperamental differences can be identified even in newborns. There are significant differences in the way babies respond to different stimuli, for instance, loud noise or gentle rocking. Related research done by Stella Chess and Alexander Thomas (1996) examined how the temperament of newborns influenced the development of their personalities in several areas.

1. **Activity level**—How active is the child? How long can he sit still?

2. **Biological rhythms**—How predictable are the child's sleeping and eating habits?

3. **Tendency to approach or withdraw**—Does the child readily join in group activities or play beside or with another child?

4. **Adaptability**—How does the child react to a new or stressful situation?

5. **Sensory threshold**—At what point does a child become bothered by too much noise, changes in temperature, different tastes, or the feel of clothing?

6. **Intensity or energy level of reactions**—How does the child respond to the emotions he feels?

7. **Mood**—Does the child have a positive or negative outlook?

8. **Distractibility and attention span**—Is the child readily distracted from a task by things going on around her?

9. **Persistence**—How does the child handle frustration or initial failure on a task? How long does he stay with a task?

> Children with different temperaments need to be treated differently.

Thanks to this research we know about the constitutional differences in children. Science also has demonstrated a related principle—that children with different temperaments need to be treated differently. For example, knowing that Carlos is easily distracted, you can offer him a quiet place to look at books and turn off the music when he is trying to concentrate. Similarly, realizing that Setsuko tends to be shy, invite her into a dramatic play episode by asking her to join you and another child at the table for "tea." While research has shown that temperament is inborn, providing suitable support for children can make a difference. An active child can calm down. An easily distracted child can expand his attention span.

Further, because environment does have an effect on temperament, you should not be surprised to learn that a child may be very different at home and at school, or that a child who likes to play actively with his peers becomes much quieter around adults.

> The important message to *Creative Curriculum* teachers is to take note of each child's temperament in a variety of settings. Doing so will help you to make appropriate decisions. Understanding how children are likely to react to the people and events in their life can make you a more responsive and effective teacher.

Interests

Another way people demonstrate their individuality is through their likes and preferences. Sometimes for no apparent reason, a particular topic interests a child and holds his attention and fancy over a length of time. One child may be fascinated by monkeys, another by helicopters or trucks. One child loves hip-hop music; another will not go anywhere without a baseball cap.

Children's interests are a built-in motivator for learning. For example, you can attract a child who is interested in monkeys to reading and language by having a book on monkeys available or reading it aloud. You can involve a child who loves to dance by having taped music available in your classroom. You can supply your Dramatic Play Area with a variety of baseball caps to motivate the cap wearer to spend time there.

Teachers who are aware of the interests of their children have a basis for building a relationship and for motivating each child to learn.

If you have a child in your group who is difficult to engage or does not use speech to communicate, try to find something that really interests him. Use that interest to help him interact with others and develop communication skills. For example, a child who is skilled at using computer programs can be encouraged to help other children with less technology experience. Teachers who are aware of the interests of their children have a basis for building a relationship with and motivating each child to learn.

Knowing individual children's interests is also a good guide for planning possible long-term study topics. If a housing development is going up across the street from your school and you've observed that Derek is fascinated by trucks and that Crystal is constructing towers with blocks, you might consider a long-term study on construction. Knowing the related interests of other children will help you think of ways to extend the study and sustain it over time.

Whether or not you are able to incorporate individual children's preferences into classroom studies, make it a practice to nurture their interests. By doing so, you convey the message that you value what is important to them. You also help them gain new skills and confidence.

Learning Styles

Every person has a preferred way of learning. Some people are visual learners. Some learn better by listening while others have to handle something physically before they can understand it. One style is not better than another—it's simply the way a person learns best.

You probably will observe at least three different styles of learning in your group of children.

Auditory learners, or children who learn best by listening, are attuned to sounds and words. They solve problems by talking about them. Auditory learners can follow verbal instructions and explanations. You can build their knowledge base by describing in words what they do: "When you added coffee grounds to the paint, it changed the way the paint feels when it dries." You also can ask open-ended questions to encourage children to verbalize their thoughts: "What's that you're making for the baby dolls' breakfast?" The more opportunities you provide listeners to hear and verbalize concepts, the more they will learn.

Visual learners, or children who learn best by looking, are drawn to color, shape, and motion. They actually think in images or pictures, taking in what they hear and see and transforming it into images in their brain. It is as if they have a movie camera in their mind.

Visual learners benefit when you show them how things are done, rather than just telling them verbally: "Come here, Jonetta. Kate can show you how to put the interlocking blocks together so that you can build with them." Visual learners also remember ideas and concepts better when they are attached to an image: "Let's make a graph of all the different types of shoes we're wearing today." "Zach, I know that you're sad that your Daddy had to go away. Why don't you draw a picture about the way you're feeling?" Children who learn by looking need to make visual representations of their thoughts and feelings to learn.

- listening
- looking
- moving

Kinesthetic learners, or children who learn best by moving, are generally well coordinated and confident in their bodies. Touching and feeling things and transforming ideas and information into movement boosts their memory and understanding.

Have you ever seen a preschooler twirl around as she tries to remember something? This twirler might be a kinesthetic learner. Something in the process of physically moving triggers her brain to learn a concept or idea. Kinesthetic learners benefit by knowing that it's okay to get up and move around. You can facilitate their learning by relating concepts to their bodies, "When I push down on your head, Setsuko, you can feel the pressure. That's what a vise does to a piece of wood . . . it holds it down and in place."

Since not all children learn in the same way, teachers should take all styles of learning into account. Traditionally, schools have appealed primarily to auditory learners, and to a lesser extent, to visual learners. Kinesthetic learners have had to adjust their natural way of learning to do well in school.

Teachers should make sure that they present information so that children who are listeners, lookers, and movers can all be successful learners.

Rather than expecting children to adjust, teachers should make sure that they present information so that children who are listeners, lookers, and movers can all be successful learners. Moreover, brain research shows that the more ways you allow children to explore a concept, the more likely they will remember what they learn. So, in addition to meeting the needs of all children, you can maximize learning by crafting learning opportunities for children with every learning style—the listeners, the lookers, and the movers.

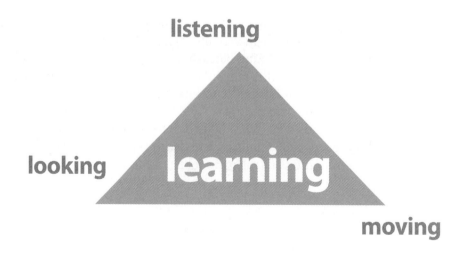

Life Experiences

In addition to other individual differences, varying life experiences contribute to the uniqueness of each child. Consider how each of these factors may affect the children you teach:

- family composition, including the number and gender of parents or guardians present in the home

- child's birth order, including the number and spacing of siblings

- presence of a chronic health problem or disability in a family member

- exposure to violence, abuse, or neglect

- home language(s)

- the family's culture and religious practices

- the type of community in which the child lives

- the kinds of work family members do

- age at which parents gave birth to or adopted first child

- economic status

- living situation, including history of moving

- parent's/guardian's level of education

- parent's/guardian's job history, including work-related travel

- special circumstances such as separation and divorce; birth or adoption of a new sibling; how many different people/places child is with each day

Life circumstances affect a child's ability to learn. Firstborn children, for example, often tend to be responsible—to follow directions faithfully and be the first to volunteer to help. The fifth child in a family of seven may crave attention and go to extremes to be noticed, including picking fights. A child with an alcoholic mother may feel that life is unpredictable and that trusting others is risky. In contrast, a child with a stable home life may be independent and confident.

Life circumstances affect a child's ability to learn.

Try to be aware of each child's life circumstances when he or she enters your program. Talking with family members and taking notes about what you learn is an important first step. During the school year you can encourage parents to communicate with you about anything new taking place in children's lives.

Culture

Culture influences the way people think and interact with others. It affects an individual's choice of words, tone of voice, facial expressions, use of gestures and personal space, and reaction time. Cultures also have different norms for asking questions, responding to questions, and conversing with adults. Sometimes cultural practices come from ethnic, racial, or religious influences. Others are specific to a geographic location or economic level.

- A child may have learned to value reflection as an approach to learning. This child has been taught that thinking about what he has just learned is more important than getting through a project quickly. If his teacher regards speed as an indication of mastery, the child will appear to be a slow learner—not the competent and thoughtful child he is.

- In some cultures, it's rude to look the teacher in the eye or to answer a question too quickly. Children in these cultural groups may be uncomfortable with these expectations and be startled if the teacher leaves no wait time between asking a question and expecting a response.

- Some children are unfamiliar with questioning as a teaching technique. They may be confused because they feel the teacher already knows the answers to the questions she asks. The children's lack of response might be interpreted incorrectly as a lack of knowledge or attention.

Children learn the norms of their culture at the same time and in the same way they learn to speak a language. Like multiple intelligences, the values and norms of one culture cannot be said to be better than those of another. Cultural norms are just the way things are done in a child's family and community.

Because the role of culture is so important, you need to learn about, understand, and respect its influence on all the children you teach. This guideline doesn't mean that you have to be fluent in every language children speak and an expert on all cultural practices. It does mean, though, that you need to learn as much as you can about each child's family background. Talk with parents and other family members to better understand their family environment and culture. Consult with colleagues and experts to help you develop appropriate expectations.

Learn as much as you can about each child's family background.

You can weave aspects of different children's cultures into the curriculum through the materials you select, the topics you choose to study, and the strategies you employ. By doing so, you give children the message that each and every child is important and worthy of respect. A *Creative Curriculum* classroom in rural Alaska, for example, would likely feature salmon fishing and its influence on people's lives. A migrant Head Start program in Maine might highlight life in a migrant camp of blueberry pickers. A military child development center in Sicily might have lots of materials and props related to shopping at the PX and living at the foot of a volcano.

> In a *Creative Curriculum* classroom, whatever is real to these children and their cultures is what you will find. For this reason, no *Creative Curriculum* classroom is exactly like any other. And no one program looks the same from year to year.

Special Needs

A child is considered to have special needs if he or she is outside the typical range of individual differences. We have to be very careful in thinking about special needs, however, because labels such as "gifted" or "disabled" can obscure important information about children. Giftedness and disabilities are both aspects of a child, not the whole child. A child may have areas of giftedness or a particular disability, but rarely does either influence every aspect of development. For example, a child might be well ahead of her peers in reading but lack social skills or the ability to think logically. Similarly, a child may have a physical disability that prevents him from walking but have well-developed language skills. Labels do not help us understand the whole child; they interfere. Teachers should look at each child as an individual.

Gifted Children

Some children in your class may be developmentally ahead of their peers. You may notice that their conversation and language are more complex. They may have learned to read and write on their own and always have a book in their hands. They may solve puzzles quickly, ask questions about big numbers, surprise you by being able to add and subtract, or have interests that seem unusual for their age.

Children with advanced intellectual skills are called "gifted." While we tend to think of only intellectual giftedness when we use the term, children can be gifted in any number of areas. Gardner's work on different kinds of intelligences shows that people can be gifted in at least eight different ways. A child in your class may be athletically advanced, a talented musician, or an incredible artist.

Even though cognitive, language, social/emotional, and physical development are all interrelated, giftedness rarely extends to all areas of development. In fact, gifted children frequently have very uneven development. Some young children who are cognitively gifted master physical tasks only when they are presented in a cognitive context. Thus, a cognitively gifted child may understand the theory behind playing cooperatively with other children. However, when it comes to doing this task in real life, he has trouble.

Because of false expectations, many adults have difficulty believing that a child who is gifted in one area is not gifted in all. Why would a child who is mature enough to read pick fights or have temper tantrums? Teachers must be careful to note areas that need strengthening in children as well as those children's gifts.

Like all children, gifted children need to be challenged or they will become bored and frustrated. The more the child feels challenged and stimulated—both at home and at school—the more confident he will be to take risks and expand his talents.

> The most important thing to remember is not to dwell on the preschool child's gifts and single her out. Rather, observe the child, follow her lead, and then create an environment where she feels supported and challenged. Attention to individual needs is what gifted children need most.

Children With Disabilities

Approximately 8 percent of American children have a disability (U.S. Department of Education, 2000). While there are many types of disabilities, most can be described as developmental delays and medical, emotional, or physical problems. In addition, increasing numbers of preschool children are being identified as having attention-related disorders and autism.

Some children will come to preschool with formal documentation of a specific disability. Since 1976, special education law and regulations have required that a child with a diagnosed disability who is eligible for special education services have an Individual Education Program (IEP). This document answers basic questions about the nature of a child's disability and what must be done to meet his educational needs. It contains goals and objectives and a description of how the disability affects access to the general curriculum. In an IEP, the types of special education services a child needs to access the curriculum are designated.

Like all children, gifted children need to be challenged or they will become bored and frustrated.

In an IEP, the types of special education services a child needs to access the curriculum are designated.

IEPs sometimes can make teachers without a special education background feel overwhelmed. To overcome any such discomfort, take a step back and reflect. Approach this child as you would any other child in your classroom. Ask yourself what special needs this child has. What behaviors does he exhibit that may be interfering with his learning? What adjustments could be made to the environment and curriculum that would enhance this child's ability to learn?

Seek out specialists (trained professionals such as occupational or physical therapists or speech-language pathologists) who work with the child, and ask for helpful strategies. Some will be based on the child's strengths, needs, interests, talents, background, learning style, temperament, and the unique nature of the classroom. Others will aim to remediate weaknesses.

A strategy or set of strategies that is effective for one child with a particular condition may not be appropriate for another child with a similar diagnosis. Together with a specialist, assess and identify children's needs for assistive technology. Such needs might include large-print books for those with visual impairments, auditory trainers for those with hearing deficits, language devices for those with communication difficulties, or physically adaptive equipment for those with orthopedic impairments.

Keep in mind that a disability, like giftedness, is only one aspect of a child, not the whole child. Think of children with disabilities as children first. A child in your room may be in a wheelchair or use a hearing aid. Rather than defining these children by their disability—e.g., visually impaired, Down's syndrome, autism—it's more helpful to think of them as preschoolers with all that being 3–5 signifies.

Children with disabilities have a wide range of abilities and needs. For instance, some children with disabilities also may be gifted. It is neither possible nor helpful to think of children with disabilities as a homogenous group. For these and other reasons, focus on what children with disabilities can do and then build on their strengths.

Whether you work with children who are disabled in self-contained classrooms or in an inclusive program, *The Creative Curriculum for Preschool* is appropriate for all 3- to 5-year-old children. The Curriculum's emphasis on organizing the physical environment to promote learning is especially important for children who require structure and predictability in their lives. Children with autism, for example, demonstrate varying degrees of need in communication, social relationships, and play content.

Seek out specialists who work with the child, and ask for strategies to help you.

Think of children with disabilities as children first.

While there are many different theories on interventions for children with autism, all of them have in common the belief that these children need to be actively engaged. Therefore, they can do very well in a *Creative Curriculum* classroom. As children talk and play together in the atmosphere of a *Creative Curriculum* classroom, they become models, supports, friends, and tutors to the child with autism.

Throughout *The Creative Curriculum*, reference to strategies that might be used to help include children with disabilities always will be related to specific behaviors, rather than any identified conditions. Therefore, you can plan and individualize for these children as you would for every other child whom you teach.

> Ultimately the goal for children with disabilities is the same as for children without disabilities: to help them access the curriculum and maximize their potential. This is what meeting individual needs is all about!

English Language Learners

Children whose primary language is not English—"English Language Learners" (ELLs)—are very likely to be in your classroom, if not now, then in the future. The number of children who speak a first language that is not English has increased dramatically and continues to increase in the United States. The Census Bureau predicts that by the year 2025, Hispanic and Asian Americans will represent one-quarter of the entire U.S. population (U.S. Census Bureau, 2000).

You may have children who are learning two languages simultaneously. Others will arrive in your classroom never having heard spoken English, except perhaps on television. You may have several non-English speakers who share a common home language. Or you may have several children whose first language varies from Turkish to Rumanian to Vietnamese. The life circumstances of these children can be very different. However, they are all children first and English Language Learners second.

The depth of children's knowledge of their primary language can vary just as it does in children who speak only English at home.

Children learning English as a second language may vary greatly in their language skills and experiences. For instance, the depth of children's knowledge of their primary language can vary just as it does in children who speak only English at home.

Some children come from language-rich home environments and arrive with strong language skills in their primary language. Others from homes where adults may not be very verbal and rarely read books to their children have a poor foundation on which to build language skills.

Teachers should be aware of cultural and individual variations that affect a child's ability to understand how to function in the school setting and to use language to communicate with others. For some, the school environment may be very comfortable; for others, it can be totally confusing and foreign.

A number of misconceptions about learning a second language can cause unnecessary anxiety in teachers and parents. The chart below dispels some of these common misunderstandings (Genesee, n.d.; Snow, 1997).

Myths About Learning a Second Language

Myth	Reality
Children who are exposed to more than one language are at a clear disadvantage.	Bilingual children are often very creative and good at problem solving. Compared to children who speak one language, those who are bilingual can communicate with more people, read more, and benefit more from travel. Such children will have an additional skill when they enter the workforce.
Learning a second language confuses a child.	Children do not get confused, even when they combine languages in one sentence. Mixing languages is a normal and expected part of learning a second language.
Learning a second language as a preschooler invariably will slow down children's readiness to read.	Actually, the opposite is often true. Bilingual children make the transition to decoding words well.
When children are exposed to two languages, they never become as proficient in either language as children who have to master only one language.	As long as they are exposed consistently to both languages, children can become proficient readily in both languages.
Only the brightest children can learn two languages without encountering problems. Most children have difficulty because the process is so complex.	Nearly all children are capable of learning two languages during the preschool years.

The preschool years are a prime time for learning languages.

Research summarized in *Preventing Reading Difficulties in Young Children* (Snow, Burns, & Griffin, 1998) stresses the importance of supporting children's continued learning in their primary language while, at the same time, fostering their ability to learn to speak English. The research on brain development shows that the preschool years are a prime time for learning languages. Keep in mind these two very important findings:

- Children who develop a sound foundation in their first language are more efficient in learning the second language.

- Concepts and skills that are learned in the first language will transfer to the second language.

Being exposed to rich experiences in two languages is a definite asset. All children can benefit from learning another language.

Stages of Learning English as a Second Language

If you have children in your classroom who are learning English as a second language, knowing the complexity of the task and the stages children are likely to go through can be very helpful (Collier, 1995). As in all areas of development, children vary in their approaches to acquiring English as well as in the rate at which they acquire the new language. Preschoolers also vary in their readiness to demonstrate what they can say in their new language.

The chart on the opposite page lists the stages you can expect English Language Learners to go through, and what you might see children do at each stage.

Stages of Learning a Second Language

Stage	What You Might See
Home language use	Children use only their home language with teachers and other children.
Non-verbal period	Children limit (or stop) the use of their home language as they realize that their words are not understood by others. This period can last from a few months to one year. Children may use gestures or pantomime to express their needs.
Early speech	Children begin using one- and two-word phrases in English and name objects. They may use groups of words such as "stop it," "fall down," or "shut up," although they may not always use them appropriately.
Conversation	Children begin to use simple sentences in English like the ones they hear in their environment. They may begin to form their own sentences using the words they have learned. Like all young children, they gradually increase the length of their sentences.
Use of "academic" language of school	Children begin to acquire English associated with specific content knowledge while they continue to develop social language.

You may see characteristics of more than one stage in a child at any time, and the length of time children remain at a given stage varies. Recognize too, that children may mix their languages. For example, a child may speak in Spanish but insert an English word he has just learned, or a child speaking English may insert a Spanish word that he needs but doesn't know in English. Sometimes children will speak phrases in one language and then switch to another language. Language mixing or switching is perfectly normal and not necessarily an indication of a language problem.

As you become familiar with the process of learning a second language, you can monitor children's progress more effectively and support their learning and development. If you view learning a second language as a valuable experience and one that can enrich your classroom, all children will benefit, not only those who don't yet speak English.

The Developmental Continuum

As a teacher, you want to know if every child is developing and learning as expected in all four areas of development—social/emotional, physical, cognitive, and language—at the same time that you are aware of each child's individual differences and needs. *The Creative Curriculum Developmental Continuum for Ages 3–5* is your road map for determining where each child is developmentally, for tracking each child's progress, and for planning learning experiences.

In the previous sections on child development, you saw that in each area, development typically unfolds in progressive steps. Children don't master a particular skill all at once. There is a sequence of steps to expect as children progress toward reaching developmental milestones. Having a way to determine where each child is on the developmental road enables you to decide what kinds of experiences will support his or her progress. The *Developmental Continuum* lays out the progression of development in each developmental area. It is made up of goals and objectives.

The Creative Curriculum® Goals and Objectives at a Glance			
SOCIAL/EMOTIONAL DEVELOPMENT	**PHYSICAL DEVELOPMENT**	**COGNITIVE DEVELOPMENT**	**LANGUAGE DEVELOPMENT**
Sense of Self 1. Shows ability to adjust to new situations 2. Demonstrates appropriate trust in adults 3. Recognizes own feelings and manages them appropriately 4. Stands up for rights **Responsibility for Self and Others** 5. Demonstrates self-direction and independence 6. Takes responsibility for own well-being 7. Respects and cares for classroom environment and materials 8. Follows classroom routines 9. Follows classroom rules **Prosocial Behavior** 10. Plays well with other children 11. Recognizes the feelings of others and responds appropriately 12. Shares and respects the rights of others 13. Uses thinking skills to resolve conflicts	**Gross Motor** 14. Demonstrates basic locomotor skills (running, jumping, hopping, galloping) 15. Shows balance while moving 16. Climbs up and down 17. Pedals and steers a tricycle (or other wheeled vehicle) 18. Demonstrates throwing, kicking, and catching skills **Fine Motor** 19. Controls small muscles in hands 20. Coordinates eye-hand movement 21. Uses tools for writing and drawing	**Learning and Problem Solving** 22. Observes objects and events with curiosity 23. Approaches problems flexibly 24. Shows persistence in approaching tasks 25. Explores cause and effect 26. Applies knowledge or experience to a new context **Logical Thinking** 27. Classifies objects 28. Compares/measures 29. Arranges objects in a series 30. Recognizes patterns and can repeat them 31. Shows awareness of time concepts and sequence 32. Shows awareness of position in space 33. Uses one-to-one correspondence 34. Uses numbers and counting **Representation and Symbolic Thinking** 35. Takes on pretend roles and situations 36. Makes believe with objects 37. Makes and interprets representations	**Listening and Speaking** 38. Hears and discriminates the sounds of language 39. Expresses self using words and expanded sentences 40. Understands and follows oral directions 41. Answers questions 42. Asks questions 43. Actively participates in conversations **Reading and Writing** 44. Enjoys and values reading 45. Demonstrates understanding of print concepts 46. Demonstrates knowledge of the alphabet 47. Uses emerging reading skills to make meaning from print 48. Comprehends and interprets meaning from books and other texts 49. Understands the purpose of writing 50. Writes letters and words

What the Developmental Continuum Looks Like

You will see in the next section how each objective is broken into developmental steps. *The Creative Curriculum Developmental Continuum* shows the developmental steps for each of the 50 objectives. In the figure below, we use one objective—40, "Understands and follows oral directions"—as an example.

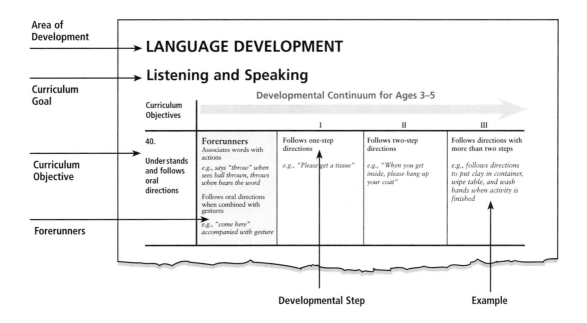

As you can see there are four columns following objective 40. The first shaded box represents Forerunners. We will return to this box below.

Steps I, II, and III: The Non-shaded Boxes

Moving from left to right, the next three boxes represent the expected developmental steps for each objective in the preschool years (children ages 3 to 5). Because children develop at very different rates, these boxes do not represent a specific age; rather they show the sequence of achieving each objective.

Step I, the first non-shaded box, approximates the beginning level. For objective 40, "Understands and follows oral directions," step I reads: "Follows one-step directions." To give you a picture of what this might look like in real life, we provide an example: *Please get a tissue.*

Step II, the second non-shaded box, identifies the next level in reaching the objective, "Understands and follows directions." Step II is: "Follows two-step directions." An example is a child who acts accordingly when told, *When you get inside, please hang up your coat.*

Steps I, II, and III represent the expected developmental steps for each objective in the preschool years.

Step III, the third non-shaded box, represents the next highest level of skill development: "Follows directions with more than two steps." An example that illustrates this step is, *Follows directions to put clay in container, wipe table, and wash hands when activity is finished.*

Children demonstrate their mastery of skills in a variety of ways. Because all of the examples presented in the Continuum are sample behaviors, you may or may not see these actual behaviors with the children you observe.

Forerunner Skills: The Shaded Box

Now let's return to the first shaded box. The stages identified in steps I, II, III apply to most children in your program. However, there may be children who, in one or more areas of development, are not in the typical range but lag behind. The first shaded box gives you a way to identify emerging skills in these children. We call them forerunners. The box is shaded to distinguish forerunners from the steps for each objective.

For objective 40, forerunner skills include

- Associates words with actions (*e.g., says "throw" when sees ball thrown, throws ball when hears the word*)

- Follows oral directions when combined with gestures (*e.g., "come here" accompanied with gesture*)

We have included forerunners out of a core belief underlying *The Creative Curriculum* that all children bring with them strengths and abilities on which you can build.

These are only examples of the many possible emergent skills a child in your program might exhibit for objective 40. For this objective, as well as every other, you are likely to observe forerunner skills that are not listed on the Continuum and that either precede or follow the ones we include. The looseness in breaking down forerunners allows for the fact that 3- to 5-year-olds with delays display a wide range of emerging skills. The forerunners do not follow a set time line; they are offered as examples of possible skills and behaviors on which you can build when planning for children.

There are many reasons why a child might be in this situation. Some children, because of lack of experience, may not have had an opportunity to develop a particular skill. For example, a child who has never had a crayon or marker in his hand may be in the very early stages of writing. Other children may have special needs or a diagnosed disability that affects one or more aspects of their development. Indeed, over the past 25 years, with federal law's emphasis on educating children in the "least restrictive environment," more children with disabilities are joining their non-disabled peers in preschool and are appearing in your classroom. We have included forerunners out of a core belief underlying *The Creative Curriculum* that all children bring with them strengths and abilities on which you can build.

Beyond the Continuum

Similarly, we recognize that you may have children who exceed widely held expectations for 3- to 5-year-olds and go beyond the scope of the *Developmental Continuum*. Such children generally are called gifted. The Continuum allows you to look at giftedness in each area of development. Calling a child gifted can be misleading. Children who are gifted generally do not excel in all areas of development. They may even be behind in some. The Continuum helps you see giftedness in particular areas rather than as an overall quality of the whole child.

While we don't include examples beyond step III, this step will give you an idea of how to increase the complexity of the task for children who are gifted in one area or another. For example, to challenge the child who is skilled at following directions with more than two steps, you might offer materials and experiences that move the child from the concrete to the symbolic or abstract. You could post picture directions to show children the procedure for turning on and using a computer or for following a recipe. Going beyond the Continuum will enable you to hold the interest of children with gifts and to support their development appropriately.

The Value of Looking at Goals and Objectives on a Continuum

Looking at goals and objectives on a continuum has a number of advantages. Specifically, *The Creative Curriculum Developmental Continuum for Ages 3–5*

- includes all children—those who are at a typical level, those who are behind, and those who are ahead

- breaks down each objective into realistic expectations to help you plan your program

- provides a framework for noting children's progress over time and, therefore, helps you observe and plan for all children in your program, including those who may not be developing typically

- fosters a positive approach to teaching by outlining what children can do and suggesting what comes next, rather than documenting what they cannot do

- gives you a wealth of information to share with families that will reassure them about their child's progress

In the remainder of this section, we present each of the 50 objectives and show you the continuum for each one. Teachers who work with children with developmental lags will find it helpful to see a further breakdown of these skills available in *The Expanded Forerunners of The Creative Curriculum Developmental Continuum for Ages 3–5.*

You may have children who exceed widely held expectations for 3- to 5-year-olds and go beyond the scope of the *Developmental Continuum.*

Social/Emotional Development

Sense of Self

Curriculum Objectives	Developmental Continuum for Ages 3–5			
	Forerunners	I	II	III
1. **Shows ability to adjust to new situations**	Interacts with teachers when family member is nearby Is able to move away from family member; checks back occasionally ("social referencing")	Treats arrival and departure as routine parts of the day *e.g., says good-bye to family members without undue stress; accepts comfort from teacher*	Accepts changes in daily schedules and routines *e.g., eagerly participates in a field trip; accepts visitors to classroom*	Functions with increasing independence in school *e.g., readily goes to other parts of the building for scheduled activities; willingly delivers a message from classroom teacher to the office*
2. **Demonstrates appropriate trust in adults**	Seeks to be near trusted adult as a "safe haven" Makes visual or physical contact with trusted adult for reassurance	Shows confidence in parents' and teachers' abilities to keep him/her safe and healthy *e.g., explores the indoor and outdoor environments without being fearful; summons adult when assistance is needed*	Regards parents and teachers as resources and positive role models *e.g., imitates parents going to work or at home during dramatic play; asks teacher's advice on how to saw a piece of wood in half*	Knows the difference between adults who can help (family members, friends, staff) and those who may not (strangers) *e.g., knows who is allowed to give her medicine; talks about why children shouldn't go anywhere with strangers*
3. **Recognizes own feelings and manages them appropriately**	Cries to express displeasure Uses facial expressions to communicate feelings *e.g., nods when asked if he is feeling sad*	Identifies and labels own feelings *e.g., says, "I'm mad at you"; "I really want to paint today"*	Is able to describe feelings and their causes *e.g., says, "I'm excited because my dad is coming home"; "I'm mad because they won't let me play with them"*	Is increasingly able to manage own feelings *e.g., calms self down when angry and uses words to explain why; chooses to go to a quiet area to be alone when upset*
4. **Stands up for rights**	Protests when slighted or wronged by crying or yelling Grabs or pushes when seeking a desired toy	Physically or verbally asserts needs and desires *e.g., continues to hold classroom pet another child wants; lets teacher know if another child refuses to give anyone a turn on the ride-on truck*	Asserts own needs and desires verbally without being aggressive *e.g., says, "It's my turn now" when sand timer runs out; tells friend who asks to paint at the easel, "I'm not done," and continues working*	Takes action to avoid possible disputes over rights *e.g., puts up "Do not knock down" sign in front of block structure; divides sandbox into area for himself and peer*

Social/Emotional Development

Responsibility for Self and Others

Curriculum Objectives		Developmental Continuum for Ages 3–5		
		I	II	III
5. Demonstrates self-direction and independence	**Forerunners** Purposefully indicates needs or wants (may be nonverbal) Selects toy or activity; plays briefly	Chooses and becomes involved in one activity out of several options e.g., during free play decides to play with giant dominoes on floor in toys and games area; after waking up from nap, takes book from shelf in library area and looks at it	Completes multiple tasks in a project of own choosing with some adult assistance e.g., makes a collage: collects materials, glue, paper, and scissors and works until done; builds a zoo with blocks, animal and people props, and cars	Carves out and completes own task without adult assistance e.g., draws one section of mural without intruding on other sections; makes a book about family trip that includes 5 pictures in sequence
6. Takes responsibility for own well-being	**Forerunners** Allows adult to attend to personal needs such as dressing or washing hands without resistance Uses self-help skills with adult assistance such as brushing teeth or putting on coat with help	Uses self-help skills with occasional reminders e.g., tries new foods when encouraged by teacher; washes hands with soap and water following procedures taught	Uses self-help skills and participates in chores without reminders e.g., goes to get a sponge after spilling juice; helps throw away trash after a picnic	Understands the importance of self-help skills and their role in healthy living e.g., tries new foods and talks about what's good for you; knows why it's important to wash hands and brush teeth
7. Respects and cares for classroom environment and materials	**Forerunners** Engages with/explores materials for brief periods of time with adult assistance or independently Participates in clean-up routines when asked	Uses materials in appropriate ways e.g., paints at easel; turns pages in book carefully without tearing	Puts away used materials before starting another activity e.g., shuts off the tape recorder before leaving the listening center; returns puzzle to shelf	Begins to take responsibility for care of the classroom environment e.g., gets broom and dust pan to help remove sand; pitches in willingly to move furniture to clear a group area
8. Follows classroom routines	**Forerunners** Allows adult to move him/her through routines Follows classroom routines with assistance such as reminders, picture cues, or physical help	Participates in classroom activities (e.g., circle time, clean-up, napping, toileting, eating, etc.) with prompting e.g., after cleaning up, goes to rug for circle time when the teacher strums the autoharp	Understands and follows classroom procedures without prompting e.g., goes to wash hands and brush teeth after lunch	Follows and understands the purpose of classroom procedures e.g., tells peer that he can't eat lunch until he's washed his hands
9. Follows classroom rules	**Forerunners** Follows simple directions and limits when told by an adult Follows classroom rules with assistance such as reminders, picture cues, or physical help	Follows classroom rules with reminders e.g., responds positively to guidance such as "speak with your indoor voice"	Understands and follows classroom rules without reminders e.g., returns puzzles to shelf before leaving the table area	Follows and understands reasons for classroom rules e.g., tells friend to put artwork on shelf so it will be safe; reminds peer not to run in classroom so that no one will get hurt

Social/Emotional Development

Prosocial Behavior

Curriculum Objectives	Developmental Continuum for Ages 3–5			
		I	II	III
10. **Plays well with other children**	**Forerunners** Tolerates being physically near others Plays alongside another child Enjoys simple back and forth games such as hide and seek	Works/plays cooperatively with one other child *e.g., draws or paints beside peer, making occasional comments; has a pretend phone conversation with another child*	Successfully enters a group and plays cooperatively *e.g., joins other children caring for babies in dramatic play center; plans with peers what they will need to set up a class restaurant*	Maintains an ongoing friendship with at least one other child *e.g., says, "We're friends again, right?" after working through a conflict; talks about another child as "my best friend"*
11. **Recognizes the feelings of others and responds appropriately**	**Forerunners** Notices expressions of feelings in others *e.g., looks or reacts by crying or laughing* Imitates other children's expressions of feelings	Is aware of other children's feelings and often responds in a like manner *e.g., laughs or smiles when others are happy; says a child is sad because her mom left*	Shows increasing awareness that people may have different feelings about the same situation *e.g., says that another child is afraid of thunder but, "I'm not"; acts out role of angry parent during pretend play*	Recognizes what another person might need or want *e.g., brings a book on trucks to show a child who loves trucks; helps a friend who is having difficulty opening a milk carton*
12. **Shares and respects the rights of others**	**Forerunners** Plays alongside another child using same or similar materials with adult assistance Plays alongside another child using same or similar materials without conflict	With prompts, shares or takes turns with others *e.g., allows sand timer to regulate turns with favorite toys; complies with teacher's request to let another child have a turn on the tricycle*	Shares toys or allows turn in response to another child's request *e.g., appropriately occupies self while waiting for others to leave swings without crying or demanding a turn; plays at sand table without grabbing items being used by others*	Shares and defends the rights of others to a turn *e.g., reminds child who doesn't want to relinquish a turn that it is another child's turn; asks teacher to intervene when two children begin to fight over a toy*
13. **Uses thinking skills to resolve conflicts**	**Forerunners** Accepts adult solution to resolve a conflict Seeks adult assistance to resolve a conflict *e.g., cries, approaches adult, or asks for help*	Accepts compromise when suggested by peer or teacher *e.g., agrees to play with another toy while waiting for a turn; goes to "peace table" with teacher and peer to solve a problem*	Suggests a solution to solve a problem; seeks adult assistance when needed *e.g., suggests trading one toy for another; asks teacher to make a waiting list for the water table*	Engages in a process of negotiation to reach a compromise *e.g., works out roles for a dramatic play episode; suggests going to the "peace table" to work out a problem*

Physical Development

Gross Motor

Curriculum Objectives	Developmental Continuum for Ages 3–5			
		I	II	III
14. **Demonstrates basic locomotor skills (running, jumping, hopping, galloping)**	**Forerunners** Walks with assistance Runs, sometimes falls Jumps and hops with hand held	Moves with direction and beginning coordination *e.g., runs avoiding obstacles; jumps forward, may lead with one foot; hops in place once or twice*	Moves with direction and increasing coordination *e.g., runs moving arms and legs; does a running jump with both feet; attempts to skip, often reverting to galloping*	Moves with direction and refined coordination *e.g., runs quickly changing directions, starting and stopping; jumps forward from standing position; gallops smoothly*
15. **Shows balance while moving**	**Forerunners** Walks on toes Easily stops, starts, changes direction, avoids obstacles Walks forward straddling line	Attempts to walk along a line, stepping off occasionally	Walks along wide beam such as edge of sandbox	Walks forward easily, and backward with effort, along a wide beam
16. **Climbs up and down**	**Forerunners** Crawls up stairs on own Walks up stairs with hand held Climbs a short, wide ladder with support from adult	Climbs a short, wide ladder	Climbs up and down stairs and ladders, and around obstacles	Climbs and plays easily on ramps, stairs, ladders, or sliding boards
17. **Pedals and steers a tricycle (or other wheeled vehicle)**	**Forerunners** Sits on tricycle or other riding toy, pushing forward/backward with feet not using pedals Pedals tricycle, difficulty with steering	Pedals in forward direction, steering around wide corners	Pedals and steers around obstacles and sharp corners	Rides with speed and control
18. **Demonstrates throwing, kicking, and catching skills**	**Forerunners** Hurls beanbag or ball Sits on floor and traps a rolled ball with arms and body Kicks a ball a short distance with hand held to maintain balance	Throws, catches, and kicks objects with somewhat awkward movements *e.g., throws ball with both hands; catches a large ball against body; kicks ball from standing position*	Throws, catches, and kicks with increasing control *e.g., throws ball overhand several feet toward target; catches bounced ball; moves toward ball and kicks*	Throws and kicks at target and catches with increasing accuracy *e.g., throws object with smooth overhand motion; catches object with elbows bent; kicks ball with fluid motion*

Physical Development

Fine Motor

Developmental Continuum for Ages 3–5

Curriculum Objectives	Forerunners	I	II	III
19. **Controls small muscles in hands**	**Forerunners** Uses self-help skills such as: finger feeds self; removes shoes/socks; washes hands with assistance Drops objects into container Touches thumb to finger to pick up object	Manipulates objects with hands *e.g., places large pegs in pegboard; buttons large buttons on own clothes; uses scissors to make snips*	Manipulates smaller objects with increasing control *e.g., eats with a fork; inserts and removes small pegs in pegboard; squeezes clothespin to hang painting; cuts with scissors along a straight or slightly curved line*	Manipulates a variety of objects requiring increased coordination *e.g., creates recognizable objects with clay; buttons, zips, and sometimes ties; cuts with scissors along lines, turning corners; cuts simple shapes out of paper*
20. **Coordinates eye-hand movement**	**Forerunners** Removes pegs from pegboard Opens a board book and turns a page Puts one block on top of another, holding the base block	Performs simple manipulations *e.g., makes a necklace with a string and large beads; rolls and pounds playdough; places pegs in pegboard*	Performs simple manipulations with increasing control *e.g., makes a necklace using small beads; pours water into a funnel*	Manipulates materials in a purposeful way, planning and attending to detail *e.g., strings a variety of small objects (straws, buttons, etc.); using table blocks, creates a tall structure that balances; completes 8-piece puzzle*
21. **Uses tools for writing and drawing**	**Forerunners** Holds large writing tool and marks with it Holds marker in palmar grasp and scribbles	Holds a marker or crayon with thumb and two fingers; makes simple strokes	Makes several basic strokes or figures; draws some recognizable objects	Copies and draws simple shapes, letters, and words including name

Cognitive Development

Learning and Problem Solving

Curriculum Objectives		Developmental Continuum for Ages 3–5		
	Forerunners	I	II	III
22. **Observes objects and events with curiosity**	Looks at and touches object presented by an adult or another child Explores materials in the environment *e.g., touching, looking, smelling, mouthing, listening, playing*	Examines with attention to detail, noticing attributes of objects *e.g., points out stripes on caterpillar; notices it gets darker when the sun goes behind a cloud; points out changes in animals or plants in room*	Notices and/or asks questions about similarities and differences *e.g., points out that two trucks are the same size; asks why the leaves fall off the trees*	Observes attentively and seeks relevant information *e.g., describes key features of different models of cars (such as logos, number of doors, type of license plate); investigates which objects will sink and which will float*
23. **Approaches problems flexibly**	Imitates adult or peer in solving problems Repeats and persists in trial and error approach	Finds multiple uses for classroom objects *e.g., uses wooden blocks as musical instruments; strings wooden beads into necklace for dress-up*	Experiments with materials in new ways when first way doesn't work *e.g., when playdough recipe produces sticky dough, asks for more flour; fills plastic bottle with water to make it sink*	Finds alternative solutions to problems *e.g., suggests using block as doorstop when classroom doorstop disappears; offers to swap trike for riding toy she wants and then adds fire-fighter hat to the bargain*
24. **Shows persistence in approaching tasks**	Remains engaged in a task for short periods with assistance Stays involved in self-selected activity such as playing with playdough for short periods	Sees simple tasks through to completion *e.g., puts toys away before going on to next activity; completes 5-piece puzzle*	Continues to work on task even when encountering difficulties *e.g., rebuilds block tower when it tumbles; keeps trying different puzzle pieces when pieces aren't fitting together*	Works on task over time, leaving and returning to complete it *e.g., continues to work on Lego structure over 3-day period; creates grocery store out of hollow blocks, adding more detail each day, and involves other children in playing grocery*
25. **Explores cause and effect**	Notices an effect *e.g., shows pleasure in turning light switch on and off, wants to do it again; repeatedly stacks blocks and watches them fall* Looks for something when it is out of sight	Notices and comments on effect *e.g., while shaking a jar of water says, "Look at the bubbles when I do this"; after spinning around and stopping says, "Spinning makes the room look like it's moving up and down"*	Wonders "what will happen if" and tests out possibilities *e.g., blows into cardboard tubes of different sizes to hear if different sounds are made; changes the incline of a board to make cars slide down faster*	Explains plans for testing cause and effect, and tries out ideas *e.g., places pennies one by one in 2 floating boats ("I'm seeing which boat sinks first"); mixes gray paint to match another batch ("Let's put in one drop of white at a time 'til it's right")*
26. **Applies knowledge or experience to a new context**	Follows familiar self-help routines at school (toileting, eating)—may need assistance	Draws on everyday experiences and applies this knowledge to similar situations *e.g., washes hands after playing at sand table; rocks baby doll in arms*	Applies new information or vocabulary to an activity or interaction *e.g., comments, "We're bouncing like Tigger" when jumping up and down with peer; uses traf-fic-directing signals after seeing a police officer demonstrate them*	Generates a rule, strategy, or idea from one learning experience and applies it in a new context *e.g., after learning to access one computer pro-gram by clicking on icons, uses similar procedures to access others; suggests voting to resolve a class-room issue*

Cognitive Development

Logical Thinking

Curriculum Objectives	Developmental Continuum for Ages 3–5			
		I	II	III
27. **Classifies objects**	**Forerunners** Finds two objects that are the same and comments or puts them together Groups similar kinds of toys together such as cars, blocks, or dolls	Sorts objects by one property such as size, shape, color, or use *e.g., sorts pebbles into three buckets by color; puts square block with other square blocks*	Sorts a group of objects by one property and then by another *e.g., collects leaves and sorts by size and then by color; puts self in group wearing shoes that tie and then in group with blue shoes*	Sorts objects into groups/subgroups and can state reason *e.g., sorts stickers into four piles ("Here are the stars that are silver and gold, and here are circles, silver and gold"); piles animals and then divides them into zoo and farm animals*
28. **Compares/ measures**	**Forerunners** Notices something new or different *e.g., a new classmate or a new toy on the shelf* Notices similarities of objects *e.g., "We have the same shoes"*	Notices similarities and differences *e.g., states, "The rose is the only flower in our garden that smells"; "I can run fast in my new shoes"*	Uses comparative words related to number, size, shape, texture, weight, color, speed, volume *e.g., "This bucket is heavier than that one"; "Now the music is going faster"*	Understands/uses measurement words and some standard measurement tools *e.g., uses unit blocks to measure length of rug; "We need 2 cups of flour and 1 cup of salt to make dough"*
29. **Arranges objects in a series**	**Forerunners** Uses self-correcting toys such as form boards and graduated stacking rings Sorts by one attribute *e.g., big blocks and little blocks*	Notices when one object in a series is out of place *e.g., removes the one measuring spoon out of place in a line and tries to put it in right place*	Figures out a logical order for a group of objects *e.g., makes necklace of graduated wooden beads; arranges magazine pictures of faces from nicest expression to meanest*	Through trial and error, arranges objects along a continuum according to two or more physical features *e.g., lines up bottle caps by height and width; sorts playdough cookies by size, color, and shape*
30. **Recognizes patterns and can repeat them**	**Forerunners** Completes a sentence that repeats in a familiar story Hums, sings, or responds to a chorus that repeats in a familiar song Completes a simple form board	Notices and recreates simple patterns with objects *e.g., makes a row of blocks alternating in size (big-small-big-small); strings beads in repeating patterns of 2 colors*	Extends patterns or creates simple patterns of own design *e.g., makes necklace of beads in which a sequence of 2 or more colors is repeated; continues block pattern of 2 colors*	Creates complex patterns of own design or by copying *e.g., imitates hand-clapping pattern (long clap followed by 3 short claps); designs a 3-color pattern using colored inch cubes and repeats it across the table*

Cognitive Development

Logical Thinking (continued)

Curriculum Objectives	Developmental Continuum for Ages 3–5			
		I	II	III
31. **Shows awareness of time concepts and sequence**	**Forerunners** Follows steps in simple routine such as in dressing or at naptime Demonstrates understanding of what comes next in daily schedule *e.g., goes to the table anticipating mealtime*	Demonstrates understanding of the present and may refer to past and future *e.g., responds appropriately when asked, "What did you do this morning?"; talks about, "Later, when Mom comes to pick me up"*	Uses past and future tenses and time words appropriately *e.g., talks about tomorrow, yesterday, last week; says, "After work time, we go outside"*	Associates events with time-related concepts *e.g., "Tomorrow is Saturday so there's no school"; "My birthday was last week"; "I go to bed at night"*
32. **Shows awareness of position in space**	**Forerunners** Moves objects from one container to another Follows simple positional directions with assistance *e.g., puts paper in trash can*	Shows comprehension of basic positional words and concepts *e.g., puts object in, on, under, on top of, or next to another object as requested*	Understands and uses positional words correctly *e.g., "Come sit near me"; "The fish food goes on the top shelf"*	Shows understanding that positional relationships vary with one's perspective *e.g., turns lotto card around so player opposite him can see it right side up; "I can reach the ring when I'm on the top step, but from here it's too far"*
33. **Uses one-to-one correspondence**	**Forerunners** Places an object in each designated space *e.g., puts a peg doll in each hole in a toy bus*	Matches pairs of objects in one-to-one correspondence *e.g., searches through dress-ups to find two shoes for her feet*	Places objects in one-to-one correspondence with another set *e.g., lines up brushes to make sure there is one for each jar of paint; goes around the table placing one cup at each child's place*	Uses one-to-one correspondence as a way to compare two sets *e.g., lines up cubes across from a friend's row to determine who has more; puts one rider next to each horse saying, "Are there enough horses for all the cowboys?"*
34. **Uses numbers and counting**	**Forerunners** Understands the concept of "one" *e.g., picks up one object when asked* Understands the concept of more *e.g., picks up more of something when directed, or asks for more cheese*	Imitates counting behavior using number names (may not always say one number per item or get the sequence right) *e.g., says the numbers from 1 to 5 while moving finger along a row of 8 items (not realizing that counting means one number per item)*	Counts correctly up to 5 or so using one number for each object (may not always keep track of what has or has not been counted) *e.g., counts out 5 pretzels taking one at a time from bowl; counts a collection of objects but may count an object more than one time*	Counts to 10 or so connecting number words and symbols to the objects counted and knows that the last number describes the total *e.g., counts 8 bottle caps and says, "I have 8"; spins dial, then moves board game piece 6 spaces; draws 5 figures to show members of family*

Cognitive Development

Representation and Symbolic Thinking

Curriculum Objectives	Developmental Continuum for Ages 3–5			
		I	II	III
35. **Takes on pretend roles and situations**	**Forerunners** Imitates simple action *e.g., picks up phone; rocks baby* With adult or peer support, imitates routines *e.g., pretends to feed doll; pours coffee; pretends to sleep*	Performs and labels actions associated with a role *e.g., feeding the baby doll, says, "I'm the Mommy"; picks up phone and says, "Hello, is Suzie there?"*	Offers a play theme and scenario *e.g., "Let's play school"; while listening to doll's heartbeat with stethoscope announces that it's time to get the baby to the hospital*	Engages in elaborate and sustained role play *e.g., suggests a play theme and discusses who will do what; discusses with peer what to buy at grocery store, takes pocketbook and goes to grocery store*
36. **Makes believe with objects**	**Forerunners** Imitates adult's or another child's use of familiar objects *e.g., rocks doll; stirs the pot* Interacts appropriately with objects with adult or peer support *e.g., responds to pretend phone call by putting phone to ear and vocalizing*	Interacts appropriately with real objects or replicas in pretend play *e.g., uses a broken phone to make a pretend phone call; puts playdough cookies on little plastic plates*	Uses substitute object or gesture to represent real object *e.g., holds hand to ear and pretends to dial phone; builds a sand castle and puts shell on top for "satellite dish"*	Uses make-believe props in planned and sustained play *e.g., pretends with a peer to be garage mechanics working on cars made of blocks; sets up scene for playing school—students sit on pillows and teacher has a box for a desk*
37. **Makes and interprets representations**	**Forerunners** Labels scribbles as people or common objects Interacts and builds with blocks Begins to use descriptive labels in construction play *e.g., "house," "road"*	Draws or constructs and then names what it is *e.g., draws pictures with different shapes and says, "This is my house"; lines up unit blocks and says, "I'm making a road"*	Draws or builds a construction that represents something specific *e.g., makes a helicopter with Bristle Blocks; draws 6 legs on insect after looking at beetle*	Plans then creates increasingly elaborate representations *e.g., uses blocks to make a maze for the class gerbil; draws fire truck and includes many details*

Language Development

Listening and Speaking

Curriculum Objectives	Developmental Continuum for Ages 3–5			
		I	II	III
38. **Hears and discriminates the sounds of language**	**Forerunners** Notices sounds in the environment *e.g., pays attention to birds singing, sirens* Joins in nursery rhymes and songs	Plays with words, sounds, and rhymes *e.g., repeats songs, rhymes, and chants; says, "Oh you Silly Willy"*	Recognizes and invents rhymes and repetitive phrases; notices words that begin the same way *e.g., makes up silly rhymes ("Bo, Bo, Biddle, Bop"); says, "My name begins the same as popcorn and pig"*	Hears and repeats separate sounds in words; plays with sounds to create new words *e.g., claps hands 3 times when saying "Su-zan-na"; says, "Pass the bapkin [napkin]"*
39. **Expresses self using words and expanded sentences**	**Forerunners** Uses non-verbal gestures or single words to communicate *e.g., points to ball* Uses 2-word phrases *e.g., "All gone"; "Go out"*	Uses simple sentences (3-4 words) to express wants and needs *e.g., "I want the trike"*	Uses longer sentences (5-6 words) to communicate *e.g., "I want to ride the trike when we go outside"*	Uses more complex sentences to express ideas and feelings *e.g., "I hope we can go outside today because I want to ride the tricycle around the track"*
40. **Understands and follows oral directions**	**Forerunners** Associates words with actions *e.g., says "throw" when sees ball thrown; throws when hears the word* Follows oral directions when combined with gestures *e.g., "come here" accompanied with gesture*	Follows one-step directions *e.g., "Please get a tissue"*	Follows two-step directions *e.g., "When you get inside, please hang up your coat"*	Follows directions with more than two steps *e.g., follows directions to put clay in container, wipe table, and wash hands when activity is finished*

Language Development

Listening and Speaking (continued)

Curriculum Objectives	Developmental Continuum for Ages 3–5			
		I	II	III
41. Answers questions	**Forerunners** Answers yes/no questions with words, gestures, or signs *e.g., points to purple paint when asked what color she wants*	Answers simple questions with one or two words *e.g., when asked for name says, "Curtis"; says, "Purple and blue" when asked the colors of paint*	Answers questions with a complete thought *e.g., responds, "I took a bus to school"; "I want purple and blue paint"*	Answers questions with details *e.g., describes a family trip when asked about weekend; says, "I want purple and blue like my new shoes so I can make lots of flowers"*
42. Asks questions	**Forerunners** Uses facial expressions/ gestures to ask a question Uses rising intonation to ask questions *e.g., "Mama comes back?"* Uses some "wh" words (what and where) to ask questions *e.g., "What that?"*	Asks simple questions *e.g., "What's for lunch?" "Can we play outside today?"*	Asks questions to further understanding *e.g., "Where did the snow go when it melted?" "Why does that man wear a uniform?"*	Asks increasingly complex questions to further own understanding *e.g., "What happened to the water in the fish tank? Did the fish drink it?"*
43. Actively participates in conver- sations	**Forerunners** Initiates communication by smiling and/or eye contact Responds to social greetings *e.g., waves in response to "hello" or "bye-bye"*	Responds to comments and questions from others *e.g., when one child says, "I have new shoes," shows own shoes and says, "Look at my new shoes"*	Responds to others' comments in a series of exchanges *e.g., makes relevant comments during a group discussion; provides more information when message is not understood*	Initiates and/or extends conversations for at least four exchanges *e.g., while talking with a friend, asks questions about what happened, what friend did, and shares own ideas*

Language Development

Reading and Writing

Curriculum Objectives	Developmental Continuum for Ages 3–5			
		I	II	III
44. **Enjoys and values reading**	**Forerunners** Looks at books and pictures with an adult or another child Chooses and looks at books independently Completes phrases in familiar stories	Listens to stories being read *e.g., asks teacher to read favorite story; repeats refrain when familiar book is read aloud*	Participates in story time interactively *e.g., answers questions before, during, and after read-aloud session; relates story to self; acts out familiar story with puppets*	Chooses to read on own; seeks information in books; sees self as reader *e.g., gives reasons for liking a book; looks for other books by favorite author; uses book on birds to identify egg found on nature walk*
45. **Demonstrates understanding of print concepts**	**Forerunners** Points to print on page and says, "Read this" Recognizes logos *e.g., McDonald's* Recognizes book by cover	Knows that print carries the message *e.g., points to printed label on shelf and says, "Cars go here"; looking at the name the teacher has written on another child's drawing, says, "Whose is this?"*	Shows general knowledge of how print works *e.g., runs finger over text left to right, top to bottom as he pretends to read; knows that names begin with a big letter*	Knows each spoken word can be written down and read *e.g., touches a written word for every spoken word in a story; looking at a menu asks, "Which word says pancakes?"*
46. **Demonstrates knowledge of the alphabet**	**Forerunners** Participates in songs and fingerplays about letters Points out print in environment *e.g., name on cubby, exit sign*	Recognizes and identifies a few letters by name *e.g., points to a cereal box and says, "That's C like in my name"*	Recognizes and names many letters *e.g., uses alphabet stamps and names the letters— "D, T, M"*	Beginning to make letter-sound connections *e.g., writes a big M and says, "This is for Mommy"*
47. **Uses emerging reading skills to make meaning from print**	**Forerunners** Uses familiar logos and words to read print *e.g., cereal logos, "exit" and "stop" signs* Recognizes own name in print and uses it as a cue to find possessions *e.g., cubby, cot, placemat*	Uses illustrations to guess what the text says *e.g., looking at* The Three Pigs, *says, "And the wolf blew down the pig's house"*	Makes judgements about words and text by noticing features (other than letters or words) *e.g., "That must be Christopher's name because it's so long"; "You didn't write enough words. I said, 'A Book about the Dog Biff,' and you just wrote three words"*	Uses different strategies (known words, knowledge of letters and sounds, patterns in text) to make meaning from print *e.g., "That word says book"; anticipates what comes next based on pattern in* Brown Bear; *figures out which word says* banana *because he knows it starts with* b

Language Development

Reading and Writing (continued)

Developmental Continuum for Ages 3–5

Curriculum Objectives	Forerunners	I	II	III
48. **Comprehends and interprets meaning from books and other texts**	Repeats words and actions demonstrated in books *e.g., roars like a lion* Relates story to self and shares information *e.g., after hearing a story about snow says, "I made a snowman"*	Imitates act of reading in play *e.g., holds up book and pretends to read to baby doll; takes out phonebook in dramatic play area to make a phone call*	Compares and predicts story events; acts out main events of a familiar story *e.g., compares own feelings about baby brother to those of character; re-enacts* Three Billy Goats Gruff	Retells a story including many details and draws connections between story events *e.g., says, "The wolf blew the house down because it wasn't strong"; uses flannel board to retell* The Very Hungry Caterpillar
49. **Understands the purpose of writing**	Watches when others write Pretends to write *(scribble writes)*	Imitates act of writing in play *e.g., pretends to write a prescription while playing clinic; scribble writes next to a picture*	Understands there is a way to write that conveys meaning *e.g., tells teacher, "Write this down so everyone can read it"; asks teacher, "How do I write* Happy Birthday?"; *says, "That's not writing, that's scribble-scrabble"*	Writes to convey meaning *e.g., on drawing for sick friend, writes own name; copies teacher's sign, "Do Not Disturb," to put near block pattern; makes deliberate letter choices during writing attempts*
50. **Writes letters and words**	Scribbles with crayons Experiments with writing tools such as markers and pencils Draws simple pictures to represent something	Uses scribble writing and letter-like forms	Writes recognizable letters, especially those in own name	Uses letters that represent sounds in writing words

conclusion

Knowing how preschool children develop is the starting point for every *Creative Curriculum* teacher. When you also know the unique characteristics of every child, you can build relationships that enable all children to thrive. And finally, looking at children's development on a continuum gives you a full picture of each child's learning and a road map for tracking children's progress. The Continuum thus serves as the teacher's primary tool for planning and guiding instruction, a topic we cover in detail in Chapter 4. In the next chapter we turn to the learning environment of a *Creative Curriculum* classroom.

References

A good beginning: Sending America's children to school with the social and emotional competence they need to succeed. (2000). Bethesda, MD: The Child Mental Health Foundations and Agencies Network (FAN) and The National Institute of Mental Health, Office of Communications and Public Liaison.

Chess, S., & Thomas, A. (1996). *Temperament: Theory and practice.* New York: Brunner/Mazel.

Collier, V. P. (1995). *Promoting academic success for ESL students: Understanding second language acquisition for school.* (No. 1-883514-00-2). Jersey City, NJ: New Jersey Teachers of English to Speakers of Other Languages-Bilingual Educators.

Genesee, F. (n.d.). *Bilingual acquisition.* Retrieved March 21, 2002, from http://www.earlychildhood.com/Articles/index.cfm?FuseAction=Article&A=38

Hanson, K. (1992). *Teaching mathematics effectively and equitably to females.* New York: ERIC Clearinghouse on Urban Education Institute for Urban and Minority Education.

Snow, C. E. (1997, November 1). The myths around being bilingual. *NABE News, 29,* 36.

Snow, C. E., Burns, M. S., & Griffin, P. (Eds.). (1998). *Preventing reading difficulties in young children.* Washington, DC: National Academy Press.

U.S. Census Bureau. Population Division. (January 13, 2000). (NP-D1-A) *Projections of the resident population by age, sex, race, and hispanic origin: 1999 to 2100.* Retrieved March 22, 2002, from http://www.census.gov/population/www/projections/natdet-D1A.html

U.S. Department of Education. Office of Educational Research and Improvement. National Center for Education Statistics. (2000). *The condition of education 2000.* (NCES 2000-062). Washington, DC: U.S. Government Printing Office. Also available at: http://www.nces.ed.gov

U.S. Office of the Surgeon General, President's Council on Physical Fitness and Sports. (1996). *Physical activity and health: a report of the Surgeon General.* Atlanta, GA, Washington, DC, Pittsburgh, PA: U.S. Government Printing Office.

inside this chapter

62 Setting Up and Maintaining the Classroom

62 Establishing Interest Areas

67 Other Aspects of the Physical Setting

73 Caring for the Classroom and Children's Work

76 Evaluating the Effectiveness of the Physical Environment

82 Establishing a Structure for Each Day

82 Daily Events

92 The Daily Schedule

97 Weekly Planning

100 Preparing for the First Few Days

102 Creating a Classroom Community

102 Promoting Positive Relationships in the Classroom

108 Developing Rules for a Classroom Community

110 Teaching Social Problem-Solving Skills

116 Responding to Challenging Behavior

123 Conclusion and References

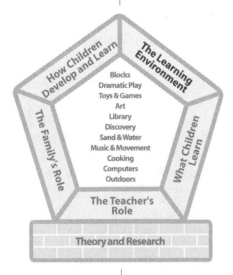

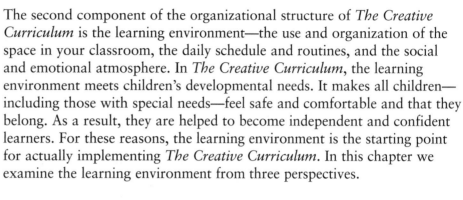

The Learning Environment

The second component of the organizational structure of *The Creative Curriculum* is the learning environment—the use and organization of the space in your classroom, the daily schedule and routines, and the social and emotional atmosphere. In *The Creative Curriculum*, the learning environment meets children's developmental needs. It makes all children—including those with special needs—feel safe and comfortable and that they belong. As a result, they are helped to become independent and confident learners. For these reasons, the learning environment is the starting point for actually implementing *The Creative Curriculum*. In this chapter we examine the learning environment from three perspectives.

Setting up and maintaining the classroom—the physical space of the *Creative Curriculum* classroom that is organized into 10 interest areas—Blocks, Dramatic Play, Toys and Games, Art, Library, Discovery, Sand andWater, Music and Movement, Cooking, and Computers—and Outdoors. Interest areas offer multiple opportunities for children to explore, discover, and grow. In each, the arrangement of furniture and the materials involves children not only in learning but also in caring for the classroom and what is in it.

Establishing a structure for each day—the daily routines and schedule that create a sense of order in *The Creative Curriculum*. Children know what to expect, and they understand what is expected of them. With the assurance that their environment is predictable and familiar, they can settle into learning and function as part of a group. The order around them creates a sense of order inside them.

Creating a classroom community—the social/emotional environment of the *Creative Curriculum* classroom. Teachers relate to children in positive ways and help them do the same with one another. The positive social climate helps children feel good about school and learn to the best of their ability.

Setting Up and Maintaining the Classroom

The physical environment in your classroom has a profound effect on individual children, the group as a whole, and you. The physical environment includes the size of the room, the colors of the walls, the type of flooring, the amount of light, and the number of windows. While you may have limited control over many of these features, you do have options about how to organize furniture, what materials to put out, and what you can bring outdoors to make the total space available to you more interesting.

A physical setting that is safe, attractive, comfortable, and well designed helps children engage in the activities you offer. Such an environment can support your goals for children and free you to observe and interact with them in positive ways.

Establishing Interest Areas

A physical space divided into interest areas is an ideal setting for preschool children who want to explore, make things, experiment, and pursue their own interests. Separate interest areas with varied materials offer children a range of clear choices. Sometimes children want to work quietly, either alone or with other children. Areas devoted to books, art activities, or toys and games provide several choices for quiet activities. Areas set aside for dramatic play, block building, woodworking, or large muscle activities provide choices for active engagement.

Interest areas, which subdivide the classroom into spaces that accommodate a few children at a time, address preschool children's preference to be in a small-group setting. With a manageable number of other children, they feel comfortable and play more positively than in larger groups. Likewise, in a smaller well-defined space, where they can concentrate on their work, children's play tends to become more complex and elaborate.

In a smaller well-defined space, where they can concentrate on their work, children's play tends to become more complex and elaborate.

As we already mentioned, a *Creative Curriculum* classroom is divided into areas for dramatic play, block building, toys and games, art, looking at books and writing, sand and water play, and a discovery table. There should also be a place for cooking activities, even if it's just a table that also serves as a "snack bar" where children can help prepare and serve themselves a snack. Ideally, children should have access to musical instruments and equipment where they can make or listen to music. Computers may have a designated space, be incorporated in the Library Area, or be located in areas of your room where they would have a natural use, such as a Discovery Area.

Interest Areas

1. Blocks
2. Dramatic Play
3. Toys and Games
4. Art
5. Library
6. Discovery
7. Sand and Water
8. Music and Movement
9. Cooking
10. Computers

Guidelines for Setting Up Interest Areas

To set up interest areas, note the location of electrical outlets, windows, doors, a sink, and storage space. See what moveable furnishings—such as shelves, tables, freestanding easels, and dramatic play furniture—are available for defining space. Take an inventory of the particular challenges in your room: built-ins, columns, radiators, exposed pipes, the locations of doors that cannot be blocked, and so on.

Space Planning Guidelines

Establish traffic patterns for entering the room, putting belongings in cubbies, using the bathroom, moving from one area to another.

Clearly define areas that need protection, such as block building and a cozy library nook, using shelves and the walls.

Locate interest areas that are relatively quiet, such as books, art, computers, and toys and games, **away from noisier ones**, such as blocks and woodworking.

Decide which areas need tables—toys and games, art, writing/book area, cooking. Because young children use the floor and open spaces for so much of their play, keep the number of tables to a minimum. Remember that you need just enough table space so everyone, including adults, can be seated at one time for snacks or meals. The tables should remain in the interest areas where they are located, not moved together cafeteria style.

Think about activities that are affected by floor coverings. Ideally, messy activities such as art, sand and water, and cooking should be on a floor that can be washed. Also assess whether you will need drop cloths, pieces of vinyl, or a shower curtain. Blocks require a comfortable, soft floor where children can sit or work on their knees.

Place interest areas near needed resources. Art, water play, and cooking activities should be near a water source; computers, CD players, and tape recorders need electrical outlets.

Reserve areas with lots of light for places where children will look at books, write and draw, care for plants.

Organize the room so you can see as much as possible from every location to ensure children's safety. Regulations on child abuse prevention require supervision of children at all times, which means always having children in full view.

Equipping Interest Areas

Interest areas work well when the materials you select are attractive, inviting, relevant to children's experiences and culture, and challenging but not frustrating. The materials should introduce children to interesting content: pets and plants to observe and care for (science); collections to sort and graph (math); resource books for looking up information (literacy); gears and clocks to take apart (technology); and more.

In general, a good rule to follow in the beginning of the year is less is better. Too many new materials at the outset can overwhelm children. Start by allowing time for them to learn how to use and care for the materials. It is important to explain this strategy to parents during the first days because the limited number of materials you have out may surprise them.

To minimize sharing problems, put out duplicates of basic materials rather than a large selection of different items, and include familiar materials such as puzzles, stringing beads, and crayons. To select materials for each interest area, turn to the sections on Creating an Environment in chapters 6 through 16.

Displaying and Labeling Materials

Everything in your classroom should have a designated place. All children benefit from this kind of order, but it is especially important for children with special needs who require consistency and predictability in their environment. When children know where things are and how and why they are grouped, they can work independently and constructively. They can also participate meaningfully in cleanup and in caring for the classroom.

While you can be flexible about where children use materials during choice time (e.g., taking colored inch cubes from the Toys and Games Area to use in decorating their block constructions), having a clearly marked place for everything makes it easier for children to return materials at clean-up time.

In the beginning of the year less is better.

When children know where things are and how and why they are grouped, they can work independently and constructively.

To show children that everything has a place, label storage places.

To show children that everything has a place, label storage places. You can use photos, pictures of toys or equipment cut from catalogs or packaging, drawings, or paper shapes made from solid-colored Contact paper (for materials such as blocks or woodworking tools) as labels.

Labels should have both pictures and words—in English and in the children's home languages. Including a sample of the object itself as part of the label (e.g., a bead or a marker) will be especially helpful for children with visual impairments or those learning English as a second language.

If you cover picture labels with clear Contact paper or laminate them, they will last longer and you can move them if needed instead of making new ones. Tape labels on containers that hold objects or directly on the shelves. When you label materials in this way, cleanup becomes a matching and literacy game that helps children learn as they find the proper place for each object.

Store materials that go together in the same place. For example, put pegs with pegboards, collage materials with glue and paper, and cars with the blocks.

Use containers such as plastic dishpans, clear plastic containers, baskets, or shoe boxes to hold materials and toys with small pieces.

Use pegs, Velcro, or a child-size clothes tree for objects that you want to hang up, such as dress-up clothes, utensils, smocks, etc.

Display materials so that children can see them easily. Place materials and toys on low shelves at children's eye level. Put books on a shelf with the covers facing out.

Store sharp items such as graters, knives, and electric frying pans for cooking out of reach. Bring them out as needed and supervise their use carefully.

Other Aspects of the Physical Setting

In addition to establishing interest areas, there are other aspects of the physical setting to consider as you set up your room. You will need to identify a place for group time, places for displays, and storage areas for children's belongings and for materials children should not be allowed to use on their own. Depending on children's needs, you may have to make adaptations to your environment so all children have access to interest areas and materials. The classroom should be as comfortable and attractive as possible so children enjoy being there.

A Place for Group Time

Establish a place in your classroom where the whole group can gather together to talk about and plan the day, listen to stories, transition from one activity to another, and participate in music and movement activities. Many classrooms are not large enough to have the luxury of an area that can be devoted solely to these whole-group activities. If your room has limited space, you can hold meetings in one of the large interest areas, for example, the Block Area or Library.

Group Time Space Guidelines

Allow sufficient floor space to accommodate all the children and adults in a circle.

Provide comfortable seating on the floor. If the area you select does not have a carpet or rug, you might use carpet squares so every child has a soft place to sit.

Allocate space for charts, such as a job chart, the daily schedule, or charts for graphing activities.

Include an easel or chart stand so you can document group discussions or display a big book as you read to the class.

Locate near electrical outlets to play tapes or CDs and **cupboards** for materials such as tapes, CDs, scarves, and rhythm band instruments.

Classroom Displays

Most of the display space in your classroom should be saved for children's work. Some teachers make a special place for each child's work on the walls and let children select the items they want to display in their space. A large sheet of construction paper can serve as a frame. Include the children's names (and a photograph if you like) to identify their work.

Invite children to tell you what it is, how they made it, what they like about it, or what they learned doing it. Write down what they say on a card and include it in the display. These practices promote literacy. They also convey the important message to children that their work is valuable and that they should protect it. Displays of children's work also let visitors to your classroom know what you are teaching and what your group and individual children are learning.

Display children's work prominently, and at their eye level, to underscore that it is important and worth protecting. Keep displays simple. When the walls and all available spaces are filled with posters and artwork, children, and even visitors, are overwhelmed and find it hard to focus on any one thing. In addition, change displays regularly. When children see the same things up week after week, they cannot see their progress, lose interest, and begin to ignore what is displayed.

Most of the display space in your classroom should be saved for children's work.

In the beginning of the year, select a prominent place to set up a display called "Classroom Community," featuring photos of the children with their family members. If you make home visits before school starts, take along a camera for this purpose. Or, take pictures as children and families arrive on the first day. Be sure to include your own picture and that of your co-teacher. As children get to know other members of the school community—the director, custodians, food service personnel, bus drivers, nurse—add their photos as well. As the year progresses, take photos of children working in different interest areas. Display these photos with a note about what children are learning. Children, as well as families and administrators, will be interested in these displays. They are an excellent way to share the Curriculum.

Be sure that store bought books and posters you display include pictures of people from many ethnic backgrounds and of both sexes. To convey that everyone has an important role to play, look for pictures showing people of all ages and abilities doing all sorts of jobs.

Consider the following places for displays:

- walls and bulletin boards

- pillars

- the tops and backs of shelves

- a clothesline and clothespins or fishnet

- easels

- room dividers

You may need to be creative about displays if regulations or other licensing codes don't allow you to secure items to the walls. A hanging bulletin board is one option.

Places for Storage

An orderly classroom requires storage space. Think in terms of three different types of storage: open storage for materials you want accessible to children; secure storage for materials you want to control; and personal storage for children and adults.

Six to eight sturdy shelves that won't tip over are ideal for materials you want children to use independently. You can supplement open shelving with plastic milk crates latched together. You also will need to find storage for cots or mats and blankets and pillows if children will be taking naps.

Use photos of the children in displays.

Look for pictures showing people of all ages and abilities doing all sorts of jobs.

Use secure storage for things like cleaning fluids, knives, etc., to ensure children's safety. Secure storage is also useful to put away materials you want to use later in the year. Organize and label what you store so you can find what you need easily, when you want it.

Designate places for children's belongings that are easily accessible and clearly labeled with a child's photo and name. Provide every child with a cubby or hook for coats, hats, mittens, boots, backpacks, and extra clothing. For treasures brought from home or work on its way home, labeled dishpans are useful. Finally, set aside a place where adults in the classroom—teachers, visitors, and family members—can store their belongings safely.

A Comfortable and Attractive Setting

Because you and the children spend a large part of the day in the classroom, it should be comfortable and attractive, with home-like touches

Take advantage of **natural light** as much as possible. Mirrors reflect light and allow children to look at the environment from a different perspective. Table lamps and floor lamps add to the coziness of the classroom.

Incorporate **softness** into the environment wherever possible—soft chairs, a crib mattress or futon covered with an attractive sheet, pillows, area rugs, and stuffed animals.

Add a variety of **textures** to stimulate children's sense of touch—bumpy, smooth, rough, squishy, prickly, silky, coarse.

Provide **quiet spaces** where children can go to get away and be alone when they need some private time—lofts, tents, an old bathtub or large box filled with pillows, a comfortable chair near a fish tank or tape deck with headphones.

Include **home-like touches**—a welcome mat at the door, fresh flowers in vases on tables, wicker baskets to hold plants or paper trash, curtains on the windows, lamps, artifacts from home, tablecloths and place mats, photograph albums, colorful soaps by the sink, magnets on a refrigerator (or any metal surface).

Bring **living things** into the classroom: plants and pets children can observe, cuddle, and care for. In the Discovery Area include natural objects such as birds' nests, pinecones, shells, an empty beehive, an ant farm.

 Adaptations for Children With Disabilities

Depending on the type and severity of children's disabilities, you may need to take the steps described in the box on the next page.

If you have children with physical or sensory disabilities in your program, you may need to adapt the space and modify materials to ensure safety and accessibility. A special education consultant can help you evaluate your classroom and outdoor areas to determine what changes, if any, are needed to encourage each child's full participation. Depending on the type and severity of children's disabilities, you may need to take the steps described in the box on the next page.

Adaptations for Children With Disabilities

Make sure **traffic patterns** between interest areas are wide enough to accommodate a wheelchair or a walker. Ramps and raised toilets may be needed to make facilities accessible.

Adjust **tables** so wheelchairs will fit underneath or equip the wheelchairs with trays. Provide tall **stools** so other children can sit comfortably at a raised table.

Provide **bolsters** or other supports so children with mobility impairments can do activities on the floor.

Allocate room for **adaptive equipment** a child uses to stand, sit, or walk.

Use **puzzles with knobs** for children with visual or motor impairments.

Investigate **hardware adaptations on computers** for children with visual disabilities, articulation problems, and manual dexterity limitations.

Include objects that a **visually impaired child** can feel.

Be aware that for a child with a **hearing impairment**, sitting close to loud areas/sounds can interfere with a hearing aid.

Caring for the Classroom and Children's Work

Maintaining your classroom should be a shared job. By having children care for their space, they will learn to be responsible. They also will become competent and organized. Teachers need to identify jobs so everyone shares in the chores that have to be done and provide ways to protect children's work.

A System for Classroom Jobs

Because the room belongs to everyone, taking care of it is a shared responsibility. Everyone has jobs. Some jobs everyone does every day: cleaning up during choice time, putting away personal belongings, scraping dishes and throwing out trash after meals are examples. Other classroom jobs—watering the plants, feeding pets, putting out cots, wiping tables, cleaning paintbrushes, setting the tables for snacks and meals—can be rotated each week. With young preschoolers, you may want to talk informally about doing jobs. Older preschoolers can handle a more formal system.

One way to introduce caring for the classroom as a shared responsibility is to have a job chart. You can discuss the different jobs and explain to the children how they can refer to the chart to learn which job they have. If children do not yet recognize their names in print, you can make cards that include a photo or symbol of each job along with the child's written name.

Talk with children about what needs to be done to keep the classroom in order. You can generate a list with older 4s and 5s, who usually understand what you mean by a job. However, you can't assume that children will come up with a complete list. You may have to add some jobs, explain about caring for the classroom, and ask leading questions. Here are some things you might say:

Our classroom looks so clean and organized today. I've been thinking about what we need to do to keep it looking this way. Does anyone have any ideas?

What kinds of jobs do we need to keep the room looking neat? I'll make a list of your ideas.

We know that plants need water to grow, so I guess we need to be sure someone is in charge of our plants.

Suppose we finish eating and there is food on the tables. What would we have to do to clean up?

After this type of discussion, you can tell the children that you will make a chart listing all the jobs and that everyone will have a job each day. When you introduce the job chart you've made at a later meeting time, review each job and talk about how many children will do each one. To reinforce the idea that each child has a role in keeping the classroom in order, include categories like "Day Off" or "Substitute" so that everyone's name appears somewhere on the chart. "Substitute" has the additional advantage of assigning responsibility when someone with a job is absent.

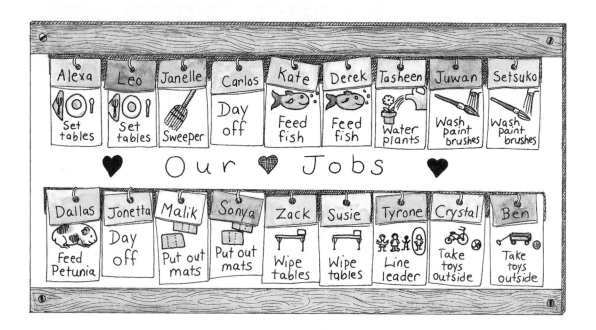

Strategies for Protecting Children's Work

The work children do in the classroom is tangible evidence of what they are learning and their competence as learners. Protecting children's work shows respect for their efforts.

Being as flexible as possible about time and materials has a positive effect on children's work habits, allows for the pride that comes from completing a project, and conveys the value you place on considering every child's needs. When teachers ask children to dismantle something they have worked hard to create—a carefully balanced block structure or a complex design made with pattern blocks—they may feel their work is not valued. Similarly, ending a work period when many children are totally engaged in their work sends a message that the work children do is not as important as the schedule. Here are some ways to protect children's work and convey respect for their accomplishments.

Provide boundaries to protect work.

Give children a concrete way to know where their work space begins and ends. For instance, in the Block Area you can define work spaces by providing sheets of cardboard on which children can build, or use hula hoops, carpet squares, or masking tape to define each building area. A large cardboard box with the top and bottom removed also can define a space in which one or more children can build (depending on the size of the box). When not in use, the boxes can be folded flat for easy storage. Similarly, in the Toys and Games Area, you can provide cafeteria trays on which children can build designs or contain a set of beads. Creating clearly marked work spaces helps children learn how to define their own work spaces, not only in school but elsewhere as well.

Preserve unfinished projects.

Because children may want to continue working on a project they have started, sometimes returning to it for several days in a row, you will need a way to preserve unfinished work. Plastic trays are excellent for holding and storing a design with table blocks, construction toys, or an art project that is incomplete. Identify a shelf in the classroom to store these trays. A project can remain on the tray as long as a child wants to work on it. However, you need to keep other children's wishes in mind. Projects should be kept only as long as a child is working on it, especially if they involve materials needed by others. If you find that a particular type of material is very popular, try to provide duplicates. Establish the rule that if another child needs some materials that are being used for a project, first ask that child if he or she still needs them. If so, help the child find something else that will work.

Take pictures.

An instant or digital camera is a valuable tool for preserving work. When a child has completed a project, you can take a picture before dismantling it and returning the materials it contains to their places. This practice is especially useful for block buildings and designs made with construction toys. Pictures enable children to share their work with the whole class and the class to be inspired by an individual child's work.

Invite children to share their work.

When you gather children together after choice time, allow time for them to talk about what they did and share their work. Don't require every child to share. You can help reluctant children, however, by describing what you observed and asking questions. "Alexa, Crystal, and Juwan, you did a lot of work on setting up our grocery store today. Want to tell us what you did?" "I saw Dallas working for the longest time on our new puzzle. It's a hard one, isn't it?"

Creating clearly marked work spaces helps children learn how to define their own work spaces.

Pictures enable children to share their work with the whole class and the class to be inspired by an individual child's work.

Evaluating the Effectiveness of the Physical Environment

You will know your classroom environment is well organized if children are able to act in these ways.

- **Make** choices and select activities on their own.

- **Use materials appropriately** and creatively once they enter an interest area.

- **Stay involved** with an activity for a sustained period of time.

- **Experience success** when they play.

- **Help care** for materials.

Take time to evaluate the physical environment. Does it convey the messages you intend? Is it working for you? Are you experiencing any problems that might be addressed by changing the environment?

Does It Convey the Messages I Intend?

Teachers who are aware of the power of the environment arrange their space purposefully to convey the messages they want children to receive. Use the messages below and methods for conveying them as a guide to assess how well your room arrangement is working.

"This is a good place to be."

- Furniture is clean and well maintained.

- Wall decorations consist mostly of children's art displayed attractively at their eye level and with large spaces of blank wall so as not to be overwhelming.

- The room includes decorative touches, including plants, displays of collections (such as shells, leaves, stones), pretty fabric-covered pillows or tablecloths, and a well-lit fish tank.

- Bright colors are used selectively on neutral-colored walls to highlight interest areas or mark storage areas on shelves.

"You belong here."

- Each child has a cubby or basket—marked with his name or picture—for keeping personal items.

- Furniture is child-size and in good condition.

- Pictures on the wall, in books, and in learning materials include people of different ethnic backgrounds and economic means, people with disabilities, non-traditional families, and women and men in different types of jobs.

- Each child's work is displayed and protected.

- Materials, equipment, and furniture are adapted so children with disabilities can be involved in all areas of the classroom.

- Materials reflect the children's home life and culture.

- Pictures of the children with their families are displayed.

"This is a place you can trust."

- Equipment and materials are arranged consistently so children know where to find the things they need.

- Shelves are neat and uncluttered, and materials are labeled so children can make choices easily.

- A well-defined, illustrated schedule is prominently displayed so children learn the order of events that occur each day and know what to expect.

- Routines such as transitions, eating, napping, and toileting are consistent.

"There are places where you can be by yourself when you want to."

- Small, quiet areas of the room accommodate one or two children.

- A large pillow or stuffed chair in a quiet corner with minimal displays invites children to enjoy being quiet and alone.

- Headphones for a CD player, tape recorders, and/or computers allow for individual listening.

"You can do many things on your own here."

- Materials are stored on low shelves so children can reach them without help.

- Materials are organized logically (drawing paper is near the markers and crayons, pegs are near the pegboards) and located in areas where they are to be used.

- Shelves are labeled with pictures and words that show children where toys and materials belong.

- Labels and printed material are in the home language of the children, if possible, as well as in English.

- An illustrated job chart (for older preschoolers) shows that everyone in the classroom has a job every day.

- Photographs of children doing interesting things in the classroom are on display.

"This is a safe place to explore and try out your ideas."

- Protected and defined quiet areas encourage small-group activities (e.g., a table with three to four chairs enclosed by low shelves containing toys and games).

- Smocks are available for art activities and water play so children can express themselves without fear of getting dirty.

- Protected floor space for building with blocks is clearly defined and out of the way of traffic.

- The outdoor area is fenced in and protected.

- Materials are displayed attractively, inviting children to use them.

- Toys that have not been used for a long time are rotated frequently and new things added to keep children's interest. Children who may find changes unsettling are prepared ahead of time.

How Is It Working?

In addition to considering the messages your classroom conveys, take time each day to assess how well the physical setting is working for children and for you. Observe children systematically during transitions, group times, and choice time when they select their own activities. Your observations will tell you what materials children typically select, how they use these materials, what they are learning, and how they relate to their peers while working. With this information, you can make the appropriate changes to the physical environment. Specific questions can help to focus your observations. Here are some examples of questions you might ask yourself.

How children select interest areas and materials

- Which interest areas and materials are most popular? Which are rarely used?

- Do any children need help in making choices?

- Does anyone need a more clearly defined work space?

- Do the traffic patterns permit children to move easily about the room, play safely, and build structures without interference?

- Are children able to find and return materials independently?

- Do children show gender-related preferences for materials or toys?

How children use materials

- Do children have the skills to use materials successfully?

- Do children use materials appropriately and creatively?

- Which types of materials seem to stimulate dramatic play? Group play?

- Which materials hold children's interest the longest?

- Are there enough materials to keep children meaningfully involved?

- Is sharing a problem?

- Are the materials reflective of children's backgrounds and home life?

- Do children know how to care for materials?

How children interact with others

- Are children able to play successfully near and with each other?

- Are any children isolated and rejected by their peers?

- Which children play together most often?

- Are children talking together about what they are doing?

- How do children ask for help from adults? From peers?

- Which play experiences seem to foster cooperative play? Individual play?

What Problems Might Be Related to the Physical Setting?

Even if you have organized the classroom and outdoor areas carefully, things don't always go according to plan. Children may fight over toys, wander about, become easily distracted, or use materials inappropriately. Although such behaviors can have several causes, the room arrangement may be one contributing factor.

If children's behavior is troublesome, a few changes in your room arrangement can make a dramatic difference. You also can involve children in finding solutions to problems. For example, during a discussion at group time you might say: "I notice that block buildings are being knocked down as people walk by. I wonder how we can fix this problem." Children are likely to be more cooperative if you involve them in coming up with a solution and then rearrange the room accordingly, than if you decide on a solution yourself. Involving children also conveys the message that they are competent to solve problems, that you expect them to take responsibility for doing so, and that the classroom belongs to everyone.

The following chart presents possible reasons for restless or disruptive behavior related to the environment and identifies strategies for rearranging the space to correct and prevent recurrences of the problem.

Challenging Behavior: Causes and Strategies

Problem Behavior	Possible Causes	Changes to the Environment
Running in the classroom	Too much space is open; room is not divided into small enough areas; activity areas are not well defined.	Use shelves and furniture to divide the space. Avoid open spaces that encourage children to run.
Fighting over toys	Too many popular toys are one of a kind; children are asked to share too often.	Provide duplicates of toys; show children when it will be their turn (e.g., use a timer with a bell, a sand timer, or a list with names of children waiting for their turn).
Wandering around; unable to choose activities	Room is too cluttered; choices are not clear; there is not enough to do.	Get rid of clutter. Simplify the layout of the room and materials. Add more activity choices.
Becoming easily distracted; trouble staying with a task and completing it	Areas are undefined and open; children can see everything going on in the room; materials are too difficult or children are bored with them.	Use shelves to define areas to minimize distractions. Separate noisy and quiet areas. Assess children's skills and select materials they can use successfully.
Continually intruding on others' work spaces	Space is limited, and poor traffic patterns prevent children from spreading out.	Define work areas for children (e.g., use masking tape or sections of cardboard for block building, trays or place mats for toys). Limit the number of areas open at one time to allow more space for each.
Misusing materials and resisting cleanup	Materials on shelves are messy; the display of materials is not orderly; children don't know how to use materials appropriately.	Make a place for everything. Use picture labels to show where materials go. Provide consistent guidance on how to clean up.

Children's behavior is a good indication of how the physical environment of your classroom is working. Once you set up the classroom as an effective learning environment, you can turn your attention to establishing the daily routines and schedule.

Establishing a Structure for Each Day

The second aspect of building an effective learning environment is establishing a structure for each day—the predictable use of time. When time is blocked out in an orderly and consistent fashion, children tend to feel safe and secure and develop increasing independence. When children don't know when things will happen, classroom life can seem chaotic.

In defining a structure for the day, think about the different events you include each day, for instance, taking attendance, gathering children together, offering choices, making transitions, and providing mealtimes and rest time. Place these events in an organized daily schedule. You also will need to develop plans for each week. We provide a Weekly Planning Form to help you do this. Because the first few days are often difficult for children, we suggest modifying the structure in the beginning as you introduce children to the program. By structuring daily and weekly time into a schedule, you meet children's developmental need for regularity and reliability.

Daily Events

Daily activities and routines in preschool programs typically include taking attendance, periods when you meet with all the children in a large group or with a few children in a small-group activity, choice times when children are free to go to interest areas and to use whatever materials they wish, as well as mealtimes and rest time. Note that activities such as story time and outdoor play are omitted from this discussion. They are covered in detail in Part II of this book, in the discussion of the interest areas where they take place.

Taking Attendance

Taking attendance is more than a practical necessity. It is an opportunity to identify all the children in the class who are present that day and think about those who are missing. If you take attendance during the first meeting of the day (which we discuss next), take time to pause after you say each child's name, have children identify themselves, and perhaps say a word or two to each one.

List children's names on a chart to promote literacy.

To involve children more and to help them recognize their own and each other's names, you might have a list of all the children's names on a chart. Linger for a moment as you point to and say each child's name. If you vary the order so children will be responding more to the print than a place on the page, this activity promotes literacy. Soon the children will be calling out the names with you.

Consider creating a "Who's Missing" chart where you write the names of any children who are absent as a concrete reminder that everyone is still a member of the community even if a child is not present. Each day when you take attendance, talk about the children who are absent and read off their names. Teachers who use this practice find that when children return, the first thing they do is cross their names off the "missing" chart. You might want to vary the way you take attendance during the year. Here are two approaches that also support literacy and mathematical thinking.

1. **Make a Velcro-backed card with each child's name and picture.** In the beginning of the year, put both the child's photograph and name on the card; later, remove the picture. Put the cards in a place where children can get to them easily. Have children select their own card and place it on a board to indicate they have arrived. When you gather your group you can count the cards together to find out how many children are at school. At the end of the day, children can place their cards in a box as they leave.

2. **Provide paper and large pencils so children can sign in each morning.** You might want to provide two clipboards: one for parents to sign their child's name and one for children. You will find that children who could only scribble their names initially learn to write clearly over time.

Large-Group Time

Large group meetings are most successful when the meeting time is kept short—five to twenty minutes, depending on the children—and children are interested in what is happening. When well structured, meetings that involve the whole class serve several purposes.

Perhaps most important, meetings provide an opportunity for children to experience a sense of belonging to a group. Children practice communication skills as they express their thoughts, ideas, and feelings and share the work they have been doing. Group time provides an opportunity to talk about and solve problems that affect the whole group. And topics that emerge in group time sometimes serve as a springboard for a new study.

Like most teachers, you probably will have a large-group time in the morning and again at the end of the day. In addition, you may want to gather the children together at other times—to read a story before rest time, to discuss plans for the next activity, to solve a problem that may have occurred during choice time, or to welcome a special visitor to your class.

The first meeting can set the tone for the day. Children are often eager to talk about a variety of topics—what happened at home, a new pair of shoes, or who they are going to play with at school. Start this meeting in a similar way each day, for example, singing a good morning song or reciting a favorite fingerplay. The sameness gives the day predictability and consistency.

Take the opportunity to teach math by having the children count how many are present that day. Touch on science by discussing the weather and drawing children's attention to the signs of the seasons, and on social studies by talking about community happenings—the opening of a new store, a fire, the arrival of the circus. At large-group meetings you also can talk about the schedule of the day. You might introduce new materials in the interest areas, or discuss a field trip, a special cooking activity, or a guest who will visit.

Whether to present a calendar depends on the developmental stage of the children in your group. Research in child development indicates that children do not truly understand time concepts until the first or second grade, even though they may use words associated with time concepts. For example, they may be able to memorize and chant the days of the week, but they lack a full understanding of what a day or time intervals such as hours, minutes, and seconds really mean. Preschoolers are focused on the here and now. They are learning the concepts of before and after, later and next. Not until age 5 do they usually begin to understand the concept of a day. Creating a consistent daily schedule—rest time, mealtime, outdoor time, work time—fosters children's learning about segments of time.

If you want to introduce a calendar, use it as a tool to show children how to keep track of important events. Mark the days when you will have a visitor, school will be closed, or a field trip is planned. This approach helps children learn the purpose of calendars and how calendars can be useful to them personally.

A group time just before children go home allows children to reflect on the day's events and provides closure. Briefly review with children the highlights of the day and what's planned for the next day. End with a closing ritual, for instance, a goodbye song or a favorite rhyme or chant. You can use the last meeting of the day to discuss the calendar by making one with large empty boxes. Fill in the boxes by asking children, "What do we want to remember about today?" and having them draw a picture in the relevant box. This activity turns the calendar into a record of classroom life. An added benefit is that children are more likely to have something to say when their families ask, "What did you do in school today?"

Start the morning meeting in a similar way each day.

If you want to introduce a calendar, use it as a tool to show children how to keep track of important events.

A group time just before children go home allows children to reflect on the day's events and provides closure.

Small-Group Time

The purpose of small-group time is to present activities briefly to a few children. The size of the group depends on the age and the individual needs of the children. Three-year-olds will benefit more from informal small-group settings of two to four children. A small group for older preschoolers can be three to six children.

Small-group times enable you to meet a variety of needs.

> - **Introduce new concepts** or new materials to children.
>
> - **Teach particular skills** to children who need individual attention.
>
> - **Focus observations** on a particular group of children and document their learning.

In small-group times, you can retell a story, conduct a science exploration, teach children a new software program, write a group story, play with a collectible, or do a limitless number of other things.

Small-group times can be held during several periods of the day. Sometimes small groups come together spontaneously, for example, during choice time when you begin working with a few children in an interest area and other children join the group. At nap time, you can work with a small group of children who get up early or don't need to sleep. If you have one or more other adults in the room, you may set up a time for everyone to work in a small group on a planned activity every day.

The makeup of small groups will not be the same every day. One day you may invite a group of children to explore an open-ended material—such as leaves, shells, or buttons. Another day, you might read rhyming books and do chants with several children who are having difficulty hearing and discriminating the sounds in words.

In planning and implementing small-group times, keep in mind how children learn best. Make sure that each child has a set of materials to use. Allow children to choose how to use the materials you provide and be prepared to follow their lead. Offer encouragement and support.

In planning and implementing small-group times, keep in mind how children learn best.

Choice Time

In choice time—sometimes called center time or work time—children choose the interest area in which they would like to work, whom they want to work with, and what materials to use. Choice time typically lasts for an hour or more, exclusive of cleanup. During this period, most interest areas are available to children: blocks, dramatic play, toys and games, sand and water, library, art, etc. When children are finished working in one area, they are free to move to another area. Teachers observe children, ask open-ended questions, and make suggestions that extend children's play and support their learning. You will find more information about what teachers do to promote learning in Chapter 4, The Teacher's Role, and in Part II of this book.

Teaching preschool children how to make choices is such an important skill that it deserves some systematic teaching with your group.

Many preschool children, especially younger preschoolers, will not understand how to make choices. This is such an important skill that it deserves some systematic teaching with your group. At a meeting before choice time, you can talk about which activities will be available. A visual cue, such as a chart with pictures of what interest areas are open, can help children focus on the choices available to them. A planning board placed in each area gives children a concrete method for managing choice time. Give children a card with their name on it to place on the planning board to indicate where they will work.

If you use a planning board, explain it to the children. At a meeting time, you can discuss the system: how the number of pegs or Velcro strips shows the number of children who can be in an area at one time; where children put their name cards; and how they should take their card with them when they decide to try another activity during choice time.

Once children become accustomed to the way the classroom operates, a planning board may not be necessary. The number of chairs, amount of materials, and available space all establish limits on the number of children an area can accommodate. If a problem comes up, use it as an opportunity to lead children through a process of deciding how to handle it:

We seem to have a problem here. Too many children want to be at the woodworking table and it's getting crowded. What shall we do? Does anyone have an idea?

If children are involved in solving a problem (whether it's having a waiting list, making more room at the table, setting up another woodworking table outside), they will be more invested in making the solution work. Soon you will find that children, on their own, will move chairs, make room for others, or remove themselves when an area is too crowded.

You may wonder whether you should be concerned if a child always selects the same activity during choice time. Because there are many ways to expand on children's interests and teach concepts in each area, this problem is handled easily. First, ask yourself why a child restricts himself to the same activity. Perhaps the child particularly loves to explore with art materials or build with blocks. Sometimes, however, a child is stuck and uneasy about trying something new. Try to make the child feel safe in a new activity by inviting him to join you or a friend in something special, like cooking or trying out a new program on the computer.

> If children are involved in solving a problem they will be more invested in making the solution work.

Transition Times

Transitions can be relaxed and provide opportunities for learning and reinforcing concepts and skills; they also can be chaotic. Here are some ways to structure transitions so they go smoothly and encourage learning in the process.

Give children notice.

Five minutes before clean-up time, for example, talk to the children in each interest area: "You have time for one more puzzle" or "There is just enough time to finish that painting but not to start a new one." Keep in mind that cleaning up some areas, such as blocks, may require more time than others. You might start children who are involved in these activities a little earlier than the rest of your group.

Allow sufficient time.

Treat transition times as valuable experiences in and of themselves, and allow enough time so children won't feel rushed.

Give children specific tasks.

Children can help set up a snack or lunch, clean up after art, and collect trash after a meal. Be specific about what you want children to do. "Please put away the plates" is not as effective as, "Please scrape the food off each plate into the trash can. Then stack the plates on the cart."

Be clear and consistent.

Provide clear directions to children during transition times and be sure that the expectations are age-appropriate. Keep the same routine each day so children learn what to do on their own.

Be flexible.

When possible, allow children extra time to complete special projects or activities in which they are particularly involved. For example, give children building a city time to complete it while other children can begin cleaning up the art materials or dramatic play props.

Meet individual needs.

Try to avoid having all children move from one activity to another as a group or requiring children to wait around doing nothing until everyone is finished. Give children who have completed their task something to do, such as getting a book to read or straightening up a display, until everyone is ready to move to the next activity.

Use transitions as opportunities to teach.

Invite all children wearing stripes, for example, to go to the next activity. Or, "If your name begins with the same sound as bike, banana, baseball, and boat, you can choose an interest area now."

Transitions can be especially difficult for some children. If children are having difficulty, make sure you have allowed sufficient time for a transition and children know what is expected of them.

If children are having difficulty, make sure you have allowed sufficient time for a transition and children know what is expected of them.

Mealtimes

Mealtimes are learning times when teachers sit with children, have them serve their own food, and carry on conversations. Good experiences at mealtimes help children to develop positive attitudes toward food and nutrition. Because food plays an essential role in family life and connects to many cultural traditions, take time to talk with families about their child's eating habits and food preferences. Find out if a child has any food allergies or a chronic health condition such as diabetes and make sure everyone in the program has this information.

Make mealtimes sociable.
Establish a calm and pleasant atmosphere. A quiet activity, such as a story before lunch, helps to set a relaxed tone. Pleasant conversation will create a comfortable atmosphere.

Be prepared.
If you continually jump up from the table to get what you need, children will start doing the same. To minimize the need for you to leave the table, keep extra foods on a cart nearby. Have extra napkins, sponges, and paper cups as well. A pair of scissors to open packets of condiments, such as ketchup, is also helpful.

Encourage children to help.
Provide small plastic pitchers, baskets, and sturdy serving utensils that children can use to pour their own milk or juice and serve their own food. Give children time to practice with the pitchers during water play, and be tolerant of spills and accidents. Keep a roll of paper towels and a sponge handy. Children can assist by setting the table, wiping the table after eating, and emptying trash from their plates into a designated can.

Allow enough time.

Some children are slow eaters. Mealtime should not be rushed. Make sure there is time for setting up, eating, and cleaning up.

Never use food to reward or punish behavior.

Threatening to withhold food or offering special food treats for doing a task contributes to unhealthy attitudes about food. If a child acts up during a meal, the best response is to deal with the inappropriate behavior.

If you serve snacks as well as meals in your program, consider setting up a self-service snack bar so children can help themselves and return to what they are doing independently.

Rest Time

In full-day programs, rest time is important for children and provides a much needed break for adults. The length of rest time varies. For children who attend six hours or more, rest time provides rejuvenation for the afternoon program. Younger children may need more rest time than older preschoolers. Even in half-day programs, children can benefit from a short quiet time or calm-down time.

Because naps are often associated with home, some children have a difficult time settling down at school. This response is normal and to be expected. Follow a regular routine at rest time so children feel safe and so they can relax. Here are some suggestions for rest time.

> Follow a regular routine at rest time so children feel safe and so they can relax.

Prepare children for rest time.

Plan a quiet activity for the group—a story, fingerplay, quiet song, or listening to music—right before rest time. Have children help set up the cots or mats as they finish eating, toileting, and brushing teeth. Allow children to bring sleep toys or special blankets from home.

Give children time to settle down at their own pace.

Children have different sleep patterns and different ways of falling asleep. Playing quiet music, rubbing a child's back, or just sitting on a cot near a restless child often helps.

Supervise rest time.

Many teachers use rest time to do paperwork and to plan. Doing desk work is fine as long as there is always an adult supervising the children.

Plan for children who wake up early and for children who do not sleep.

Allow non-nappers to get up after 15 minutes or so and engage in quiet activities. You might create "nap bags" with quiet activities such as magic slates, books, and small toys or games that children can bring to their cots or mats.

Allow time for children to wake up at their own pace.
Children who regularly are still sleeping at the end of rest time may need more sleep. If you place their cots away from the center of activities, they can continue to sleep. These children may need extra help when they get up.

If you are having a particular problem with a child during rest time, consult the child's family. Perhaps they could offer some insights that would help you meet the child's needs.

We have discussed the basic activities and blocks of time in a preschool classroom: taking attendance, large and small group times, choice time, transitions, meal and rest time. You put them together in a predictable sequence by planning and following a daily schedule.

The Daily Schedule

The daily schedule blocks out time and establishes a sequence for the activities in your classroom. When the daily schedule suits the developmental and individual needs of the children, classroom life proceeds smoothly and is enjoyable for everyone. A good schedule for preschool children offers a range of different types of activities:

- active and quiet times

- large-group activities, small-group activities, and time to play alone or with others

- indoor and outdoor playtimes

- time for children to select their own activities and for teacher-directed activities

A daily schedule establishes the consistency that helps young children to predict the sequence of events and thus to feel more secure and more in control of their day. They delight in reminding you that "snack comes next" or telling a visitor that "now we go outside." In addition, a schedule helps children to develop time concepts as they anticipate what comes first in the day, second, next, and last.

Consistency does not preclude flexibility or spontaneity, however. Nor does it mean that the clock rules the day. A special occurrence can be reason enough to alter the daily routine. For example, an unexpected snowfall might inspire you and the children to pause in the middle of choice time, put on jackets and hats, and go outdoors. Similarly, on a day when children are particularly engrossed in their chosen activities, you may decide to extend choice time. Keep in mind what's most important: you want children to be excited about and engaged in what they are doing. Be flexible about time when children are working well and engaged.

In putting together your schedule, start with the fixed times for events in the day that can't be changed. A fixed period might be lunch or the time when a shared playground is available for your class's use. Keep in mind the developmental abilities of your children. Waiting times should be kept to a minimum, and adequate time should be allotted for putting on coats and hats, eating meals and snacks, and cleaning up. Work periods should be long enough to give children a chance to select materials and activities, plan what they want to do, and clean up afterward without feeling rushed.

Daily Schedule Guidelines

Try to **schedule more challenging activities in the morning**, when most children are freshest.

Plan at least 60 minutes a day for each choice time so that children can become deeply involved in their play.

Allow 45–60 minutes for each outdoor period.

If possible, **schedule nap time directly after lunch**. Children tend to be sleepy after eating.

Arrange for a quiet activity after nap time, so sleepy children can continue to nap while those who are up can play.

If your program includes lunch and nap, **make sure children have a play activity in the afternoon** as well as in the morning. Getting up from a nap and going home immediately is hard for children.

To give you an idea of how to organize a full-day program, we provide a sample schedule on the following pages. We realize, however, that not all programs operate for the same number of hours a day. Some preschools have a 5–6 hour day, others are half-day (typically 3 hours), and child care programs serve children all day. You can adapt the sample schedule to suit your program.

How you order your day may change as children grow and as you need more flexibility or time for certain kinds of activities.

Also, don't feel locked into the time periods or the sequence of activities we list. For example, you might like to have a story time right before nap to help children settle down instead of having it before lunch. You may want to begin the day with a morning meeting, or let children ease into activities as they arrive and hold your group meeting after choice time. How you order your day also may change as children grow and as you need more flexibility or time for certain kinds of activities.

DAILY SCHEDULE

30 minutes (8:00–8:30 a.m. or earlier in child care programs)	**Planning/preparation time:** Review the plans for the day. Conduct health and safety check (e.g., refill bathroom supplies, remove any broken or torn materials, check outside for trash). Prepare interest areas (e.g., mix paint, place puzzles on a table, display new books). Set out name cards in sign-in area. Think about individual children, any special needs, current projects. Set out self-serve breakfast.
30 minutes (8:30–9:00 a.m. or longer in child care)	**Arrival:** Greet families and children individually. Help children store belongings, select a quiet activity, or serve themselves breakfast.
10–15 minutes (9:00–9:15 a.m.)	**Group meeting:** Give signal to gather the group and lead children in singing songs and fingerplays and sharing news. Read a poem, talk about the day's activities, and talk about the choices for the morning. Consider the needs of children who are not ready for large-group activities (e.g., hold two smaller groups, have one teacher sit close to children who need extra attention).
60–75 minutes (9:15–10:15 or 10:30 a.m., depending on how snack will be served)	**Choice time and small groups:** Guide children in selecting interest areas. Observe and interact with individual children to extend play and learning. Lead a short, small-group activity that builds on children's skills and interests. Work with children engaged in study activities.
	Cleanup: Help children put away materials in each interest area.
15 minutes (10:15–10:30 a.m.)	**Snack time:** Sit with children and enjoy a snack together or supervise the "snack bar." *Note:* Self-serve snacks can be incorporated into indoor or outdoor choice time (in warm weather).
10 minutes (10:30–10:40 a.m.)	**Group time:** Invite children to share what they did, lead music and movement activity, read aloud (e.g., story, poem), record ideas, or write experience story.
60 minutes (10:40–11:40 a.m.)	**Outdoor choice time:** Supervise the playground toys and materials (swings, climbers, slides). Observe and interact with children as they jump rope, play ball games, blow bubbles, make nature discoveries, and so on. Extend study work outdoors, if appropriate. Help children to put away or carry in toys and materials, hang up jackets, toilet, and wash up.

DAILY SCHEDULE

10 minutes
(11:40–11:50 a.m.)

Story time: Read and discuss a storybook. Use props to help children retell stories.

55 minutes
(11:50 a.m.–12:45 p.m.)

Lunch: Help children to prepare the tables for lunch. Encourage conversations about the day's events, the meal itself, and topics of interest to children. Guide children in cleaning up after lunch, brushing teeth, setting out cots/mats, and preparing for rest.

60–90 minutes
(12:45–2:15 p.m.)

Rest time: Help children relax so they can fall asleep. Supervise rest area, moving about so each teacher gets a break. Provide quiet activities for children who don't sleep. Adjust length of rest time to suit age of group and needs of individual children.

30 minutes
(2:15–2:45 p.m.)

Snack/quiet activities: Set up snack so children can serve themselves and prepare some quiet activity choices.

15 minutes
(2:45–3:00 p.m.)

Group activity: Lead group meeting/activity. Help children reflect on the day and prepare for home. Read aloud.

60 minutes
(3:00–4:00 p.m.)

Outdoor choice time: Supervise and interact with children. Plan some special activities.

60 minutes
(4:00–5:00 p.m.)

Choice time and small groups: Set out a limited number of choices for children such as computers, library, toys and games. Lead a small-group activity.

60 minutes
(5:00–6:00 p.m.)

Closing and departures: Lead group discussion about the day and plans for the next day. Involve children in quiet activities, hanging up their artwork, and preparing for the next day. Greet parents and share something about the child's day.

As time allows during the day

Planning and reflection: Discuss how the day went, progress of individual children (skills, needs, interests); work on portfolios and observation notes related to *The Developmental Continuum*. Review and make plans for the next day.

To focus children's attention on the flow of activities and the consistency of their days, take time to talk about the schedule throughout the day. Use it to guide children as they move from one activity to the next and to think about the choice they will make: "We've just finished group time. Next we're going to work in interest areas. Think about whether you want to work in the Block Area, the Discovery Area, Dramatic Play, or Toys and Games."

To help children learn the order of the day, you can display your schedule at their eye level, with illustrated pictures or actual photographs of the scheduled activities. If you put Velcro on the back of pictures, you can move them around easily when the schedule changes to include a special event such as a field trip. Illustrating the schedule in pictures promotes both literacy and an understanding of sequence.

Weekly Planning

Day-to-day teaching is done in the context of weekly planning. A weekly plan helps you to implement *The Creative Curriculum* in manageable chunks of time, to determine what will happen during group activities and in each interest area, to prepare the environment for that week's work, and to allocate time. Decisions regarding the week are based in part on what topic children are studying at that time. For example, suppose you are studying shoes and planning a field trip to a shoe store for the end of the week. On Monday, you might do an activity with children where they take off and sort their shoes. On Tuesday, you decide to read the fairy tale, "The Shoemaker and the Elves" (The Brothers Grimm), and on Wednesday, you introduce a tool to measure feet so children can use it in their dramatic play.

Observation is the basis for weekly as well as all other planning. By observing children, you can find out if the activities you have been planning and the materials you have been providing are producing the desired outcomes. For example, were children able to come up with different categories for sorting their shoes? Do they know how to use the foot measurer? Have they incorporated it into their play? Should other props be added? Answers to these questions enable you to adjust your plans if needed.

The classroom teaching team should review the weekly plan daily to see that everyone is prepared. Each member of the team may have different observations of children to share and will have important suggestions for adjusting the plan.

The planning form developed for use with *The Creative Curriculum* gives you a structure for planning each week and preparing materials and activities ahead of time. The form has several sections.

Planning Changes to the Environment

As you observe children, you can decide if materials are appropriate and if the children are using them constructively. In the course of a study, you may want to add new materials related to the topic.

"To Do" List

List arrangements to make, materials to secure, and coordination needed to implement your plans.

Weekly Planning Form

THE CREATIVE CURRICULUM®
FOR PRESCHOOL

Planning Changes to the Environment

Week of:_____   Study/Project:_____

Teacher:_____   Assistant:_____

Blocks	Dramatic Play	Toys and Games	"To Do" List
Art	Library	Discovery	
Sand and Water	Music and Movement	Cooking	
Computers	Outdoors	Family/Community Involvement	

Family/Community Involvement

List ways to include children's families and community resources into the program.

Large-Group Times

Write down what you want to prepare, such as the songs, stories, games, and materials you need to have ready for each group time.

Story Time

Write down the titles of books you plan to read to the whole group during the week. Review the story and think of ways to make it an interactive read-aloud time.

Small-Group Times

List the activities and materials you want to use during small-group times and which children you will include.

Weekly Planning Form

CREATIVE CURRICULUM®
FOR PRESCHOOL

Planning for Groups

	Monday	Tuesday	Wednesday	Thursday	Friday
Group Time (songs, stories, games, discussions, etc.)					
Story Time					
Small-Group Activities					
Special Activities (site visits, special events, etc.)					

Notes *(reminders, changes, children to observe)*

Special Activities

List activities such as a field trip, celebrations, a nature walk, or an invited guest that require prior planning. You won't necessarily have a special activity every day.

Notes

Use this space to list the children you want to observe, record plans that worked well, and changes you want to make in the future.

The Creative Curriculum Weekly Planning Form can be found in the Appendix (p. 526). We also show a completed planning form to give you an idea of how a topic that children are investigating influences weekly planning. The topic we picked, a study of worms, is described in detail in Chapter 4 in the section on planning long-term studies.

Preparing for the First Few Days

Planning carefully for the first few days of school can help children make the necessary transition and feel comfortable. Try to anticipate their needs and structure their arrival. Some children who have been in group settings since infancy may have learned skills to relate to other people. Others may be having their first experience away from home or in a group. In either case, expect that the children are wondering about what lies ahead. If they could put their concerns into words, they might ask:

- Will I be safe?

- Can my mommy and daddy stay with me?

- Are my teachers going to like me?

- Will my teachers be nice to me?

- Will the other kids like me?

- What will I do here?

In addition to the concerns children have, they are required to digest a lot of new information in the first few weeks of a new program year. They have to learn

- the names of a whole group of strangers

- to trust adults they are just meeting

- to interact with children they have never met before

- what they can do and what they cannot

- where things are located

- how to use and care for materials

- how to follow a set of daily routines

- what it means to make choices

- where to find and return materials

All of the strategies for setting up the classroom and planning each day will help children to feel comfortable and welcome. Even so, you may want to do a few things a little differently during the first few days.

Guidelines for the First Few Days

Keep groups small. Try to stagger entry dates so children can get used to the classroom and routines in small groups. If you can't, have enough adults available so you can divide the class into smaller groups as you teach children about routines and practices.

Allow time for hellos and goodbyes. At the beginning of the year, you can expect some children to have difficulty with separation. Allow time for transitions from home to school by encouraging family members to stay for a few minutes and help children ease into an activity. Reminders of home also can be helpful as well. Invite children to bring a special object such as a stuffed animal or blanket for rest time or have parents record an audiotape of a favorite story, poem, or song.

Select activities children can do independently. Activities during the first few days of school should follow the rule that simple is better. Plan for the kinds of activities that allow children to be successful independently. For example, put out simple puzzles, self-correcting toys like pegboards with pegs, crayons and plain paper, and—depending on your class—home-related props such as a wok or tortilla maker in the Dramatic Play Area.

Teach children your signal for getting their attention. Decide what will work for you: strumming an auto harp or guitar, or holding one arm in the air until everyone does the same and stops talking. Whatever signal you choose, teach it to children and practice it. Talk about how important it is to stop and listen. Explain that the classroom is a busy place that is often noisy. For safety reasons having a way to get everyone's attention quickly is important.

Hold a group meeting. Bring the group together for an active and brief (about 5 to 10 minutes) meeting. Remember that some children will not be ready to participate, so allow them to watch from a safe distance. Teach one or two simple songs or fingerplays using children's names and repeat them each day.

Take children on a tour of the classroom. Talk about the different activity areas and what children can do in each one. In the beginning, it's best to limit the number of activity choices. Point out that everything has a place and that the labels show where things go.

Keep in mind that many children probably won't remember most of what you say. Therefore, be prepared to repeat everything you say over and over again during the first days and weeks. With your daily program organized, a plan for the first few days, and a way to plan for each week in place, you are ready to focus on building a classroom community.

Creating a Classroom Community

The developmental theory behind *The Creative Curriculum* teaches that children learn best in the context of relationships. Because relationships with peers and teachers influence how children feel in school and how they learn, the social climate of your classroom is critically important. Just as you purposefully organize the space in your classroom and establish a daily schedule and routines, you need to set the tone for how children will treat one another, how you will treat them, and how problems that inevitably come up will be resolved.

The *Creative Curriculum* classroom is a community. By community we mean a place where people feel safe, help one another, and see themselves as part of a group. A community also nurtures social competence by helping children to understand how to treat other people and how they want to be treated by others; to acquire the skills to cooperate, negotiate, and make and keep friends; and to resolve problems and conflicts. In a community children learn which behaviors are acceptable and which are not, and they develop self-discipline. These are not easy skills to acquire—they take a lifetime—and they deserve time, patience, and, often, direct teaching. A classroom does not become a community automatically or quickly.

Creating a classroom community begins with learning about each child so you can build positive relationships. Also from the start, you will need to teach children how to relate positively to others. You will have to establish rules and clear and consistent limits so children learn what behavior is acceptable and what is not. You need to teach children how to solve problems on their own, because problems always come up, and you don't want to spend much of your time arbitrating. Even so, you are likely to encounter challenging behaviors from time to time, and it's best to be prepared to deal with them.

Promoting Positive Relationships in the Classroom

Positive social relationships in preschool—the core of a classroom community—create the best environment for children's learning. When they feel comfortable, children are free to do the work of learning. Who you are and how you relate to children—and their families—probably makes more of a difference than anything else you do. The relationships you build with each child, and the guidance you provide to help children develop friendships and work cooperatively with others, can have lasting and positive results.

Building a Relationship With Each Child

Every child is unique, but the one thing every child needs to flourish is to feel accepted and appreciated. Your influence extends beyond the bounds of your classroom and continues long after children have moved on through the grades. The quality of children's relationships with their teachers in preschool is an important predictor of children's future social relationships and academic success in school (Peisner-Feinberg et al., 1999). In other words, how children feel in your classroom is as important as how they think (Shonkoff & Phillips, 2000).

Your ability to form a positive relationship with each child, and to appreciate what's unique and special about that child, conveys both your respect and caring. Strong relationships ready children's minds for learning. As Loris Malaguzzi, the founder of the Reggio Emilia system has said, "The way we get along with children influences what motivates them and what they learn" (Malaguzzi, p. 68).

In a *Creative Curriculum* classroom, teachers treat every child with respect and acceptance, viewing all children as capable, competent learners. They convey the message that it is okay to explore and experiment, and that there is more than one solution to a problem. Mistakes are viewed as opportunities to learn. For these reasons, children experience a sense of belonging to a community that gives them the self-confidence to tackle new tasks and seek answers to questions.

Some children are easy to get to know and immediately draw adults into a warm relationship. Others are more difficult to understand, making it hard for teachers to see their positive attributes and build a relationship. Learning about children's unique qualities—what they like to do, how they learn best, what skills they are developing, what challenges they face, and whom they like to be with—can open the door to appreciation and respect for each child, which, in turn, becomes the basis for building a relationship. Here are some specific steps for getting to know children and building a relationship.

Observe, observe, observe.
The best way to get to know what is special about each child is to make purposeful observation an everyday practice, documenting what you see and discussing your observations about children with other staff members. When you observe with an open mind, you uncover surprising information. Set yourself a goal of knowing every child in your classroom well enough to be able to answer the question, "How is this child special?"

Strong relationships ready children's minds for learning.

- observe
- respect
- be sensitive
- validate

Talk to children respectfully.

Talk with each child just as you would talk to another adult. Avoid talking down or using baby talk. Use your best manners so children learn from your example. If you are not sure how you are doing, tape yourself one day and then listen to how you sound. Ask yourself, "Would I talk this way to another adult?" You may be surprised at what you discover!

Be sensitive to children's feelings.

Children, like adults, want their feelings to be valued and recognized, not ignored or put down. Sometimes, in an effort to be reassuring, we make little of a child's pain or upset: "Oh that's not such a big problem" or "Where's your smiley face today?" Instead of making comments like these, use your eyes and ears to gauge how a child is feeling and reflect back what you see and hear.

When you listen to and accept children's feelings without making value judgments, you convey respect and understanding.

Sometimes you can pinpoint a problem from your observation and make a specific, relevant statement: "It's hard when your best friend is busy playing with someone else. It doesn't mean she's not your friend anymore." At other times, you won't know what the problem is without asking: "You look like something is bothering you. Want to talk about it?" When you listen to and accept children's feelings without making value judgments, you convey respect and understanding. You also teach children how to interpret their own feelings and the feelings of others.

Validate children's accomplishments and progress.

Because young children want approval, adults have to be careful and thoughtful about making them too dependent on adult affirmation. For instance, Alfie Kohn cautions us to avoid too much praise—"Good girl." "I like the way you did that." This approach tends to make children seek and depend on adults for validation of their behavior and their work (Kohn, 2001). Conversely, praise involves judgments about a child's actions. A child may think, "If I get praise one day, I could just as easily be criticized the next." The point is to promote children's confidence in their own abilities and skills at making sound judgments of their work. You can help by being specific:

Avoid empty praise such as saying, "Good girl."

You got your coat on all by yourself!

That was a hard puzzle and you did it. You didn't give up.

You figured out how to make the car go faster down the ramp.

Another alternative to empty praise is to ask questions to help children identify for themselves what they have accomplished:

How did you figure it out?

What was the hardest part?

What helped you?

However you phrase your responses to children, be sure that your words nourish their self-confidence and sense of their own competence.

Helping Children to Make Friends

A classroom is not a community unless every child has at least one friend. Children who do not have friends, who are rejected repeatedly by their peers, are in a cycle of rejection that they often cannot break on their own. They may approach other children in ways that invite rejection: showing off, acting silly, playing too roughly, bullying others, or being aggressive. The more they are rejected, the harder they try using the same behaviors that didn't work in the first place. Or, they may simply withdraw.

To break this cycle, children need the help of a caring adult. The preschool years are a prime time to head off the negative consequences of being friendless. The longer a child remains socially isolated, the greater the likelihood that the child will demonstrate increasingly disruptive behavior and poor academic achievement.

Children who are very shy also may have trouble making friends. Because they are quiet and not disruptive, their isolation many go unnoticed by their teachers (Asher & Coie, 1990). Some children with disabilities may need extra help developing friendships if they do not form friendships naturally. In a classroom community, all children relate positively to each other and enjoy a real friendship with at least one other child.

Children need three types of skills to make and keep friends. They must know how to establish contact with another child, maintain a positive relationship, and negotiate when a conflict arises (Kostelnik, 1990).

A classroom is not a community unless every child has at least one friend.

By coaching and specific teaching, you can help children see how their behavior causes them difficulties and provide them with positive alternatives.

Skills Children Need to Make and Keep a Friend

Establishing contact.

To make contact, a child has to use the same behaviors that are required in any community and that are accepted by other children. These behaviors include smiling, asking questions, offering ideas, making positive comments, inviting someone to join them, or offering to share something.

Children who are rejected at the initial stage in making friends often have not learned acceptable ways to establish contact with their peers.

Maintaining a positive relationship.

To maintain a friendship, children must know how to cooperate, share, show empathy, express affection, offer ideas, help, take turns, and express enthusiasm. Children who have these skills are key members of their community, and are viewed as reliable and fun to be with. The behaviors that cause trouble and isolation from the community at this stage include aggression, unwillingness to cooperate, showing off, trying too hard, and acting in ways that annoy others.

By coaching and specific teaching, you can help children to see how their behavior causes them difficulties and, at the same time, provide them with positive alternatives so they may become fuller members of the classroom community.

Negotiating a conflict.

Like all communities, classrooms are the site of disagreements. Since disagreements inevitably arise in any friendship, children must know how to resolve differences. Children who resort to either physically or verbally violent outbursts, or who withdraw from the conflict entirely, fail to maintain and deepen their friendships.

Socially successful children express their ideas, explain how they feel, listen to another's point of view, and work out solutions to problems. As each child masters these strategies, the whole community benefits.

Classroom Strategies That Support Friendships

When you purposefully build a community in your classroom, you give children many opportunities to practice the skills they need to make friends. It also may be necessary to take specific steps to overcome the rejection some children encounter.

Have discussions about making friends.

One way to start a discussion about making friends is by reading a book on the topic. For instance, *Will I Have a Friend?* (Miriam Cohen) or *The Rainbow Fish* (Marcus Pfister and T. Alison James) can help you introduce the subject and begin a discussion.

Coach children.

Both neglected and rejected children can have trouble entering groups. To help them, model and practice how to ask questions, make positive comments, and offer help. As children master these skills, coach them on how to share, offer trades, take turns, and make conversation. The more their overtures produce good results, the more they'll be willing to try, and the better the classroom community will function as a whole.

Pair children to work on a task.

Partnering provides opportunities for children to work with someone they normally wouldn't choose and to establish friendships. Therefore, use opportunities to have two children who are not usually together share a job or help you set up for a cooking activity. Soon they may work together at their own initiative, and the classroom will be a more productive community.

Interpret children's actions.

Children who have trouble making friends often don't know what they are doing that alienates others. By describing their actions in words, you help them become more conscious of and, therefore, better able to change the behaviors that cause them trouble: "Did you notice that when you sat down in the middle of the floor you were in the way of the block builders? Next time try asking the others: 'Where can I play?' Let's see if that works better." You may find you need to stay with the child and continue to model and help him practice. The help you provide will contribute to a positive atmosphere in the classroom community.

Point out the benefits.

"Look at the smile on Crystal's face. You can tell she is happy that you shared the markers with her." A child who recognizes the positive consequences of a behavior is more likely to share in the future, not because she is seeking attention from an adult, but because the sharing skill pleased another child and paves the way for her to become integrated more fully into the classroom community.

> It may be necessary to take specific steps to overcome the rejection some children encounter.

Minimize rejection.

In any preschool classroom, rejection is a powerful (and hurtful) issue. One well-known teacher, Vivian Paley, noticed that some children in her class had all of the power and were excluding others. Feeling that this arrangement was unfair, she decided to put an end to the issue by establishing a simple rule: "You can't say you can't play" (1992). Paley discovered that having this rule was an effective way to minimize the instances of rejection and promote a sense of belonging to a community. At the same time, she helped children to be more assertive.

Through your observations, you'll usually find some reason that a child is regularly excluded. Find out what the problem really is and develop a plan to help the child. Have a goal that every child has a friend and that your classroom is a community in which children relate to each other respectfully.

Developing Rules for a Classroom Community

A classroom community is a safe place, where children know that no harm will come to them—physically or emotionally. Therefore, a classroom needs a few basic rules that create a safe community.

Involving children in deciding on rules is a powerful way to convey a shared responsibility for life in the classroom community. Children are more likely to understand and follow rules they helped to establish. You probably will have to lead them through the rule-making process by first discussing why they need rules and then helping them to come up with ideas. Using the Continuum, you should take into account the developmental abilities of preschool children. Most 3- and some young 4-year-olds may be on step I of objective 9, "Follows classroom rules." The concept of a "rule" has limited meaning, so you need to make the discussion as short and as concrete as possible. Older 4s and 5s may be on step II or III. They will understand what rules are and have more ideas to add. All children, however, will understand the concept of staying safe, and that's the most important message in a discussion of rules.

Think about categories for essential rules before you meet with children to generate classroom rules.

Before you meet with children about classroom rules, give some thought to what rules are absolutely essential to you—your non-negotiables. It may be helpful to think about specific categories first instead of the actual rules you want. Categories might include:

- maintaining physical safety

- respecting the rights of others

- not hurting the feelings of others

- caring for the classroom

A discussion with children about rules

our class...

Ms. Tory: *Our classroom has to be a safe place for everyone. I think we need some rules to make everyone feel safe here. Does anyone know what a rule is?*

Carlos: *It's something you can't break.*

Ms. Tory: *Tell us what you mean Carlos.*

Carlos: *It means you have to do it, what it says.*

Ms. Tory: *So a rule is something that tells you what to do.*

Carlos: *Yeah.*

Ms. Tory: *What kind of rules make you feel safe? Take a minute to think to yourself.*

Tasheen: *I don't like it when people hit me. It hurts.*

Ms. Tory: *So, for Tasheen to feel safe, we would have a rule that says, "We keep our hands to ourselves." Would that make anyone else feel safe?*

Zack: *Yeah. No kicking either.*

Ben: *And no biting.*

Ms. Tory: *So everyone would feel safer if we were nice to each other. I'm going to write down your ideas on this chart to help us remember them. "We treat others nicely."*

Susie: *And no spitting. That's yucky!*

Ms. Tory: *OK. I think no spitting is covered. What happens when people run in the classroom? Is there a lot of room here for running?*

In the example on the previous page, the teacher guides children to think about possible problems and to identify some key rules for the classroom. She restates children's ideas in positive terms so children know what to do, rather than focus on what not to do. Cognitively, children can grasp the positive long before they understand negatives. Besides, emphasizing the positive sets a better tone. Limit the number of rules to about four and keep them simple:

- Be kind to others.

- Keep the room neat.

- Walk in the classroom. Run outside.

- Help each other.

Post the rules in the meeting area, where you can review them with the children. You will probably need to remind children of the rules on a regular basis. When a rule isn't working, ask children what they think the problem is. You may be surprised by how seriously they begin to approach problem solving when they are part of a community that treats their ideas with respect.

Teaching Social Problem-Solving Skills

Conflicts are a way of life. They come up all the time in every classroom. Because children get frustrated easily, it's tempting for adults to solve the problem quickly by offering a solution. Yet a quick solution from an adult doesn't teach children how to solve problems on their own. Rather, it ensures that children will depend on adults continually to solve their problems. So, in addition to having general rules, you will need to teach social problem-solving skills directly. Take the opportunity each time a conflict comes up.

Some conflicts will involve two children. Others may involve the entire class. Below we describe the procedures for handling each of these situations.

Handling Problems Between Children

Preschool children typically fight about actions or things: "He took my book" or "She pulled my hair." Whenever possible, try to settle a conflict before it escalates. As soon as you hear voices rising, try to calm the situation by getting close to the children involved. Once a conflict has begun, the following steps can be taken to resolve it.

Help children calm down.

When emotions are hot, the first step is to defuse the situation. You might suggest a cooling-off time or describe what you think the children are feeling so they know they have been heard and their concerns are valid:

> *I can see you're having a hard time waiting for your turn. It's hard to wait. It makes you feel angry.*
>
> *Let's take a few minutes to calm down. Take a few deep breaths.*

Many people think that batting a pillow is a good way to release anger, but the opposite is true. Hitting a pillow or punching bag increases aggression. Calming down is better. Techniques for calming down include breathing deeply, counting slowly, and using positive self-talk: "Calm down. I can handle this." You can teach these techniques during group time, when no one is angry and children are likely to be more receptive. Later, when stressful situations arise, you can remind children to use the techniques they learned in group time.

Another good approach is to establish a calm-down place in the classroom where children can go to cool off, relax, or take a break. Such a place gives children a positive alternative to acting out or falling apart during a conflict. A calm-down place is not the same as a time-out chair in a corner. Rather, a calm-down place might be the classroom library, a loft, or a listening area. The designated area ideally will contain soft furniture: a rocking chair, beanbag chair, rug, covered mattress, or pillows. Just flopping onto a bean bag chair, curling up with a book, staring at tropical fish, or listening to a favorite tape can be calming.

At first, you may have to tell children when they need to retreat and cool off. The goal is for children to recognize their own strong feelings and know when they need to take a break in a quiet space. In this way, children become increasingly responsible for their own feelings and behavior.

Hitting a pillow or punching bag associates anger with hitting, a bad combination. Calming down is better.

Identify the problem.

Many childhood disagreements arise out of confusion or misunderstandings. These can be addressed once children have calmed down. Let each child have a chance to speak. The goal is to have all parties to the conflict listen. Children are no different from adults. They can listen better if they feel they have been heard themselves and understood:

> *We need to be able to hear what both of you have to say. Tell us what happened, Leo. When you finish, then it will be Setsuko's turn to talk.*

> *Did you hear what he said?*

> *Do you need to hear it again?*

> *Do you have a question to ask him?*

Staying calm and neutral is important, even if you have strong opinions. Listen with your eyes as well as your ears. Repeat what you hear so children have a chance to correct any misconceptions:

> *So you're saying. . .*

> *And you're feeling. . .*

> *What I hear you saying is. . .*

Have children restate what they heard. Then review each step of what happened, who did what, how each action made the other person feel, and what resulted. Putting your arm around each child can be reassuring (though not for all children). Open-ended questions encourage children to give their view of the situation:

> *What do you think happened?*

> *What made Kate upset?*

Some teachers identify a peace table in the classroom for conversations like these. Children know to go there to work out a problem together.

Generate solutions.

Once children have talked through their problem, encourage them to come up with several possible solutions. You can start this process by asking questions:

> *What can we do about this?*
>
> *Do either of you have any ideas?*

If the same type of conflict took place recently, or you discussed a similar situation during group time or after reading a book, you can remind children of the solutions they generated:

> *Remember the other day when. . .? Think about what you did then and see if that gives you an idea for solving your problem.*

If children are stuck, you might have to suggest some ideas, or ask if they would like help:

> *What do you think would happen if. . .?*
>
> *What do you think about. . .?*
>
> *Would it help if we. . .?*

The goal is to come up with as many ideas as possible. One technique for encouraging a variety of solutions is to give neutral responses to children's suggestions by saying something like:

> *That's one idea. What's another?*

This approach helps you to avoid making premature judgments.

Review solutions and choose one.

Remind children of the ideas they suggested and ask which one they think will work best. Begin by listing the ideas. Then ask:

> *What solution do you think would work best?*
>
> *Would this idea be fair to both of you?*

The goal is to arrive at a solution that each child can live with, so both children feel their needs have been met.

Check back.

Once a solution is implemented, it's a good idea to check with the children to see how it's working. If the solution isn't working well, they will probably let you know on their own! Reassure them that they are experimenting to find the best solution—just as scientists do. You might invite them to share what happened at a group meeting time and to talk about their new plan.

Solving Problems That Involve the Whole Class

In addition to problems that occur between two children, some problems affect the whole class, for instance, fighting on the playground, excessive noise during choice time, or superhero play that gets out of control. Teachers sometimes think they have to solve these problems for children. In a classroom community, a better alternative is group problem solving.

When the group is involved in solving problems, children learn the responsibilities required for community living, even if every idea offered is not relevant or even helpful. In addition, children will be more likely to accept and follow their own solutions.

These steps for group problem solving are similar to the steps in helping two children resolve conflicts (Levin, 1994). They are described below.

Discuss the situation.

Present the problem in simple terms without making a judgment about what you think or what you feel is right. Share why it's a concern:

I've been thinking about a problem and I need your help in solving it. Lately, I've been noticing that there's a lot of superhero play in our classroom. It's a problem because it's very noisy and someone is always getting hurt. Remember we said this has to be a safe place for everyone. Does anyone have some ideas of what we might do?

Invite children to offer their thoughts about the problem. Restate what each child says to clarify and make sure all ideas are validated:

So, you think that . . .

> Children will be more likely to accept and follow their own solutions.

Generate possible solutions.

Summarize the ideas children offer and invite them to think of possible solutions. Let them know there is no one right answer; many solutions might work:

> *So, some of you think that superheros only fight. But others think superheros could do different things, such as fixing things that get broken, or giving out reminders when people forget our class rules. Any other ideas?*

Encourage everyone to contribute.

Write down the ideas and ask children to explain ideas that are not clear:

> *Can you say more about that?*

> *Tell us more about your idea.*

Make a plan.

Review the list of solutions and ask children to think about which one they would like to try. Describe how the solution would work and make sure everyone has the same understanding:

> *A lot of children think the idea of having superheros give out rule reminders would be good. Let's think about what we need to have to make it work.*

Let children know that every solution to a problem doesn't always work. Explain that everyone will try out the plan and observe what happens. Agree on a time to come back and review the situation.

Assess the results.

Evaluate what happens. If the problem is not solved, generate some solutions. Encourage everyone to contribute and make a new plan. Even in situations when a solution is working, encourage children to reflect on why it worked:

> *Has the reminder idea worked? What have you noticed?*

Establishing a classroom environment where conflicts are minimal and where children acquire the skills to solve social problems when they emerge is part of building a community. A smoothly running classroom helps children feel that they are in control, that their feelings and concerns are respected, and that together they can solve problems and create a peaceful place for everyone.

Responding to Challenging Behavior

In spite of all the positive steps you take to create a classroom community and help children to develop social problem-solving skills, from time to time in almost every group you will be faced with challenging behaviors. How you respond sends a powerful message to everyone in the class.

Imagine how children in a classroom feel when, day after day, they hear their teacher say:

Haven't I told you a hundred times not to do that?

I don't care what happened, I'm angry with both of you.

Don't you know better than that? You should know the rules by now!

Instead of going outside, I want you to sit in the time-out chair and think about what you just did!

You know we have a rule about sharing. I'm going to just put this toy away and no one will get to play with it. I hope you're both satisfied!

You're making life miserable for all of us.

These negative statements reflect a teacher's frustration at being unable to establish control in the classroom.

These kinds of statements put everyone on edge and do little to help children change their behavior. Most likely they reflect a teacher's frustration at being unable to establish control in the classrooms. The better alternative is to have a repertoire of strategies for dealing with challenging behaviors and establishing control in the classroom.

Common Challenging Behaviors

Testing limits, physical aggression, biting, temper tantrums, and bullying are among the most common challenging behaviors. Many caring teachers struggle to deal with these behaviors every day. They are up against a society that glorifies violence in many ways. Just look at the TV programs children watch and the toys marketed to children. Sadly, too many children experience violence first hand, and their behavior shows the profound impact of these experiences.

Here are suggestions for responding firmly and positively when these types of behaviors appear in your classroom.

Testing limits is one of the ways preschool children discover how much power they have and the kind of authority they are dealing with. Some children will test limits repeatedly, and they need adults who understand children's need to test limits. A clear framework for managing difficult behavior is helpful. Here is a framework recommended by Dr. Becky Bailey in her book, *There's Gotta Be a Better Way* (1997, pp. 202–212).

Steps in Setting Limits

Acknowledge the child's feelings and wishes. A child who feels acknowledged and understood is more open to hearing what you have to say. Therefore, the first step is to figure out what the child is trying to accomplish and reflect back what you believe is the child's intention: "You feel like climbing today." "Those small beads are frustrating for you."

Clearly state the limit. In simple terms, convey what behavior is not permitted. Be very specific and direct. "We use tables for our work and for eating. Tables are not for climbing." "You can play with the beads and string them. They are not throwing toys."

Say what behavior is acceptable. Give the child alternative ways to behave that address a need or wish. "You can climb up to the loft or stand on the hollow blocks. Which one would you like to do?" "Let's pick up these beads first. If you want to throw something, we have bean bags you can throw. Or I can find some large beads for you to use that won't be so frustrating. What's your choice?" When children have choices that address their needs, they are more willing to comply.

Offer a final choice. If a child is determined to test the limits and does not end an unsafe behavior and/or choose one of the acceptable options you have offered, that child needs additional patience and consistency. Keep your message consistent and firm. The child must understand that the behavior must stop. "If you continue to climb on the table, you will have to leave this area and play in one without tables. It's your choice." Should the child continue, lead him gently away saying, "I see you decided to go to another area. I'll help you find a place you can play safely. When we go outside, we can be sure you get a chance to do some real climbing." To the child throwing beads, you could say, "It looks like throwing is more important to you right now than stringing the beads. You can come back here when you are ready to use them for stringing. Meanwhile, let's find something for you to throw."

The most important message to communicate is that the classroom is a safe place. Stop immediately any behaviors that may injure a child. Try to keep in mind that misbehavior of any kind is an opportunity to identify the limits and clarify which behaviors are acceptable and which are not.

Physical aggression—hitting, scratching, kicking—must be stopped immediately. Likewise, the victim needs immediate attention. Intervene by getting down to the aggressor child's level and clearly stating the rule regarding physical aggression. "Alexa, stop now! I cannot let you hurt people." Involve the aggressor child in comforting the one who was hurt (if the hurt child permits this). Using this technique helps children to understand the connection between their actions and the victim's pain. "Please get the ice pack from the freezer right away so Sonya can put it on her leg."

Children feel scared when they lose control, and your firm arms can help that child feel safe because you have taken charge of the situation.

When a child uses physical aggression and is out of control, you may need to hold her until she calms down. Children feel scared when they lose control, and your firm arms can help that child feel safe because you have taken charge of the situation. A few minutes may be required, but the child will quiet down. Then you can discuss what happened: "Do you want to talk about what made you feel so angry? I could see that you were upset." Reassure the child that you want to listen to her feelings. Let the child recover before discussing alternative ways to handle anger and frustration.

Biting, like other forms of aggression, requires an immediate response. Clearly state the rule about not biting. Involve the child who did the biting in comforting the one who was bitten, and talk about what caused the problem.

Avoid the idea that biting a child back teaches a child what it feels like to be bitten. This sometimes popular strategy only reinforces aggression. Instead, think of a way you can channel the child's energy positively. Since some children have great difficulty controlling their urge to bite, it may help to provide something that can be bitten (for example, a clean washcloth) until a child learns to control this behavior.

Observe, anticipate, and redirect biters before they reach their target!

If a child bites often, talk with the parents to find out if the child bites at home. Purposefully observe the child to see if you can pinpoint when the behavior occurs and what might be at the root of the problem. Develop a plan to stop it by, for example, intervening before a child reaches the frustration level. Observe, anticipate, and redirect biters before they reach their target!

Temper tantrums are a child's way of expressing frustration by screaming, kicking, and crying. Tantrums often occur when children have very strong feelings they can't express through words, or when they are frustrated because they can't control a situation. When a child is having a temper tantrum, you have to act quickly to protect the child as well as other people and things in the environment. Some children calm down when you hold their arms and legs firmly. Others need you to be nearby and to hear your calm voice. Once a child relaxes, you can talk about what happened and what the child could do differently in the future:

I could tell you were really mad. Your arms were going like this and your face looked like this [demonstrate]. Your whole body was telling me that you were angry. You really wanted to play with the truck. Next time, try telling Juwan, "Let me play with the truck when you are finished."

Many tantrums can be avoided by providing a developmentally appropriate and engaging program in your classroom. Children who are tired and frustrated are more likely to have tantrums than those who are well-rested, fed nutritious meals and snacks before they get too hungry, and provided with age-appropriate materials and activities. Observe children to determine when and why they lose control. Learn to recognize the signs that a child is getting tired and frustrated. When a sign appears, direct the child to a soothing activity such as water or sand play or listening to music.

Bullying is a way some children exert control over others. Often the biggest bullies are the most fearful children. Their behavior has to be stopped and redirected. The longer children are allowed to get their way by bullying others, the harder it is to change this behavior. When you see a bullying incident, be ready to step in. Help children to say what they need to say until they can monitor themselves independently.

Bullies sometimes pick on certain children. They know which children will not stand up for themselves so they disrupt their play, grab their toys, and push them around. Children who are victimized time after time can become targets of aggression and suffer from low self-esteem. They learn to be helpless and dependent on adults to defend them, and it may become a vicious cycle that is hard to break (Slaby, Roedell, Arezzo, & Hendrix, 1995).

You can stop the bullying and teach victims to be assertive when an incident occurs, or at a more neutral time such as a group discussion. For example, you might read a story on the topic and have children practice how to respond to teasing. Involve children in role-playing what to say if someone does something mean to them: "Stop pushing!" "I'm still playing with it." "Stop calling me that name."

When a child is having a tantrum, you have to act quickly to protect her, as well as other people and things in the environment.

Often the biggest bullies are the most fearful children.

Stop the bullying and teach victims to be assertive.

Coaching children on how to be assertive

Derek grabs the truck that Jonetta is playing with and wheels it away. Mr. Alvarez notices that Jonetta just sits there as tears well up in her eyes. Typically, Jonetta does not defend herself, so Mr. Alvarez steers Derek back to where Jonetta is sitting and says: "Hold on just one minute. What happened here? Jonetta, you were playing with the truck. Tell Derek, 'No. I'm using the truck. You can't have it now.'" He then coaches Jonetta: "You try it now." When she doesn't respond, Mr. Alvarez says, "Let's try saying it together first."

Determining the Causes of Challenging Behavior

Challenging behaviors, such as the ones described above, are often cries for help. Children who exhibit these behaviors may not know how to express their feelings in constructive ways. Focus attention on what a child may need rather than on what the child is doing. Try to imagine what these children might say if they had the words.

"I don't feel well." Health problems and conditions such as illness, allergies, lack of sleep, poor nutrition, or hunger can be a cause of children's misbehavior. If you suspect a physical problem, talk with the children's families and consider having the child evaluated by a health professional.

"I don't know what I'm supposed to do." Give children brief instructions: "Clean up." "Get ready." "Use the brush properly." If they don't comply, avoid assuming they understand and they are resisting on purpose. Young children don't necessarily understand vague words such as "properly" and aren't likely to ask what the strange word means. They need a teacher to show them what to do and how to do it, for example, how to hold a brush so the paint doesn't drip down the page or onto hands and clothing.

"I want you to notice me." Children need to feel important and valued. When they don't receive enough positive attention, they may seek out negative attention. They have learned that when they act up, adults notice them and spend time with them. Unfortunately, once children are successful in getting attention by misbehaving, they are likely to continue their unacceptable behavior unless the cycle is broken.

Focus attention on what a child may need rather than what the child is doing.

"I'm bored." Even in the most interesting and varied environment, some children will be bored because they can't find something to do. Making an extra effort to consider their unique characteristics and interests when planning activities and selecting new materials helps to alleviate boredom.

"I want more control." Some children have very few opportunities to make decisions or to exercise control over their lives. When children are given choices—which materials to use, whom to play with, alternative ways to express strong feelings—they feel more powerful and they begin to develop self-discipline.

"I'm scared." Often the child who is aggressive toward others and challenges adults is a fearful child. To overcome his fears, the child acts as if he is powerful. To help this child, try to find out what his fears are and what is causing them. Make a plan to address them and reassure him that he is safe.

Helping Children to Regain Control

When children lose control, you can help them compose themselves by modeling calm behavior. This approach is not always easy because you need to work against your own frustration. Being human, you may get angry as well when a child's behavior is particularly challenging.

Keep in mind that you can't help children develop self-control if you, yourself, are out of control. Screaming at children, isolating them when they are out of control, and making them feel bad and incompetent rarely produces positive results. These approaches only fuel the fire. Once you are in a power struggle with a child, you have lost the battle. Instead, keep the ultimate goal in mind: to help children develop self-control, not just to behave when adults are present and they fear the consequences of getting caught.

Sometimes, reframing the situation and talking yourself into a more positive way of feeling helps. Suppose, for example, that a child is running around the room, screaming at the top of her lungs, turning over chairs, and throwing things.

The interpretation you choose will affect the way you respond.

You could say to yourself: *Just what I would expect from her. I've had it. I'm going to show her who's boss.*

Or, you could say: *She is testing me. She needs my help. I need to be consistent.*

The second choice can help you remain calm so you can respond in a positive and constructive way. There are several steps to take in responding to challenging behaviors and helping a child regain control.

Intervene to stop dangerous behavior. Your job is to keep everyone safe. You cannot reason with a child who is out of control.

Establish a relationship with the child. A child who knows you care will be much more likely to respond to the help you offer.

Observe to seek more information. Systematic observations over time reveal a great deal of valuable information about what sets the child off and which of his needs are not being met.

Talk with others who know the child. Family members can provide insight, as can other teachers and program staff who know the child. With multiple perspectives you can build a more complete picture.

Develop a plan. With a particularly difficult child, hold a meeting with those who share responsibility for the child. In this way you are likely to come up with a plan that will be implemented consistently by all involved.

Implement the plan and evaluate its effect. The first plan may take time, and it may not be the best one. If it is not working, develop a new plan.

When you are dealing with challenging behaviors of any kind, keep in mind that there is an underlying reason behind all behavior.

When you are dealing with challenging behaviors of any kind, keep in mind that there is an underlying reason behind all behavior. Children who misbehave may not feel safe or connected to others. They may lack the foundation of trust necessary to experiment with doing constructive activities of their own. They need adults who care and form a relationship with them and rebuild their trust. They need opportunities to express their fears and anger appropriately—through creative art, dramatic play, storytelling, and talking with caring adults. They need you to remain calm and be helpful. Only then will they be ready to learn.

conclusion

In this chapter we described the second component of the organizational structure of *The Creative Curriculum,* the learning environment—how to set up and maintain the classroom, establish a structure for each day, and create a classroom community where all children feel safe and know they belong. When the learning environment meets children's needs and supports them, teachers can teach and children will learn. We turn to this component of the organizational structure of *The Creative Curriculum* in the next chapter—What Children Learn.

References

Asher, S. R., & Coie, J. D. (Eds.). (1990). *Peer rejection in childhood.* New York: Cambridge University Press.

Bailey, B. A. (1997). *There's gotta be a better way: Discipline that works!* (Rev. ed.). Oviedo, FL: Loving Guidance.

Kohn, A. (2001). Five reasons to stop saying "Good job!" *Young Children, 56*(5), 24–28.

Kostelnik, M. (1990). Social development: an essential component of kindergarten education. In J. S. McKee (Ed.), *The developing kindergarten: Programs, children, and teachers* (pp. 170–172). East Lansing, MI: Michigan Association for the Education of Young Children.

Levin, D. E. (1994). *Teaching young children in violent times: Building a peaceable classroom.* Cambridge, MA: Educators for Social Responsibility.

Malaguzzi, L. (n.d.) History, ideas and basic philosophy: an interview with Lella Gandini. In C. P. Edwards, L. Gandini, & G. E. Forman, (Eds.), (1998). *The hundred languages of children: The Reggio Emilia approach—advanced reflections* (2nd ed., pp. 49-97). Greenwich, CT: Ablex.

Paley, V. G. (1992). *You can't say you can't play.* Cambridge, MA: Harvard University Press.

Peisner-Feinberg, E. S., Burchinal, M. R., Clifford, R. M., Culkin, M. L., Howes, C., Kagan, S. L., et al. (1999). *The children of the cost, quality, and outcomes study go to school: Technical report.* Chapel Hill: University of North Carolina at Chapel Hill, Frank Porter Graham Child Development Center.

Shonkoff, J. P., & Phillips, D. A. (Eds.). National Research Council, & Institute of Medicine (2000). *From neurons to neighborhoods: The science of early childhood development.* Washington, DC: National Academy Press.

Slaby, R. G., Roedell, W. C., Arezzo, D., & Hendrix, K. (1995). *Early violence prevention: Tools for teachers of young children.* Washington, DC: National Association for the Education of Young Children.

inside this chapter

126 Literacy
126 Components of Literacy
132 Connecting Literacy Content, Teaching, and Learning

134 Mathematics
134 Components of Mathematics
140 Connecting Math Content, Teaching, and Learning

142 Science
142 Components of Science
144 Connecting Science Content, Teaching, and Learning

146 Social Studies
146 Components of Social Studies
150 Connecting Social Studies Content, Teaching, and Learning

152 The Arts
152 Components of the Arts
154 Connecting Content in the Arts, Teaching, and Learning

156 Technology
156 Components of Technology
159 Connecting Technology Content, Teaching, and Learning

161 Process Skills

163 Conclusion and References

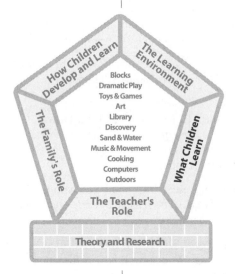

What Children Learn

The Creative Curriculum organizational structure's third component is content—what preschool children learn. Experts have developed standards defining what children should know and be able to do by certain grade levels. States and local school districts have adapted these standards. The content children learn in *The Creative Curriculum* is guided by these standards.

Preschool teachers have always taught content. When they made recipe cards so children could count the cups of flour needed to make a cake, they were teaching math. When they challenged children to find out what kinds of leaves a caterpillar liked to eat, they were teaching science.

Today, because of the standards movement, the knowledge base in each content area is more systematic. Also, the emphasis on teaching content is greater than in the recent past. These changes have set a new challenge for the preschool teacher—knowing what to teach and how to present it. *The Creative Curriculum* explains how to teach content in ways that respect the developmental stages of preschool children. This chapter defines the body of knowledge included in each content area and the process skills children use to learn that content.

Literacy—vocabulary and language, phonological awareness, letters, words, print, comprehension, books, and other texts

Mathematics—numbers, patterns and relationships, geometry and spatial awareness, measurement, and data collection, organization, and representation

Science—the physical properties of objects, living things, and the earth and the environment

Social Studies—how people live, work, get along with others, shape, and are shaped by their surroundings

The Arts—dance, music, dramatic play, drawing and painting

Technology—tools and their basic operations and uses

Process Skills—observing and exploring; problem solving; and connecting, organizing, communicating, and representing information

Literacy

Becoming literate doesn't just happen. Teachers thoughtfully and purposefully interact with children and plan experiences that support emerging literacy. A print-rich environment that allows children to practice literacy skills in real-life experiences, combined with explicit teaching of key concepts, is the foundation of literacy learning in preschool. As children's excitement about their newfound ability to read and write increases, teachers create multiple opportunities for continued literacy learning.

Components of Literacy

Over the past few years, researchers and practitioners (Snow, Burns, & Griffin, 1998; National Institute of Child Health and Human Development, 2000) have studied how children learn to read, write, and understand written language. They have identified what concepts children need to become competent and confident readers and writers and the kinds of experiences that help them make progress. Based on this research, we describe seven components of literacy for preschool children ages 3–5:

- increased vocabulary and language
- phonological awareness
- knowledge of print
- letters and words
- comprehension
- understanding books and other texts
- literacy as a source of enjoyment

Increased Vocabulary and Language

When children are exposed to rich vocabulary, they learn the words they will need to read and write. In addition, research has shown that children who have large vocabularies and lots of experience using language are more successful in school(Hart & Risley, 1995). A *Creative Curriculum* classroom provides many opportunities for children to develop vocabulary and use language. These include

- informal conversations—talking with peers and adults throughout the day
- songs, rhymes, fingerplays, or movement activities
- firsthand experiences—hearing new words to describe what they are doing
- read alouds—listening to books and talking about new words in the story

Preschool children demonstrate increased vocabulary and language when they

- point to one of the trucks and say, "That's a frontloader."

- share at group time: "I'm going fishing with my dad tomorrow and we're going to bring fishing poles and a big net and catch 100 fish."

- describe a scary dream as a "nightmare" after the teacher reads *There's a Nightmare in My Closet*.

If you have children whose primary language is not English, you should know that a strong base in a first language promotes school achievement in a second language (Snow et al., 1998). Children who are learning English as a second language are more likely to become readers and writers of English if they understand the vocabulary and concepts in their primary language first. These children need special attention to increase their vocabulary and language abilities. The long-term goal is for children to be able to understand, speak, read, and write in both the primary language and English. Therefore, you want to support children's first language as you help them acquire oral proficiency in English.

Phonological Awareness

Phonological awareness is hearing and understanding the different sounds of spoken language. It includes the different ways oral language can be broken down into individual parts, for instance, separate sounds and syllables. A key finding in recent research has been the importance of developing phonological awareness during the preschool years.

The skills that make up phonological awareness lie on a continuum of complexity. The simplest level of phonological awareness includes skills such as playing with rhymes, noticing how words begin with the same sounds, or clapping out individual words or syllables of a song, rhyme, or chant. Playing with sounds in speech paves the way to phonemic awareness —the most advanced level of phonological awareness. Phonemic awareness is the ability to hear, identify, and manipulate the individual sounds— phonemes—in spoken words (National Institute of Child Health and Human Development, 2000). Phonemic awareness typically is addressed in kindergarten and first grade.

It is common to confuse phonological awareness with phonics, but they are not the same. Phonics is connecting a printed symbol with a sound, unlike phonological awareness, which is hearing sounds. Phonics activities become appropriate for preschool children only if they understand that speech is made up of a sequence of sounds. The preschool teacher's role in promoting phonological awareness is to draw children's attention to the separate sounds of spoken language through playful songs, games, and rhymes.

Children learning English as a second language are also developing phonological awareness through the activities you do. They may not reproduce sounds exactly as they are made in English, however. These children are still learning to hear and discriminate the sounds of English and need you to acknowledge (rather than correct) the sounds they are trying to make while you continue to model correct English pronunciation.

Preschool children demonstrate phonological awareness when they

• join in saying rhymes, poems, and rhyming songs

• make up nonsense words or silly names (e.g., "Silly Willy," "funny bunny")

• clap along with each word or syllable of a song or rhyme (e.g., clapping twice while saying the name Kel-ly)

• notice that several words or names begin with the same sound (e.g., Jonelle, Juwan, Jonetta)

Knowledge of Print

This component of literacy involves connecting print with meaning. Children acquire a knowledge of print by seeing it in the environment and using it in their play. By drawing children's attention to the features of print, you help children to develop print concepts such as the following:

• Print carries a message.

• Each spoken word can be written down and read.

• Print follows conventions (e.g., left to right, capital/lowercase letters, punctuation).

• Books have common characteristics (e.g., front, back, author, illustrator).

Preschool children demonstrate knowledge of print concepts when they

• point to a printed label and say, "Cars go here."

• make a grocery list in the Dramatic Play Area, writing the words from left to right and top to bottom

• read a big book to a group of stuffed animals, pointing at the words and turning the pages from front to back

Letters and Words

This component of literacy is more than being able to recite the ABC song. Really knowing about letters involves understanding that a letter is a symbol representing one or more of the sounds in the English language; that these symbols can be grouped together to form words; and that these words have meaning.

The most important letters to children are the ones in their names, particularly the first letter. For example, Setsuko points to the "S" on a stop sign and says, "That's my letter!" Many children do not begin experimenting with spelling until they are 5 or 6 years old. You know a child has an understanding of beginning and ending sounds when he writes "PG" above his drawing of a pig. Some people call this stage "invented spelling," "temporary spelling," "developmental spelling," or "phonetic spelling." Research has shown that early forms of spelling indicate that children are making important sound-symbol connections. Other stages will follow.

Preschool children demonstrate their understanding of letters and words when they

- use magnetic letters or other alphabet materials to form their name

- attempt to write a phone message in the dramatic play area

- say, "That says 'w,'"-pointing to the first letter of each word in "wishy-washy, wishy-washy"

Comprehension

Comprehension is understanding the meaning of spoken and written languages. Children with comprehension skills may ask questions or make comments on the topic of a story you are reading, or act it out in their play.

How you read to children is very important to the development of comprehension skills. Pausing at the end of a sentence to let children join in, asking open-ended questions, and helping children make connections to prior experiences are all effective teaching strategies for developing comprehension skills. In the Library chapter we outline specific strategies for reading aloud to individuals and groups of children.

Preschool children demonstrate comprehension skills when they

• retell the story of *The Very Hungry Caterpillar* using felt pieces of fruit on the flannel board

• explain, "They ran away from the kids 'cause they were scared," after hearing the teacher read *Goggles*

• talk about their own experiences after hearing the teacher read *Ira Sleeps Over*

• re-enact *Caps for Sale*

Understanding Books and Other Texts

Understanding books and other texts involves knowing how to read and write signs, menus, letters, shopping lists, newspapers, invitations, messages, journals, and books. Books take many forms—narrative storybooks, predictable books (books with rhyme, repetition, and predictable language patterns), informational books, number books, alphabet books, poetry books. You can help children learn about different forms of literature by making sure you keep a variety of books in your classroom and calling children's attention to their specific characteristics. Storybooks especially offer particularly important learning opportunities. Children can learn many things:

• A story has a beginning, middle, and end.

• There are different characters in a story.

• The story has a setting where it takes place.

• There is a sequence of events in a story.

• A conversation might be taking place.

Understanding books and other text also involves learning how to handle books in ways such as holding the book right side up, turning the pages front to back, and knowing specific words related to books such as author and illustrator.

Preschool children demonstrate their understanding of concepts about books and other texts when they

• retell the story of *The Three Little Pigs*: "The second pig built his house of wood, but the wolf huffed and puffed and blew it down. So the third pig made his house out of bricks."

• place a sign that reads "Do not move!" on a design made with pattern blocks

• refer to a book about castles while building one with blocks

• ask for a book on butterflies so they can find out the name of the one they found

• draw a picture, write some letters on it, and say, "It's a letter for Grandma."

Literacy as a Source of Enjoyment

Motivation is also an aspect of literacy and one that is particularly important. Children read because they are motivated to learn something new that interests them, uncover the plot of a story, or discover something that makes them laugh. The more they read, the better readers they become, and the more motivated they are.

In the Library chapter, you can find many ideas and strategies for making that area inviting and attractive. In addition, you will find many ways to instill a love of reading in your classroom.

Preschool children demonstrate their enjoyment of literacy experiences when they

• ask the teacher to read a favorite book

• join in the refrain "Brown bear, brown bear, what do you see?" as the teacher reads the book

• scribble across the top of the page after finishing a picture and then read the story to the teacher

• listen to a story and ask questions about it

• use books to get answers to their questions

Connecting Literacy Content, Teaching, and Learning

The chart below shows how to connect literacy content, teaching, and learning. The first column outlines the content of literacy for preschool children. The second column shows some of the ways teachers present this content effectively. The last column lists the objectives on the *Developmental Continuum* that you should be watching for as children work. As you watch children you will be able to observe and identify their progress. This information will help you to determine the kinds of content to introduce and the methods you should use.

Literacy Content	What Teachers Can Do	*Creative Curriculum* Objectives
Increased Vocabulary and Language (Acquire new words and use them to communicate)	Engage in frequent one-on-one conversations with children. Provide children with many firsthand experiences and give them the words that describe what they are doing. Introduce new words during story time using various strategies: explaining; pointing to pictures; using expression, body language, or tone of voice.	3. Recognizes own feelings and manages them appropriately 38. Hears and discriminates the sounds of language 39. Expresses self using words and expanded sentences 40. Understands and follows oral directions 41. Answers questions 42. Asks questions 43. Actively participates in conversations
Phonological Awareness (Hear and discriminate between the separate sounds of spoken words; recognize words that sound the same and words that sound different)	Lead children in singing songs, saying rhymes, and fingerplays. Sing songs, play language games, and say rhymes that encourage children to play with words. Talk about words and sounds during daily activities: "Tasheen and Tyrone—Your names both start the same way!" Read books that play with the sounds in words, such as those by Dr. Seuss.	38. Hears and discriminates the sounds of language 46. Demonstrates knowledge of the alphabet 50. Writes letters and words
Knowledge of Print (Learn how print works)	Talk about features of print (top-to-bottom, left-to-right) while writing experience charts. Occasionally run your finger under the words as you read a story. As you write with children, draw their attention to symbols such as periods and question marks: "I better put a period here so others will know to stop when they are reading it." Post a sign with pictures and words on what to take for snack. Post sign up sheet for activities.	45. Demonstrates understanding of print concepts 46. Demonstrates knowledge of the alphabet 47. Uses emerging reading skills to make meaning from print 48. Comprehends and interprets meaning from books and other texts 49. Understands the purpose of writing 50. Writes letters and words

Literacy Content	What Teachers Can Do	*Creative Curriculum* Objectives
Letters and Words (Identify and write some letters and words)	Display the alphabet at children's eye level and have alphabet cards available for children to use during play. Add materials such as alphabet puzzles, magnetic letters, foam letters, paper, and pencils to the interest areas. Draw children's attention to letters and words in the environment as they come up in everyday activities.	21. Uses tools for writing and drawing 37. Makes and interprets representations 46. Demonstrates knowledge of the alphabet 47. Uses emerging reading skills to make meaning from print 49. Understands the purpose of writing 50. Writes letters and words
Comprehension (Understand and follow what is going on in a book, story, or conversation)	Add storytelling props to the Library Area for acting out a story. Leave off a word at the end of a sentence when reading a predictable book. Ask children open-ended questions while reading: "What do you think will happen next?" "How would you feel if that happened to you?" Encourage children to recall important events in a story: "Do you remember what happened when the wolf blew on the house of straw?"	44. Enjoys and values reading 45. Demonstrates understanding of print concepts 47. Uses emerging reading skills to make meaning from print 48. Comprehends and interprets meaning from books and other texts
Understanding Books and Other Texts (Learn how to use a book and the purpose of books; gain a sense of story; learn about the uses of other texts such as signs, menus, magazines, newspapers, etc.)	Model how to handle books properly and teach children to care for them. Help children find books and magazines to learn more about topics of interest. Add magazines, signs, pamphlets, telephone books, menus, and newspapers to dramatic play areas. Talk about the author and illustrator when introducing a story.	44. Enjoys and values reading 45. Demonstrates understanding of print concepts 47. Uses emerging reading skills to make meaning from print 48. Comprehends and interprets meaning from books and other texts 50. Writes letters and words
Literacy as a Source of Enjoyment (Enjoy being read to, reading and writing)	Arrange the Library Area attractively and include high-quality literature and soft, comfortable furniture. Read books to children and encourage them to talk about the story. Place books in all interest area on topics that are relevant. Add interesting materials to the writing area to encourage writing attempts—pencils and pens, stationery, stamps, envelopes, etc.	35. Takes on pretend roles and situations 38. Hears and discriminates the sounds of language 44. Enjoys and values reading 45. Demonstrates understanding of print concepts 47. Uses emerging reading skills to make meaning from print 48. Comprehends and interprets meaning from books and other texts 49. Understands the purpose of writing 50. Writes letters and words

Mathematics

Just as preschool teachers cultivate literacy in children, they use multiple opportunities during the day to help child build competence in math. When children give each person at the table a cracker, pour water from one container to another, put all the big buttons in one pile and the smaller ones in another, or clap a rhythmic pattern—they are learning math. Everyday experiences such as these provide the context for preschool children to progress in math. In addition, teachers' knowledge of the substance of math content provides facts and concepts needed to promote and extend children's mathematical thinking.

Components of Mathematics

National standards in mathematics (NCTM, 2000) describe what children should learn in preschool. The key components of math include

- number concepts

- patterns and relationships

- geometry and spatial sense

- measurement

- data collection, organization, and representation

Number Concepts

Number concepts are the foundation of mathematics. These concepts develop gradually over time as children explore, manipulate, and organize materials and as they communicate their mathematical thinking with adults and peers.

Children are said to have number sense when they have a good intuition about numbers and their relationships. As children gain a sense of numbers, they understand, for example, what "three" really means, and that "threeness" can be represented by a number "3," the word "three," or a set of three objects. They begin to explore the relationships between quantities such as more, less, and the same.

Counting is one of the earliest number concepts to emerge. It begins with the development of oral counting skills or rote counting sometimes as early as age 2. Rote counting simply means memorization of a sequence of numbers. Rote-counting skills develop as children join in songs, fingerplays, and rhymes involving numbers.

One-to-one correspondence follows rote counting. One-to-one correspondence means linking one, and only one, number with each item in a set of objects. This technique should be modeled throughout the day in interest areas and daily routines, and often must be taught directly. Sometimes children count an object twice. You can model strategies to help children keep track of what they are counting by showing them how to move each object to the side after they have counted it.

Other number concepts include quantity, comparisons, and number symbols. Quantity is the concept of an entire set (knowing that the last object counted represents the entire set of objects). If you ask a child to bring you three cookies and he brings you all three rather than just the third cookie counted, he probably has an understanding of quantity. A child who understands number order knows whether he counts a row of three cookies from left to right or goes in a different order, the amount is still three. Making comparisons involves knowing the meaning of such terms as *more than*, *bigger than*, *less than*, and *the same as*.

Young children can learn the names of numbers without having any idea what the symbol represents. The concept of number symbols involves seeing a numeral, for instance 3, and associating that numeral with three objects. Number symbols only have meaning when they are introduced as labels for quantities. Rather than teaching children to recognize number symbols in isolation, link the number symbols to a quantity.

Preschool children demonstrate understanding of number concepts when they

- notice that it takes five scoops of sand to fill a cup

- predict it will take 10 blocks to make a fence, then count to see if the prediction is correct

- count five children and then set the table with five plates, napkins, and forks

Patterns and Relationships

Patterns are regular arrangements of objects, shapes, or numbers. Pattern recognition allows children to recognize relationships among objects and then to make generalizations about number combinations and to count.

Recognizing patterns and relationships is not just an important math objective but one that children will use in science and in literacy. For preschoolers, the goal is to recognize and analyze simple patterns, copy them, create them, and make predictions about them by extending them. Preschool children can readily grasp the concept of recognizing simple patterns. As you "read" a pattern of beads—red, blue, red, blue—children can join in. After recognizing simple patterns, they can copy a pattern they see or hear. To extend a pattern, children must figure out what comes next and continue on with the sequence. They also can create a pattern on their own, but often the rules they create are not consistent.

Preschool children demonstrate understanding of patterns and relationships when they

- line up small cars in a red, black, red, black, red, black pattern

- sponge paint a patterned border around a picture

- create a rhythmic pattern such as clap-clap-snap, clap-clap-snap

- make a pattern with interlocking cubes (white, blue, green, white, blue, green)

Geometry and Spatial Sense

Geometry and spatial sense is recognizing the shapes and structures in the environment. Children learn about and use their knowledge of two- and three-dimensional shapes when you give them the opportunity to create designs with pattern blocks; draw, paint, and cut shapes in their artwork; return blocks to the shelves by sorting them; and locate shapes in the outdoor environment. First, children learn to recognize simple geometric figures like triangles, circles, and squares. Next, they learn characteristics of shapes (e.g., a square has four sides). At a higher level, they begin to apply reasoning as they work with shapes (e.g., this must be a triangle because it has three sides). You reinforce their understanding by describing the shapes that you see children create or locate.

Children gain spatial sense as they become aware of themselves in relation to the world around them. Through the experiences you provide, they learn about location and position (*on, off, on top of, under, in, out, behind, below*), movement (*backward, forward, around, through, across, up, down,* etc.), and distance (*near, far, next to*). As you give children the opportunity to manipulate objects and shapes, they also learn to make predictions (e.g., What will happen if I turn this shape upside down?).

Preschool children demonstrate their understanding of geometry and spatial sense when they

• use a geoboard to create geometric shapes with rubber bands

• say, "You put your horse inside the fence. I'm going to make mine jump over the fence."

• note that bubbles look like circles

• use empty boxes, tubes, and containers to build an imaginary playground

Measurement

The focus of measurement activities in preschool is on developing an understanding of the principles and uses of measuring. Children learn measurement from opportunities to use materials and participate in hands-on activities.

As a first step, children make comparisons without any measurement tools. Using the materials you provide to play, children learn concepts such as longer, shorter, heavier, lighter, faster, and slower. Next, children learn to use non-standard measures such as a shoe, a piece of string or ribbon, or even a hand to measure an object.

Formal instruction in measurement using standard measures such as clocks, rulers, scales, thermometers, and measuring cups comes later, typically toward the end of kindergarten and in the primary grades. However, if these measuring tools are made available to children, they will explore and use them in their play and investigations.

Preschool children demonstrate their knowledge of measurement when they

• realize that only a short time is left to clean up when the teacher turns over the sand timer

• measure a table using a unit block

• count how many cups of sand it takes to fill a bucket

• use a piece of ribbon to measure the length of a rug

Data Collection, Organization, and Representation

Data collection, organization, and representation in preschool involve sorting, classifying, graphing, counting, measuring, and comparing. Instruction in each of these areas can build on children's natural interest in making collections.

As part of collecting, children may begin to sort and make sets without any plan in mind. Then they sort more purposefully—for example, by properties such as color, shape, or size. As children develop and refine their sorting skills, they can sort by more than one attribute. This ability is strengthened when you encourage them to talk about their sorting rules.

Graphing is a direct extension of sorting and classifying. A graph presents information in a visually organized way that helps children to see relationships. Graphing is a way for children to display many different kinds of information in different forms. A simple graph of the kinds of shoes children are wearing could develop from a concrete representation to a symbolic one.

• Concrete—shoes with ties, Velcro, or buckles, and slip-on shoes

• Symbolic—pictures representing the types of shoes

Our Leaves

Maple		Elm	Dog-wood		Birch		Oak	Pine

After children make a graph, they can use it to analyze and interpret the data. This step involves comparing, counting, adding and subtracting, and using terms such as greater than, less than, equal to, and not equal to. This graph was made after the children in one classroom collected leaves on a walk.

To help children interpret this graph, a teacher might ask these questions:

> *What does this graph tell us?*
>
> *Which kind of leaf did we collect the most of? The least? How do you know that?*
>
> *Which leaves did we collect the same number of? How do you know that?*

Preschool children demonstrate their ability to collect, organize, and represent data when they

- sort a collection of dolls into a group with shoes and a group with no shoes

- make a graph of a sticker collection, sorting them by color

- make tally marks under "yes" and "no" on a clipboard while doing a survey of what the group prefers for snack—juice or milk

- draw a picture of each object that floats and each that sinks after testing them in the water table

Connecting Math Content, Teaching, and Learning

In *The Creative Curriculum*, math content is presented in ways that preschool children learn. The chart below shows how to connect math content, teaching, and learning. The first column shows the content of math for preschool. The second column shows some of the many ways teachers can present this content effectively. The last column lists the objectives on the *Developmental Continuum* you should be watching for as children explore concepts in math. As you watch children engage in these activities, you will be able to observe and identify children's developmental progress. This information will help you to determine the kinds of math content to present and the methods to use.

Math Content	What Teachers Can Do	*Creative Curriculum* Objectives
Number Concepts (Understand numbers, ways of representing numbers, and relationships between numbers)	Teach children counting songs, rhymes, and chants: "1, 2, 3, 4, 5, I caught a fish alive." Count during daily activities—the children present, the cups needed for each child, the paintbrushes needed for each container. Encourage child to compare relationships between quantities: "Do we have more red caps or more blue caps?"	22. Observes objects and events with curiosity 23. Approaches problems flexibly 28. Compares/measures 33. Uses one-to-one correspondence 34. Uses numbers and counting
Patterns and Relationships (Recognize, copy, extend patterns; make predictions about patterns in the environment)	Clap hands then pat thighs in a pattern (clap, pat, clap, pat). Later move to more complex patterns (clap, clap, pat, clap, clap, pat). Create "people patterns" with children (stand, sit, stand, sit) and help them describe the pattern. Draw children's attention to various patterns in the environment: "I see a pattern in your shirt today—red, blue, red, blue." Describe patterns you see children creating: "You made a pattern with the blocks—square, triangle, square, triangle."	22. Observes objects and events with curiosity 23. Approaches problems flexibly 27. Classifies objects 28. Compares/measures 30. Recognizes patterns and can repeat them 37. Makes and interprets representations

Math Content	What Teachers Can Do	*Creative Curriculum* Objectives
Geometry and Spatial Sense (Recognize, name, build, draw, describe, compare and sort two- and three-dimensional shapes; recognize and describe spatial relationships)	Talk about the geometric shapes as children use blocks or shape blocks. Provide empty boxes, tubes, and containers for children to use in creating and constructing. Take children on a walk looking for shapes in the environment. Describe spatial relationships you notice as children play: "You're putting the horse inside the fence you made."	22. Observes objects and events with curiosity 23. Approaches problems flexibly 27. Classifies objects 28. Compares/measures 32. Shows awareness of position in space 37. Makes and interprets representations 39. Expresses self using words and expanded sentences
Measurement (Use non-standard units to measure and make comparisons)	Show children how to use objects to measure things: "Look. This table is five blocks long." Use a sand timer or kitchen timer to let children know that there are only five minutes left until clean-up time. Ask open-ended questions during measurement activities: "I wonder how many cups of water your pitcher will hold." Use words like before, after, next, yesterday, today, tomorrow throughout the day: "Tomorrow is Leo's birthday."	22. Observes objects and events with curiosity 23. Approaches problems flexibly 27. Classifies objects 28. Compares/measures 29. Arranges objects in a series 31. Shows awareness of time concepts and sequence 34. Uses numbers and counting
Data Collection, Organization, and Representation (Pose questions to investigate, organize responses, and create representations of data)	Pose a "question of the day." Show children how to make tally marks under "yes" or "no" on a clipboard: "Do you like to wear your shoes at nap time?" Graph collections of objects found in the classroom such as stickers, leaves, rocks, shells, buttons, etc. Have the children form a "people graph" in response to your questions: "Are there more children here with brown hair than blonde hair?" Ask questions such as, "How did you make your group?" "Where does this one go?" "How are these two alike?"	22. Observes objects and events with curiosity 23. Approaches problems flexibly 27. Classifies objects 28. Compares/measures 29. Arranges objects in a series 30. Recognizes patterns and can repeat them 33. Uses one-to-one correspondence 34. Uses numbers and counting 37. Makes and interprets representations

Science

Science content is more than isolated facts such as the stages in the life of a butterfly. Scientific facts are important, but how they are put together into meaningful ideas is more significant. For example, learning about the development of a butterfly should lead to the big idea that all living things develop in a series of stages called a life cycle. Preschool children learn science by exploring the world around them. When you provide an environment with many varied materials, they try out things to see how they work, they experiment, they manipulate, they are curious, and they ask questions. As they seek answers to their questions, they learn to enjoy and appreciate their surroundings. These activities are science.

Components of Science

To decide which concepts children should learn, observe children's scientific interests and what they see and do every day. Your observations will fall into three categories that are the components of science (National Research Council, 1996):

- physical science
- life science
- earth and the environment

Physical Science

Physical science is about the physical properties of materials and objects. Through exploration of materials, children learn about weight, shape, size, color, and temperature. They explore how things move and change. When children make a block ramp to race cars, look through a kaleidoscope, or pick up objects with magnets, they are learning about the physical properties of objects. Think about these questions to help children learn physical science:

What does this look like? Big or little, striped or polka dotted, bright or dull?

How does this smell? Like perfume or burned like toast?

How does this taste? Sweet, salty, bitter, or bland?

How does this sound? Loud or soft, fast or slow?

How does this feel? Slimy, squishy, hard, sharp, or tickly?

How can you make this move? Can you roll it, twist it, blow it, swing it, or push it?

How can you make this change? Can you mix it, pour it, smash it, or shake it?

It is not necessary to set up specific science experiments for children. You can create opportunities to learn about physical science in all interest areas.

As you talk with children, they can demonstrate their understanding of physical science when they

• use a magnet to pick up metal objects buried in the sand table

• tilt ramps to make cars go down faster in the block area

• use a pulley to lift a basket of books into the reading loft

• say, "Look! My blue paint ran into the yellow paint and it turned green."

 ### Life Science

Life science is about living things. You are teaching life science when you ask children to care for plants and animals in a classroom. Key ideas emerge from exploring the immediate environment. Therefore a preschool in Louisiana might explore crawfish, while in Alaska children might learn about salmon or caribou. In Arizona, children could learn about cactus and in rural Nebraska, about corn. No matter what topic children study, these are the concepts to think about as you plan learning experiences:

How do living things get food?

What are characteristics of plants and animals?

What do plants and animals need to grow?

How do plants and animals depend on each other?

How do living things change as they grow?

Which animals lay eggs?

What plants and animals live in our neighborhood?

Life science also includes knowledge about one's body and how to keep it healthy. These topics can be taught by exploring these big ideas:

How do your bodies grow and change?

How do you use your senses to make discoveries?

Why do you need different kinds of food?

How do you stay safe and healthy?

Preschool children demonstrate their knowledge of life science when they

• point out, "Our gerbil sleeps all day long. I wonder if he stays awake at night?"

• water plants after observing that their leaves are drooping

• notice that their hearts beat faster after running on the playground

Earth and the Environment

The component of science called earth and the environment is about the world of nature. In preschool, earth and the environment are about natural settings that children can experience directly. The goal is for children to understand those settings, learn key ideas, and develop respect for their natural surroundings. Think about how you might address these questions in your daily activities:

What is the land like in this community? Is there water, grass, sand, or rocks? Are there lakes, ponds, mountains, deserts, rivers, or fields? What are these things like?

What can you see in the sky? How do the things in the sky affect the world around you?

What is the weather like here? How does it affect you?

How can you take care of the world around you?

Preschoolers learn about the earth and the environment when they

• play shadow tag

• talk about things they do during the day and at night

• add water to dirt while making mud pies

• paint with water on the sidewalk and notice that the picture soon disappears

Connecting Science Content, Teaching, and Learning

The content of science in *The Creative Curriculum* is geared to children's interest in the world around them. The chart that follows shows how to connect science content, teaching, and learning. The first column shows the general content of science for preschool. The second column shows some of the many ways teachers might present this content effectively. The last column lists the objectives on the *Developmental Continuum* you should be watching for as children work on science content. As you watch children engage in these activities, you will be able to observe and identify children's developmental progress. This information will help you to determine the kinds of science content to present and the methods to use.

Science Content	What Teachers Can Do	*Creative Curriculum* Objectives
Physical Science (Explore the physical properties of the world by observing and manipulating common objects and materials in the environment)	Include science materials such as magnets, magnifying glasses, balance scales, pulleys, and mirrors to encourage exploration. Use open-ended questions to further investigations: "I wonder why this big toy boat floats but the penny sinks." Describe physical changes you see taking place: "When your blue paint ran into the yellow paint, it turned green!" Include old small appliances or broken toys on a "take-apart" table to help children learn how things work.	22. Observes objects and events with curiosity 25. Explores cause and effect 26. Applies knowledge or experience to a new context 27. Classifies objects 28. Compares/measures 29. Arranges objects in a series 30. Recognizes patterns and can repeat them 32. Shows awareness of position in space
Life Science (Explore living things, their life cycles, and their habitats)	Add living things such as plants and pets to the classroom environment and study them. After planting seeds with the children, provide markers and paper so they can observe and record the growth over time. During a study of houses, talk with children about different kinds of animal homes such as bird's nests, beehives, anthills, etc. Observe and discuss life cycles of animals such as butterflies and frogs. Help children learn about health and their bodies every day: "Can you feel your heart pounding after running so much?" "Those carrots you're eating are so good for you."	7. Respects and cares for classroom environment and materials 12. Shares and respects the rights of others 22. Observes objects and events with curiosity 25. Explores cause and effect 26. Applies knowledge or experience to a new context 31. Shows awareness of time concepts and sequence
Earth and the Environment (Explore the properties of the world around them, notice changes, and make predictions)	Lead a discussion about things we do during the day and things we do at night. Paint with water on the sidewalk and talk about why it disappears. Talk about the seasons as you notice the changes in your environment: "I can tell fall is here. The leaves are turning red, yellow, orange, and brown." Discuss the weather each day while preparing to go outdoors: "Jeremy, will you check the weather outside today? Do we need to wear sweaters?"	7. Respects and cares for classroom environment and materials 25. Explores cause and effect 26. Applies knowledge or experience to a new context 27. Classifies objects 28. Compares/measures 31. Shows awareness of time concepts and sequence 32. Shows awareness of position in space

Social Studies

Social studies is the study of people—how people live today and how they lived in the past, how they work, get along with others, solve problems, shape and are shaped by their surroundings. Children begin learning social studies in infancy. They explore physical space by crawling, climbing, digging, and splashing. In preschool, board games or the challenge of riding around a tricycle path teach mapping skills. Children learn about time (history) from the daily predictable routines you establish—a story before rest time, circle time after interest areas, and outdoor play after lunch. When you set up a play grocery store and help children learn about jobs and buying and selling, you help them learn economics. This learning continues as they visit the supermarket, the doctor, the hardware store, and the shoe store. Preschoolers learn about civics as you teach them to cooperate to resolve differences in a classroom setting. Everyday experiences pertinent to children's lives are the foundation for learning social studies.

Components of Social Studies

Social studies standards focus on history, geography, economics, and civics. We have organized the components of social studies for preschool children into the following categories:

- spaces and geography

- people and how they live

- people and the environment

- people and the past

Spaces and Geography

Geography for preschool children includes the characteristics of the place where they live, and the relationships between that place and other places. It also includes the physical characteristics of the children's world and mapping. The materials for teaching this content area are the slides, the swings, and the grassy area by the tree—and the method is talking about how to navigate these areas. You can talk about mapping by discussing directions—how to get to the bathroom, the playground, the carpool line. You can encourage children to recreate their neighborhood in the Block Area and draw or paint maps of places they go. An important goal is for children to begin to understand that maps represent actual places.

These kinds of questions can help you think about ways to build understanding of spaces and geography:

Where do you live? What is your community like?

How do people move from one place to another?

Where are you in relation to other people and objects (e.g., near, far, next to, outside, behind)?

What is a map and how can it help us?

Preschool children demonstrate their understanding of spaces and geography when they

• move a piece in the right direction while playing board games like *Candyland*

• mold wet sand to make mountains, hills, and streams

• figure out how to maneuver around a bike path or an obstacle course

• use blocks to represent roads and buildings

People and How They Live

People and how they live is the component of social studies that includes physical characteristics of people; similarities and differences in habits, homes, and work; family structures and roles; and the exchange of goods and services. Preschool children can begin to explore these concepts by studying themselves and their families and by thinking how classroom rules help people live together and get along.

These questions about people and how they live may help you design experiences for children to learn these ideas:

Who are the people in your family? What do they do?

How do you make and keep a friend?

What are the jobs of people in our community?

How do people use money to get goods and services?

What are some of the rules in your home, school, and community?

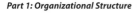

Preschool children demonstrate their growing understanding of people and how they live when they

• talk about family members living in the same house

• describe what jobs their parents do

• point out that their hair color is the same as a friend's

• use a toy cash register to "sell" shoes

• invite a child in a wheelchair to play catch with a ball

People and the Environment

People and the environment covers the ways people change the environment and protect it. For preschool children topics in this component of social studies are, for example, building cities, making roads, building highways or dams, cleaning up a park, recycling, or preserving some green space. In preschool the method for teaching people and the environment is to draw out what children learn by exploring the area around their home and school and to build on that information.

Here are some questions you can think about to help children explore about how people affect the environment:

How can we respect and care for our world?

What are some bad things that people do to the environment? How do they affect all of us?

Preschool children demonstrate their understanding of people and the environment when they

• place trash in the wastebasket in the classroom and the playground

• note, "If they cut the tree down on our playground, we won't have any shade."

• help collect trash from the playground

People and the Past

People and the past is about history. Preschool children focus on the here and now. They do not have the true understanding of chronological time that is essential to understand history. Instead they learn about time in relation to themselves, including their daily schedule, what they did yesterday, and what they will do tomorrow.

Preschool children love to consider what they can do now that they couldn't do when they were "babies." They can appreciate stories about other times and places—if the topics are relevant to their own experiences. Consider these questions to help you think about how to teach preschool children about people and the past:

How do things and people change over time?

How do we measure the passage of time?

What is the difference among past, present, and future time?

Preschool children demonstrate their knowledge of people and the past when they

- hold up a baby shoe and say, "My foot used to be this little, and now it's all grown-up!"

- say, "A long, long, long time ago I went to my Aunt Susie's house."

- use a sand timer while taking turns

Connecting Social Studies Content, Teaching, and Learning

The *Creative Curriculum* teacher focuses social studies instruction on the world of the children in their class—where they live and what they see around them. The chart below shows how to connect social studies content, teaching, and learning. The first column outlines the general content of social studies for preschool. The second column shows some of the many ways social studies teachers can present this content effectively. The last column lists the objectives on the *Developmental Continuum* you should think about as children work on social studies content. As you watch children engage in these activities, you will be able to observe and identify children's developmental progress. This information will help you to determine the kinds of social studies content to present and the methods to use.

Social Studies Content	What Teachers Can Do	*Creative Curriculum* Objectives
Spaces and Geography (Learn about the physical world around us and how we move about the world)	Provide board games like *Chutes and Ladders* as a way of introducing beginning mapping skills. Create an obstacle course for children to maneuver around and through. Mark the shadow of a tree or a flagpole at different times of the day and talk about why it changed. Draw children's attention to the physical properties of the earth as they dig in the dirt and create mud by adding water: "There are lots of small rocks in the dirt you're digging. Would you like a sifter?"	22. Observes objects and events with curiosity 23. Approaches problems flexibly 25. Explores cause and effect 26. Applies knowledge or experience to a new context 32. Shows awareness of position in space 37. Makes and interprets representations
People and How They Live (Recognize and respect likenesses and differences in people; recognize how people rely on each other for goods and services; learn social skills; understand the need for rules)	Create rules about getting along and cooperating in the context of real problems as they come up: "There seemed to be a problem at the sand table today. Is there a rule we could make so everyone has enough room to play?" Provide paint, crayons, markers, and construction paper in various skin tones. Invite families to participate in the classroom and share aspects of their culture. In the Dramatic Play Area introduce new props that focus on jobs—flower shop, auto repair, restaurant, grocery store. Visit different stores in the neighborhood and discuss the jobs people do.	1. Shows ability to adjust to new situations 3. Recognizes own feelings and manages them appropriately 4. Stands up for rights 9. Follows classroom rules 10. Plays well with other children 11. Recognizes the feelings of others and responds appropriately 12. Shares and respects the rights of others 13. Uses thinking skills to resolve conflicts 26. Applies knowledge or experience to a new context

Social Studies Content	What Teachers Can Do	*Creative Curriculum* Objectives
People and the Environment (Learn how people affect the environment by changing it and protecting it)	Provide junk that can be used to create sculptures. Plant trees in the schoolyard and help children collect trash. Talk about changes that take place in the immediate environment (a fire that destroys the woods, fish that die as a result of pollution, trees that are cut down to make way for a road or a parking lot). Set aside and sort plastic, paper, and metal to be picked up for recycling. Recycle cardboard tubes and boxes, and use in the Block or Art Area.	7. Respects and cares for classroom environment and materials 22. Observes objects and events with curiosity 23. Approaches problems flexibly 25. Explores cause and effect 26. Applies knowledge or experience to a new context
People and the Past (Learn how things and people change over time)	Invite grandparents to talk about their lives as children. Ask children to bring in pictures of themselves as a baby or an article of their baby clothing. Discuss how they have changed over time. Ask children questions that will help them recall the past: "What did you do yesterday when you got home?" Explore toys from long ago. Teach children games you played as a child.	22. Observes objects and events with curiosity 25. Explores cause and effect 31. Shows awareness of time concepts and sequence

The Arts

Art is designing, creating, and exploring. Children mix paints; pound and shape clay; build structures with blocks, boxes, and Legos; dance; dramatize stories; clap rhythms; and sing chants and songs. Preschool children like to get their hands into materials and to move their bodies. Preschool teachers can expose children to a wide variety of experiences in the arts throughout the day.

Components of the Arts

National Standards for Arts Education (Consortium of National Arts Education Associations, 1994) includes four components:

- dance

- music

- theater or performing arts (what we would call dramatic play in preschool)

- visual arts

You will find that these four components of the arts are emphasized throughout *The Creative Curriculum*. Chapter 9 on Art provides guidance on the visual arts. Chapter 13 on Music and Movement describes appropriate experiences in music and dance. Throughout the entire Curriculum, emphasis is placed on the important role of symbolic and pretend play. Components of the drama standards can be found in the Dramatic Play Area, the Block Area, the Library Area, and the Music and Movement Area. In addition, group time activities provide opportunities for dramatizations. A discussion of how the standards in the Arts apply to preschool follows.

Dance

Dance is using one's body to express ideas, to respond to music, and to convey feelings. When you encourage children to vary their responses to different musical phrases, they learn about the body's ability to move, and they use time and space in many different ways.

Preschool children demonstrate knowledge of dance when they

- use scarves and streamers to move to the music

- imitate movements of animals after a trip to the farm

- move quickly to a polka, and slowly to a lullaby or spiritual

Music

Music is combining voice and/or instruments to create melodies and pleasing sounds. Children learn music by listening to and interacting with many kinds of sounds. Therefore, you should provide children with opportunities to play with musical instruments, learn and make up songs, listen to recordings, and talk about sounds. When preschool children explore instruments, create melodies, learn songs as a group, and make up songs, they develop appreciation for different kinds of music and become comfortable with different forms of musical expression.

Preschool children demonstrate their understanding of music concepts when they

- make different sounds with musical instruments

- play musical games such as "Farmer in the Dell" and "Hokey Pokey"

- create a song while pounding clay

- say, "That music makes me think of a parade."

Drama

Drama is telling stories through action, dialogue, or both. Preschool children recognize that movement can communicate messages and represent actions. Preschool teachers are teaching drama when they provide children with clothing they can use to dress up and pretend, props that can transform blocks into a city, and puppets that can act out a story. As children play with materials such as these, they express their feelings and inhabit and learn about worlds beyond the limits of their immediate surroundings.

Drama also has a direct impact on other learning, such as language development and literacy. In *Preventing Reading Difficulties in Young Children* (Snow et al., 1998) the writers report that children benefit from play-based instruction in which they invent dramatic play scenarios. This kind of sociodramatic play not only increases oral language use and enables children to practice storytelling skills, but it also offers a challenge for children to work together to negotiate their play ideas. In turn, each of these skills promotes reading comprehension.

Preschool children demonstrate drama skills as they

• gather props and act out "Goldilocks and the Three Bears" in the dramatic play area

• pantomime someone who is happy, sad, angry, tired, excited, and scared

• make up a puppet show for others to watch

• ask, "Guess who I am?" and then pretend to walk like an elephant

Visual Arts

The visual arts are painting, drawing, making collages, modeling and sculpting with clay or other materials, building, making puppets, weaving and stitching, and printmaking with stamps, blocks, or rubbings. Children benefit from opportunities to work with different kinds of paint and paper; draw with crayons, markers, and chalk; put things together with paste and glue; cut with scissors; mold playdough; and clean up with mops, sponges, and brooms. The more exposure you give children to all kinds of materials—and to discussions about different ways to use the materials—the more children become able to express their ideas through the visual arts.

The visual arts also promote an understanding of the world. Children learn to draw and draw to learn. Using markers, clay, collage, wire, or wood, children represent what they have learned about a topic. In so doing, they master drawing materials and learn about different perspectives, part/whole relationships, size, position, and the characteristics of people and things.

Preschool children demonstrate understanding of the visual arts when they

• create a torn-paper collage after looking at books illustrated by Leo Lionni

• use bright paint colors at the easel

• try different ways to balance a mobile

• create a get-well card for a friend

Connecting Content in the Arts, Teaching, and Learning

In a *Creative Curriculum* classroom, the arts are addressed throughout the day. The chart on the next page shows how to connect the arts content, teaching, and learning. The first column outlines the content of the arts for preschool. The second column shows some of the many ways teachers can provide learning experiences for children. The last column lists the objectives on the *Developmental Continuum* you should be watching for as children work on arts content. As children engage in these activities, you will be able to observe and identify children's developmental progress. This information will help you to determine the kinds of experiences to offer and the ways to offer them.

Arts Content	What Teachers Can Do	*Creative Curriculum* Objectives
Dance (Learn about the body's ability to move and use time and space in different ways)	Offer children scarves and streamers to use as they dance to music. Invite children to move in different ways. Play different kinds of music that inspire children to move quickly (polka) or slowly (lullaby or spiritual). Teach new vocabulary words such as smooth, jerky, gallop, and glide.	14. Demonstrates basic locomotor skills (running, jumping, hopping, galloping) 15. Shows balance while moving 30. Recognizes patterns and can repeat them 35. Takes on pretend roles and situations 37. Makes and interprets representations 40. Understands and follows oral directions
Music (Develop an awareness of different kinds of music and become comfortable with different forms of musical expression)	Set up an area where children can explore instruments, listen to and create music. Introduce children to music words—rhythm, beat, steady, fast, slow, loud, soft. Teach children songs that might be familiar to their families—folk songs, ballads—so they can sing together. Create songs or chants while pounding clay. Clap rhythmic patterns to music.	25. Explores cause and effect 30. Recognizes patterns and can repeat them 31. Shows awareness of time concepts and sequence 34. Uses numbers and counting 35. Takes on pretend roles and situations 38. Hears and discriminates the sounds of language 40. Understands and follows oral directions
Drama (Communicate a message or story through action or dialogue)	Participate in and encourage children's pretend play. Gather props and invite children to act out familiar stories such as *Caps for Sale*. Have children show you facial expressions of someone who is happy, sad, angry, tired, excited, or scared. Provide puppets and props and encourage children to act out a story you have read.	3. Recognizes own feelings and manages them appropriately 11. Recognizes the feelings of others and responds appropriately 32. Shows awareness of position in space 35. Takes on pretend roles and situations 38. Hears and discriminates the sounds of language 39. Expresses self using words and expanded sentences
Visual Arts (Use a variety of media for communication and expression; solve problems using art materials; appreciate many forms of art)	Provide materials children can use to represent their ideas—markers, crayons, paints, clay, collage, wire, wood scraps. Talk about illustration techniques in books, such as torn-paper pictures, watercolors, pastels. Provide materials in the Art Area for children to experiment. Add mirrors to the Art Area and encourage children to look at their own facial features when they draw people. Encourage children to draw pictures to show what they have learned. Display children's work attractively and prominently in the classroom.	3. Recognizes own feelings and manages them appropriately 7. Respects and cares for classroom environment and materials 19. Controls small muscles in hands 21. Uses tools for writing and drawing 22. Observes objects and events with curiosity 25. Explores cause and effect 30. Recognizes patterns and can repeat them 32. Shows awareness of position in space 37. Makes and interprets representations

Technology

Technology is the study of tools, machines, materials, techniques, and sources of power that make work easier and that solve problems. Children learn technology by exploring how things work. When they figure out what kind of tools they need to build a structure using wood scraps they are solving technological problems. When children sing songs into a tape recorder or create colored lines on the screen by dragging a mouse, they are using tools. If you view technology from a broad perspective, you can see how it can be integrated into all aspects of the preschool classroom.

For children with disabilities, the use of technology opens new avenues for learning. A child who is unable to speak can use communication devices to interact with others. A child who is physically impaired can use switches to control battery-operated toys. Special assistive devices allow children with a handicapping condition to have equal access to the learning environment.

Components of Technology

Standards in technology (International Society for Technology Education, 1998) outline the skills, concepts, knowledge, and attitudes that children in preschool through grade 12 should demonstrate. The standards focus on both the basics of using computers and the uses of technology to communicate, to learn new information, to solve problems, and to create. Equally important, the standards also stress social skills, such as working cooperatively with peers and using technology responsibly.

We have identified four components of the technology standards that apply to preschool children:

- awareness of technology
- basic operations and concepts
- technology tools
- people and technology

Awareness of Technology

For preschool children technology is knowing how technology is used at home, at school, and at family members' work sites. You can teach technology by asking children to name the tools and machines they use every day and to think about how tasks might be accomplished if this equipment were not available. You also can encourage children to find out how people use technology to do their jobs.

Preschool children demonstrate an increasing awareness of technology when they

- pretend to scan merchandise while playing store

- notice how computers are used during a field trip to the fire station

- suggest making a video of their trip to the grocery store

Basic Operations and Concepts

This component of technology includes the basics of using technological tools. For example, if children are using tape recorders, they need to know how to insert a tape, turn the machine on and off, and use the play and rewind buttons. The basics of using computers are turning on the computer, starting up a program, navigating through software, and exiting the program. The Computer chapter describes in detail how to introduce children to computers and how to interact with children so they can acquire knowledge and concepts about this technology.

Preschool children demonstrate knowledge of basic operations and concepts when they

- use a mouse, keyboard, or touch screen to operate the computer

- use a drawing program to create a picture

- rewind a tape they have listened to so another child can hear it from the beginning

Technology Tools

This component includes the different forms of technology, ranging from computers, digital cameras, and VCRs to wheels and shovels. By using various tools, children learn that each serves a different purpose.

- To draw a picture, I need crayons, markers, paint, or a computer drawing program.

- To write a story, I need a pencil, pens, markers, or a word processing program.

- To examine a tiny insect, I need a magnifying glass.

Preschool children use technology tools when they

- retell a story into a tape recorder and ask others to listen

- use a drawing program to create a picture

- use a simple word processor program to type a name

- use tools such as a magnifying glass, balance scale, or binoculars to explore and investigate

People and Technology

This component is about using technology responsibly and safely, caring for equipment, and using it appropriately. Because technology is part of everyday life and is often taken for granted, it is important for children to understand that people, including themselves, control technology.

For example, children can control how they navigate through a software program, change the volume on a tape recorder, or flip a light switch. When children learn how to handle floppy disks and CD-ROMs properly, how to exit a software program before turning the computer off, or to keep things away from equipment that might damage it, they are controlling technology.

This component of people and technology also includes helping young children to learn how people can work together to use technology. For instance, you can have a group of children solve problems together on the computer. If they can't figure out how to do something, they find a friend or adult who can help them.

Preschool children demonstrate their understanding of people and technology when they

- drag a mouse or create a line on a paint program

- say, "You can't eat your snack next to the computer because crumbs can make the keyboard break."

- click on icons (picture cues) to navigate through a software program

Connecting Technology Content, Teaching, and Learning

In *The Creative Curriculum*, teachers can make learning about technology an appropriate part of the preschool classroom. The chart on the next page shows how to connect technology content, teaching, and learning. The first column outlines the technology content for preschool. The second column shows some of the many ways teachers can present this content effectively. The third column lists the objectives on the *Developmental Continuum* you should be looking for as children work on this content.

As you watch children engage in these activities, you will have an opportunity to observe and identify children's developmental progress. This information will help you to determine the kinds of content to present and the methods to use.

Technology Content	What Teachers Can Do	*Creative Curriculum* Objectives
Awareness of Technology (Gain awareness of technology as a tool for finding information, communicating, and creating)	Offer toy cell phones, cameras, microphones for children to use during play. Point out how technology is used while on field trips: "The computer helps firefighters see a map leading them to the fire." Take videos of children during play and replay them.	22. Observes objects and events with curiosity 35. Takes on pretend roles and situations 36. Makes believe with objects 39. Expresses self using words and expanded sentences 42. Asks question
Basic Operations and Concepts (Learn basic skills to operate technology; use appropriate terminology to communicate about technology)	Show children how to use a mouse, keyboard, or touch screen to operate a computer. Teach children about the picture cues (icons) that will help them navigate through a software program. Use computer terminology when showing children how to use a software program: "I'm going to paste the picture here." Teach children how to exit a program before turning off the computer.	5. Demonstrates self-direction and independence 7. Respects and cares for classroom environment and materials 19. Controls small muscles in hands 22. Observes objects and events with curiosity 23. Approaches problems flexibly 25. Explores cause and effect 37. Makes and interprets representations 46. Demonstrates knowledge of the alphabet 47. Uses emerging reading skills to make meaning from print
Technology Tools (Understand that there are different tools of technology, and they can be used in a variety of ways)	Encourage children to retell a story into a tape recorder and ask others to listen. Set up a drawing program so children can create a picture to represent what they have learned. Show children how they can use a simple word processing program to type their names or words. Provide tools such as magnifying glasses, balance scales, binoculars to explore and investigate.	22. Observes objects and events with curiosity 23. Approaches problems flexibly 25. Explores cause and effect 26. Applies knowledge or experience to a new context
People and Technology (Understand that technology is controlled by people; use technology safely and responsibly; work collaboratively while using technology)	Show children that by dragging the mouse, they create a line on a paint program. Encourage children to work with a friend to figure out how to navigate through a software program. Develop rules with the children for using the computer safely and properly.	5. Demonstrates self-direction and independence 22. Observes objects and events with curiosity 23. Approaches problems flexibly 25. Explores cause and effect 26. Applies knowledge or experience to a new context

Process Skills

When children learn content in literacy, math, science, social studies, the arts, and technology, they are learning more than facts. They are learning methods of communicating, thinking mathematically, doing what scientists do, conducting social science research, creating as artists, and using technology. Methods of learning are called process skills.

Children use process skills as they work on learning concepts in each of the content areas covered in *The Creative Curriculum*. The cognitive and language objectives in the *Developmental Continuum* include process skills that have been described in many standards documents. Below we provide an overview of process skills and show how they apply to the content areas described on the previous pages. We also pinpoint which *Developmental Continuum* objectives relate to each process skill.

Observing and exploring. Observing and exploring involves noticing things in the environment and noticing how and when they change. These process skills also include manipulating objects to understand their properties and how they work. As an example, a child notices that a car goes down a ramp faster if the ramp is tilted and then explores tilting it at different angles (Science).

Creative Curriculum objectives related to observing and exploring include

> 22. *Observes objects and events with curiosity*
> 24. *Shows persistence in approaching tasks*
> 42. *Asks questions*

Connecting. Connecting involves linking new learning to prior experience. Connecting anchors new learning and puts it into a broad context. For instance, a child talks about bedtime routines after hearing the story, *Bedtime for Frances* (Literacy).

The *Creative Curriculum* objective related to connecting is

> 26. *Applies knowledge or experience to a new context*

Problem solving. Problem solving involves identifying a problem, thinking of ways to solve it, and trying out solutions. Problem solving is related to creative thinking. It involves generating new ideas, using materials in a different way, and taking risks to try something new. At the sand table, a group of children want to create a fence around their hill. They decide which materials they could use, guess how many they'll need, and test out their solutions (Math).

Creative Curriculum objectives related to problem solving include

> 23. *Approaches problems flexibly*
> 25. *Explores cause and effect*
> 26. *Applies knowledge or experience to a new context*
> 28. *Compares/measures*
> 30. *Recognizes patterns and can repeat them*

Organizing information. Organizing information includes breaking a whole idea or problem into parts, classifying, and comparing. Organizing makes gathering, tracking, and using information possible. At group time, children create a graph by placing their name either by a picture of feet or by a picture of a car to show if they walked or rode to school (Social Studies).

Creative Curriculum objectives related to organizing information include

> 27. *Classifies objects*
> 28. *Compares/measures*
> 29. *Arranges objects in a series*
> 30. *Recognizes patterns and can repeat them*
> 34. *Uses numbers and counting*

Communicating and representing. Communicating involves talking about observations with a friend or adult. Communicating also includes using representations, such as drawings, dramatizing, graphing, or making a model out of clay. For example, a child uses clay to create the new class pet, a hedgehog (The Arts and Science).

Creative Curriculum objectives related to communicating and representing include

> 21. *Uses tools for writing and drawing*
> 37. *Makes and interprets representations*
> 39. *Expresses self using words and expanded sentences*
> 41. *Answers questions*
> 42. *Asks questions*
> 43. *Actively participates in conversations*
> 50. *Writes letters and words*

conclusion

In this chapter we described what is appropriate content for preschool children and what you can do to help them learn it. We also described the process skills children use as they work to master content knowledge. With an understanding of content and how children learn it, teachers can expand the opportunities they offer children to acquire knowledge and understand concepts. They can make a direct link between the preschool curriculum and what children will learn in elementary school. When the content of the curriculum is taught with children's developmental stages in mind, children are more likely to be successful learners who feel excited about and challenged by what they are learning. The next chapter explains the teacher's role in observing, guiding, and assessing children's learning.

References

Consortium of National Arts Education Associations. (1994). *Dance, music, theatre, visual arts: What every young American should know and be able to do in the arts: National standards for arts education.* Reston, VA: Music Educators National Conference.

Hart, B., & Risley, T. R. (1995). *Meaningful differences in the everyday experience of young American children.* Baltimore: P.H. Brookes.

International Society for Technology in Education. (1998). *National educational technology standards for students.* Eugene, OR: Author.

National Council of Teachers of Mathematics. (2000). *Principles and standards for school mathematics.* Reston, VA: Author.

National Institute of Child Health and Human Development. (2000). *Report of the National Reading Panel: Teaching children to read: An evidence-based assessment of the scientific research literature on reading and its implications for reading instruction.* Washington, DC: Author, National Institutes of Health.

National Research Council. (1996). *National science education standards.* Washington, DC: National Academy Press.

Snow, C. E., Burns, M. S., & Griffin, P. (Eds.). (1998). *Preventing reading difficulties in young children.* Washington, DC: National Academy Press.

inside this chapter

166 Observing Children

166 How, When, What to Observe

167 Being Objective

169 Using the *Developmental Continuum*

173 Guiding Children's Learning

173 Using a Range of Teaching Approaches

179 Adapting Instruction to Include All Children

183 Working With Groups of Children

187 Promoting Learning in Interest Areas

188 Exploring Content in Interest Areas

190 Integrating Learning Through Studies

199 Assessing Children's Learning

199 Collecting Facts

204 Analyzing and Evaluating the Collected Facts

206 Using What You've Learned to Plan

209 Conclusion and References

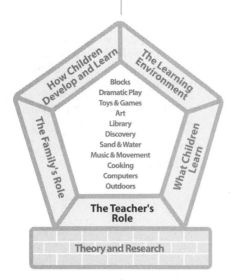

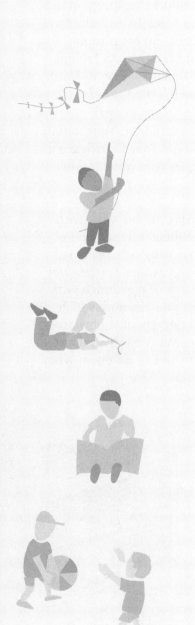

4 The Teacher's Role

In previous chapters, we touched on the teacher's role. In this chapter we focus exclusively on the teacher's role, the fourth component of the organizational structure of *The Creative Curriculum*. We describe how teachers can put together knowledge of children's development with the content they want to teach. The *Creative Curriculum* teacher is engaged in an ongoing cycle of observing, guiding learning, and assessing children's progress. During this cycle teachers interact with children continuously and make decisions about when and how to respond to meet individual and group needs. The chapter is organized in three sections, one for each part of the cycle.

Observing children—how teachers look at and listen to children to learn about them and begin to build a relationship with them. We describe how, what, and when to observe in an objective way and demonstrate how to use the *Developmental Continuum* in this process.

Guiding children's learning—how teachers use a range of teaching strategies to interact with individual children, children with special needs, and with the group as a whole. We give an overview of the 11 interest areas of the *Creative Curriculum* classroom and in each show how teachers can guide children's learning and integrate learning by engaging children in studies on topics that interest them.

Assessing children's learning—how teachers track children's progress using a systematic approach that supports learning and is consistent with the goals and objectives of the Curriculum. We illustrate three steps in the assessment process: (1) collecting facts, (2) analyzing and evaluating the collected facts, and (3) using what you have learned to plan for each child and the group.

Observing Children

Observation is an objective look at what a child does and says. In a *Creative Curriculum* classroom, teachers observe children regularly. When you use observation to find out what is unique and special about children, you have a basis for building relationships with them and for planning experiences that will enable every child to grow and flourish. As Jablon, Dombro, & Dichtelmiller state, "There is always something new to learn about a child—even a child you think you know well"(1999, p. 12).

How, When, What to Observe

The purpose of observing children is to get to know children. Your initial observations may be very informal. Gradually, you use your knowledge of the *Developmental Continuum* as the lens to sharpen your observations and make good decisions about guiding learning.

Most observations can occur naturally during the day as you work with children and take note of what they do and say. In these instances, take a moment to absorb the scene at hand. Think about what is happening. You are likely to see behaviors that relate to specific *Creative Curriculum* objectives. For instance, you might be making a batch of playdough with a group of children. As you follow a picture recipe, you can note which children are able to count the number of cups and tablespoons (objective 34) and the kinds of questions children ask and answer (objectives 41 and 42). Keep some file cards or sticky notes handy so you can jot down what you see and hear at the time.

In addition to spontaneous, informal observations, try to schedule regular formal observation times. Formal observations involve watching one or more children systematically and recording what you see and hear. This way of observing allows you to slow down and notice things you might otherwise miss. Try to arrange with your co-teacher or a parent volunteer to be with the children so you can free yourself to do planned observations.

You may follow one child for a period of time and jot down behaviors you observe. Later you can reflect on how these behaviors relate to *Creative Curriculum* objectives. Or, you may observe a group of children playing and document the behavior of several children. You may review these notes later to see what objectives apply. There may be times when you want to observe a child with a particular objective in mind. Your observation notes yield rich information that will help you in your later analysis and evaluation when you use the *Developmental Continuum*.

Your observation notes yield rich information that will help you in your later analysis and evaluation when you use the Developmental Continuum.

Being Objective

To use your observations to reflect on and assess children's learning, you should write them down. To be useful, observation notes should be objective and factual. When your notes include words like *shy, aggressive, upset, hyperactive,* or *angry,* they reveal your impressions, interpretations, or assumptions rather than what a child actually did or said. These judgmental words may or may not tell an accurate story. Interpretations, impressions, or assumptions include

- labels (shy, vivacious, creative)

- intentions (wants to. . .)

- evaluations (good job)

- judgments (beautiful, sloppy)

- negatives (didn't, can't, won't)

To be useful, observation notes should be objective and factual.

Objective and accurate notes include only the facts about what you see and hear. Factual observations include

- descriptions of an action

- quotations of language

- descriptions of a gesture

- descriptions of a facial expression

- descriptions of a creation

A series of objective, factual observations collected over time accumulate into a useful evaluation. As you observe, you may discover something completely unexpected.

Compare the following two examples of observation notes on a child at the water table.

Example 1

Carlos is being mischievous today. He purposely splashes the water on the floor and on others. He checks to see if I am watching him, then laughs at other children.

Example 1 is not an objective note. It uses a label ("mischievous") and makes judgments ("he purposely splashes the water," "checks to see if I am watching him," "laughs at the other children"). The teacher could not know if Carlos was watching out for her or if he was laughing at the other children.

Now consider another recording of this same event.

The more aware you are of what objective notes look like, the more skilled you will become at writing them.

Example 2

Carlos plays with the waterwheel. Some water falls on two of the other children's shoes. He looks at me, then looks at the other children and begins to giggle.

Example 2 is an objective note. It includes only the facts of what Carlos did ("plays with waterwheel"), what happened ("Some water falls on the other children's shoes"), and his reaction ("He looks at me, then looks at the other children and begins to giggle"). Accurate notes include all the facts about what a child did and said in the order they happened.

Writing objective notes takes practice. The more aware you are of what objective notes look like, the more skilled you will become at writing them.

Here are two examples of objective observation notes.

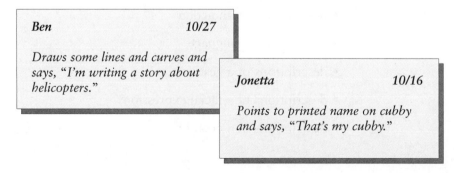

Ben   *10/27*

Draws some lines and curves and says, "I'm writing a story about helicopters."

Jonetta   *10/16*

Points to printed name on cubby and says, "That's my cubby."

Using the Developmental Continuum

The *Developmental Continuum* is your guide for making the observation process systematic. Collect observation notes that relate to all of the 50 objectives. This does not mean, however, that you need to conduct 50 separate observations on each child in your class! One observation can yield information about many objectives.

The more familiar you are with the goals and objectives, the more efficient you can be in observing and recording what you see. You may find it helpful to display the poster of *The Creative Curriculum* Goals and Objectives where it will be a visual reminder. There is also a chart with this title in the Appendix (p. 530) that you can keep on a clipboard to use for taking notes. If an objective comes to mind as you record your observation notes, jot down its number.

The *Developmental Continuum* is your tool for planning instruction and assessing learning because information you gain from observing children and thinking about their developmental level is the basis for supporting their learning appropriately. Using the Continuum, you will have a perspective, for example, on how many options to offer, how much independence you can reasonably expect, how many directions a child can handle at a time, whether the classroom routines and rules are working, how well a child works with others, and a child's level of persistence and curiosity. All of this information will help you decide what academic content to teach and how to teach it. You can think about teaching in a way that challenges children rather than frustrates them.

In the following chart you see how a teacher observes children throughout the day. Her knowledge of the objectives and the developmental steps of the Continuum enable her to organize what she sees, consider how she might respond, how she will plan and interact with individual children and the group, and think about what teaching strategies she will use.

> The more familiar you are with the goals and objectives, the more efficient you can be in observing and recording what you see.

Observation	Reflection	Response
Arrival Crystal says: "Ms. Tory! Guess what? I got a new puppy and his name is Sparky. He's white with some black spots and he licks my face."	Crystal transitions into the classroom easily. *(Objective 1, Shows ability to adjust to new situations)* She can describe her new puppy. *(Objective 39, Expresses self using words and expanded sentences)* How can I use her interest in her new puppy to strengthen her skills in literacy?	Engage Crystal in conversations about her new puppy. Show her books in the Library about puppies. Suggest that she represent her ideas about her new puppy using props in the Dramatic Play Area, drawing a picture of her puppy, or creating one with clay. Listen to conversations among the children to see if this might be good topic for a study.
Group Meeting Setsuko sits still and looks at others sing and march. She looks down without responding when other children ask her why she doesn't want to join in.	Setsuko seems to feel uncomfortable participating in group music and movement activities. *(Objective 8, Follows classroom routines)* She doesn't express her feelings in words. *(Objective 3, Recognizes own feelings and manages them appropriately)* Would she feel comfortable exploring music and movement with just one other child?	Talk to Setsuko's family to find out more about her style of responding. Invite her to participate in a different way, such as turning on the tape recorder or beating a drum. Provide opportunities for her to explore music independently or with a friend.
Choice Time Derek pretends to be a police officer writing a ticket: "Pull over, lady. You're going too fast." He scribbles on a piece of paper from left to right and top to bottom of the page.	Derek organizes others to join him in playing police officer. *(Objective 10, Plays well with other children; and 35, Takes on pretend roles and situations)* He attempts to write to convey meaning and imitates how print is written on a page. *(Objective 49, Understands the purpose of writing; 45, Demonstrates understanding of print concepts; 50, Writes letters and words; and 21, Uses tools for writing and drawing)*	Observe Derek's play to determine how it unfolds. Enter into the play without interrupting the flow. Say, "What's the speed limit officer? I don't want to break the law. Maybe we need to make a sign so we'll know how fast we can drive." At group time, talk about what police officers do and why. Invite a police officer to visit the classroom. Take a walk in the neighborhood to find traffic signs.

Observation	Reflection	Response
Snack Time Zack counts the number of children at his table and says, "We need five straws." He gets the straws and gives each child one.	Zack uses self-help skills to get the group what they need. *(Objective 6, Takes responsibility for own well-being)* He uses his knowledge of numbers in a purposeful way—to count the number of children at the table accurately and distribute the straws. *(Objective 33, Uses one-to-one correspondence; and 34, Uses numbers and counting)*	Acknowledge Zack's helpfulness. Observe how he counts collections of objects to find out if he gets confused with numbers greater than five. Show him how to touch each object as he counts. Challenge Zack to count bigger quantities (e.g., "Will you get seven paintbrushes for the easel?").
Outdoor Time Tasheen tells Kate, "Let's play 'Follow the Leader.' You follow me." She walks along the edge of the sandbox, hops to the fence, and crawls through the tunnel."	Tasheen leads others in play. *(Objective 10, Plays well with other children)* She uses gross motor skills *(Objective 14, Demonstrates basic locomotor skills; and 15, Shows balance while moving)* How can I build on her physical skills to extend her learning?	Challenge Tasheen physically by suggesting more complex tasks (e.g., a balance beam, walking backwards). Help her to learn positional words by describing what she is doing (e.g., "You're going through the tunnel. Now you're going around the tree.").
Story Time Tyrone asks me to read *The Hungry Thing*. When The Hungry Thing asks for "feetloaf" to eat, Tyrone says, "He wants meatloaf!"	Tyrone selects a favorite story and then participates actively in story reading. *(Objective 44, Enjoys and values reading)* He plays with sounds to figure out what The Hungry Thing wants. *(Objective 38, Hears and discriminates the sounds of language)*	Offer Tyrone food props from the Dramatic Play area so he can retell the story on his own. Read other books that involve playing with language such as *Bread and Jam for Frances* or *Alphabite: A Funny Feast from A to Z*. Teach songs, rhymes, and chants that build phonological awareness.

Observation	Reflection	Response
Small-Group Time/ Choice Time A small group of children works on sorting a collection of toy cars. Leo take all the red cars and lines them up from smallest to largest.	Leo participates in small-group activities. *(Objective 8, Follows classroom routines)* He comes up with an idea and completes the task. *(Objective 24, Shows persistence in approaching tasks)* He groups cars by color. *(Objective 27, Classifies objects)* Leo uses problem-solving skills to line up his cars according to size. *(Objective 29, Arranges objects in a series)*	Observe Leo closely and ask questions or make statements that will extend his thinking (e.g., "How did you decide to put this car on the end?"). Challenge Leo by inviting him to think of new ways to sort his red cars, such as cars with two doors and cars four doors. Use other opportunities throughout the day for sorting, classifying, and arranging objects in a series.
Rest Time Sonya wiggles on her cot, hums a song, and tickles another child who is beginning to fall asleep.	Does Sonya understand the rules during nap time? *(Objective 8, Follows classroom routines)* Is there a reason she may be trying to disturb others? *(Objective 12, Shares and respects the rights of others)* Perhaps Sonya doesn't need to nap as much as the other children. How can I meet Sonya's needs to be active and still be respectful of other children's need to nap?	Place Sonya and other children who tend not to sleep in a separate area of the classroom. Give her the opportunity to rest for a short period of time. Offer her quiet materials (e.g., books, magic slates) to use while on her cot.
Closing/Departure While discussing the day, Juwan says, "Me and Tasheen dug a hole outside and found a bug. We're gonna find that bug again tomorrow."	Juwan recalls the events of the day and shares with others. *(Objective 43, Actively participates in conversations)* While his grammar isn't perfect, he uses complete sentences. *(Objective 39, Expresses self using words and expanded sentences)* How can I support Juwan's language development and maintain his interest in engaging in conversations? How can I build on Juwan and Tasheen's new interest?	Give attention to Juwan as he speaks. Use eye contact and facial gestures to let him know I am listening. Rephrase some of Juwan's words using correct grammar (e.g., "Oh, you're going to dig again tomorrow? Do you think that bug will be in the same place?"). Offer tools—shovels, magnifying glass, or a bug catcher— to help with their exploration.

Guiding Children's Learning

Learning in a preschool classroom is full of contradictions. It is calm, yet dynamic; predictable, but full of surprises; active and hands-on, but sometimes quiet and reflective. The contradictions require a range of teaching approaches. What works to introduce, reinforce, and extend learning in one situation may be ineffective in another. Therefore, good teaching requires a range of teaching approaches.

Using a Range of Teaching Approaches

In the past, some teachers believed that a well-designed environment and allowing children to play were enough to support learning. Others suggested that the best way for children to learn was for teachers to instruct them directly and to have them practice what they learned. Fortunately, we now have research that clearly addresses this debate. The National Research Council report, *Eager to Learn: Educating Our Preschoolers* (2001), makes a clear case for the use of a wide range of teaching strategies, including both child-initiated learning and direct teaching. There is also room for many teaching approaches that use elements of each.

Because children have unique learning styles and needs, you should use the full range to guide their learning. In addition, the various skills and concepts to be learned require different teaching approaches.

Child-Initiated Learning

When you want children to explore and construct an understanding on their own, child-initiated learning is effective. Here, children choose the activity and the action. Playing alone, with one or more children or perhaps in a small group, they interact with materials freely, in many different ways.

> *Dallas experiments with objects at the sand table, pouring sand from one container to the next and adding water to some containers.*

> *Setsuko takes her sick baby to see Dr. Kate in the Dramatic Play Area who uses a stethoscope to check her heartbeat.*

In child-initiated learning, children choose the activity and the action.

In each instance, the child is developing concepts through highly engaged and complex play. Dallas is learning about measurement (math) and what happens to sand when water is added (science). Setsuko is learning about jobs (social studies) and the importance of tools (technology). The teacher makes a decision about how to scaffold the child's learning by building on these explorations to further learning either at the moment or at a later time. For example, she might decide to engage Dallas in a conversation using comparative words—more, less, the same as—as well as plan to add more measurement tools to the sand table.

Child-initiated learning, however, is not a matter of chance. It occurs when teachers think about children's development and their knowledge of content to intentionally prepare an interesting and rich environment that offers children choices. All of the considerations regarding the environment outlined in Chapter 2 must be in place. The arrangement of the furniture and selection of materials, the carefully planned daily routines and schedule, and the positive social climate of a community all support child-initiated learning. Also, substantial teacher involvement is required. Because children learn best when they are self-motivated, effective *Creative Curriculum* teachers create extensive opportunities for children to make discoveries and initiate learning on their own. In each of the interest area chapters we show how teachers guide child-initiated learning.

Substantial teacher involvement is required.

Teacher-Directed Learning

While children learn through their play, not all play experiences lead to meaningful learning. Some things require explicit teaching. In these instances, direct teaching makes the most sense. Direct teaching involves planning how to teach a concept or skill; the materials needed; whether it is best taught to an individual child, in a small group, or to the whole class; and then teaching it.

Suppose, for example, that you want children to begin using woodworking materials and tools. Because safety issues are involved you cannot let children explore these materials without specific instruction on how to proceed safely. So, you make a decision to show children in small groups how the tools can be handled safely and to discuss the rules that must be followed in this area of the classroom. Through direct instruction, children learn how to put on safety goggles and use a hammer and saw.

Some things require explicit teaching.

Learning the alphabet is another example where direct teaching is appropriate. Children can't learn the alphabet by themselves—someone has to tell them the names of the letters. So you place the alphabet at children's eye level in the classroom, provide magnetic alphabet letters, and teach the names of the letters, relating them to the letters in children's own names.

Direct teaching also can be useful during an unplanned teachable moment. Say, for example, the children have just returned from a walk in the neighborhood. At circle time, their teacher records the children's recollections about the experience on a chart.

A teachable moment

our class...

Crystal: "We saw a digging machine."

Ms. Tory: "That's right, Crystal. It's called a bulldozer."

Derek: ". . . and a big bus."

Juwan: ". . . and lots of bugs!"

Ms. Tory writes the words, "bulldozer, big bus, bugs," on the chart paper and asks everyone to say them with her as a group.

Tasheen: "Hey, those all start the same."

Ms. Tory: "They sure do—bulldozer, big bus, bugs." She draws a line under each b and says, "They all start with the letter b. I'm thinking of something else we saw on our walk that starts with a b sound. It sounds like utterfly."

Children: "Butterfly!"

Whenever teachers want to communicate information and facts that children need because they can't get to the next level of understanding on their own, it makes sense to use a direct teaching approach. Whether specifically planned—such as teaching a small group how to use woodworking tools or introducing individual children to the alphabet—or taking advantage of a teachable moment, direct teaching helps children build a knowledge base.

Interacting With Children to Promote Learning

Child-initiated and teacher-directed learning each involve different kinds of teacher interaction with children. In reality, life in the classroom always requires a range of teacher involvement. Much like a scaffold supports the framework of a building under construction, teachers support children's learning using a range of approaches.

When teachers talk with children about what they are doing, or ask questions that challenge their thinking, they are guiding their learning.

As you interact with children throughout the day, you will have to determine the right degree of involvement. You will need to observe what children are doing, encourage their efforts, and intervene thoughtfully to support additional learning. For example, you might take an action such as moving a notepad into the Dramatic Play Area, to allow a child to expand her literacy learning by writing a prescription for a baby doll. Another time you notice what children are doing as they engage in an activity and comment on it. "I see you decided to use the tubes we added to the water table. I'm curious to see what you decide to do with them."

On another occasion you may decide to model a skill or behavior—for example, by showing a child how to use a tweezers to pick up small objects that he has had difficulty grasping with the tongs. When teachers talk with children about what they are doing, or ask questions that challenge their thinking, they are guiding their learning.

Talking With Children About Their Work

The least intrusive teaching strategy is simply to describe what you see a child doing. This approach makes children more aware of their actions and encourages them to reflect on what they are trying to do and why. It also lets children know that you are interested in them and their work. The following kinds of comments help children reflect on their work:

> *That's an interesting group of animals you've taken out to use. It looks like they are all animals you would see on a farm—except for one.*

> *I see you are mixing yellow and blue paint. I wonder what new color you will create.*

> *When you clicked the computer mouse, stars went off in the sky.*

Another approach is to engage children in conversation to encourage them to put their actions and ideas into words. Conversations help children to clarify for themselves what they are doing and reinforces what they are learning. If they have to explain an action, they have to make sure that what they're doing makes sense to them. Conversations of this type also develop children's language skills. Here are some examples of what you might say:

> *Adding water to the sand really changed what you could do with the sand. What did you want to happen when you added the water?*

> *You've spent a long time on this building. Tell me about it.*

> *What made you decide to feed the guinea pig now instead of at the end of the day?*

Asking Children Questions

Questioning children not only extends learning, it also gives you insight into children's progress in the learning process. There are two basic kinds of questions: closed and open. A closed question has one right answer. It can be answered with a yes or no or one or two words. In the majority of cases, the teacher already knows what she wants the child to answer. Here are some typical closed questions teachers ask:

> *What color is this?*   *How many are there?*

> *What is this called?*   *Is this yours?*

Describe what you see a child doing.

Engage children in conversation to encourage them to put their actions and ideas into words.

There are two basic kinds of questions: closed and open.

Open-ended questions ask a child to give more than a one- or two-word response and have many possible right answers.

Most teachers are comfortable asking closed questions. They are easy to ask and the answers give insight into what a child knows. Open-ended questions ask a child to give more than a one- or two-word response and have many possible right answers. They also generate critical thinking. If you ask a child, "What happened to the playdough when we left it uncovered?" you're bound to get a far more insightful response than asking, "Is it OK to leave the playdough uncovered?" Here are some different types of open-ended questions you can ask to extend children's thinking.

To put thoughts into words: *Why do you think the little boy in the story was sad?*

To observe: *What do you see, hear, feel? What did you notice?*

To make predictions: *What do you think will happen if you keep adding blocks to your tower?*

To think about similarities and differences: *How are these two blocks the same? What makes these things go together?*

To apply knowledge to solve a problem: *What could you do to keep the paint from dripping on the floor?*

To stretch thinking: *What would happen if there were no cars, trucks, buses, planes, or boats? How would we get around?*

To consider consequences: *What would happen if you left your drawing outside and it rained?*

To evaluate: *What made you decide to pick this book to read? How did this make you feel?*

To assess feelings: *How would you feel if that happened to you?*

Questions that ask children to consider consequences, make predictions, and apply what they already know to new situations are especially effective in building children's understanding. They challenge children's thinking and lead to more meaningful learning. By listening to children, understanding their thinking, and supporting them in taking the next steps in making discoveries, teachers provide the scaffolding to extend children's learning.

Adapting Instruction to Include All Children

Often teachers think they have to do something dramatically different in the classroom to accommodate children with special needs or learning challenges. Usually, this is not the case. As you develop relationships with children and use a variety of teaching strategies, you will be able to judge how children respond and which strategies seem to work best in which situation. In the following sections we offer additional guidance about ways to think about the needs of children who are gifted, those with disabilities, and children who are learning English as a second language.

Teaching Children Who Are Gifted

The teacher's role in working with gifted children is to provide challenging and stimulating experiences. Gifted children are often eager to explore a topic in greater depth and approach studies that interest them with a high level of enthusiasm and intensity. Here are a few suggestions for working with gifted children.

Stock interest areas with interesting and challenging materials. Create a room environment that promotes investigations, inquiry, and independent exploration.

> Provide challenging and stimulating experiences.

Follow the child's interests. If a child is keenly interested in dinosaurs or helicopters, help him explore those topics by providing books, web sites, and other resources. It's not necessary to involve the entire class in this topic, but do include others who share a similar interest.

Teach to the child's strengths. If a child is advanced mathematically, don't waste her time teaching her to recognize number symbols. Find out what she does know and offer her challenging problems to solve. Boredom can be a gifted child's greatest enemy. Many teachers find they can compress the essential elements and allow gifted children to move beyond the original goals and objectives in some areas. This means that a gifted child will likely progress beyond Step III on the *Developmental Continuum* objectives.

> Boredom can be a gifted child's greatest enemy.

Have realistic expectations. Keep in mind that being gifted in one area is no guarantee that a child is gifted in all areas of development. The mathematically gifted child may be physically or socially at an average—or even below average—level of development. You need to individualize your approach to match the child's individual profile of skills.

If a child can read, find books that are at or slightly below his reading level for pleasure reading. For instructional purposes, find books that are slightly above his reading level. The important point to remember in selecting books for this child is that while he may be a reader, he's still a preschooler. The content of books written for older children may not be appealing to or appropriate for a 3- to 5-year-old child, so you will have to choose thoughtfully.

> Remember that gifted children are children first. Keep in mind that children who are gifted intellectually sometimes feel different and have special needs socially and emotionally. These children need adults to accept their intellectual differences and help them to feel understood and supported.

Teaching Children With Disabilities

Thoughtful planning can help you address the needs of children with disabilities so they can be included fully in the program. Think about your environment, how your day flows, and what obstacles keep children from participating and feeling competent. This analysis will help you determine what adjustments to make. Here are some ways to help children with disabilities—or any child who is struggling with learning.

Use clear visual cues to help children understand where to place coats, bags, etc., when they arrive in school (such as color-coded cubbies). Be consistent with closing routines at departure time to facilitate predictability and independence.

Use transition-preparation techniques throughout the day. Object or picture cues that show activities may be helpful for children with learning and language difficulties when they want to change what they are doing. Children with attention or behavior challenges might benefit from five-minute, two-minute, or one-minute warnings about upcoming transitions. Children with hearing impairments would benefit from visual cues such as hand gestures. Most children will benefit from a review of the schedule upon arrival and at various points during the day.

Use peer buddies in interest areas as teaching models. This technique not only facilitates interaction, but also builds peer mentoring capabilities in children who have strengths in certain developmental areas. Children who receive such mentoring typically learn more from it than from adult teachers.

Thoughtful planning can help you address the needs of children with disabilities so they can be included fully in the program.

Use visual cues at mealtimes to indicate how things should be arranged when setting the table (such as a placemat with outlines for plate, fork, spoon, napkin, cup; potholders for placement of large bowls, plates, etc.).

Use visual and tactile props to accompany stories and songs at circle time, so children have multisensory ways to help them understand.

Encourage active participation and energy release in outdoor and other gross motor play. Then plan for calming activities before returning to more sedentary activities (such as swinging on swings, blowing bubbles, or massaging a child's shoulders).

Have a child's attention before giving new directions or rules. Use visual and tactile cues as necessary to encourage a child to look at the speaker, and use gestures or demonstrations as needed to help children understand verbal messages.

Assess and identify children's needs for assistive technology with a specialist. Such needs might include large-print books for children with visual impairments, auditory trainers for children with hearing deficits, language devices for children with communication difficulties, or adapted equipment for children with orthopedic impairments.

> Be willing to reflect on the effectiveness of your teaching strategies. You may find that you need to regroup and try other approaches. With your perseverance, children with disabilities can grow and thrive in a *Creative Curriculum* classroom.

Teaching English Language Learners

As outlined in Chapter 1, children who are learning English as a second language go through specific stages as they learn English. You can support them in working through these stages by using teaching strategies that respond to their needs at each stage.

Learn some words in a child's home language and use them as well as English to label materials. Seeing and hearing their home language will make children feel welcome and safe in an environment where people are speaking a new language.

Use concrete objects and gestures to communicate with children going through the non-verbal period. They may be feeling their way through a strange situation, so keep in mind that they are still actively learning and absorbing what is going on around them. Make them feel included in the classroom.

Use objects and hands-on experiences to underscore the connection with language to help children make the transition from nonverbal communication to using a few words. Focus on the child's intent and extend, expand, or imitate what the child says.

Offer encouragement as children feel more confident and begin communicating conversationally in English. Avoid correcting the child's grammar, but model correct language in your conversations with the child.

Use pictures and gestures that will help children delve further into the complexities of English when they begin to use more formal language.

In addition to these stage-specific strategies, there are general strategies you can use to help English Language Learners—and all children—to improve their communication skills. These include the following practices (Tabors, 1997; De Houwer, 1999; Gosnell, 2001).

Establish a classroom community where everyone sees it as his or her responsibility to help others, and children can become language models for each other. You can teach them specifically how to be helpful to one another.

There are general strategies to help English Language Learners.

Create a language-rich environment in which materials are labeled in English and the children's home languages. Stock interest areas with magazines and reference books in children's home languages. Children need to have ongoing experiences in both languages.

Use lots of repetition, running commentary, and actions as you talk, e.g., "Now I'm putting the block on the shelf." Describing the actions they are doing will help to increase the children's vocabulary.

Establish familiar daily routines in your schedule so children will know "what comes next" and connect events with language.

Assist children in sociodramatic play. Provide background information, introduce props, and explain roles. Sometimes children whose first language is not English need "scripted" dialogue to get them started.

Be patient. Give children time to get their words together and express themselves; don't rush them.

Provide books in the children's home languages. If you don't understand the language, scan the books' illustrations and length of text to see if they look appropriate.

Choose predictable books for story time. These books tend to repeat phrases and are written in simple language. Bring concrete props and act out the words as you read the story. Read the same books to children many times. Encourage children to "read" to one another.

Involve families by encouraging them to continue speaking their primary language when they visit the classroom and at home. Invite them to record books on tape or to help make signs and books for the classroom in their home language.

> Keep in mind that your attitude is most important. If you view learning a second language as a valuable experience and one that can enrich your classroom, all children will benefit—not only those who don't yet speak English.

Working With Groups of Children

There are many times during the day when teachers plan to work with groups of children. Sometimes you bring the whole class together. At other times you decide to work with a small group of children. Each is a choice you make based on the needs of children and the content to be addressed. Whether working with a large or small group, think carefully about teaching approaches that will be most effective in the group situation.

Large-Group Instruction

Large-group instruction involves the whole class. Certain kinds of activities lend themselves to large-group instruction. The first or last meeting of the day, when you want children to experience being a part of a community, is one such activity. Use this time to have all children greet one another. At other times the whole class may be together to listen to a story, to participate in a music and movement activity, or to learn about the choice activities or materials that will be available that day. These activities are important for children to learn to be part of a large group as well as to learn specific information.

In the following example of large-group instruction, Mr. Alvarez wants to teach children how to use and care for materials. He knows he can't assume that children know how to do this and recognizes that it is something he has to teach.

Introducing materials to the class

our class...

Mr. Alvarez decides to introduce unit blocks to the class. Because he wants the children to see blocks as materials to explore, he structures the meeting with that idea in mind. He brings a selection of blocks to the meeting area and invites each child to pick several blocks to explore.

Mr. Alvarez: *What do you notice about these blocks?*

Ben: *Smooth. They're smooth.*

Mr. Alvarez: *Ben noticed how smooth the blocks are.*

Carlos: *Pretty heavy.*

Mr. Alvarez: *They're kind of heavy, aren't they?*

Kate: *Mine have points.*

Mr. Alvarez: *Kate noticed her blocks have points or corners on them.*

Sonya: *I have a triangle.*

Leo: *Two little ones fit on this long one.*

Mr. Alvarez: *Yes. So, if you run out of long blocks, Leo noticed that you can use two of the smaller blocks to make a long one. That's a good thing to know.*

He then invites the children to think of ways to use the blocks and comments on what they have built. After several children have demonstrated their ideas, he concludes the discussion.

Mr. Alvarez: *In our classroom, there is not one right way to use many toys. You just saw that there are many ways you can use our unit blocks. These blocks will be here every day. During choice time, the Block Area is one of the areas you can choose, and you can make whatever you want with the blocks. When you are finished, there's a special way you can tell where the blocks go on the shelf. Who thinks they know where this long unit block goes on the shelf? Can you show us, Janelle? When we put blocks away in their right place, children who want to use them will know exactly where they are.*

When you introduce materials at the beginning of the year, and each time you put out something new, you have an opportunity to talk about how to use them properly and where they will be kept in the classroom, and to brainstorm creative uses with the children. When you introduce materials, you generate interest and often motivate children to try an activity they otherwise might have ignored or avoided. You can also take the opportunity to reinforce the idea that materials are everyone's responsibility. Therefore, introducing materials is an important opportunity to interact with the large group.

Small-Group Instruction

In the course of each day teachers work with a variety of small groups. Sometimes the group is self-selected, and you interact with the group of children who happen to be in one interest area. At other times you gather the children you want to work with you on a given activity or project.

Even though they are in a small-group setting, each child may be working on a different skill such as counting, patterning, classification, or shapes. Your knowledge of where each child is in relation to the 50 objectives on the *Developmental Continuum* will help you to determine which children to work with on a given activity and how to interact to further learning.

See an example on the following page of how a teacher might guide learning in a small-group activity.

A small-group activity

our class...

During choice time, Ms. Tory invites five children to join her on the rug for a small group activity. She brings a collection of bottle caps and invites each child to take a pile and explore them. Ms. Tory has a set of caps as well. As she begins using her set of bottle caps, she observes how the children are using theirs and listens to what they are saying. She says, "Leo, you have put all the red caps, blue caps, yellow caps, and orange caps together. I'm going to try that with mine." Leo says, "You have more blue caps than you have orange." Ms. Tory responds, "You're right Leo. I have more blue caps."

Janelle draws Ms. Tory's attention to her caps: "Look, I've made a pattern! Red cap, white cap, red cap, white cap." Ms. Tory says, "I wonder what will come next? Blue? Yellow?" Janelle responds, "Noooo. Red will come next!" Ms. Tory notices that Janelle has become very skilled at making patterns and does so each time she works with collectibles. Ms. Tory says, "I'm going to try to make a pattern and I bet I can trick you! Watch this." Ms. Tory lines up her caps as follows: red, blue, yellow, red, blue yellow, red, blue. Janelle touches each one, and names the color, and then says, "You can't trick me! I know what comes next . . . it's yellow!" While Janelle is making patterns with her caps, Ben is watching and says, "Look Ms. Tory, I can make a pattern too!"

Kate has organized her caps into a long line and begins counting them. She counts to ten correctly, but gets confused abut which caps she has already counted. Ms. Tory asks, "May I count them with you?" Carlos, who has been making towers out of his caps, wants to join in too. "One, two, three . . ." Ms. Tory moves each cap aside as they count.

Ms. Tory announces to the group that clean-up time will be in a few minutes. She then makes a game of clean up time. "Find all your caps that have writing on them and put them into the bucket." Carlos says, "I want to try. Find all the caps that are black and put them in the bucket." Janelle takes a turn: "Find all the caps that open and close and put them in the bucket." The children continue taking turns until all of the caps are put away.

While the children finish cleaning up, Ms. Tory takes a few minutes to jot down notes about her observations of children working with the bottle caps.

Here's what made this small-group activity successful:

- The activity was short—less than 10 minutes.

- The teacher used the materials and modeled for children.

- All children had materials to use.

- Children worked at their own developmental level.

- The teacher observed how the children used the materials and extended their learning with open-ended questions or comments.

- The children observed each other and shared ideas and problem-solving strategies. They learned new ways to use the materials by watching each other.

- Skills related to multiple objectives were addressed during this activity: patterning, one-to-one correspondence, counting, classifying, and problem solving.

Using the *Developmental Continuum* will help you to determine where each child is in relation to the Curriculum objectives so you can plan increasingly challenging activities. By documenting what you observe, you will be able to extend children's learning and help each child make progress.

In *The Creative Curriculum*, interest areas are the primary setting in which children learn. This is where child-initiated learning usually begins and where teachers observe children to consider what kinds of teacher-directed learning is needed and what teacher interactions will best guide learning.

Promoting Learning in Interest Areas

Interest areas offer opportunities for teachers to teach content as children explore materials. When children observe a caterpillar in the Discovery Area, and you talk with them about how it moves and eats leaves, they gain science knowledge. When they arrange wooden community worker figures through a city of blocks they've built, and you talk about the jobs people do, they learn about social studies. When they look at books in the Library Area and retell the story, they learn reading skills. As they make finger paint and mix bread dough, children measure ingredients and talk with you about how properties change states, learning about math and science.

In the chart that follows, we give examples of how teachers provide materials to initiate and then guide learning in literacy, math, science, social studies, the arts, and technology in each interest area. Use this chart to inspire your thinking about how to teach content throughout the day.

Exploring Content in Interest Areas

	Blocks	Dramatic Play	Toys & Games	Art	Sand & Water
Literacy	Have paper, markers, and tape available for children to make signs for buildings. Hang charts and pictures with words at children's eye level.	Include books and magazines in the house corner. Introduce print (shopping lists, receipts, message writing, etc.).	Talk about colors, shapes, pictures in a lotto game. Provide matching games for visual discrimination.	Invite children to dictate stories to go with their artwork. Share books about famous artists and their work with children.	Add literacy props to the sand table such as letter molds or road signs. Encourage children to describe how the sand and water feel.
Math	Suggest clean-up activities that involve sorting by shape and size. Use language of comparison such as taller, shorter, the same length.	Add telephones, menus, and other items with numbers on them. Participate in play, talking about prices, addresses, and times of day.	Provide collections for sorting, classifying, and graphing. Have children extend patterns with colored cubes, beads, etc.	Use terms of comparison (the piece of yarn is longer than your arm). Provide empty containers of various shapes for creating junk sculptures.	Provide measuring cups, spoons, containers of various sizes. Ask estimation questions ("How many cups will it take to fill the container?").
Science	Talk with children about size, weight, and balance. Encourage children to experiment with momentum using ramps, balls, and marbles.	Introduce props such as a stethoscope or binoculars. Model hygiene skills by washing "babies" or dishes.	Talk about balance and weight as children use table blocks. Sort, classify, and graph nature items such as rocks, leaves, twigs, and shells.	Describe the properties of materials as they interact (wet, dry, gooey, sticky). Use water and brushes for outdoor painting so children can explore evaporation.	Make bubble solution and provide different kinds of bubble-blowing tools. Put out magnifying glasses and sifters so children can examine different kinds of sand.
Social Studies	Include block people who represent a range of jobs and cultures. Display pictures of buildings in the neighborhood.	Include props related to different kinds of jobs. Add multicultural dolls and props such as cooking utensils, foods, and clothing.	Select puzzles and other materials that include diverse backgrounds and jobs. Play board games that require cooperation, following rules, and taking turns.	Include various shades of skin tone paint, crayons, markers, and construction paper. Encourage children to paint and draw what they saw on a site visit.	Invite children to describe roads and tunnels created in sand. Hang pictures of bodies of water (rivers, oceans, lakes, streams) near the water table.
The Arts	Encourage children to build props, such as a bridge for *The Three Billy Goats Gruff* for dramatization. Display artwork posters that include geometric shapes and patterns.	Display children's artwork or posters of artists' work in the dramatic play area decor. Provide props for children to dramatize different roles.	Include materials that have different art elements (pattern or texture matching, color games, etc.). Add building toys that encourage creativity such as Legos, Tinker-toys, etc.	Provide different media for children to explore clay, paint, collage, construction, etc. Invite a local artist to share his or her work.	Create sand sculptures; display photographs of sand sculptures created by artists. Use tools for drawing in wet sand.
Technology	Include ramps, wheels, and pulleys. Take pictures (using digital, instant, or regular cameras) of block structures and display in the area.	Include technology props such as old cameras, computers, keyboards, microphones, etc. Encourage children to explore how tools work—eggbeaters, can openers, etc.	Add toys (gears, marble mazes, etc.) that encourage children to explore how things work. Use a light table to explore transparent shapes.	Include recyclable materials for children to create an invention. Use technological tools for creating items such as a potter's wheel or spin art.	Include props with moving parts at the water table—such as waterwheels, eggbeaters, pump, etc. Use toy dump trucks, loaders, cranes for outdoor sand play.

Exploring Content in Interest Areas

Library	Discovery	Music & Movement	Cooking	Computers	Outdoors
Keep an assortment of good children's books on display. Set up a writing area with pens, markers, pencils, paper, stamps, envelopes, etc.	Keep science related books (e.g., insects, plants, seeds, etc.) on hand. Include paper and markers for recording observations.	Write words to a favorite song on a chart. Have children use instruments for the sound effects in stories.	Use pictures and words on recipe cards. Talk about words and letters on the food containers during a cooking activity.	Illustrate and write the steps in using a computer. Use a drawing or simple word processing program to make a book.	Bring colored chalk and other writing materials outside. Have children observe street signs in the neighborhood.
Add number stamps to the writing area. Include books about math concepts: size, number, comparisons, shapes, etc.	Have tools on hand for measuring and graphing. Provide boxes for sorting materials by size, color, and shape.	Play percussion games emphasizing pattern: softer, louder. Use language that describes spatial relationships—under, over, around, through.	Use a timer for cooking. Provide measuring cups and spoons.	Include software that focuses on number concepts, patterning, problem solving, shapes, etc. Use a drawing program to create patterns.	Have children look for patterns in nature. Invite children to make collections on a walk, then sort, classify, and graph the items collected.
Include books about pets, plants, bodies, water, inventions, etc. Provide a variety of objects for experimentation with floating and sinking.	Include pets and plants that children can care for. Include tools such as a magnifying glass and a microscope that children can use to observe the properties of objects.	Set out bottles with different amounts of water so children can investigate the sounds they produce. Use a tape recorder to record children's voices; play them back for children to identify.	Encourage children to taste, smell, touch, listen, and observe at each step of the cooking process. Discuss how heating and freezing changes substances.	Have children observe cause and effect by hitting a key or dragging a mouse. Allow children to observe as you connect computer components.	Take pictures of a tree the children see every day and discuss how it changes during the year. Have children feel their heartbeat after running or exercising.
Include books that reflect diversity of culture and gender. Show children how to use nonfiction books, picture dictionaries, and encyclopedias to find information.	Take nature walks and post the places where collected leaves and flowers were found. Set up a recycling area where children sort paper, glass, and plastic into bins.	Show videotapes reflecting songs and dances of many cultures and languages. Include instruments from different cultures.	Encourage parents to bring in recipes reflecting their cultures. Visit stores that sell foods of different cultures.	Encourage children to work cooperatively on software related to a study topic. Develop rules with the children for using computers and post them in the area.	Take many trips in the neighborhood and talk about what you see. Invite children to make maps of outdoor environments using chalk on concrete.
Talk about art techniques used by illustrators (e.g., torn paper collage by Leo Lionni). Include children's informational books of famous artwork.	Provide kaleidoscopes and prisms and have children draw the designs they see. Use the materials children have collected on nature walks for collages.	Provide a variety of musical instruments to explore. Add scarves, streamers, and costumes to encourage dancing.	Encourage children to be creative while preparing their snacks. Dramatize foods being cooked —a kernel of popcorn being popped; cheese melting.	Include drawing and painting software. Include software that allows children to create musical tunes.	Bring art materials outdoors for creating pictures and sculptures. Provide streamers and scarves for outdoor dance and movement activities.
Set up a listening area with books on tape. Include books about how things work.	Introduce scientific tools and see if children can figure out what they do. Provide clocks, watches, and gears that children can take apart and put together.	Add an electronic keyboard that produces different sounds. Include tape recorders, CD player, headphones, etc.	Cook a recipe in a microwave and a conventional oven and compare cooking times. Examine how different kitchen gadgets work.	Set up a computer area with open-ended software programs for children to use. Add an inexpensive camera to the computer so children can see themselves on the screen.	Point out examples of technology while on a walk in the neighborhood. Provide tools for investigating outdoors such as magnifying glasses, binoculars, periscopes.

Integrating Learning Through Studies

In addition to setting up interest areas and interacting with children around the materials you provide, you can promote children's learning by studies, particularly in-depth or long-term ones. Studies allow teachers to integrate different content areas and address developmental goals.

In the past, the standard approach to tying curriculum content together was through the use of themes. Theme topics often came from the teachers' experiences, shared ideas from colleagues, or published guides and activity books. A common practice was to use the same themes year after year, whether or not the topic and experiences suited the interests and skills of a new group of children. Although some themes worked well, and teachers were able to implement them in a developmentally appropriate way, others were not appropriate for all classrooms. When teachers in Hawaii tried to do a "fall" theme in October—even though the local temperature was a constant 80 degrees and the leaves on the palm trees outside didn't change color or fall off—the material was not meaningful or relevant to children's experiences.

We believe a meaningful way to teach content is to build on children's knowledge and interests. We call this approach to integrating content *studies*. Educators Lilian Katz, Sylvia Chard, and Judy Helm use the term project approach. Much like a study, a project is

> *an in-depth investigation of a topic worth learning more about. . . . The key feature of a project is that it is a research effort deliberately focused on finding answers to questions about a topic posed either by the children, the teacher, or the teacher working with the children.* (Katz, 1994 quoted in Helm & Katz, 2001, p. 1)

The strongest feature of a study is its ability to support children's inborn dispositions to be curious, to explore the world, and to make sense of their experiences in a meaningful context.

Whether you call it a study or a project, this approach involves organizing the daily curriculum in a way that is both relevant and exciting for children. The strongest feature of a study is its ability to support children's inborn dispositions to be curious, to explore the world, and to make sense of their experiences in a meaningful context.

Throughout the study, you can observe and record children's comments and questions, their involvement with materials, their successes, and their confusion. Samples of children's work, photographs of their constructions, and photocopies of their writing can be collected and reviewed as you reflect on each child's learning. Using documentation and reflecting on children's progress on the *Developmental Continuum* helps you to plan for the group and for each child.

Studies begin with a good topic. Unlike a preset theme, study topics are unique to each class you teach. Ideas may originate from any source—teachers, children, or families. The topic may center on something children are curious about (how our bodies change), a social concern (food we eat), or an unexpected event (ants in the classroom).

No matter where the idea comes from, to be a good study topic, it must generate excitement in the children and have enough parts that can be investigated and explored. Here are some questions to ask yourself in assessing the appropriateness of a topic.

Selecting a Good Study Topic

Does this topic address children's **interests** or potential interest?

Is this topic real/relevant to children's experiences and is it **age-appropriate**?

Do enough of the children have **experience** with the topic so they can come up with questions to investigate and explore? Does the topic **build** on what children already know?

Can children **explore** the topic firsthand? Can real objects be manipulated?

Are **resources**—such as people to talk to, places to visit, objects or living things to observe and explore, books—available?

Can children do some research for this topic **independently** without depending entirely on the teacher's assistance?

Can the topic be explored in a variety of ways over an **extended period**?

Will the topic permit children to use **literacy** learning and **math** in real-life contexts?

Will the topic allow children to explore key components of **science** and **social studies**?

Can the **arts** and **technology** be incorporated readily into the topic?

Does the topic lend itself to representation in a variety of **media** (e.g., dramatic play, writing, constructions)?

Will the topic facilitate communication with **families**? Are family members likely to want to get involved with the project?

Is the topic respectful of **cultural differences**?

Is the topic worth **studying**?

Once you decide that a topic will work, you can begin mapping out how content might be addressed. Then you can collect resources and find appropriate experts and ideas for field trips. You'll also want to consider how families can be involved.

The length of a study depends on many factors, including the children's ages, interests, and focus. Studies run on their own momentum, not a calendar's schedule. In general, a study should be able to sustain children's interest for three weeks to a month.

Steps in Planning a Study

While studies are flexible and unique by nature, they are not without a structure. In fact, every good study will share common structural features. All of the teaching strategies we described earlier are used in engaging children in a study. We suggest that you follow these 10 steps when implementing a study.

Beginning the Study

Step 1: Select an appropriate topic.
Based on the criteria presented above, choose a topic for a study that you believe will hold the children's interest and has meaningful content worth knowing.

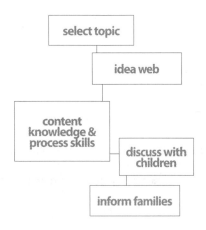

Step 2: Create a web of important ideas.
Use this web to anticipate the concepts that may be learned and the investigations that may take place. Using small pieces of paper, write down every word you can think of related to this topic. Next, organize these words into groups on chart paper. Write a statement that describes each group. These statements are the important ideas you hope children will learn. For example, in a study about insects, the big ideas might include how insects move, what insects eat, where insects live, or how insects help us. (See Chapter 3 for examples of key concepts in science and social studies.)

Step 3: Determine how content knowledge and process skills can be learned through this study.
Brainstorm ways that you can address literacy, math, science, social studies, the arts, and technology in this study.

Step 4: Discuss the topic with children.
Find out what understandings children already have. Lead discussions and encourage children to put their thoughts and memories into both words and pictures. Ask children what they want to know about the topic and make a list of their questions.

Step 5: Inform families of the proposed study topic.
Encourage parents to discuss the topic at home with their children and to share any expertise they might have with the class. Involve families as active participants in the study.

Investigating the Topic
Step 6: Use the Weekly Planning Form to organize materials and plan activities.
Think about how children might investigate this topic in interest areas, daily routines, and group time activities. Record only the activities or strategies that will help children gain a deeper understanding of the topic, not just cute ideas related to the topic. For example, in a study about cars children will learn more about the topic by building a dashboard out of recyclable materials than by sponge painting car shapes on paper.

Step 7: Assemble relevant materials and resources.
Think about what children need to conduct their investigations. Bring together the necessary research tools (books, materials, and technology) and arrange for field trips and visiting experts to support children's learning.

Step 8: Facilitate investigations.
Divide children into small groups to investigate particular research questions. Use open-ended questions to encourage further discoveries. Observe how children are investigating and suggest additional materials and resources. Decide if there is particular content material that you should teach directly. Bring the groups back together to share findings and give each other ideas.

Step 9: Document findings.
Encourage children to document what they have learned by making representations (drawings, writings, diagrams, maps, graphs, collections, constructions, and the like) and displaying them around the room. You also may wish to display some of this documentation in the classroom's entry hall to share with families and school visitors.

Concluding the Study
Step 10: Plan a special event to end the study.
Before the children start to lose interest, think about a way in which you can end the activity on a high note. Some teachers have a celebration, in which children share their investigations with others in the school, the community, and their families. You can help children review and evaluate their work and think of imaginative ways of presenting their findings to others. Use the children's ideas and cues to lead you to the next study.

A Sample Study of Worms

To illustrate how a study comes to life in the preschool classroom, we show you what each step looks like using our class of children ages 4–5 taught by Ms. Tory and Mr. Alvarez.

A sample study of worms

our class...

Step 1. Select an appropriate topic.
The children are excited about the earthworms they discovered where a piece of outdoor equipment had been removed. Ms. Tory and Mr. Alvarez provide an aquarium with dirt and invite the children to bring the worms inside the classroom.

Step 2. Create a web of important ideas.
For several days, Ms. Tory and Mr. Alvarez let the children independently explore the worms in the Discovery Area. They make a web of ideas to help them decide if worms would make a good topic for a study. By doing the web, they could see that many important ideas related to life science could be explored.

Step 3. Determine how content knowledge and process skills could be learned.
They next explore whether a study of worms would address the academic content that they want to cover. They develop the following chart.

A Possible Study of Worms

Literacy	Look at informational books about worms Read storybooks about worms (e.g., *Inch by Inch* by Leo Lionni)	Learn new vocabulary words about worms (slimy, wiggly, tunnels, compost) Sing songs/do fingerplays
Mathematics	Compare sizes and lengths of worms Guess the number of worms and then count them	Talk about the pattern of the worm's skin
Science	Investigate what worms like to eat Use a magnifying glass to watch how worms move	Compare different kinds of worms Observe worm eggs hatch Make a worm bin
Social Studies	Find out how worms help us Create a worm composting pile, adding leftover food from meals	Learn how to care for worms Visit a worm farm
The Arts	Use clay to make a representation of a worm Pour a puddle of colored water or mud on paper and let a worm crawl through it, creating worm tracks	Listen to the song, "Glow Worm," and move around the room like a worm
Technology	Use tools to explore the worms (magnifying glass, computer microscope, etc.) Look at video on Internet of worms hatching	Send questions about worms via e-mail to a worm expert

The process of making such a chart enables teachers to think about how to teach content knowledge and process skills as part of a study. Confident that they have a good topic, the teachers are ready to discuss the topic with children.

A sample study of worms, *continued*

Step 4. Discuss the topic with children.

At the next day's morning meeting, Ms. Tory brings the aquarium of worms to the meeting area and encourages the children to observe the worms and pick them up if they want. She asks the children to comment on what they see or had seen in earlier observations of the worms. These were a few of the comments they made:

Jonelle:	*"They wiggle when they move."*
Dallas:	*"They don't have any eyes."*
Crystal:	*"They don't have arms and legs."*
Zack:	*"They like to dig."*
Malik:	*"They like to crawl under things like on our playground."*
Alexa:	*"They can go upside down."*
Jonetta:	*"They leave black yucky stuff on your hands when you pick them up."*
Carlos:	*"Worms like to hide."*

After a discussion with the children about how worms would make a good topic for them to study, they talk about how they could learn about worms. Ms. Tory helps them to come up with a list of questions they would like to investigate:

> *What do worms eat?*
>
> *Why do fish like worms?*
>
> *Do worms have a smell?*
>
> *How do they dig if they don't have arms and legs?*
>
> *How deep can a worm go?*
>
> *How do worms see if they don't have eyes?*
>
> *How big can a worm get?*

At story time that week, Mr. Alvarez and Ms. Tory read books about worms and introduce songs about worms.

Step 5. Inform families of the proposed study topic.

The teachers send a note home to families about the new study of worms and encourage them to think of ways in which they might become involved in the study. Tyrone's father, who works at a sporting goods shop that sells fishing worms, says he could come in and talk about worms. Jonetta's grandmother says she will bring in worms from her garden.

A sample study of worms, *continued*

Step 6. Use the Weekly Planning Form to organize materials and plan activities.

Ms. Tory and Mr. Alvarez use the Weekly Planning Form to record investigation options in interest areas and during group times.

Step 7. Assemble relevant materials and resources.

Ms. Tory locates a number of web sites that the children can use to study worms, and she makes sure there are magnifying glasses, tongs, and other tools available for the children's investigations. She also asks the children's librarian to help her locate books the children might want to check out.

Step 8. Facilitate investigations.

Children are interested in investigating different questions so the teachers help them to form groups. One group studies what worms look like. Another group tracks how they move. A third group explores what worms eat.

Step 9. Document findings.

Over the next month the children seek answers to their questions about worms. They make drawings, paintings, and sculptures of the worms. They dictate stories about what they observed to their teachers and record worm anecdotes. The class takes a trip to a nearby worm farm. The children interview Tyrone's father and compare the worms in Jonetta's grandmother's yard to the ones at school.

The children learn about worms for many weeks. They create a number of constructions, homemade books, plays, and murals to represent their findings.

Throughout the study, Ms. Tory and Mr. Alvarez document the children's progress. They make observational notes that they put in the class binder. They take photos of the children's creations and representations, and keep copies of the books, drawings, writings, and audiotapes the children make for their portfolios. They use the documentation to help them track the children's progress on the Developmental Continuum.

Step 10. Plan a special event to end the study.

When the children have answered many of the questions they chose to investigate, the study starts to lose momentum. The teachers decide it is time to conclude the study. They ask the children to think about all of the work they have done and how they want to share what they have learned with others.

The children decide to hold a Worm Fest and to make an exhibit featuring their projects. Families, other classes, and school staff are all invited for a celebration of the worm study. Following the study, the class decides to keep the worm viewer in the Discovery Area and the compost near the recycling bins. The worms join the class guinea pig and fish as pets.

A study of worms worked for Ms. Tory's and Mr. Alvarez's class that year. It appealed to the children's interests because of what they found in the environment near their school. The teachers built on this broad base of interest and crafted a study that could be used to guide learning well.

In a rich learning environment, teachers promote development and learning in interest areas and use studies to integrate the learning of key components of the content areas. As you interact with children in meaningful ways, you further support children's growth. The strategies you use help children to become motivated learners who are eager to continue learning. The critical factor in ensuring that children are learning and making progress is the assessment system you put in place and your use of the information you gather to plan for each child and the group. This is the topic we address next.

Assessing Children's Learning

Assessment is the process of gathering information about children in order to make decisions. Assessment can serve many different purposes. The report, *Eager to Learn: Educating Our Preschoolers*, identifies four purposes (Bowman et al., 2001, p. 234):

1. Assessment to support learning

2. Assessment to identify special needs

3. Assessment for program evaluation and monitoring trends

4. Assessment for program/school accountability

While all of these purposes apply to *The Creative Curriculum*, the first—to support learning—is most important in the curriculum organizational structure. In *The Creative Curriculum*, teaching and assessment go hand-in-hand. Through assessment teachers obtain useful information about children's knowledge, skills, and progress by observing, documenting, analyzing, and reviewing children's work over time. At each step of the way you are systematic to ensure that you are meeting the needs of every child.

> Through assessment teachers obtain useful information about children's knowledge, skills, and progress by observing, documenting, analyzing, and reviewing children's work over time.

Assessment to support learning works best when it is linked closely to the goals and objectives of your curriculum. *The Creative Curriculum Developmental Continuum* Assessment System has been designed specifically for this purpose. If you are using this system you will want to refer to *A Teacher's Guide* that comes with the Assessment Toolkit, or the on-line version, which explains how to use all the forms that enable you to link assessment with guiding children's learning.

If you are using a different assessment system, be sure it is compatible with the *Creative Curriculum*'s goals and objectives for children. Whatever system you use, there are three essential steps to the assessment process: (1) collecting facts, (2) analyzing and evaluating the collected facts, and (3) using what you've learned.

Collecting Facts

The first step in assessing children to support learning is collecting facts. One very effective way to do this is by ongoing observation. Teachers document what they observe so they can review this information at a later time. Another way is to collect children's work samples and maintain a portfolio for each child.

Documenting Your Observations

Earlier in this chapter we discussed how, what, and when to observe. We showed you how the *Developmental Continuum* guides your observations, helps you to recognize where a child is developmentally, and gives you an idea of what the next steps are. Documenting your observations means having a system that enables you to keep carefully written records.

In order to use observation notes for later analysis and evaluation, teachers need multiple observations that apply to all the objectives.

A system is an organized way to keep track of your observations and to make sure that you have observed each child in each developmental area for all of the *Creative Curriculum* objectives. Some teachers use a large binder with a section for each child, divided into the four developmental areas. Whenever they have an observation note on a child, they put the dated note in the appropriate section for later review.

To use observation notes for later analysis and evaluation, teachers need multiple observations that apply to all of the objectives. When you have several observation notes, for example, that demonstrate how a child approaches problems flexibly (objective 23) in the Block Area as well as the Dramatic Play Area, you can be sure that the conclusions you draw about what developmental step a child has reached are likely to be valid. You can also examine your notes to see whether a particular behavior on a particular day was not reflective of a child's general level of functioning.

Collecting Children's Work in Portfolios

In addition to documenting your observations by keeping written records, another major way to collect information about children over time is to keep a portfolio. A portfolio is a system for organizing samples of a child's work to document progress over time. It is a purposeful collection containing items such as dated samples of a child's art and writing and photographs of the child's completed work, for example, block constructions, a design with pattern blocks, a graph, or outdoor tunnel. The items in a portfolio are concrete and representative examples of a child's efforts, achievements, and approaches to learning. Taken together, these materials provide a picture of each child's progress over time.

A portfolio is a system for organizing samples of a child's work in order to document progress over time.

You can use portfolios to

- share information with families—"It's easy to see Juwan's progress when we compare the drawings he made six months ago to the ones he made last week."

- help children to reflect on their work and recognize their own skills and progress—"Tell me about the picture you drew for your story."

- review a child's progress, set goals, and plan instructional strategies

Each sample of a child's work reveals a great deal of information about that child's development. While you don't need a large number of work samples in a portfolio, you do need sufficient variety to tell the whole story. In collecting a child's work for a portfolio, take time to write an observational note and clip the note to the back of the work sample.

To show growth, collect similar samples over a period of time. For instance, comparing a child's attempt to write her name throughout the course of the year would be one excellent way to document writing development. But it would be hard to document growth if you were to compare a writing sample, a painting, a photograph of a block structure, and a dictated story. At the beginning of the year, think of two or three items—such as writing samples or paintings—that would be good for documenting development in particular areas and set a goal for yourself to collect these three to five times throughout the year.

Also, refer to the stages of development in each interest area in *The Creative Curriculum,* found in Part II of the book. Collect samples of children's work or photographs that show growth as children progress through these stages. For example, Chapter 6 outlines the four stages of development in building with blocks. A series of photos of a child carrying blocks, making bridges, and, finally, making elaborate constructions is an excellent way to show growth over time.

To help you think of the variety of items you can include in a child's portfolio, consider the following suggestions and the ways you might make use of technology to document children's work and preserve it.

> In collecting a child's work for a portfolio, take time to write an observational note and clip the note to the back of the work sample.

Completed work samples that can be compared over time:

- drawings, paintings, collages, weavings

- writing (scribbles, labels, letters, names and words, numbers, signs and messages)

- a story dictated to a teacher and/or illustrated by the child

- a book made by the child

- computer printouts

- graphs or drawings of a science experience

If you photocopy or scan a drawing or writing sample for the child's portfolio you can enlarge or reduce it to fit easily in whatever storage system you have developed. If you have a scanner attached to your computer, you can scan children's work and use it for many purposes besides the portfolio, such as newsletters, children's books, etc. Sometimes it is easier to capture a child's activity, such as block building, with a photo than it is to write a description. Here are some ideas for photographs.

Photographs of a child's work and play activities:

- block building or other block structure

- a construction made by a child doing woodworking

- a sculpture made from clay or recyclable materials

- shells, leaves, or other natural objects sorted by size and color

- indoor/outdoor murals or other group projects the child has participated in

Photographs showing a child's physical development:

- standing on the top of a climber
- swinging

- riding a tricycle
- completing a puzzle

Photographs showing a child involved in everyday routines and activities:

- using a serving spoon
- cleaning up

- brushing teeth
- listening to a story

When you use photographs, number a set of adhesive labels 1–24 (or however many pictures are on the roll). Write a brief note about the picture you are taking on the label, then place it on the back of the photo once it has been developed. Before photographing children, make sure you have the parents' written permission.

Sometimes you'll want to write a note about what a child said or did to go along with something in the portfolio. At other times, the best way is to make a recording of an event.

Written records of a child's interests:

- questions—asked or answered during a small-group activity
- favorite books

- descriptions of drawings and other work
- comments after a field trip

Video and audio recordings of a child's language development:

- singing, telling a story, or playing with others
- conversing during a family-style meal

- engaging in dramatic play
- identifying a solution to a problem

You can use a small cassette recorder to capture children's oral language development. In addition to learning about children's language, you can gain insight into their thought processes. With a recorder, you can stay in the action without having to be writing. You'll save yourself a lot of time if you use a recorder with a counter and jot down the counter number so you can find what you've recorded, at a later date. If you have access to a video recorder, you can videotape children in action, for instance, when they are engaged in dramatic play or during a story retelling. An advantage to videotaping is that you take very accurate notes and use the time you need to reflect and study what children are saying and doing.

Storing Work in Portfolios

Portfolios start with a few items but grow quickly. You'll need to have a storage space large enough to hold the items and a system for organizing them. Children's work and other items can be stored in a number of ways:

- accordion files
- magazine files
- hanging file folders
- pocket folders
- empty pizza boxes (unused, donated by a local business)
- X-ray folders
- plastic containers with lids
- folder made from tagboard or poster board, folded and stapled on two sides

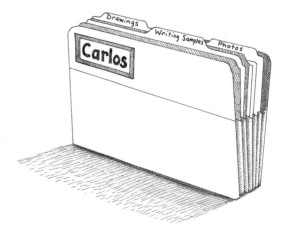

File the items you have collected by date and group them by categories that make sense for your program. It might be helpful to you to group them by the areas of development—social/emotional, cognitive, language, and physical development. This will make reviewing your documentation easier when it is time to complete the *Individual Child Profile*.

Keep in mind that the chief purpose of collecting facts is to get to know children well—their interests, needs, and challenges. The next step is to reflect on this information to make instructional decisions.

Analyzing and Evaluating the Collected Facts

By systematically analyzing and evaluating your observation notes as well as portfolio samples, you will have a picture of where each child is on the *Developmental Continuum*. You will know what the next steps for learning are related to the 50 objectives. You can organize your observation notes as well as the information in children's portfolios by asking yourself, on a regular basis, "What does this mean?" Using the goals and objectives decide which objective(s) apply and jot down the number right on the note or on the back of a work sample. Here's how you might analyze the sample notes we showed earlier (on page 168).

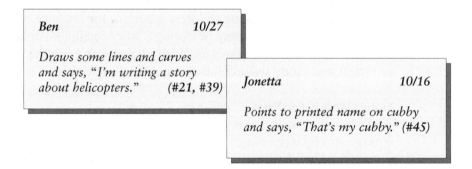

Ben   10/27

Draws some lines and curves
and says, "I'm writing a story
about helicopters."   (#21, #39)

Jonetta   10/16

Points to printed name on cubby
and says, "That's my cubby." (#45)

The observation note on Jonetta was very clearly related to objective 45, "Demonstrates understanding of print concepts." The observation note on Ben, however, relates to more than one objective. It applies to physical development (21, "Uses tools for writing and drawing"), but in analyzing it further, you see it also reveals evidence of Ben's language development (39, "Expresses self using words and expanded sentences"). You can use this note for both objectives.

To evaluate children's progress you have to decide what developmental step each child has reached on an objective on the *Developmental Continuum*. Let's see how this works using the observation note on Jonetta shown above. Looking at this note, plus your other observation notes and portfolio items on Jonetta, you decide that for objective 45, "Demonstrates understanding of print concepts," Jonetta "knows that print carries the message" (step I). Record this information.

Curriculum Objectives	Developmental Continuum for Ages 3–5			
		I	II	III
45. **Demonstrates understanding of print concepts**	**Forerunners** Points to print on page and says, "Read this" Recognizes logos *e.g., McDonald's* Recognizes book by cover	Knows that print carries the message *e.g., points to printed label on shelf and says, "Cars go here"; looking at the name the teacher has written on another child's drawing, says, "Whose is this?"*	Shows general knowledge of how print works *e.g., runs finger over text left to right, top to bottom as he pretends to read; knows that names begin with a big letter*	Knows each spoken word can be written down and read *e.g., touches a written word for every spoken word in a story; looking at a menu asks, "Which word says pancakes?"*

In the same manner, you can complete all of the 49 other objectives, using your observation notes and Jonetta's portfolio. Evaluate where every child is in relation to the objectives. Repeat this process by examining your notes and the portfolios of everyone in your class.

After noting where Jonetta and the other children in your class fall on the *Developmental Continuum*, you will want to have a system for documenting each child's progress over time. We recommend that you record progress at three times during the year. Programs using *The Creative Curriculum* Developmental Continuum Assessment System can use the *Individual Child Profile* for this purpose. With this collection of information you can plan your teaching and make changes to the environment appropriately.

Using What You've Learned to Plan

The wealth of information you have on each child is only meaningful if it is linked to decisions about teaching. It can help you to plan for children individually and for your group as a whole.

Planning for Each Child

The *Developmental Continuum* is the tool to help you to identify where a child is in relation to each of the Curriculum's objectives and how to support the next step in development. Here are some examples of how you might use the Continuum to plan.

Jonetta is now aware that print carries the message (*Objective 45, step I*). She is noticing print in the environment. To help her get to step II, "Shows general knowledge of how print works," I'm going to call attention to how I read from left to right and from the top of the page to the bottom the next time I read with her.

Setsuko is beginning to engage more in conversations by responding "to comments and questions from others" (*Objective 43, step I*). She seems very excited about having a guinea pig in the class. We can build on this new interest to promote her language development and literacy learning by reading books about guinea pigs and encouraging her to talk about what she has observed the guinea pig doing.

Leo has been building, knocking down, and rebuilding the same block structure for weeks (*Objective 25, "Explores cause and effect"*). Does he just like to watch what happens when he knocks it down—or is he angry, frustrated, or stuck at step I, "Notices and comments on effect"? We'll have to observe him in other interest areas to think about what he knows about cause and effect and take him to the next step of testing out possibilities with intention.

Alexa seems to be at the forerunner level of *Objective 24, "Shows persistence in approaching tasks,"* because she remains engaged with materials for only brief periods of time. I think she really might like to work with playdough if there are rolling pins and cookie cutters available, so I'm going to put these materials in the Art Area. Then I can see if she will explore further and complete a task (step I, Sees simple tasks through to completion) if I stay in the area and interact with her while she uses it.

As you can see, teachers' purposeful observations of children help them to make decisions daily about what an individual child might need. Even more valuable is the comprehensive picture of development you obtain when you summarize all your observations for each child related to the 50 Curriculum objectives. Because the *Developmental Continuum* covers all areas of development, it gives you a developmental portrait of the whole child.

We recommend that you summarize children's progress three times during the year and use the information you've collected to plan for each child. If you are using *The Creative Curriculum* Assessment System, you can use the forms specifically designed for this purpose. Teachers who are using a different approach to assessment will need a system to summarize the information they have collected. For each child in your class, you will make a global assessment of that child's skills in all areas of development.

Using Jonetta as an example, you might begin by reviewing her progress in **social/emotional development** (objectives 1–13). Think about her strengths and challenges related to these 13 objectives. Your summary will give you insight into how to further her social/emotional development.

Next, look at what you learned about Jonetta related to **gross motor and fine motor development** (objectives 14–21). Note what Jonetta is able to do and where she is struggling. Then do the same for **cognitive development** (objectives 22–37) and **language development** (objectives 38–50). For each developmental area, try to summarize Jonetta's development in that area in three or four sentences.

Together, these summaries of the four areas of development will give you a good idea of Jonetta's overall development. You'll have a picture of what she has accomplished and where her skills are just emerging. This knowledge will help you to think about the activities and instructional supports to further Jonetta's growth and development. In Chapter 5 we discuss in detail how you can share this information with families and together develop a plan (see pages 231–234).

Because the *Developmental Continuum* applies to all children ages 3–5, and to children who are not at a typical level of development, you cannot expect that every child in your program will progress to the higher levels for each objective. Over the course of the year, however, you would hope to see evidence of progress in every child.

Planning for the Group

Another important use of the information you have collected in the assessment process is to plan for the group. You may find, after reviewing the progress of the class as a whole on the *Developmental Continuum*, that work on certain skills could benefit everyone.

Three times during the year summarize children's progress and use the information you've collected to plan for each child.

Now you can think about when and where to teach these skills. Some you'll teach in large- and small-group settings. For example, let's take a look at one objective, objective 38, "Hears and discriminates the sounds of language." In a classroom of 20 children ages 4–5, suppose you find:

- Two children are at the Forerunner level. They notice sounds in the environment and participate in some parts of singing songs.

- Nine children play with words and rhymes (step I).

- Seven children invent their own silly rhymes (step II).

- Two children can hear and repeat separate sounds in words (step III).

Reflecting on what this information means, you conclude that the majority of children are still developing the skill of hearing and discriminating sounds. You decide to work on phonological awareness with the whole group. To make objective 38 a group focus, you might try these strategies:

- Stock the Library Area with tapes of poems and chants with lots of repetition and rhyming words for children to listen to on their own.

- Lead a small group of children who are at the first developmental step in singing some finger plays and simple songs.

- During routines play games such as "If your name begins the same sound as these words—table, toes, turnips, tickle—you may select a book."

- Teach children to clap to the rhythm of the music.

- Encourage children to make up silly rhymes with words: "apple, papple, bapple; car, bar, mar, dar, far."

- Call attention to words that begin with the same sound.

- Read aloud books that contain rhyme, rhythm, and repetition, such as *Brown Bear* by Bill Martin, Jr. or any of the Dr. Seuss books.

Based on what you learn from your review of children's progress on the Continuum, you can identify which children would benefit from more focused instruction and practice on certain skills. This information will help you to plan small group activities. The *Developmental Continuum* is a teaching tool that lets you learn about each child so you can plan for individual children and the group.

Based on what you learn from your review of children's progress on the Continuum, you can identify which children would benefit from more focused instruction and practice on certain skills.

conclusion

As you can see, observing, guiding, and assessing children's learning is an ongoing process. You collect facts, analyze and evaluate what they tell you about the child's development, then use the information you've learned to plan for each child and for a group of children. You then implement your teaching plans, continue to observe and document what children do, and so the cycle goes.

References

Bowman, B. T., Donovan, M. S., & Burns, M. S. (Eds.). (2001). *Eager to learn: Educating our preschoolers.* Washington, DC: National Academy Press.

De Houwer, A. (1999). *Two or more languages in early childhood: Some general points and practical recommendations* (No. EDO-FL-99-03). Washington, DC: ERIC Clearinghouse on Languages and Linguistics Center for Applied Linguistics. (ERIC Document Reproduction Service No. ED433697)

Gosnell, E. S. (2001). *Classroom culture and children whose home language is other than English: Negotiating meaning in preschool special education.* Unpublished doctoral dissertation, George Mason University, Fairfax, VA.

Jablon, J. R., Dombro, A. L., & Dichtelmiller, M. L. (1999). *The power of observation.* Washington, DC: Teaching Strategies.

Katz, L. G. (1994) The project approach. Champaign, IL: ERIC Clearinghouse on Elementary and Early Childhood Education. In J. H. Helm & L. Katz (2001), *Young investigators: The project approach in the early years* (p. 1). New York: Teachers College Press.

Tabors, P. O. (1997). *One child, two languages: A guide for preschool educators of children learning English as a second language.* Baltimore: Paul H. Brookes, Pub.

inside this chapter

212   Getting to Know Families

212 Appreciating Differences

214 Using Initial Contacts to Learn About Families

218   Making Families Feel Welcome

218 Creating a Welcoming Environment

220 Introducing Your Program

221 Building Trust

222 Reaching Out to All Family Members

223   Communicating With Families

223 Daily Exchanges

224 Formal Communications

225   Partnering With Families on Children's Learning

225 Offering a Variety of Ways to Be Involved

228 Making Classroom Participation Meaningful

231 Meeting With Families to Share Information and Plan

235   Responding to Challenging Situations

235 Families Under Stress

236 Dealing With Misunderstandings

239 Addressing Differences Constructively

241   Conclusion and References

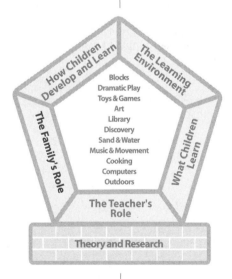

The Family's Role

5

Home and school are a young child's two most important worlds. Children must bridge these two worlds every day. If home and school are connected in positive and respectful ways, children feel secure. But when the two worlds are at odds—because of apathy, lack of understanding, or an inability to work together—children suffer. Teachers who truly value the family's role in a child's education, and recognize how much they can accomplish by working with families, can build a true partnership.

Start with the idea that parents are already involved. They have been raising their children since birth. They demonstrate a commitment by enrolling their children in your program and getting them to your classroom each day. Instead of expecting them to give time they don't have, choose a different goal. Focus instead on developing a relationship with every family so you can work together to support children's healthy development and learning. This chapter will help you by addressing the following topics.

Getting to know families—recognizing differences in families and making the most of initial contacts to learn about each family

Making families feel welcome—creating a welcoming environment, introducing families to your program, building trust, and reaching out to all members of a child's family

Communicating with families—taking advantage of informal daily exchanges and more formal methods of communication to share information and keep families up-to-date on your program

Partnering with families on children's learning—offering a variety of ways for families to contribute, involving families in the program, and conducting conferences to discuss children's progress and to plan together

Responding to challenging situations—recognizing families that are experiencing stress, dealing with misunderstandings, and handling differences that are based on strongly held philosophical and cultural beliefs

Getting to Know Families

Just as you get to know each child and use what you learn to develop a relationship that helps every child learn, you begin building a partnership with families by getting to know and appreciate each family. Every family is different. If you try to relate to all families in only one way, you will reach only a small percentage of the families who respond to that approach. By contrast, if you vary the ways you communicate with families and involve them in the program, you will be more likely to reach every family.

Appreciating Differences

One obvious difference in families is in **structure**. The traditional family—two parents and their children—is not as common as it once was. Many children are growing up with one parent. Some are being raised in foster homes or by grandparents or other relatives. Other children live with two mothers or two fathers. To appreciate differences among the families you serve, start by keeping an open mind about what constitutes a "family." And remember that however non-traditional a family may seem to you, children's families are the most important people in the world to them.

Personality and temperament are among the ways families are different. Some families are easy to get to know. They feel comfortable in the school environment and they are eager to communicate with their children's teachers. Others are uneasy and shy in a school situation. They may have unhappy memories of their own school experiences and are unsure of how to relate to their children's teachers. Regardless of these differences, you can convey to all families that you value them and that your classroom is a safe place for them to visit.

> However non-traditional a family may seem to you, children's families are the most important people in the world to them.

Life experiences such as level of education, socio-economic status, health issues, and length of time in this country also account for differences in families and influence how they relate to their children's teachers. Some parents not only care for their children but also care for elderly or ill family members. Some are facing challenging circumstances such as unemployment, substance abuse, unstable or unsafe housing, depression, or lack of access to a phone or transportation. Your sensitivity to these life circumstances can go a long way in helping you to accept and appreciate all families.

Cultural differences are sometimes less obvious but no less important than structure, personality, and life circumstances. Culture has been defined as the beliefs, values, and practices we have learned from our families, either through example (watching what others do) or through explicit direction (being told what is expected). Cultural background affects how people communicate and interact with others and their expectations of how others will respond. Because every culture has its own set of rules and expectations, different cultures interpret what people do and say differently.

To appreciate how and why families respond as they do, it's helpful to be aware of your own personal experiences and how they have influenced your thinking and your actions.

Gaining Self-Awareness

Think about the messages you may have received growing up and the experiences you had in your own family and community. Considering these questions may help you begin (or continue) your own process of self-awareness.

- How did you become aware of your personal identity—nationality, culture, ethnicity?

- What early messages did you receive about other groups?

- How did you define a "family" when you were growing up? Has your definition changed today?

- What messages did you receive about your family's socio-economic status?

- Were girls treated differently from boys in your family? What do you think your family's expectations were for you?

- How and when were you encouraged to express your ideas and feelings?

- Was it acceptable to be noisy and active in your home, or were children expected to be seen and not heard?

- How was discipline handled?

- Was independence encouraged?

If you were to share your experiences with someone from a similar background, you would probably find many similarities in beliefs and practices, but also many differences. You might not want to be labeled as belonging to the same group as this person. For this reason, it is not helpful to try to generalize about any group's characteristics. Labels only perpetuate stereotypes and are often inaccurate. It is far better to learn as much as you can about and from the families in your program than to depend on group stereotypes that may be entirely wrong. Consider the many factors that influence the practices and values of an individual family, including the family's country of origin, its social class there and here, the parents' educational background, and whether extended family members live in the home.

Using Initial Contacts to Learn About Families

Initial contacts with children's families are opportunities to get to know a little about each one. Depending on your program's procedures, your first contact with families may be at enrollment or during a home visit. Because these initial contacts make a strong impression, use them to learn about families and to begin building a positive relationship.

Think about what will make families feel comfortable right from the start. How can you convey that you are eager to get to know them and their child? Ask yourself, is it appropriate to serve something to eat or drink? Do you need to arrange for someone who speaks the family's home language to be present? Be guided by the principal idea that in these initial contacts, you want to make families feel comfortable with you.

Enrollment

Most programs have an enrollment form with specific questions about the child's history and about the family. Before meeting with a family, find out, if you have any doubt, how to pronounce the child's name correctly. During enrollment, explain how the information on the form will be helpful to the program. Try to leave time to speak informally with families about their children. You will probably gain valuable insights by asking open-ended questions:

- What would you most like us to know about your child?

- What are your child's favorite activities?

- Does your child have a favorite toy?

- What would you say are your child's greatest strengths?

- Are there any concerns that we should know about?

- What are your hopes and dreams for your child?

- What do you most want your child to learn in our program?

If appropriate, you might use the child's enrollment to learn a little about the family's culture and heritage. Here are some questions that might give you some valuable insights:

- Are there any special traditions, celebrations, or songs, that are especially important to your family and your child?

- How would you like us to support your child's heritage and cultural identity at school?

- How can I learn more about your heritage and culture?

- Would you be willing to share something about your culture with the program?

You may find that you are collecting a lot of information by speaking informally with families during enrollment. To keep track of what you learn, you might create a web for each child (a process we describe in detail in Chapter 4 when we discuss planning a study). In the middle of a piece of paper, write the child's name. As parents respond to the questions and the discussion evolves, write down a few representative words in a web format. Take time to share the web with the child's family at the end of the session and explain how you will use the information to get to know and teach the child.

To keep track of what you learn, you might create a web for each child.

Enrollment also might be an appropriate time to explain how much you value the involvement of families in your program. Talk about ways you intend to communicate with and involve family members. Find out what special talents and interests families would be willing to share with your class.

Home Visits

One of the best ways to get to know children and families is to make home visits before the school year begins. Families are often more comfortable in their own setting than at school. Home visits are an excellent way to build a bridge to school for a child who has never been in this kind of environment.

Here is a true story of how one teacher learned the power of home visits.

The Power of Home Visits—A True Story

As I approached Gabriel's house, I saw a motorcycle in the side yard. Close by were two child-sized motorcycle-like wheeled riding toys, and on the patio sat a collection of toy motorcycles. Before parking my car, I already knew that one way to engage Gabriel was to include motorcycle activities in my classroom. I made a mental note to put toy motorcycles in the block center and a motorcycle book in the book center.

Gabriel led me to the back of the house to see his room. I noted the stuffed animals on his bed and the toys he'd been playing with. I knew I could refer to these in class. Before I left, his parents proudly announced that Gabriel would have a new brother or sister in six months. Now I had another piece of information that might lead him to talk to his classmates and me. In a ten-minute visit, I learned more about this child and his background than I had learned previously about some children in an entire year as their teacher. Since that time I've made a commitment to visit every child's home before each school year.

Parents benefit from home visits, too. They receive information about the beginning of school, the school's discipline policy, my classroom management techniques, field trips, and class routines. Many of the parents I work with were once poor students in school, and some were school dropouts. Their memories of school and teachers aren't pleasant, and they have bad feelings about sending their own children to school. They associate parent/teacher conferences with bad news and school problems, but realize I'm visiting because I'm interested in their child's success.

Children benefit most from the visit. Taught to be wary of strangers, students meet me in their own homes, with their parents present. When they walk in the classroom door, my face is familiar. The snapshots I took of them and their families are on the bulletin board. Because I've met every child, I can greet each one by name.

If you've never made a home visit, I urge you to try it. You'll find it to be one of your most valuable teaching tools (Backer, 2001).

Before making a visit, send a welcoming postcard to or call the child's family, letting them know you would like to visit. Then set up a time. Go with the intention of getting to know each family and building a relationship, not judging. Invite families to talk about themselves by asking open-ended questions. Briefly share a personal story if you feel that will put families at ease.

Just as you may bring flowers or a gift to a friend's house when you are invited for dinner, consider bringing something from the classroom such as a book or paper and crayons for the child or a guide to the program for parents. If possible, bring something for the child that he can keep until the first day of school. It will serve as a concrete connection to the program and make entering the classroom easier.

You also might bring a camera so you can take a picture of the child alone and one with family members who are present. You can use both kinds of pictures in classroom displays. Some teachers bring an instant camera so the family can take a picture of the teacher with the child to be kept in the home. These snapshots, often displayed on the household refrigerator, are a natural way to connect home and school.

Visiting all children at home is not always possible. In these cases, make an effort to talk with families on the phone, at least, before their children come to the program, or try to meet at a neutral public place, such as a coffee shop or a park. These options often work well because some parents are intimidated by being in a school setting. But no matter where you first meet with family members, they can teach you a great deal if you are genuinely open and eager to learn from them. The insights you gain will help you to build a relationship with each child and family and to be a better teacher.

Go with the intention of getting to know each family and building a relationship, not judging.

Making Families Feel Welcome

All you have done to get to know families will help you welcome them. Families that feel welcome in your classroom are more likely to return and to become involved in the program. The environment you create in your classroom and the ways you introduce the program can make families feel they belong and they have a role to play. Over the course of the year you can build trust through the ways you communicate with and reach out to all family members.

Creating a Welcoming Environment

The most important message families can receive when they enter the building and your classroom is that this is also a place for them. The environment can carry positive messages.

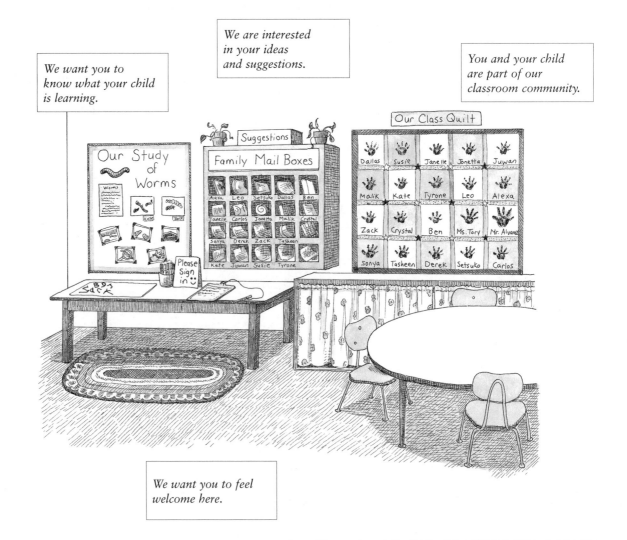

We want you to know what your child is learning.

We are interested in your ideas and suggestions.

You and your child are part of our classroom community.

We want you to feel welcome here.

How to Convey Positive Messages

Make the **entranceway** attractive, neat, and inviting. Include decorative touches such as plants, pictures, and displays of children's work.

Provide space for **mail/message boxes** for each family. To help you sort messages easily by language, color-code the mailboxes according to the home languages of the families in your program. This practice will make it easy to put the messages in the right place.

Incorporate **artifacts** that represent your families' cultures into your displays such as handmade quilts, weavings, musical instruments, masks.

Provide **places for family members** to hang their coats and store their belongings during their visit.

Keep a **bulletin board** with up-to-date information on program activities, upcoming meetings, and community events that may be of interest to families.

Place a **suggestion box** in a prominent place and provide slips of paper and pens.

Mount an attractive display of **photographs** of the children in your class and their families.

Place an **adult-size rocking chair** in the Library Area.

Have a **sign-in sheet** for families to sign in their children each morning. Children can sign in themselves on a separate sheet.

Display **books and pictures** that reflect the diversity of your program.

Offer **resources** that parents can read and check out.

Post **signs** in the classroom showing what children are learning in each interest area and how adults can support what the children do.

Take time to assess continually whether your environment conveys the messages you intend. Let families know their ideas and contributions are always welcome.

Introducing Your Program

When children first enter the program, their parents are likely to be especially interested in finding out what their child will be learning and what each day will be like. Make them feel welcome by responding to their interests. Some programs develop a booklet that introduces their philosophy and goals for children, describes the kinds of experiences children will have, and outlines policies and procedures. Programs implementing *The Creative Curriculum* can give parents *A Parent's Guide to Preschool Education*. Explain what the **booklet** contains so that parents feel familiar enough with the content to read it later. If parents have shared with you what they want their children to learn, you can refer them to specific sections of the booklet that address their goals.

Take families (and children) on a **tour of the classroom** and talk about how you have set up different interest areas, what the day is like, where children place their belongings, and what to expect on the first day of school. This might be a good time to invite families to share something from home that might be displayed in the classroom.

You also can consider holding an **open house** for families at the beginning of the year. You can describe your program briefly, distribute and go through a parent's guide, and recreate the day for families. Start with everyone in a circle to demonstrate circle time. Welcome everyone by name. Go over a typical schedule and then explain the concept of choice time. Invite each person to select an interest area and explore the materials you have set out. As they do, move from one area to another. Comment on what people are doing and explain what children learn from the same activities.

The **Letter to Families** you will find at the end of each interest area chapter of *The Creative Curriculum* describes what children do, how teachers support their learning, and how families can help at home. You can send these letters home over a period of time, perhaps once a week, so that parents don't feel overwhelmed with too much information. Alternatively, you can distribute the appropriate letter at a meeting during which you are talking about a particular topic, such as cooking with children.

Another way to share what and how children are learning is to create an attractive **display** at the entrance to your classroom or school. Take photographs of children engaged in meaningful work. Display the photos along with samples of children's work and brief descriptions of what children are doing and what they are learning.

> When children first enter the program, their parents are likely to be especially interested in finding out what their child will be learning and what each day will be like.

Building Trust

To feel welcome, families need to trust you. Trust between teachers and families grows over time and is based on many experiences that are positive and respectful. Some parents may be uneasy in a school environment and unsure of how they will be treated. You can build trust by conveying positive messages to families. Here are some suggestions.

Conveying Positive Messages to Families

To convey to families...	You can...
They are welcome as soon as they enter the building.	Greet each family member by name and say something positive—about the child, the family, or the program.
They are capable of making a contribution to the program.	Find a way to uncover and then use each person's special skills and interests in your program. Acknowledge the expert insights and information parents have about their child and how valuable these are to you as the teacher.
They are competent.	Make sure all written communication is in simple language and translated if necessary. Avoid the use of jargon in both written and spoken communication. Learn and use at least a few words in the family's home language so you can communicate directly.
Their views are valuable and they have a role to play.	Find out what topics are of interest to parents. Create a relaxed atmosphere, share children's strengths, invite parents' views on the child's progress, and make conferences a joint planning time.
They understand what is happening in the classroom.	Take the time to explain how children are learning through play and reassure parents that research confirms that children in a high-quality program make progress toward learning important skills in literacy and math, even if the classroom is different from what they expected to see.

All families come with expectations—some positive, some negative, and some neutral. Responding in a positive and respectful manner will help them to trust you enough to engage in open exchanges.

Reaching Out to All Family Members

Parents are not the only family members who should feel welcome in your classroom. All members of a child's family can be involved in the program and their involvement can make a big difference. Grandparents, for example, may have more free time to share than parents and often (though not always) a great deal of patience. Their participation in the classroom can be valuable: reading to children, playing games, assisting in special activities, and more. Schools that have partnered with senior citizen homes or groups such as Foster Grandparents find that intergenerational programs benefit both older citizens and the children.

You probably will need to make a special effort to welcome and involve fathers, who sometimes feel uncomfortable in early childhood settings where women predominate. Once fathers discover that their presence and their contributions are appreciated by the program staff and are important to their child, they are more likely to take an active role. And there are substantial benefits to getting fathers involved in the child's life at school.

Research (U.S. Department of Education, 1999) has shown that young children whose fathers are involved in their education do better in school. Moreover, the children of involved fathers are more likely to enjoy school and are less likely to be expelled or suspended than children whose fathers are not involved in their schooling. By "father" we do not necessarily mean only the child's biological father. A father figure may be another significant male—the mother's partner or husband, an uncle, older sibling, grandfather, another relative, or a family friend—who is a steady influence in the child's life.

> The most important thing to keep in mind is that all children need caring adults in their lives who take an active interest in their learning.

The most important thing to keep in mind is that all children need caring adults in their lives who take an active interest in their learning. Find out which adults are important in a child's life and think creatively about how you can extend a welcome to them. Learn about their interests, what jobs they do, any special hobbies that might be tapped, and what they would like to share with the children. Describe what others have contributed to the program. Some adults are more likely to come to an activity that involves the whole family rather than one that is designed specifically for parents. You also may be successful if you create special projects or events to interest different family members. For example, you might invite grandparents or special friends to come and read or tell stories, and those interested in construction projects to help with a fix-it day. Or you might ask family members about topics of interest to them and arrange for a special speaker or activity.

The steps you take each day to make all families feel welcome in your program and classroom set the stage for a partnership. You can build on this foundation by communicating regularly with every family so they become knowledgeable about their children's lives at school.

Communicating With Families

Good communication is essential for building partnerships. Families want to know what experiences their children are having at school and what you have learned about their child. Often they have information to share as well. Daily exchanges are just as valuable as the formal methods you may use to communicate with families. When young children observe respectful and genuine interactions between their families and teachers, they see that their two worlds—home and school—are connected.

Daily Exchanges

In most programs serving preschool children, teachers have opportunities to communicate with family members each day. Make it a point to note something a child has done during the day and jot it down so it doesn't slip your mind at the end of the day. Here are some suggestions for making the most of daily exchanges with families.

Making the Most of Daily Exchanges With Families

Make families feel welcome. Greet them personally and by name. Tell them something their child has done or comment on your plans for the day.

Have something specific to say to each one. "Good morning, Ms. Lewis. I know Derek wants to show you the clock he's been taking apart in our Discovery Area."

Share an event or something the child has done recently. "Let me tell you about the building Janelle made with our blocks yesterday. It was pretty amazing."

Solicit parents' advice about their child. "We've been encouraging Tyrone to try new foods at mealtimes but he is still very reluctant. Is there anything he particularly likes that we should know about?"

Give support to parents when needed. "It's hard for Leo to say goodbye to you today. Is there any reason you can think of? Perhaps he just needs an extra hug. I know he'll be fine once he gets busy and we have lots planned for today."

Be a good listener. Active listening skills convey that parents' concerns and ideas are being taken seriously. "I can understand how upset you were about the biting incident. I can assure you that we are taking steps to prevent another incident."

Talk about what children are learning. The end of the day can be a perfect time to talk with families about what their child has done that day and to explain its value. "We saved the design Kate made with the pattern blocks to show you. Her ability to create and repeat patterns is an important skill in math and in reading."

Check out communication. If there is uncertainty about a parent's statement, clarify your understanding. "Let me see if I'm hearing you correctly. What I heard you say is . . ."

Formal Communications

In addition to conferences and progress reports, discussed later in the chapter, there are many ways to keep family members knowledgeable about what is happening in your program. As always, try to communicate in a language the family will understand, and if some family members are not readers, show sensitivity by speaking directly with those families.

Ways to Communicate With Families

Daily or weekly bulletins. A brief note about what took place at school each day (or week) is one way to keep families connected. Write a short message and reproduce it for each family. It could be as simple as a form that says, "Ask me about …" with a highlight filled in. Bulletins give families topics to discuss with their children about school.

Telephone calls. Set up a schedule to call each family monthly to say hello and say something positive about the child's progress. Call to convey your concern if a child has been out sick. Some teachers give out their home phone numbers and encourage families to call any time; others set limits on when they will be available for phone calls at home.

E-mail. More and more families—and programs—have access to e-mail. Sending e-mail is an excellent way to stay in touch. You can also update families through a listserv.

Internet. Introduce families to CreativeCurriculum.net (if you are using this system), where they can participate in a parent-to-parent message board, view their child's portfolio, and add comments or upload pictures.

A class web site. You, a colleague, or a parent can build a class web site. If you have digital cameras or scanners, you can include photos of the children and their work. A web site is a good way to keep families informed about long-term studies and class events.

Thank-you notes. Each week, send a brief thank-you note to a few families telling them you appreciate something they have done that contributed to their child's life at school.

Journals. Provide each family with a journal that travels between home and school. Parents and teachers can write entries in the journal and share information.

Notices. There are times when you send a written notice so that every parent quickly gets the same information. Some examples might be a policy change, a special event, or a contagious disease in a child or staff member.

Telephone tree or electronic messages. With an automated phone messaging system, you can send a message or alert to everyone's phone on any topic.

Whatever methods you adopt, it is important to have a variety of ways to communicate with families and to choose manageable approaches that keep you in touch with your partners—children's families.

Partnering With Families on Children's Learning

When parents are involved, children do better.

Parents have been teaching their child since birth—they are already your partners in supporting their child's learning. You have much to gain by recognizing their role and including them as partners in the education of their children. Numerous studies have documented the academic benefits to children of a parent-school-teacher partnership. When parents are involved, children do better. These findings hold true regardless of the educational background of the parents or their income level (Henderson & Berla, 1994).

To partner effectively with parents, you will need to get them involved and keep them involved. But what exactly do we mean by parent involvement? Traditionally, parent involvement meant having parents attend meetings at school, volunteer time in the classroom, and help with fund-raising efforts. Success was measured by the number of parents who attended an event or gave time to help in the classroom or with an activity.

Today, most parents work full time. Some have more than one job, and others work at night. They are not always able to participate in their child's school program. Therefore, teachers need to think of parent participation in new ways.

Involvement can take many forms—from contributions parents can make at home to volunteering in the classroom and sharing information on children's progress. Through the process of partnering, teachers learn a great deal about children and how to teach them. Parents come to appreciate how much they've already taught their children. And the biggest winners of all are the children who thrive on the cooperative relationships between their families and teachers.

Offering a Variety of Ways to Be Involved

Although the strengths and talents of parents and other family members may not be immediately evident, every family has something positive to offer. Try to discover the special interests and abilities of all family members and think of ways you can incorporate them into the program. Ask yourself, "What does this person bring to our relationship that enhances our ability to work together?" The more options you provide for families to contribute to your program and to be involved with their children's life at school, the more likely you are to succeed in reaching every family.

Early in the year during a home visit, at enrollment, in a phone call, or at an open house let families know how helpful it would be to have them involved in the program—and how much their involvement would mean to their children. Ask family members what they enjoy doing with their children, what interests them, and what they are most comfortable doing. Explain that there are many ways to contribute and offer ideas.

Ways for Families to Be Involved

Making things for the program. Family members can do projects at home that will benefit all the children in the program. They can help collect "beautiful junk" to be used in the art area (such as fabric scraps, ribbons, yarn, pieces of soft wood for woodworking), objects for sorting and classifying (such as buttons, shells, keys, bottle caps), or props for dramatic play. Families may be willing to make things for the classroom such as matching games, sewing doll clothes or curtains, or taping stories for the Library Area.

Sharing their culture. Families that are willing to share aspects of their cultural heritage can enrich the program greatly. They might lend art objects and come in to talk with the children about what they mean, how they were made, and their significance. You might invite a family member to cook a traditional dish with the children, teach them dances or songs, tell stories, or share photographs of their country of origin. Families that cannot come into the classroom during the day might tape songs or stories.

Sharing a talent or job. Once you learn about the special talents and interests and what family members do for a living, you can invite them to share their knowledge and experiences with the children. The possibilities are endless: playing an instrument; preparing a garden; teaching children about animals or insects; applying carpentry skills to a project for the program; and so on.

Participating in a study. Families can be a great source of information and ideas if the topic of a study is something they are knowledgeable about. You might send home a note describing what you will be studying and inviting families to be part of the planning. They might join you on a field trip, contribute materials (such as old shoes for a study of shoe stores), or participate in special activities you plan related to the study.

Contributing to the curriculum. In some programs, it is a requirement that parents have a say about the curriculum. Although the program has already adopted a curriculum (such as *The Creative Curriculum*), it may set up an Education Committee and invite interested parents to participate. The committee typically meets several times during the year to discuss topics, such as what children are learning, what training is being offered for the staff, positive outcomes of the program that have been documented, and what program improvements should be considered.

Parent participation in curriculum planning can be somewhat controversial. Some teachers fear that families will suggest practices that are not developmentally appropriate, or make requests that are not in the best interests of the children. Rather than responding defensively, take the view that families that participate in curriculum planning are showing their interest and willingness to give their expertise and opinions. Even if their ideas may not be appropriate, try to find something about their suggestions that you can accept and build on in a positive way. Ask questions to get an idea of what is important to them, and then describe ways you address their goals in your program.

Take the view that families are showing their interest and willingness to give their expertise and opinions.

View exchanges about curriculum as an opportunity, rather than a battleground. For example, if a father says an important goal of the curriculum is for children to know the alphabet and learn how to sound out words, don't get caught up in the fact that all children won't be able to do these things. Instead, you can confirm how important these skills are in *The Creative Curriculum* and show how the Curriculum helps to develop them.

- Show the goals and objectives that relate to these skills and share the *Developmental Continuum* to explain the steps in development.

- Share the strategies we describe in Chapter 3 for Literacy, and the chapter on the Library Area in Part II of this book.

- Talk about what you do every day and validate all the ways families help their children to develop skills: talking with their children, reading together, pointing out signs and naming the letters, helping their children write their names.

- Invite families to share other ideas.

If you keep in mind that teachers and families have similar goals—namely, to ensure children's success in school and in life—you usually can find common ground. In addition, families often have wonderful ideas for enriching the curriculum, particularly when they know a great deal about the topic. When you describe how you intend to address their expectations or use their suggestions, they feel a sense of ownership, which often leads to enthusiastic support.

You can usually find common ground.

Whatever families offer to do can enhance your program. The size of the contribution is not important. What families learn by contributing and the positive message their involvement conveys to children are what count most.

Making Classroom Participation Meaningful

Some families will be able to participate in your daily program. Doing so enables them to see firsthand how you work with children and promote learning. In addition, there are many benefits for children. Seeing their parents in their classroom is exciting and a source of pride, and an extra adult in the room means more individual attention for all children.

Reassure parents that you do not expect them to be teachers. Explain that your primary goal is to give them an opportunity to learn about what goes on in the classroom, and that their assistance will be very helpful. Prepare them for the possibility that at first their child will want their full attention. Explain that this is very normal.

Talk with families ahead of time—at a parent meeting or individually— about ways in which they can work with children: playing with a group in an interest area; playing one-on-one with their child or another child; leading a small-group activity; giving a demonstration; or serving as an expert on a topic. Some teachers have found it helpful to post signs or posters in each interest area that explain what children do and what they are learning. If you have a special need for assistance in an activity or an interest area, contact the parent in advance so he or she will have the opportunity to ask questions, make suggestions, or make necessary preparations. However, also allow for family members to select an area of interest to them during choice time.

In general, there are ways families can participate that apply to all interest areas and activities. Think about developing a short, one-page flyer highlighting the following tips for family members:

- Observe what children do and show you are interested by describing what you see. ("I notice you put all the red pegs in a row.")

- Follow children's lead without taking over. ("I'm going to try making the waterwheel turn just like you did.")

- Ask open-ended questions to find out what a child is thinking. ("How many ways can you use this?" "What will it do?" "How does it feel?" "What do you like best?" "What do you think will happen next?" "How did you decide to do it that way?")

- Offer assistance when it is needed.

The chart that follows offers suggestions of what you can tell families about the importance of each interest area and what they might do when they participate.

Interest Area	What You Can Tell Families About Each Interest Area	What Families Might Do When They Participate
Blocks	Blocks are designed in mathematical units. Children's building goes through distinct stages. Children create designs and build what they see around them—roads, houses, a zoo.	Talk with children about the different shapes and how many blocks they need. Help children find and return blocks to their designated place. Suggest props a child might like to use.
Dramatic Play	Pretend play is the way children make sense of their experiences. Children take on roles and pretend about a situation, use props, and play with other children.	Pretend with children by taking on a role. Help children find and return the props they need. Suggest ideas to extend make-believe play.
Toys and Games	These materials teach math, develop eye-hand coordination, and promote small muscle skills. Some are self-correcting and some are open-ended.	Play games with children. Help a child who is having trouble completing a task such as a puzzle. Comment on the pattern a child makes.
Art	Children need time to explore and experiment with different art materials. Creative art is the way children express their own ideas and feelings. Adults should not impose their own ideas on children. There are predictable stages in children's artwork.	Encourage children to experiment with paint, markers, clay, dough, and collage materials. Help with a special activity such as making playdough. Help children write their names on their artwork or write down what children dictate.
Library	Children develop valuable literacy skills and a love for books. It is a quiet place to get away and enjoy books. The most important letters are the ones in children's names.	Read and enjoy looking at books with children. Encourage children's writing and take dictation. Tell stories and listen while children retell stories.
Discovery	This is an area where children can make discoveries and experiment with materials. Adults can encourage and share a sense of wonder with children.	Be curious about children's discoveries. Help children take apart an old small appliance (e.g., clock, tape recorder).

Interest Area	What You Can Tell Families About Each Interest Area	What Families Might Do When They Participate
Sand and Water	These are soothing materials that calm children. There are scientific and mathematical discoveries children can make.	Make sure the sand and water stays in the tubs. Offer props and talk about what children are discovering. Help with a special activity like blowing bubbles, testing what floats/sinks.
Music and Movement	Children develop coordination and learn concepts through songs. They develop listening skills and an appreciation of different kinds of music.	Share an instrument they can play or music they enjoy, or teach children a dance. Explore the sounds of different instruments. Participate in group-time activities.
Cooking	Children learn literacy and math skills following recipes. Children make scientific discoveries in cooking. Preparing and eating food is very satisfying. There are rules and procedures for safety.	Help collect materials needed. Remind children of the rules for safety. Assist children in following recipe cards. Make a favorite recipe with the children.
Computers	Computers are a part of everyday life. The software selected engages children in active learning. Children can work together on the computer.	Assist children in following the procedures for using computers. Help children find programs they want and learn how to use them. Participate in playing a game on the computer.
Outdoors	Outdoor time is important for children's health and well-being. Children can learn about nature firsthand. They develop their large muscle skills and coordination.	Help supervise children at play. Play a game with children. Take an interest in discoveries (e.g., watching a caterpillar, collecting leaves). Share a special skill or interest (e.g., woodworking, gardening, basketball, ring toss).

Families that have a positive experience when they participate in the classroom are more likely to come again. A meaningful role in supporting their child's learning will have a far greater effect than tasks such as washing paintbrushes or preparing snacks. Be sure to let family members know how much you appreciate their help and how important it is to their child. It's always nice to follow up with a brief thank-you note or phone call to thank them again.

Meeting With Families to Share Information and Plan

Most programs hold conferences with families several times a year to share information and discuss the children's progress. In the previous chapter we described how teachers individualize the curriculum by observing and documenting children's progress using the *Developmental Continuum* as a guide. Families will be interested in finding out what you learned, and you, in turn, can learn a great deal about children from talking with their families.

Involving families in planning for their children is a powerful way to convey that this is a true partnership. Here are some of the benefits you can expect:

- You obtain a richer, more accurate assessment of a child's development by exchanging observations with families.

- You gain valuable insights about a child's culture, background, interests, and temperament that will aid you in planning appropriate experiences.

- You have a shared vision of a child's strengths and challenges.

- You agree on what objectives and teaching strategies are important.

- You have shared expectations for a child's growth and development.

- You encourage parents in their role as their child's first and most important teacher.

- Children are more likely to receive common messages both at school and at home.

- Education becomes a team effort.

Try to schedule a planning meeting with each child's parents at least three times a year, or whenever you report to parents.

Preparing for a Conference

The more prepared you are for conferences, the more positive the experience will be for both you and children's families and the more you will be able to accomplish. In the previous chapter where we discussed assessment, we described the value of maintaining a portfolio for each child and tracking children's progress on the *Developmental Continuum*.

Before meeting with families, go through the child's portfolio and your ongoing observations of each child. Be sure the portfolio and your observations are up-to-date. Review what you have learned about the child from completing the *Developmental Continuum*. What have you learned about the child's social and emotional skills? Fine and gross motor skills? Cognitive development? Language skills? Pull out the information you feel will be of most interest to each child's family. A written report that summarizes the child's progress, such as the *Child Progress and Planning Report,* can be a useful tool for presenting this information.

Before you meet with the family...

- review the portfolio

- consider the family's interests and values

- pull out information that will be of most interest to child's family

- think about which areas of development, objectives, and strategies you will discuss with the child's family

Think about what you know of each family's background and consider what may be most important to them. Some of the *Creative Curriculum* objectives that you see on the Continuum reflect certain values of Western/American cultures. For example, under Social/Emotional Development, you will find several objectives (e.g., Objective 3, "Recognizes own feelings and manages them appropriately"; Objective 4, "Stands up for rights"; Objective 5, "Demonstrates self-direction and independence") that some families would not value as goals for their children. They may value obeying authority over expressing one's own views, sharing over respect for personal property, and interdependence over independence.

What do these differences mean to you as a teacher as you assess children's progress and attempt to partner with families? First, acknowledging differences underscores the importance of listening to and learning from families. Take time to find out what each family wants most for its child, what behaviors are important, and how the family views its role in the child's education. Second, take this information into consideration as you decide what objectives to focus on for each child. Finally, keep in mind what are important values for a family as you prepare for a conference so you can emphasize the child's progress in those areas first. For example, in some families, social and emotional skills are valued more highly than cognitive skills. Knowing this, you can begin your conference by sharing the child's progress in this area of development.

A final step in preparing for a conference is giving some thought to the areas of development and particular objectives you want to focus on and the strategies you will discuss with the child's family. Ask yourself, "How can I help this child move to a higher developmental level for specific objectives? What new skills is this child ready to learn? How can I build on this child's interests and strengths?" You won't have all the answers before meeting with families, but you will have some ideas to offer as a starting point.

Conducting a Conference

A good way to begin talking with families about their child's progress is by sharing work samples. Pictures of block structures the child has made, samples of writings and drawings, and dictated stories are concrete evidence of a child's accomplishments. Take time to explain a little about each work sample and what it shows about the child's interests and strengths. Most important, share something positive that shows you really know what's unique and special about the child. Starting off a conference in this way can put families at ease.

Review what you have written about the child's development.

Invite families to share their own observations and identify objectives important to them.

Discuss specific objectives you want to focus on.

Share work samples and offer positive comments.

Provide families with a copy of the plan.

Next, review what you have written about the child's development. Highlight the child's strengths as well as any areas of concern, and share specific examples from your observation notes or the child's work samples.

Invite families to share their own observations. Questions such as the following will encourage families to share their perspective:

- What does your child like or dislike about coming to school?

- What changes have you seen?

- What are your child's special interests?

- What would you like your child to experience at school this year?

After hearing what families say, share some specific objectives you want to focus on for the child and invite families to identify any that are important to them. Describe several strategies you will be using and ask the family what it might enjoy doing at home with the child.

Provide families with a copy of the plan so it becomes a true blueprint for supporting the child's development and learning. When you meet next, you and the family can assess how the plan worked, review new evidence of the child's progress, and revise the plan together.

Responding to Challenging Situations

In spite of all the positive steps you take to build a positive relationship with every family, you will still encounter challenging situations that work against a partnership. Some families are coping with basic needs and experiencing ongoing stress that makes it difficult for them to be available to their child. Others choose not to get involved, thinking that their child's education is a professional matter only. As always, it's important to understand what is causing a challenging situation so you can address the real issues.

Families Under Stress

Increasingly, teachers deal with families under stress. A large number of families are headed by single parents who must seek employment or job training without knowing who will be caring for their young children. Ongoing and unrelenting stress can come from many other sources as well. Here are just a few:

- living in a community plagued by violence

- unemployment

- long commutes to a demanding job that does not allow flexibility in work hours to accommodate family needs

- meeting the daily needs of a family member with a disability or chronic illness

- domestic and/or substance abuse

- adapting to a new culture and/or language

- substandard, overcrowded housing or living in a shelter

- depression that has not been diagnosed or treated

- lack of health insurance to address medical issues

Parents who are under stress from these or other life situations do not always have the emotional energy or physical resources to provide nurturing care for their children—sometimes even to meet their children's most basic needs. They may not be able to solve problems, communicate with their children, or give them the attention and affirmation they need. Their discipline may be inconsistent, overly punitive, or nonexistent. For children in these circumstances, life is unpredictable and dangerous, and their confusion may manifest itself in anger, withdrawal, or fearfulness in your program.

Recognize the the signs of a family under stress.

What Can a Teacher Do?

First, do not feel that you need to solve families' problems by yourself. Begin by recognizing when a family is under stress. Avoid adding to the stress by being overly critical (e.g., if a parent has forgotten to bring boots for her child in spite of several reminders) or by reporting on a problem you are having with their child if you can wait for a better time. At the same time, let the family know that resources are available that can help them and that you will ask your supervisor or colleagues for advice. Your program might have social services and family support workers who can conduct a family needs assessment to learn about each family's situation and then help find the resources the family needs. At a minimum, every program can put together information they can share with families such as:

- an up-to-date list of community agencies and hot lines for referrals

- brochures and resources families can borrow

- a listing of support groups that deal with the issues facing families

Research and share important resources with the family.

Parenting is one of the most important jobs in the world, yet there is very little training for this critical role. Parents who were fortunate enough to have caring, nurturing experiences in their own childhood have a solid foundation for becoming good parents themselves. Those who had less constructive experiences still want the best for their children and are doing what they think is needed. Although there will be things you see parents doing—or failing to do—that will distress you, hold to the belief that most are doing the best they can. Learn as much as you can about the strengths and needs of each family so that you have realistic expectations and can individualize your approach to partnering. What works with one family will not necessarily work with another.

Dealing With Misunderstandings

If you work with families that share your values and beliefs and that have similar life experiences and personal characteristics, you are more likely to interpret what they say and do accurately. But if you work with families that are very different from you—and if you know little about their beliefs and practices—miscommunication and misunderstandings can easily take place. Understanding and respecting practices that are different from your own help you to build positive relationships with all families and involve them in your program.

The following chart illustrates how miscommunication between parents and teachers can occur. It shows differences in perspective about the same situations.

Miscommunication—Different Perspectives

Situation	The Teacher's View	The Family's View
Sonya's teacher describes how pleased she is that Sonya has begun to speak up more in class and share her ideas. The parents say nothing when they leave the conference.	Talking in class is an important goal for all children. Initially, Sonya rarely spoke up in a group, so the change is an exciting development. She will learn more if she participates actively and puts her ideas into words to express what she knows.	Speaking up in a group means Sonya is boasting and we do not approve of this behavior. We want our daughter to be respectful and quiet so she can learn.
After conducting a workshop on ways that parents can help their children learn at home, and providing written suggestions, teachers find that several parents do not follow through.	Parents who don't spend time on activities with their child at home just don't care very much about their success at school. The more families are involved, the better children will do in school.	It's the teacher's job to teach my child, not mine. I don't know how to do what the teacher is asking.
After careful observations over time, a teacher is concerned that a child's language is delayed and suggests an evaluation. The parents fail to make an appointment with a specialist.	If a real problem exists, it should be identified as early as possible. Parents should want to get all the help they can get for their child.	In life, we must accept what we are given. Why interfere?
Carlos' mother unzips his coat and hangs it in his cubby along with his mittens and boots. The teacher says, "Carlos, you can unzip and hang up your own coat, can't you? Tomorrow, show your Mom how you can do things for yourself."	Self-help skills and developing independence are important objectives for children. Carlos' mother is treating him like a baby.	Helping my child is one way I show him how much his family loves him. I want to care for him, especially just before I have to say goodbye for the day. There's plenty of time for him to learn to take care of himself.
Setsuko reluctantly looks up, then quickly looks away when the teachers asks her to look her in the eye as she explains the rules about running in the classroom.	I can't be sure she is listening to me if she is not looking at me when I speak to her.	We have taught our child that looking into an adult's eye when being reprimanded is a sign of disrespect. Doing so is going against what we have taught her.

Parents who do not understand what their children's teachers want, or who feel that their values and goals for their child are not respected, cannot be comfortable and involved with their child's life at school. And when the values and skills children learn at home are not respected or understood at school, children become confused about what to do. Identifying most strongly with their home culture, children may reject the school culture because it is so unfamiliar. In doing so, they also reject the goals and values of the education system, feel alienated, and often drop out of school. The opposite can happen as well: children may identify more with the school culture and reject their own heritage, becoming increasingly isolated from their family and their community.

You can avoid making children feel they have to choose between the practices they learn at home and the ones they are expected to follow at school. Sometimes this means accepting what a child does. For example, knowing that a child has been taught that looking directly at an adult who is giving directions is disrespectful helps you appreciate why it would be upsetting and confusing to the child if you said, "Look me in the eye when I am talking to you." For this child, you would understand her behavior and perhaps check out whether she has paid attention to you by asking her to indicate she has understood.

In other situations you may need to find a compromise that still shows respect for the family's values without accepting the practices at school. If you know, for example, that for some families, doing things for a child, even if he is capable of doing them independently, is a sign of love, you can validate a mother's practice of unzipping, removing, and hanging up her son's coat. At the same time, you might share with the parent that when she is not available, her son is learning to care for himself, which is an important life skill.

Another example is the situation of the family that resists the recommendation to have the child's language development assessed by a specialist. Here you may be more successful if you first acknowledge the family's viewpoint—that we must accept what exists and make the best of it. Confirm that while this is true, it's also true that many problems can be overcome if they are identified early, thus giving the child an opportunity to overcome the difficulty and be successful. Once an agreement has been reached, you can find out what would be most comfortable for the family. Perhaps offer to have someone from the program go along to see a specialist, or to have the child observed at the program itself.

> Through a combination of acceptance, compromise, and sensitivity to the family's culture, you can avoid making children feel that they have to choose between the practices they learn at home and the ones they are expected to follow at school.

Addressing Differences Constructively

Some differences are hard to reconcile because they are so against your program's philosophy and your own strong beliefs.

Some differences are hard to reconcile but must be addressed directly because they go against your program's philosophy and your own strong beliefs. One common example concerns spanking. Some parents want you to spank their child for any misbehavior. They firmly believe that hitting is good for children: "Spare the rod, spoil the child." "If you hit your child, society won't." They may tell you, "My parents hit me and I turned out okay." Spanking a child, however, goes against what we know from research on the negative effects of corporal punishment. This practice is also against the law in most states. In a *Creative Curriculum* classroom, where teachers strive to create a peaceful classroom community, hitting anyone is not tolerated. Rather, the object is to guide children's behavior in positive ways so they learn self-discipline.

In situations where a family's wishes and values conflict with those of the program, the following steps may be helpful in resolving differences constructively.

Seek first to understand the family's position.

Ask open-ended questions and listen to learn what concerns the parents may have. "Tell me a little about what concerns you have for your child. What would you like your child to learn here?" These questions can help you discover the real issues behind parents' requests. More than likely, they want their child to behave well and practice self-discipline.

Validate the family's concerns and wishes.

Restate what you hear them say to be sure you understand and to let the family know you hear them. "What I hear you say is that you want to be sure your child learns how to control himself and how to behave. This is an important goal for us as well. We spend a lot of time building children's skills in this area."

Explain how your program addresses the family's concern.

Acknowledge that there are different points of view on any topic. Without negating their request, talk about your shared vision for children. You both want to help children learn how to behave in acceptable ways and relate to others in a caring and respectful manner. You might begin by sharing the specific objectives on the *Developmental Continuum* that relate to self-discipline. (These objectives are included under social/emotional development.) If parents are interested, show them the steps children are likely to go through in reaching specific objectives, and discuss the examples under each one. Describe the practices in your program that support children in acquiring the skills they need. If possible, share the research on topics of concern to parents.

Make a plan to check in with one another to assess progress.
Leave parents with the assurance that you will monitor their child's progress and stay in touch. Reassure them that their concerns will remain on your mind and be addressed. Again, if you are using the *Developmental Continuum*, you can pinpoint where the child is in relation to relevant objectives, and you can discuss what all of you can do to support the child.

In some situations, you may decide that a compromise can be the best solution and that you should put aside your own beliefs to accomplish something more important. An example is the issue of a graduation ceremony at the end of the year before children leave the program.

You may feel a graduation is not developmentally appropriate, particularly if it means a formal ceremony in which children perform, wear caps and gowns, and receive diplomas. Parents, many of whom had negative school experiences and never graduated themselves, may attach special significance to a graduation ceremony. The ceremony represents evidence that their child's experiences in school have been different and the hope that this may be the first of many graduations. You may decide, therefore, to have a modified graduation celebration, a party to which all families are invited and share food together. The compromise conveys respect for parent's wishes and allows everyone to enjoy the celebration.

By suspending judgment, you can convey to families that you are eager to learn from them and gain a deeper understanding of what they want and value. With this information in hand, you can try an approach that suits them and gains their trust and respect without violating the values, goals, and principles of your program.

By suspending judgment, you can convey to families that you are eager to learn from them and gain a deeper understanding of what they want and value.

conclusion

Building a partnership with families and ensuring that they have a role in their children's education is the last component of *The Creative Curriculum*. Together, these five components—knowing how children develop and learn, creating the learning environment, knowing what content children need to learn, and understanding the teacher's role and the family's role—will help you to be effective in providing all children in your classroom with learning experiences that will promote their development. In Part 2, we show how the five-part organizational structure described in the preceding chapters is applied to each of the 10 interest areas of a *Creative Curriculum* classroom and the Outdoors.

References

Backer, B. (2001, January 28). Home Visits. Message posted to ECENET-L@LISTSERV.UIUC.EDU (First appeared in *First Teacher* magazine, September/October 1994. Retrieved February 14, 2002, from http://www.awod.com/gallery/rwav/bbacker/articles/homevisits.html)

Henderson, A. T., & Berla, N. (1994). *A new generation of evidence: The family is critical to student achievement*. Columbia, MD: National Committee for Citizens in Education.

U.S. Department of Education. Office of Educational Research and Improvement. National Center for Education Statistics. (1999). *The condition of education 1999*. (NCES 1999-022). Washington, DC: U.S. Government Printing Office. Also available at: http://www.nces.ed.gov

inside this chapter

243　How Block Play Promotes Development
244　Connecting Block Play With Curriculum Objectives

246　Creating an Environment for Block Play
247　Selecting Materials
251　Displaying Blocks and Props
252　Cleanup—A Special Challenge

253　What Children Learn in the Block Area

255　The Teacher's Role
255　Observing and Responding to Individual Children
261　Interacting With Children in the Block Area
267　Frequently Asked Questions About Blocks

269　A Letter to Families About Block Play

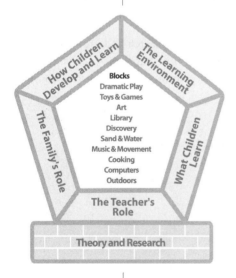

Blocks

How Block Play Promotes Development

Blocks, especially hardwood unit blocks, are standard equipment in a *Creative Curriculum* classroom. Wooden blocks naturally appeal to young children because they feel good to the touch, are symmetrical, and invite open-ended explorations. When children construct, create, and represent their experiences with blocks, they grow in each area of development.

Social/emotional development. In the Block Area, children negotiate for materials they want to use, determine how many children can work in the area, care for materials, and follow the rules for building safely. They also exchange ideas. Since one child's idea of how to build a zoo, for instance, may differ from another's, children expand their knowledge and learn to respect viewpoints different from their own.

Physical development. Children's small muscles develop when they carry and carefully place blocks together to form a bridge or make an intricate design. They gain strength in their large muscles using hollow blocks, and improve eye-hand coordination when they carefully balance blocks so they won't tumble.

Cognitive development. As children experience the world around them, they form mental pictures of what they see. Playing with blocks gives them an opportunity to recreate these pictures in concrete form. The ability to create these representations of their experiences is the basis for abstract thinking. Moreover, block play promotes a concrete understanding of concepts essential to logical thinking. Children learn about sizes, shapes, numbers, order, area, length, patterns, and weight as they select, build with, and put away blocks.

Language development. Children are very willing to talk about their constructions when adults ask questions and show genuine interest. They increase their vocabularies when adults give them new words to describe what they are doing, and develop their writing skills by making signs for their buildings.

Connecting Block Play With Curriculum Objectives

Your familiarity with the *Creative Curriculum* goals and objectives will help you identify what children are learning as they build and create with blocks. You can document children's growth on the *Developmental Continuum* based on your observations. In the chart below, we list selected objectives and show what children might do that demonstrates their growing abilities.

Selected Curriculum Objectives	What a Child Might Do in the Block Play Area
Social/Emotional Development	
4. Stands up for rights	Says, "I don't like it when you knock my blocks down."
5. Demonstrates self-direction and independence	Looks at a picture of a bridge and begins to construct one.
7. Respects and cares for classroom environment and materials	Arranges blocks on shelves labeled with size and shape outlines and places props in containers with picture labels.
9. Follows classroom rules	Cautions a friend, "Don't build too close to the shelf or someone may step on your building."
10. Plays well with other children	Suggests making a gas station to go with a road two children have built.
12. Shares and respects the rights of others	Divides up remaining long blocks so each child has some to use.
13. Uses thinking skills to resolve conflicts	During a struggle over blocks, offers: "You can use this block. It's just like the one I'm using."
Physical Development	
15. Shows balance while moving	Creates balance beam out of hollow blocks and walks across.
19. Controls small muscles in hands	Carefully balances small blocks on tall tower without knocking down the structure.
20. Coordinates eye-hand movement	Places people figures on each floor of an apartment house built with blocks.
21. Uses tools for writing and drawing	Draws picture of completed block structure.

Selected Curriculum Objectives	What a Child Might Do in the Block Play Area
Cognitive Development	
23. Approaches problems flexibly	When the blue rug sample he wants as a pond is being used, goes to Art Area for blue construction paper.
25. Explores cause and effect	Says, "If I add one more block, my building will fall."
27. Classifies objects	Sorts blocks according to type and shape.
28. Compares/measures	Gets a piece of string to measure two structures.
29. Arranges objects in a series	Notes that blocks on shelf are organized from large to small.
30. Recognizes patterns and can repeat them	Creates a wall by alternating short and tall blocks.
32. Shows an awareness of position in space	Says, "I'm going to put the animals inside the fence. You make a road outside the fence."
34. Uses numbers and counting	Reminds another child, "You can't have more than four hollow blocks on top of each other."
37. Makes and interprets representations	Builds a house and names the rooms.
Language Development	
39. Expresses self using words and expanded sentences	"I'm making a drawbridge for our castle."
41. Answers questions	Explains, "I'm making a zoo. Don't you see the animals?"
42. Asks questions	Asks, "How do you make steps?"
43. Actively participates in conversations	Discusses with another child how to build their airport.
47. Uses emerging reading skills to make meaning from print	Places stop sign along block road and says, "When your truck gets here, it has to stop."
49. Understands the purpose of writing	Brings paper and pencil to teacher and asks for help in making a "Do not knock down" sign.

Creating an Environment for Block Play

How you set up the Block Area, the materials you provide for children, and the procedures you establish for using and caring for blocks set the stage for children's learning. To maximize the potential of blocks as effective learning materials, give children sufficient room to build, a clearly defined space for block play, appropriate flooring, and a variety of props and open-ended materials. In the illustration below, we show a Block Area that is designed for imaginative, constructive play.

Note that blocks and props are all neatly arranged so children can easily find what they need and return them.

Tape on the floor defines a "no-building zone" near the shelf which prevents children from building where their constructions might be knocked over by other builders who are taking blocks off the shelf or returning them.

Setting up the Block Area	Suggested Materials
Location:	Hardwood unit blocks (about 390 pieces total). Put out 3–4 basic shapes at first.
Away from line of traffic, preferably in a corner of the room and defined by shelves	Set of hollow blocks (48 pieces)
Ample space so children can build without getting in each other's way	People props (multi-ethnic family sets, multi-ethnic community figures sets)
	Animal props (farm, zoo, pets)
Near other noisy activities such as the Dramatic Play Area	Road signs
Set up:	Small cars, trucks, trains, buses, boats
Smooth, flat carpeting on the floor if possible	Wooden train set with trains
Three shelves—two for blocks and one for props	Books related to construction

Selecting Materials

A good supply of blocks and accessories to enhance children's constructions will make the Block Area interesting for children. While several types of blocks are recommended for use in implementing *The Creative Curriculum*, we feel that unit blocks and hollow blocks are essential.

Unit Blocks

Hardwood unit blocks are durable, have no rough edges, and are easy for children to manipulate. There are 25 different sizes and shapes of unit blocks. The basic unit block is 5-1/2" x 2-3/4"x 1-3/8". All blocks in the set are proportional in length or width to this basic unit; for example, the double-unit block is 11" long and the half-unit is 2-3/4" long. The two triangles equal one square, and the four quarter-circles equal one circle. This design aids children in learning math concepts as they select, build, and return blocks. For example, if a child needs a long block and it isn't available, he could substitute two smaller blocks.

We recommend purchasing a classroom set of unit blocks (about 390) for a group of 15 to 20 children. This total should include as wide a range of sizes and shapes as possible, such as ramps, curves, and cylinders. With a large variety of blocks, you will find that children's building can become truly creative.

For young children or inexperienced block builders, introducing just a few basic shapes and sizes at the start of the year, such as the unit, half-unit, and double-unit blocks is preferable. As soon as children become comfortable and skilled at building and putting blocks away, you can add additional block shapes until the full set is available.

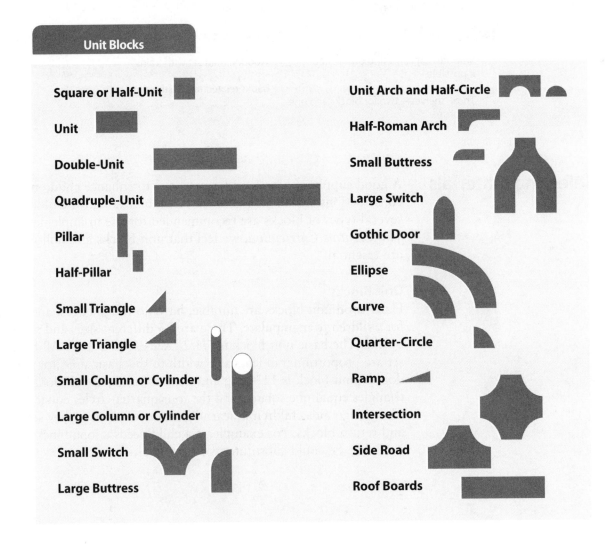

Unit Blocks

Square or Half-Unit	Unit Arch and Half-Circle
Unit	Half-Roman Arch
Double-Unit	Small Buttress
Quadruple-Unit	Large Switch
Pillar	Gothic Door
Half-Pillar	Ellipse
Small Triangle	Curve
Large Triangle	Quarter-Circle
Small Column or Cylinder	Ramp
Large Column or Cylinder	Intersection
Small Switch	Side Road
Large Buttress	Roof Boards

Adequate space, storage, and labeling ensure that blocks are well-housed and not thrown against each other during the clean-up process. Unit blocks, however, are an investment and require some care if they are to last for many years.

Sand blocks periodically to eliminate rough or splintered edges. Use sandpaper, then apply commercial wood polish or linseed oil to provide a protective coating. Wash dirty blocks with oil soap and then scrub with a stiff brush and soap and water. Blocks should be dried thoroughly before they are polished. Think about involving children and families in some of these chores.

Hollow Blocks

Hollow blocks are made of wood and are much larger than unit blocks. The basic square is 5-1/2" x 11" x 11". A classroom set contains 48 pieces and seven different shapes, including a half-square, a double square, two lengths of flat board, and a ramp. Hollow blocks are open on the sides so that they can be carried easily. Because children typically enjoy carrying hollow blocks from one place to another, these blocks are excellent for children's large muscle development. Young children also enjoy the sense of power they feel by moving something large.

With hollow blocks, children can construct large structures—a boat, an airplane, a rocket—and then climb inside and pretend to be the captain, pilot, or astronaut.

Other Types of Blocks and Construction Materials

You can add other types of blocks and materials to the Block Area.

Cardboard brick blocks, best suited for young preschoolers, allow children to create large structures safely. They now come with a plastic-like coating so they can be wiped clean with a damp sponge or cloth. While not as sturdy as wooden hollow blocks, a 44-piece set is inexpensive and a nice addition to the classroom inventory.

Foam blocks are quiet, safe, building materials made from foam rubber.

Large plastic blocks come in all sizes and shapes. They are colorful and sturdy.

PVC pipes are the large white plastic tubes you can get in hardware stores. If you purchase the connector pieces, children can build large structures. They are great for outdoors or a large open area.

Props and Accessories

Including props and accessories in the Block Area encourages children to extend their block play into dramatic play. Group props by category (e.g., people, animals, cars, traffic signs) and keep them in labeled containers.

In addition to the basic props, you can add new materials throughout the year to inspire children's creativity. Here are some suggestions:

Including props and accessories in the Block Area encourages children to extend their block play into dramatic play.

- a dollhouse with furniture in small containers
- multi-ethnic wooden figures
- traffic signs, gas pumps
- telephone wire
- paper towel rolls
- thin pieces of rubber tubing
- paper, markers, and scissors
- popsicle sticks
- hats (construction worker, police, firefighter)
- tiles, linoleum squares, rugs
- pulleys and string
- toy carpentry tools
- vinyl rain gutters

- books, magazines, or postcards with pictures of buildings, roads, bridges
- floor map of city
- castle blocks
- shells and pebbles
- cardboard boxes and shoeboxes
- play money
- large fabric scraps
- logos from local businesses
- driftwood or small logs
- styrofoam or cardboard packaging materials
- old blueprints

Displaying Blocks and Props

Blocks should be stored on low shelves and grouped by size and shape so children can find what they want easily and return them when they have finished. In this way, cleanup becomes a sorting and matching game, not just a task children have to complete before they can go on to the next activity.

Solid-colored Contact paper is ideal for indicating the place for each block shape. You can trace the shape of the block on the back, cut it out, and place it directly on the shelf. Labels for long blocks should be placed lengthwise on the shelves starting in the left-hand corner (to reinforce the concept that we read from left to right). For blocks that stand up, such as arches, place the label behind the blocks on the back of the shelf.

Props should be organized and labeled as well. Larger props such as trucks can be placed on the shelf, but those with many pieces are best stored in containers with picture and word labels. Be sure to include paper and markers, either in the area or easily accessible, so children can make signs or blueprints, or draw a picture of what they have built.

Finding space for hollow blocks can often be a challenge when space is limited. Some teachers close off another area for a day or two to make room for hollow block play, or keep hollow blocks stacked in a hallway where children can use them as long as they can be supervised. (Be sure to check any fire regulations that may apply.) Another alternative is to keep hollow blocks stored in a protected shed outdoors, perhaps on a cart so they can be moved easily to a building area.

Cleanup— A Special Challenge

Cleanup takes place both during and at the end of choice time. When children leave the area to go to another activity, they should put away any blocks they have used, unless they are part of a construction they are leaving up. If children don't follow this rule, cleanup can seem like an overwhelming task. Because cleaning up blocks presents a special challenge, teachers have to be flexible and get more involved.

Block Area Clean-Up Suggestions

Give children a five-minute warning that clean-up time is coming. If necessary, tell each child individually how much time is left: "You have enough time to finish the road."

Allow extra time for cleanup so children don't feel quite as rushed. If you help children get started, the task usually becomes more manageable.

Let children continue working if they are truly engrossed in block play. Children appreciate having their work respected in this way and will learn that everyone gets the privilege when it is needed.

Help children get started. Remind them that the shapes on the shelves tell them where the blocks go. Assign each child a shape or prop to put away. After doing this for several days, the children should be able to organize the task on their own.

Cleanup is more fun if you make it into a game. Here are some examples:

- Give each child a "ticket" with a block shape on it. Children put away all blocks that match that shape.

- Tell children, "Bring all the blocks to me that look like this one." As they bring all blocks of one shape, show them where on the shelf the shape belongs by having them compare the shape to the labels.

- Declare a number for the day: "Today we'll clean up the blocks by threes." Each child then collects three blocks at a time and puts them away.

When you convey respect for children's block structures and help in the cleanup, you encourage children to use blocks creatively, so they benefit from their play. The way you organize blocks and props, the space you provide for block play, and the routines for cleaning up are critically important factors in how well children use the blocks. You want to maximize children's access to these materials. In this way, the Block Area will become a vital part of your plan for children's learning.

What Children Learn in the Block Area

The Block Area offers many opportunities for learning through play. All the content areas we discussed in Chapter 3 can be explored through block play if teachers consciously think about each of the components of literacy, math, science, social studies, the arts, and technology. Here are some examples of what you do to support children's learning with blocks.

Literacy

Expand children's **vocabulary and language** by talking about their buildings. Introduce new words (e.g., front-end loader, cylinder, arch) as they use blocks and props. Invite children to talk about their work (e.g., "Tell me about your building." "Where do your cars go when they run out of gas?").

Promote **understanding of books and other texts** by displaying books in the Block Area related to children's interests and constructions. Help children find books to answer their questions (e.g., a book on bridges, farms, or how to build a house).

Teach children about **print and letters and words** by placing writing tools and paper in the Block Area and encouraging children to make signs for the buildings. Display pictures and labels with words and include props such as traffic signs.

Mathematics

Teach **number concepts** by suggesting that children put away blocks in sets ("Everyone take three blocks at a time to put away"). Ask number questions ("How many square blocks would you need to make one as long as this double-unit block?" "How could you divide up the ramps so each of you has the same number?").

Encourage children to explore **patterns and relationships** by pointing out patterns children have made in their constructions ("Look how balanced your fence is. It goes tall, short, tall, short, and just keeps on going."). Suggest that children draw a picture of their block design.

Emphasize concepts about **geometry and spatial sense** by organizing blocks by size and shape on the shelf and making a label for each shape. Teach children the names of block shapes (e.g., triangles, squares, rectangles, cylinders). Talk about positions in space (e.g., over, under, next to, beside, through, below, inside, on top of).

Nurture children's interest in **measurement** by offering materials such as string and rulers so children can measure their buildings.

Science

Encourage children to explore **physical science** by providing balance scales, pulleys, mirrors, and pipes. Take an interest in children's explorations of blocks (e.g., how smooth they are, how heavy, which ones stand up best).

Expand children's knowledge of **life science** by adding plastic or wooden animals so children can build animal homes such as farms, zoos, caves, or cages. Provide artificial plants and flowers to encourage children to create different animal habitats.

Promote understanding of the **earth and environment** by providing telephone wires and pipes as props for building and talking about how electricity and water get into buildings. Include natural materials such as rocks, acorns, shells, pinecones, and twigs to use in buildings.

Social Studies

Encourage learning about **spaces and geography** by talking about roads children are making and where they go. Display maps and help children to figure out how to reproduce their neighborhood with blocks.

Explore concepts related to **people and how they live** by learning about different stores and jobs in the neighborhood. Provide props that show people engaged in a range of jobs. Display books and pictures about how people live and work and talk with children about them.

The Arts

Promote **drama** skills by encouraging children to use block structures as the setting for dramatic play. Provide props such as hats, empty food containers, or a steering wheel to use with hollow blocks.

Nurture the **visual arts** by allowing time for children to create original designs and structures with blocks. Suggest that children draw pictures of their structures as a way of preserving them.

Technology

Help children explore **basic operations and concepts** by including ramps, wheels, and pulleys. Talk with children about what makes a building stable.

Provide **technology tools** for children to use to take pictures of block structures and display them. Help children to create building plans on the computer that they can recreate in the Block Area.

As you learn more about each of the components of the content areas we described in Chapter 3, you will find more ways to extend children's learning as they play with blocks.

The Teacher's Role

Blocks have the potential for stimulating a broad range of creative, imaginative, constructive play, from arranging simple designs to building actual representations of such complex structures as bridges, skyscrapers, and whole neighborhoods. As in all interest areas, your involvement in children's play is what makes block play meaningful. Caroline Pratt, the educator who designed unit blocks in the early 1900s, cautioned that blocks will "simply remain pieces of wood unless they are infused with information gleaned from experience" (Windsor, 1996, p. 4). Children benefit the most from their play with blocks when teachers help them to organize and express their ideas.

The first step is to observe what children do so you can determine how best to respond to each child. You use a variety of teaching strategies as you interact with children to support their learning.

Observing and Responding to Individual Children

You are likely to see children playing with blocks in a variety of ways, some more advanced and productive than others. This is because children's use of blocks goes through a series of predictable stages and children progress through these stages at different rates. A child first using blocks is likely to carry them around and manipulate them but not use them to construct anything. An experienced block builder may build an intricate tower or an elaborate design. Each child is exhibiting behaviors appropriate to his or her current stage of development.

Stages of Block Play

Understanding the stages of block play gives you realistic expectations of what children do as they carry, stack, manipulate, and build with blocks. Watch children as they play and build and soon you will be able to identify the four stages in children's use of blocks. This knowledge will guide you in knowing how to help children advance to a higher stage of block building so they get the full benefit of playing with blocks.

Stage I: Carrying Blocks

Young children who haven't played with blocks before are likely to carry them around or pile them in a truck and transport them. At this point, children are interested in learning about blocks—how heavy they are, what they feel like, and how many can be carried at once. By experimenting with blocks, children begin to learn their properties and gain an understanding of what they can and cannot do with blocks.

Stage II: Piling Blocks and Making Roads

Children in Stage II continue to explore the properties of blocks and how they can be used. They make towers by piling blocks on top of each other and discover what different arrangements look like as they place blocks on the floor.

At this stage children also begin to use their imagination and apply important cognitive skills. To young builders, flat rows of blocks on the floor typically suggest a road. They use props such as cars and trucks if they are available to elaborate on their constructions. Making roads during Stage II marks the transition from simple piling to using blocks to make actual constructions. Children who have been building roads find they can use roads to link towers. This discovery leads to an active stage of experimentation and problem solving.

Stage III: Connecting Blocks to Create Structures

In Stage III children use their experience with blocks to expand their construction techniques.

Typical techniques used by children in Stage III are the following:

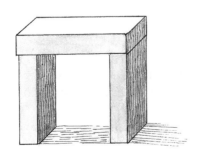

Bridging. To make a bridge, children set up two blocks, leave a space between them, and connect the two blocks with another block. Like enclosures, bridges first begin as an experiment in construction and later are used for dramatic play. When children make bridges, they practice balance, explore spatial relationships, and improve their eye-hand coordination.

Making enclosures. Children put blocks together to enclose a space. At first, simply making the enclosure is a satisfying experience. Later, the enclosure may be used for dramatic play with zoo or farm animals. (Making enclosures also helps children think about mathematical concepts, particularly area and geometry.)

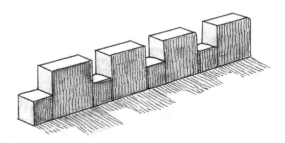

Designs. Children are fascinated with symmetry, balance, and patterns and use blocks to form decorative patterns and symmetrical layouts. Once they have combined a few blocks in a design, they may continue the same pattern until their supply of blocks runs out, or they may try variations. Blocks become an art medium for children to express their creative ideas.

Stage IV: Making Elaborate Constructions

Experienced builders are able to put blocks together with dexterity and skill. Children learn to adapt to changes in their building area by curving structures and by building them above, around, or over obstacles. Children in Stage IV often create artistic and complex structures.

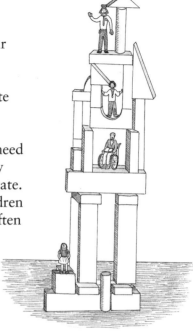

During this stage of block play, children need a variety of block sizes and shapes so they can make their constructions more elaborate. Another hallmark of Stage IV is that children use them as a setting for dramatic play, often labeling them and even asking for signs so everyone will know what they built.

Responding to Each Child

In observing children's individual growth, the stages we described provide a way for you to evaluate children's experiences with blocks. You can use the information you gather to decide whether a child needs more time to practice a particular stage, or should be helped to move to the next stage. While observing a child, notice

- what stage of block building the child has achieved

- if the child is aware of different shapes and sizes and able to return blocks to their proper place

- whether the child talks about structures and responds to questions

- what props and materials the child uses in building

Your observations will help you plan experiences to facilitate further learning. You may find, for example, that a child needs more encouragement to use blocks or an idea to get her started.

To make the best use of your observations, keep *The Creative Curriculum Developmental Continuum* in mind as you observe children and reflect on what you learned. When teachers take the time to consider what their observations tell them about a child, their responses are more likely to be effective in promoting learning. The chart on the next page gives examples of how this process works in the Block Area.

Observation	Reflection	Response
Alexa builds a tall structure with a road around it and moves toy cars along the road, parking them by the building. (Stage IV)	She uses blocks to build a construction that represents something specific. *(Objective 37, Makes and interprets representations)* She knows how to use objects in pretend play. *(Objective 36, Makes believe with objects)* How can I encourage her to engage in elaborate and sustained dramatic play? *(Objective 24, Shows persistence in approaching tasks)*	Say, "I see you have some cars parked near your building. Is that a parking lot? How do people know where to park?" Offer new materials such as people figures and traffic signs. Encourage her to involve other children: "I wonder if Juwan could build a gas station in case your cars run out of gas."
Leo stands the double unit blocks on end, one on top of the other, and they fall down. He tries this four times with the same result. (Stage II)	He continues to work on a task even when encountering difficulties. *(Objective 24, Shows persistence in approaching tasks)* He notices the problem but doesn't seem to understand what is causing it. *(Objective 25, Explores cause and effect)* How can I help him figure out what to do to solve the problem?	Ask, "What do you think is causing the blocks to fall down?" Offer a suggestion: "I wonder how you could make the bottom of your building more sturdy." Provide hard surfaces for building (e.g., cardboard, linoleum tile). "Let's see what happens if you build on this instead of the rug."
Carlos places blocks around a fire engine and explains to another child, "This is a fire station. Don't you see the fire engine parked inside?" (Stage III)	He plays cooperatively with one child. *(Objective 10, Plays well with other children)* He uses longer sentences to communicate. *(Objective 39, Expresses self using words and expanded sentences)* How can I help him elaborate on his construction and involve other children?	Offer additional props such as fire trucks, people figures, child-size firefighter hats, toy ambulance, and books on firefighters. Make a suggestion: "Tell us about your fire station. Who works there and how do they know when there is a fire?"
Janelle puts blocks away, sorting some but not all correctly.	She takes responsibility for cleaning up. *(Objective 7, Respects and cares for classroom environment and materials)* She participates in activities like cleanup. *(Objective 8, Follows classroom routines)* She has beginning skills in sorting and classifying. *(Objective 27, Classifies objects)* Have I organized the arrangement of blocks, labeled the shelves, and explained the organization to the children?	Clearly label all the blocks and talk to the children about how they are arranged and why. Incorporate some math learning by making a suggestion: "Let's put away all the triangle blocks first. Can you find all the blocks that look like this?"

Interacting With Children in the Block Area

There is no right or wrong way to build with blocks—children can create whatever they want. Sometimes children start with an idea of what they want to make; at other times three-dimensional designs grow as children place blocks together randomly or in patterns. When children's block structures begin to resemble things they have seen, they will start to name what they build—a road, a farm, or spaceship—and use them in dramatic play.

Your observations will help you determine when to intervene and what to say to support children's learning.

Talking With Children About Their Structures

One of the most effective ways to reinforce children's block play is to talk to them about their structures. This suggestion may sound easier than it actually is, especially when children are just beginning to explore blocks and their constructions are minimal. For example, talking to a child about the construction shown below might prove challenging for many teachers.

The easiest response to this builder would be to say, "That's a nice building" or "Good job." These statements say nothing at all about what the child did, nor do they give the child a chance to tell you something about the arrangement of the blocks. They also imply that the goal is to make something you think is "nice" or "good."

The key to talking to children about their block play is to use statements that describe what a child has done, or to ask open-ended questions that encourage children to talk about their work. This technique is also helpful for children who have difficulty expressing themselves and may be unable, at least in the beginning, to describe what they have built.

What you say, of course, will depend on what the child has created. Here are the types of positive and constructive comments you might make about a child's work.

Choice of blocks: *You found out that two of these blocks make one long block.*

The arrangement: *You used four blocks to make a big square.*

The number used: *You used more than ten blocks to make the road.*

The similarity: *All the blocks in your road are exactly the same size.*

Noteworthy designs: *Your building is as tall as the shelf. Those long blocks are holding up the short ones. It took careful work to be sure the blocks wouldn't fall.*

Descriptions such as these validate the importance of children's work, build concepts in math, and expand their vocabularies. Below are two sample buildings and some possible comments a teacher might make to reinforce the child's work:

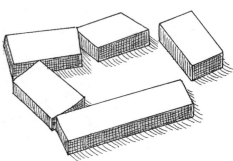

I see you used one block that is longer than the others.

Look, your blocks make a space in the middle.

All of your blocks except one are touching.

You used five blocks. You made the whole building with just five blocks.

All your blocks are rectangles, but they're not all the same size.

Similarly, for the block structure pictured to the left, you might make the following comments:

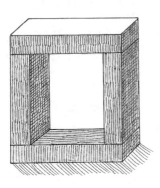

You made the top block balance. I bet that wasn't easy.

Some of your blocks lie down and some stand up.

If I get down on my knees, I can look through it.

You had to be very careful when you made this building.

Comments such as these serve several purposes. First, these types of comments focus on the process of building rather than emphasizing a final product as the major goal in building. They demonstrate that you value what the child has done and encourage the child to experiment with new ideas and materials and to learn from mistakes. In addition, you build verbal skill by introducing specific words to describe what the child did. By repeatedly hearing words such as *under*, *on top of*, *beneath*, *through*, *less than*, and *more than*, children learn their meaning. They begin to use these words themselves, thus enlarging their vocabularies which helps them progress as readers.

Supporting Children in Moving to the Next Stage

Often children need a teacher's help to move on to the next stage of building and to expand their ideas. However, determining when to intervene is not always easy. You may wonder what to do, for instance, if a child simply piles up blocks day after day. Should you step in and help the child to move to the next developmental stage?

Keep in mind that piling up blocks isn't just busywork; it's an important and natural stage in block building. Children gain understanding and mastery by repeated interactions with materials, and they gain self-confidence when they have time to practice their new skills.

Most children will move on to the next stage when they are ready, often by observing how other children build with blocks. However, if a child truly seems to need help or encouragement to move on, try the following suggestions:

Ways to Support Children

Get down on the floor with a child who is frustrated over a problem and offer support in solving the problem. For example, you might say, "Let's see if we can find another way to make those blocks stand up."

Help the child solve a problem. For example, ask a leading question: "Do you think another block shape might work there?"

Display and discuss pictures of constructions to inspire a child who has built the same construction every day for a week.

Add new accessories and props to expand construction ideas.

Ask questions about the type of structure and what might belong with it. For instance, you might ask: "Who can live in that building?" or "How will people get to that building?"

Sometimes just a word of encouragement or a small suggestion can inspire a child. Other times more is needed. Here is an example that illustrates how a teacher's support encourages a child to recall her experiences and expand her work with blocks. This is known as scaffolding children's learning.

Four-year-old Tasheen began by getting the basket of zoo animals and some unit and double-unit blocks. She built simple enclosures and put the animals inside.

At this point, Mr. Alvarez joined her, and the following dialogue took place:

> **Mr. Alvarez:** *Tell me about these animals.*
>
> **Tasheen:** *They're at the zoo.*
>
> **Mr. Alvarez:** *Have you been to the zoo?*
>
> **Tasheen:** *Yes.*
>
> **Mr. Alvarez:** *What did you see at the zoo? What kinds of buildings do they have?*
>
> **Tasheen:** *Cages for the animals—where they can go inside and outside.*
>
> **Mr. Alvarez:** *It looks like you've made an outside yard for the giraffe and the elephant. Do they have an inside house, too?*
>
> **Tasheen:** *Yes. [She starts to make one.]*

When Mr. Alvarez returned five minutes later, Tasheen had constructed a round house with a roof and an outdoor enclosure that in fact resembled the elephant/giraffe house at the local zoo.

Tasheen was able to remember what the cages looked like because she had been to the zoo. If she hadn't had any ideas from her own experience, Mr. Alvarez could have offered a book to look through. Realizing that Tasheen could extend her building even more, he asked other questions:

Mr. Alvarez:	*Did you see any people at the zoo?*
Tasheen:	*Of course. Mommies and Daddies and kids. [She goes to the block accessories and takes four wooden block figures, which she lines up in front of the building.]*
Mr. Alvarez:	*How will people know what this building is?*
Tasheen:	*It would say "elephant house."*
Mr. Alvarez:	*I have some paper and crayons here. Would you like to make a sign?*
Tasheen:	*Yes. It should say "elephant house."*
Mr. Alvarez:	*Do you want to make the sign?*
Tasheen:	*No, you write "elephant house." [Mr. Alvarez makes the sign and Tasheen tapes it on the building.]*

Mr. Alvarez:	*How do people get to the zoo from their homes?*
Tasheen:	*They drive in cars.*
Mr. Alvarez:	*And where do they park their cars while they walk around to see the animals?*
Tasheen:	*There's a parking lot and it costs a dollar to park there.*
Mr. Alvarez:	*Maybe you could make a parking lot for your visitors.*

Mr. Alvarez left Tasheen for a short while. When he returned, Tasheen had added walkways around the building and a parking area with cars.

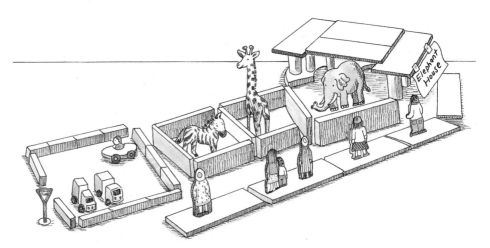

By talking with Tasheen about visitors and by naming the buildings, Mr. Alvarez encouraged her to think about the zoo from several perspectives—who comes to visit the zoo, how they come, where they walk, and where else they go. This example shows how a teacher supported child-initiated learning and extended Tasheen's block play in the following ways:

- observing what she did

- asking questions to help her recall experiences

- listening to what she said

- making suggestions based on her experiences

- supplying props and making signs

To encourage this type of more extensive block building, we suggest that you leave block structures standing for a day or two so that the children can continue their play. You might say: "I know you want to keep working on your apartment house, but it's time to clean up. Why don't you just put away the blocks you haven't used and we can leave the building up. Then you can work on it again tomorrow (or this afternoon)." Keep a "Do not knock down" sign available for children's use. By actively participating with children in the Block Area, teachers can effectively promote the use of blocks and props as valuable learning materials.

Frequently Asked Questions About Blocks

Some children never use the blocks. What should I do?

First ask yourself why a child may avoid the Block Area. Is the child generally afraid to try new things? Uncomfortable with noisy activities? One way of easing a reluctant child into the Block Area is to invite that child to join you playing with blocks. Choose a time when only a few children are in the area, sit down on the floor, and begin building.

In some classrooms the boys establish the Block Area as "boys only" territory. They tell the girls in words and actions that they aren't welcome. Moreover, girls may get the message from society that construction work is primarily for men, so they feel that they don't belong in the Block Area. As a result, they lack experience with blocks and may be at an earlier developmental stage of building than boys of the same age.

If you find that girls tend to avoid the Block Area, you may need to make a concerted effort. From the very beginning of the year, convey the message, "In our class, everyone can build with blocks." Make a point to display pictures of female construction workers or read a book at story time about female builders. (Try *Mothers Can Do Anything* by Joe Lasker, *Mommies at Work* by Eve Merriam, or *Joshua's Day* by Sandra Lucas Surowiecki and Patricia Riley Lenthall.) Adding dollhouse furniture and plastic animals to the area often encourages more girls to start building.

Should I allow children to bring materials from other areas (e.g., table blocks, telephones, hats, pinecones) into the Block Area?

Children tend to do this when they want to decorate their buildings or use them as settings for dramatic play. Since you want to encourage children to create elaborate buildings and to engage in sociodramatic play, we recommend allowing them to borrow materials. This is one reason for locating the Block Area near the Dramatic Play Area. Bringing materials from other areas should not be a problem as long as children understand that when no longer needed, materials go back to where they are stored.

Having a place for everything in the classroom makes it easier to enforce this rule. However, you may want to put some limits on what materials can be brought to the Block Area. For example, it is not a good idea to allow puzzle pieces to be moved from place to place in the classroom. A puzzle with missing pieces is no longer a satisfying toy.

Children don't want to spend time building because they know they have to take it down at clean-up time. What should I do?

Sometimes when children have made a building that is very special to them, it's difficult for them to dismantle it when it's time to clean up. If possible, try to leave buildings up overnight or even for a week. This allows children to work on a construction over time, which leads to more elaborate building and, often, to dramatic play.

If this is not possible in your room, offer to take a picture of the building so children can preserve their work in photos. These pictures can be displayed in the Block Area, which often encourages children to create, reproduce, and build more complex structures. Taking pictures of a child's work over a period of time creates a visual record of the child's progress to include in the portfolio. Another alternative is to invite children to make a drawing of their building and display it on the wall.

How high should children be allowed to build?

There is something very intriguing and empowering about building tall structures. The issue, of course, is safety. Therefore, we recommend developing classroom rules about tall buildings. For hollow blocks, a good rule is not to build higher than four blocks tall. For unit blocks, you will have to use your best judgment. Some teachers establish the rule that structures cannot be taller than the builder. Talk with children about making their constructions strong so they are less likely to topple over, building away from other buildings and from traffic, and not knocking blocks down.

Should I intervene when children use blocks as guns?

Given the increasing level of violence in children's lives, we suggest making the classroom a "gun-free zone." Children make guns when they can't think of more creative things to do with blocks. Just saying "no gun building" does not solve the problem. Going into the Block Area and helping children come up with other construction ideas has a more lasting effect. Having pictures around the wall of constructions in the community helps. Take photos of children's work and display them around the area to inspire children.

A LETTER TO FAMILIES ABOUT BLOCK PLAY

Dear Families,

The hardwood unit blocks you see in our classroom are one of the most valuable learning materials we have. They come in exact sizes and shapes. For this reason when children build with blocks they learn math concepts such as the number of blocks that fill a certain space. They compare the height of their buildings and learn about geometric shapes (triangles, squares, and rectangles). When they lift, shove, stack, and move blocks, they explore weight and size. Each time they use blocks, children are making decisions about how to build a structure or solve a construction problem.

Children often use blocks to recreate the world around them—a road, a house, the zoo. They work together and learn to cooperate and make friends. We encourage children to talk about what they are doing to promote language development. We also talk with children and ask questions to expand on their block play. For example, we might say:

> *I see you built a tall apartment house. How do the people get to their floor?*
>
> *Where do people park their cars when they come to visit the shopping center?*
>
> *Would you like to make a sign for your building?*

These questions and comments make children more aware of what they are doing and encourage them to try out new ideas.

What You Can Do at Home

You can encourage your child to learn through block play by taking an interest in what he or she does at our program. Come spend time in our Block Area to see your child building and caring for blocks. When you take a walk in your neighborhood, point out roads and interesting buildings. You may want to purchase table blocks, colored wooden cube blocks, or cardboard brick blocks to have at home. You can also make a set out of milk cartons, which come in different sizes. Store them in shoe boxes or plastic tubs and containers and put a picture and written label on the container so your child knows where these materials belong.

Identify a place where your child can build and play with the blocks safely. Props such as clothespins, small plastic animals, and cars and trucks will extend your child's play and inspire new ideas. The settings your child creates can be used for pretend play as well.

inside this chapter

271 How Dramatic Play Promotes Development
272 Connecting Dramatic Play With Curriculum Objectives

274 Creating an Environment for Dramatic Play
275 Selecting and Displaying Materials
276 Creating New Settings for Dramatic Play

280 What Children Learn in the Dramatic Play Area

282 The Teacher's Role
282 Observing and Responding to Individual Children
287 Interacting With Children During Dramatic Play
291 Frequently Asked Questions About Dramatic Play

293 A Letter to Families About Dramatic Play

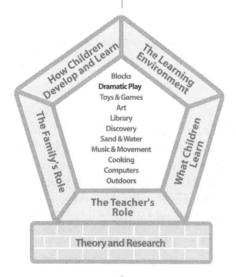

Dramatic Play

How Dramatic Play Promotes Development

Dramatic play is central to children's healthy development and learning during the preschool years. For this reason, every *Creative Curriculum* classroom includes an area designed to inspire creative and imaginative play. In the Dramatic Play Area, children break through the restrictions of reality. They pretend to be someone or something different from themselves and make up situations and actions that go along with the role they choose. When children engage in dramatic play they deepen their understanding of the world and develop skills that will serve them throughout their lives.

Social/emotional development. To engage in dramatic play with others, children have to negotiate roles, agree on a topic, and cooperate to portray different situations. They recreate life experiences and try to cope with their fears by acting out roles and situations that worry them. For example, a child who anticipates going to the hospital for an operation can pretend to be the doctor. By assuming this role, the child can switch from feeling out of control to being in charge. Research shows that children who engage in dramatic play tend to demonstrate more empathy toward others because they have tried out being someone else for a while. They have the skills to cooperate with peers, control impulses, and are less aggressive than children who do not engage in this type of play (Smilansky, 1990).

Physical development. Children develop small muscle skills when they button and snap dress-up clothes and dress the dolls. They practice hand-eye coordination and visual discrimination skills when they put away props and materials.

Cognitive development. When they pretend, children create pictures in their minds about past experiences and the situations they imagine. These images are a form of abstract thinking. When children set the table for a meal for two or use play money to purchase food at their grocery store, they explore math concepts. They also learn from one another as they share ideas and solve problems together.

Language development. To engage with others in dramatic play, children use language to explain what they are doing and ask and answer questions. They choose the language that fits the role they have selected. They use reading and writing skills when literacy props are included in the Dramatic Play Area.

Connecting Dramatic Play With Curriculum Objectives

Your familiarity with the *Creative Curriculum* goals and objectives will help you identify what children are learning as they play. Using the *Developmental Continuum*, you can pinpoint exactly what each child can do and how to support the child in moving to the next step. In the chart below, we offer some examples of what children might do or say that would indicate their developmental progress on selected objectives.

Selected Curriculum Objectives	What a Child Might Do in the Dramatic Play Area
Social/Emotional Development	
1. Shows ability to adjust to new situations	Replays scenes of a mother leaving her baby to go to work to gain control of fears about separation.
4. Stands up for rights	Says, "That's not fair. You always get to be the mommy. I want a turn too."
7. Respects and cares for classroom environment and materials	Hangs dress-up clothes before leaving area, matching each piece with its picture and word label.
10. Plays well with other children	Invites another child to join him and asks, "Do you want to be the Daddy?"
11. Recognizes the feelings of others and responds appropriately	Comforts another child and says, "Sure, you can have a turn."
12. Shares and respects the rights of others	Sorts out the play money so everyone gets some to use in their store.
13. Uses thinking skills to resolve conflicts	Says, "Okay, we can both be firefighters. I'll drive the truck and you hold the hose."
Physical Development	
19. Strengthens and controls small muscles in hands	Buttons and snaps dress-up clothes and helps another child.
20. Coordinates eye-hand movement	Carefully pours water from a pitcher into teacups, without spilling.
21. Uses tools for writing and drawing	Writes shopping list before going to the grocery store to shop.

Selected Curriculum Objectives	What a Child Might Do in the Dramatic Play Area
Cognitive Development	
23. Approaches problems flexibly	Gets gray and green construction paper, markers, and scissors to make coins and dollar bills for the shoe store.
26. Applies knowledge or experience to a new context	Says, "When you give a shot, first you have to get some cotton and rub the arm clean."
31. Shows awareness of time concepts and sequence	Looks on the calendar and says, "What day do you want to come see the doctor?"
33. Uses one-to-one correspondence	Sets the table for four people, putting a spoon and plate at each chair.
34. Uses numbers and counting	Says, "We need four cups. Look, one, two, three, four chairs."
35. Takes on pretend roles and situations	Puts on a firefighter's hat and says, "I'm the fire chief. Call me if you have a fire at the house."
36. Makes believe with objects	Picks up a block and says, "Here's your hamburger. Do you want some ketchup?"
37. Makes and interprets representations	Gets a cardboard box, draws windows on each side, and announces, "Here's a house for the dog."
Language Development	
39. Expresses self using words and expanded sentences	Gives out menus and says, "Today we have meatballs and spaghetti. Only four dollars. Who wants it?"
41. Answers questions	Says, "I'm the bus driver. I'll get the steering wheel," when asked whom he wants to be.
42. Asks questions	Says, "Can I use the suitcase now? I'm going on a trip."
43. Actively participates in conversations	Asks another child, "What would you like to eat? I'm going to the store to buy dinner."
46. Demonstrates knowledge of the alphabet	Points to K on cereal box and says, "My name starts the same way."
49. Understands the purpose of writing	Takes out a pad and writes a prescription for the patient, saying, "Here. Take this to the drugstore and get some pills."
50. Writes letters and words	Copies words from coupons to make a list of foods to buy at the store.

Creating an Environment for Dramatic Play

Think of the Dramatic Play Area as a stage. Children can enter the area and immediately take on a role and pretend. Initially it is set up to look like a home with props and furniture that represent a kitchen and perhaps a bedroom and living room. This is because children are most familiar with themes related to family life. All children share common experiences such as taking care of babies, cooking and serving food, and talking on the telephone. Before long, children extend these themes to situations like shopping at the grocery store, and going to the doctor, the post office, and more. To maintain children's interest and support them in extending their ideas, teachers regularly change the props and enhance the setting to incorporate new experiences and interests of the children.

The area includes a home setting and a small grocery store. Children can extend their play to include going shopping for food (social studies).

Literacy materials such as magazines, signs, food boxes, telephones, paper, and writing tools invite children to incorporate reading and writing into their play.

Children explore math concepts by setting the table, using the cash register with play money, and talking about time.

Setting up the Dramatic Play Area	Suggested Materials
Location: Near the Block Area so materials can be shared and sociodramatic play encouraged Defined by walls, shelves, and furniture to create a secluded area and separate spaces—kitchen, living room, bedroom **Set up:** Familiar furniture: doll bed, child-size wooden stove, refrigerator, sink, chest of drawers, table and chairs, small couch, sink, ironing board and iron, doll carriage or stroller, high chair, full-length mirror Flexible furniture that can be used to create new settings (e.g., cartons, a puppet theater that can be converted to a store)	Dress-up clothes for men and women, hung on low hooks, and accessories like hats, shoes, boas, jewelry Pots, pans, dishes, and other kitchen equipment relevant to different cultures, stored on shelves and/or hung on pegboard Dolls representing different ethnic groups with clothes and blankets Child-size broom and mop Telephones Pocketbooks/briefcases Plastic food, empty food boxes relevant to different cultures Calendars, memo pads, address book, phone book, pencils, cookbooks, message board Home-like touches such as curtains, a tablecloth, photographs, a small rug, a plant

Selecting and Displaying Materials

In selecting materials and props for the Dramatic Play Area, consider the developmental abilities of the children in your classroom and what will be most familiar to them. While too many props can be overwhelming, you will find that appropriate and interesting materials stimulate imaginative and constructive play.

Children at a beginning stage of dramatic play depend on concrete and realistic objects. Therefore, the younger the children, the more important it is to begin with realistic props and actual materials like pots and pans or a telephone. For older children, who are better able to rely on their imaginations in their use of props, you can provide more open-ended materials such as empty boxes, Styrofoam, and fabric scraps. As always, it's best to begin with a limited selection. More can be added as children gain the skills to use props well and care for them.

Look for props and materials that reflect the cultural and ethnic backgrounds of the children in the group.

In equipping the Dramatic Play Area, look for props and materials that reflect the cultural and ethnic backgrounds of the children in the group. You want children to receive the message that "this is just like my home." In addition, be sure to include items that traditionally are used by both men and women.

When children can easily find the props they need, less time is spent searching for materials and more time is devoted to dramatic play.

Finally, all props should be clean and safe. Children quickly lose interest in dolls that are falling apart or in dress-up clothes that cannot be tied or snapped into place. As props get broken or torn, repair or replace them.

Because there are many different kinds of props in the Dramatic Play Area, it's important to organize them. Arranging them in a logical way encourages children's creativity, enables them to work independently, and helps them to make choices. An orderly area conveys the message that this is a special place, and the items in it are to be taken care of and valued. When children can find the props they need easily, less time is spent searching for materials and more time is devoted to dramatic play.

Ways to Display Props and Materials

Use hooks, set on a board tacked to the wall or on a pegboard on the back of a shelf to hang hats, bags, and dress-up clothes.

Use a small shelf unit or chest with drawers to hold doll clothes and small dress-up items.

Provide a shoe rack or hanging shoe bag to store shoes and other small items.

Set up a pegboard with hooks to display pots, pans, and kitchen utensils.

Place a small coatrack to store hanging clothes and bags.

Hang three-tiered wire baskets from hooks to store plastic foods.

Choose plastic storage bins for costume jewelry and plastic food.

Creating New Settings for Dramatic Play

While most of the home-related props and furniture remain in the Dramatic Play Area throughout the year, you can extend children's play by incorporating new settings. Because dramatic play is one of the important ways preschool children recreate their own life experiences, this interest area is an ideal place for them to explore new ideas and concepts they are learning. The more extensive and varied their experiences, and the more adults talk with them about these experiences, the richer their dramatic play is likely to be.

For children to play together successfully, they need a common set of experiences. A study, which is a valuable way of exposing all children to information about the world around them, provides such experiences. When you then offer props related to the study topic, children have an idea of how to incorporate them into their play and use them appropriately.

As discussed in Chapter 4, study topics often emerge from children's interests. Suppose, for example, you notice that several children are talking about their experiences going to the doctor. At story time, you read a book on this topic and lead a discussion. Then you plan a trip to a clinic. To focus children's attention on what they will see, you stock the Library Area with picture books on the topic.

The day before the trip, discuss with children what they think they will see and what questions they have about the clinic. To help children recall afterward what they learned, bring a camera on the field trip and take pictures. (You also might take a few disposable cameras so children can take their own photographs. If you do this, take time beforehand to teach children how a camera works and how to take a picture.)

After the trip, display the photographs in a prominent place. At a group meeting, children talk about what they saw. They respond positively when you suggest setting up a clinic in the Dramatic Play Area. When you ask what to include, the children come up with lots of ideas:

- chairs, table, and magazines for the waiting room

- an eye chart

- prescription pads and pencils

- folders and clipboards for patients' charts

- an appointment book and a calendar

- stethoscope, blood pressure cuff, syringes (without needles), ace bandages, empty pill bottles

- cot or mat with blanket

- white shirts for nurse's cap, masks, lab coats

- flashlight

- X rays

- telephones

- dolls (for patients)

When you offer props related to the study topic, children have an idea of how to incorporate them into their play and use them appropriately.

When you use the children's suggestions to add new props to the Dramatic Play Area, children are more likely to use the materials you provide. They also begin to feel they are directing their own learning, which builds their confidence as learners.

Once you have started collecting props for different study topics, you will want a way to store them for possible future use with new groups of children, or to bring out again at another time. While you vary what you study with each new group of children, some topics come up often enough to merit keeping a box of props in storage so you don't have to start from scratch each year. Here are some examples.

Supermarket. Children often accompany their parents to buy food. Hence, the supermarket theme evolves quite naturally from the home setting. The following props and materials can be used to set up a supermarket:

- table or crates to create sections of the supermarket
- shopping baskets and/or child-size carts
- signs for different sections—meat, dairy
- empty food containers—boxes and cans with labels
- plastic food items
- paper bags for groceries
- crayons, markers, scissors, and construction paper to make signs
- stick-on price tags or stamp pads with number stamps
- cash register and tape
- paper or plastic money
- coupons and supermarket ads

Post Office. A visit to the post office can lead to a study of how mail gets from one place to another and the different jobs of people in the postal service. Props related to this topic might include the following:

- telephone books, zip code directories, sample charts from the local post office
- junk mail, letters, greeting cards
- envelopes, stationary, pencils and pens
- ink pads and stamps (e.g., first class, priority mail, next day)
- stamps (stickers) and return address labels
- scale to weigh letters and packages
- clock
- signs (e.g., Open, Closed, Stamps)

Some topics come up often enough to merit keeping a box of props in storage so you don't have to start from scratch each year.

Shoe Store. All children have had the experience of getting new shoes. They may be interested in different kinds of shoes—flip-flops, running shoes, boots, dress shoes. This interest can lead to a visit to a shoe store and then the addition of props such as the following:

- assorted old shoes and shoe boxes (labeled and priced)
- signs from a shoe store
- cash register and play money
- a shoe-shine kit with clear polish and rags
- a ruler to measure feet or a real foot measurer from a shoe store

Office. An office workplace is another natural extension of house play, particularly for children with family members who work in an office. To set up an office, include the following props:

- pads of paper, pens, and pencils
- calendars and old planners
- stapler, hole punch, paper clips, rulers
- typewriter and/or computer
- briefcases
- adding machine or calculator
- telephone and telephone books
- business cards
- ink pad and stamps

Creating new settings for dramatic play sets the stage for learning, and children learn content as they engage in dramatic play.

What Children Learn in the Dramatic Play Area

Each of the content areas described in Chapter 3 can be addressed in the Dramatic Play Area. Here are some examples of how teachers purposefully plan experiences and provide materials that involve children in learning meaningful content through their dramatic play.

Literacy

Promote **vocabulary and language** by introducing and teaching children the names of props (e.g., stethoscope, briefcase, hard hat, menu). Ask questions (e.g., "You look all dressed up. Where are you going?") and read stories on topics that children use in their dramatic play, such as buying new shoes or going to the clinic.

Encourage children to explore **print and letters and words** by placing writing tools and paper in the Dramatic Play Area (e.g., note pads, prescription pads, eye charts, posters, stationery, and envelopes). Participate in children's play to demonstrate the uses of writing. Encourage children to use writing tools and paper as part of their play. Offer props such as telephone books and empty food boxes with labels.

Promote understanding of **books and other texts** by including story books, phone books, calendars, cookbooks, newspapers, magazines, and other print materials in the Dramatic Play Area. Encourage children to use these props in their play. Read storybooks that inspire dramatic play such as *Roxaboxen* (Alice McLerran), *Miss Tizzy* (Libba Moore Gray), and *Aunt Flossie's Hats* (Elizabeth Fitzgerald Howard).

Mathematics

Guide **problem solving** by helping children to find solutions to problems they encounter (e.g., what they can use for food, how to make a balance scale, what to do if two children both want to be the doctor).

Promote understanding of **number concepts** by asking number questions (e.g., "How many plates do you need to put on the table?"). Offer props such as play money, scales, measuring tapes, cash registers, and calculators.

Encourage children's interest in **measurement** by providing props such as a foot measurer for a shoe store, sand timers, height charts, and a bathroom scale.

Science

Encourage children to explore **physical science** by providing balance scales, eggbeaters, kitchen magnets, can openers, timers, and fishing rods (without hooks).

Expand children's knowledge of **life science** by including plants in the Dramatic Play Area. Talk about what kinds of foods are good to eat. Discuss the names of pretend fruits and vegetables.

Promote understanding of the **earth and the environment** by including telescopes and thermometers. Discuss weather reports and talk about recycling.

Social Studies

Encourage learning about **spaces and geography** by including maps. Take trips to neighborhood stores and help children set up a store in the Dramatic Play Area.

Explore concepts related to **people and how they live** by providing props that encourage children to role-play family life and different kinds of jobs. Display photographs of families and community helpers.

The Arts

Encourage children to explore **drama** by teaching them the skills they need to pretend. Read familiar stories that children can act out. Provide puppets and encourage children to put on a puppet show.

Promote the **visual arts** by providing materials children need to make their own props for dramatic play, such as cardboard boxes, collage materials, construction paper, scissors, paint, and markers.

Technology

Raise children's **awareness of technology** by including old cameras, calculators, different types of phones, typewriters, and computers in the Dramatic Play Area. Talk with children about how these objects are used.

Promote understanding of **people and technology** by taking on a role and demonstrating how to use different tools in play episodes. Visit people or invite guests to your classroom who use technology in their work and encourage children to use what they learn in their dramatic play themes.

There are many ways teachers can help children to develop knowledge and skills in the different content areas through dramatic play. We expand on the teacher's role next.

The Teacher's Role

While pretend play is considered natural—something all young children do on their own—it is less common today than it was in the past. Teachers in all types of settings are finding that young children do not necessarily engage in dramatic play on an advanced level. Because the ability to engage in and sustain imaginative play is so central to children's development—particularly cognitive and social/emotional development—we recommend that teachers take an active role in teaching the skills to make-believe. Your role, as in all interest areas, is to observe what children do and individualize your response. Based on what you learn, you can interact with children and support their play.

Observing and Responding to Individual Children

To get the most from their play, children need specific skills and a range of experiences to give them ideas for make-believe. It is therefore useful to familiarize yourself with the six skills children use to pretend at a high level. Children who have and use all six skills are engaging in what Sara Smilansky calls "socio-dramatic play." Here are the six skills that she identifies (Smilansky & Shefatya, 1990).

Role-play. Children have to be able to pretend to be someone or something else and mimic typical behaviors and verbal expressions. At a beginning level of role-play, children simply imitate one or two actions of familiar people or animals: a mommy feeding her baby or a dog eating out of a dog dish. On an advanced level, children think of many different actions relevant to their chosen role and expand the types of roles they play.

Use of props. Children elaborate their role-play by incorporating objects into their make-believe. At a beginning level, they rely on real or realistic objects. Then they use objects to represent a prop (e.g., a paper plate for a steering wheel). Children at the advanced level of pretend ability can substitute words and actions for real objects (e.g., they use hands in circular motion for a steering wheel).

Make-believe. In early dramatic play, children imitate actions they have seen others do, such as picking up a toy phone and talking on it. At a higher level, they are able to use words to describe and then re-enact real-life actions or events. For example, a child might point to the table and say, "I'm the doctor. Pretend this is my office. You be the Mommy and bring your baby for a checkup." Children may also engage in fantasy—enacting situations that aren't drawn from real life such as slaying dragons or battling monsters.

Length of time. At first their involvement in dramatic play may just last a few minutes before children move on to something else. They are not able to sustain their play. As children become more adept at role-playing, they can remain in play episodes for increasing amounts of time.

Interaction. Notice when and why children interact with one another in the Dramatic Play Area. At an early stage, several children may be pretending at the same time but not interacting with each other except if they need a prop someone else is using. At a more advanced level, children have agreed on what roles they are playing and they relate to one another from the perspective of their chosen role.

Verbal communication. Listen to what children say when they are engaged in dramatic play. If they are talking from the perspective of the role they are playing, and communicating with others about the make-believe situation, they are playing at a high level.

Knowing these skills gives you a framework for observing children's play and deciding when and how to intervene. The following chart shows the progression from a beginning level of simple dramatic play to the more advanced level of sociodramatic play for each of the six essential skills.

Knowing the six skills gives you a framework for observing children's play and deciding when and how to intervene.

Levels of Dramatic Play

Dramatic Play Skills	Beginning Level	Advanced Level
Role-Play		
Role Chosen	Role relates to child's attempts to understand the familiar world (e.g., mommy, daddy, baby, animals)	Child selects roles related to the outside world (e.g., firefighter, police officer, doctor)
How Child Plays Role	Child imitates one or two aspects of role (e.g., child announces, "I'm the mommy," rocks the baby, and holds a bottle)	Child expands concepts of role (e.g., child says, "I'm the mommy," feeds the baby, goes to a meeting, prepares dinner, reads the newspaper, goes to work, talks on the phone, etc.)
Use of Props		
Type of Prop Needed	Child uses real object or replica of object (e.g., real or toy phone)	Child uses any object as prop (e.g., block for phone) or holds hand to ear and pretends it's a telephone
How Child Uses Prop	Child enjoys physically playing with objects (e.g., banging receiver of phone, dialing)	Prop is used as part of play episode (e.g., child calls a doctor on phone because baby is sick)
Make-Believe	Child imitates simple actions of adult (e.g., moves iron back and forth on ironing board, holds phone receiver to ear)	Child's actions are part of a play episode of make-believe (e.g., "I'm ironing this dress now so I can wear it for the party tonight")
Length of Time	Involvement in play is fleeting (e.g., child enters area, plays with doll, puts on hat, and leaves area)	Child is engaged in dramatic play for more than 10 minutes (e.g., child dresses up as a doctor, examines a "patient," writes a prescription, and asks, "Who's next?")
Interaction	Solitary play (e.g., child pretends to be a mommy rocking a baby, paying no attention to what others are doing) Functional cooperation (e.g., child agrees to take turns using the steering wheel)	Cooperative effort (e.g., child agrees to be a passenger on a bus, gives the driver a ticket, and asks for change)
Verbal Communication	Verbalization centers around the use of toys (e.g., "Bring me that phone" or "I had the carriage first")	Dialogue about play theme—constant chatter about roles children are playing (e.g., restaurant scene: "What do you want to eat?" "Do you have hamburgers?" "Yup. We have hamburgers, french fries, and cokes."

Responding to Each Child

The six skills children use to engage in dramatic play provide a focus for observing children's play and determining the type of intervention that will be most effective with each child. Keeping these skills in mind, notice whether a child

- selects the same role day after day, or experiments with different roles and thinks of many different aspects of the role

- uses props to make believe, or uses movements and/or words to substitute for real objects (such as pretending to punch the buttons on an imaginary phone)

- makes up a situation and plays out a sequence of events

- spends 10 minutes or longer in a dramatic play episode

- collaborates with other children in dramatic play

- uses language to communicate ideas

Observing these aspects of dramatic play allows you to compile a profile of each child's skills. Based on what you learn, you can make decisions on when it is appropriate to intervene and how.

To make the best use of your observations, also keep in mind the *Creative Curriculum* goals and objectives. Watch what a child does and consider which objectives are most relevant to what you learned about the child. Ask yourself a series of questions before you decide how best to respond. Your observations and reflections will help you to identify where a child is on the *Developmental Continuum* so you can pinpoint the next steps for that child. This may lead you to plan new experiences, to change the environment in some way, or to provide more focused instruction to support the child's learning. The chart that follows gives examples of how you might use your observations of a child to respond appropriately.

Observation	Reflection	Response
Jonelle places a dress on the ironing board, runs the wooden iron over it, and says, "I'm getting ready for a party."	Jonelle uses real objects and is able to make believe as part of a play theme. *(Objective 35, Takes on pretend roles and situations; and 36, Makes believe with objects)* How can I encourage her to extend her make-believe play and involve other children?	Ask questions to sustain the play: "Are you giving the party? Will you be cooking some food?" Make her aware of other children: "I bet Sonya would like to come to the party. Look, she's trying on a dress right now."
Tyrone rocks back and forth on rocking chair holding a doll, watching the other children but not interacting.	Tyrone may not know how to approach other children. *(Objective 10, Plays well with other children)* He is at the stage of imitating what he has seen *(Objective 35, Takes on pretend roles and situations)* How can I intervene to extend his dramatic play skills and help him feel more comfortable interacting with other children?	Point out what other children are doing: "Look, Jonetta is feeding her baby. Let's find out what she's giving her baby." Become involved by asking, "Is your baby hungry? Do you want me to hold your baby while you warm up a bottle?"
Using scissors, Dallas cuts out coupons from a coupon book and copies letters from the coupons on a note pad.	Dallas can cut on a line with a scissors. *(Objective 19, Controls small muscles in hands)* He writes by copying letters to make a list. *(Objective 49, Understands the purpose of writing; and 50, Writes letters and words)* What new props can I add to extend his interest in reading and writing and involve other children?	Place empty food containers, food posters, and play money in the area. Involve other children by asking, "Are you planning to go shopping? I wonder who will be at the store to help you." Plan a trip to a grocery store.
When another child says there is no food in the house, Susie goes to the collage box, brings back Styrofoam pellets, and says, "Here are some beans for dinner."	Susie finds multiple uses for classroom objects to solve a problem. *(Objective 23, Approaches problems flexibly)* She can use a substitute object to represent something she needs. *(Objective 36, Makes believe with objects)* How can I support her eagerness to help other children and extend her play theme?	Validate what she did: "You figured out a way to have some food. Do you have enough beans for me too?" Involve other children to sustain the play: "Tasheen, would you like to join us for dinner? Do you have something to bring?"

Interacting With Children During Dramatic Play

To maximize opportunities for children to gain social/emotional, physical, cognitive, and language skills, teachers should take an active role in supporting children's dramatic play. Your ongoing observations will help you know when it's appropriate to let children be and when it would be helpful to intervene. If your observations tell you that children appear to be stuck in their choice of dramatic roles, they simply may need your help in coming up with new ideas. And they will be more likely to re-enact and clarify new concepts they are beginning to explore firsthand if the Dramatic Play Area incorporates materials related to a study. There are several approaches you can take.

By talking about what children are doing, you make them more aware that they are pretending.

Making Suggestions to Stimulate Dramatic Play

One effective strategy for stimulating dramatic play is to observe what is happening and comment or ask questions about what you see. By talking about what children are doing, you make them more aware that they are pretending. You can also make a suggestion that will extend their play.

Ms. Tory observes Alexa place a doll in the carriage and push it around the room. She says, "I see you are taking your baby for a walk. Where are you going?" Alexa continues pushing the carriage without responding. Ms. Tory asks, "Are you taking your baby to the park or to the store?" Alexa responds, "To the store." Ms. Tory responds, "Uh oh, I think you forgot your pocketbook and you'll need money at the store. I see a purse on the shelf but we may need to make some money."

Crystal is playing shoe store. She measures Derek's foot and says, "Here are your new shoes." When Derek doesn't respond, Mr. Alvarez says, "How much are those shoes? Derek, do you need a shoe box for your shoes?"

In each of these situations the teachers observed what was going on and made suggestions to help children focus on their make-believe situation and their use of props, and to extend their ideas in a positive direction.

Participating in Children's Play

You may find that there are times when taking on a more active role in children's play is necessary. This step is more appropriate when children are at a beginning level of dramatic play. For example, you may observe children engaged in pretend play but not interacting with one another. In this situation you can encourage interaction by participating in the play episode and helping children connect to one another.

An active role is appropriate when children are at a beginning level of dramatic play.

Kate is standing by the stove stirring a pot. Leo is sitting on the rocking chair holding a doll. Ms. Tory sits down near Leo and says to Kate, "You've been very busy cooking. What are you making?" When Kate doesn't respond, Ms. Tory says,"Mmm, it smells a lot like chicken soup. Am I right?"

When Kate nods her head, Ms. Tory says, "Oh good. I love chicken soup and I'm hungry. Leo, are you hungry too? I wonder if Kate can make us some dinner. Kate, do you have enough soup for all of us?"

For children who seem to be running out of ideas for a play episode, you can help them extend the role-playing situation, make the theme more complex, or include more actions for the role being played. Here are two examples.

Three children are playing restaurant. Dallas and Crystal are sitting at the table eating and Alexa is serving the food. Ms. Tory, noticing that the episode is ending because the children have run out of ideas, says, "Does anyone besides me want to order dessert? Waiter, what kind of desserts do you have?"

Setsuko has a stethoscope around her neck and is examining Kate's "baby" but doesn't seem to know what else to do. Mr. Alvarez suggests some ideas: "What's wrong with the baby, doctor? She won't stop crying? Do you think she needs some medicine? Can you write a prescription? Let's call the drugstore and see if anyone is there."

As these examples show, teachers can take an active role in promoting children's pretend play by noticing what children are doing and extending their ideas.

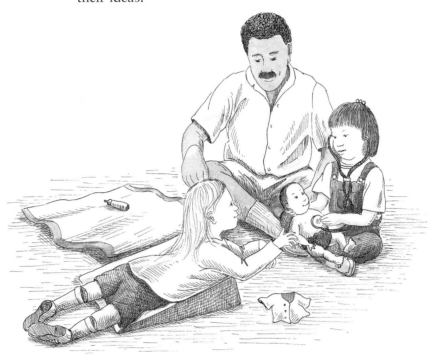

Introducing New Props to Enhance a Study

As we discussed earlier in this chapter, props can inspire children to apply what they've learned and to extend their play. When props are introduced as part of a study topic, children are able to recreate and explore the experiences they've had. Here is an example of how a teacher introduced new props after taking the children on a trip to the post office.

Ms. Tory brings her prop box labeled Post Office to the meeting area. She says to the children, "Now that we have been to the post office, I think you might be able to use the things we have in this box. Before I show you what's in the box, let's think about the people we saw at the post office and what they were doing. Who has an idea?"

The children share ideas such as mail carrier, person buying stamps, mail clerk weighing letters, mail truck driver. Ms. Tory responds, "I'm going to take some things out of this box. See if you remember who uses them and what they do."

Taking out one item at a time, she invites children to share what they know about each one. Then she says, "I'll leave this box out in case anyone wants to make a post office."

Sometimes children's play gives you a chance to teach them about using pretend props and leads to an in-depth study.

During choice time Malik puts a hat on his head and lines up five chairs. He sits in the first chair, and announces, "I'm the bus driver. Who wants a ride?" Mr. Alvarez says, "It looks like you need a steering wheel. I wonder what we could find." He looks around the classroom and finds a paper plate. Over the next few days, this play continues, with other children becoming involved.

Mr. Alvarez arranges for a "real" bus driver to bring a bus into the parking lot and takes the children in small groups out to investigate it. The children take photographs of the bus and draw pictures of its different parts. They return to the classroom with their drawings and photos and decide to turn a large refrigerator box into a bus.

The project takes several weeks, with many more investigations and lots of dramatic play once the bus is complete.

As stated before, the introduction of new props is most effective when you select them based on a topic children are already interested in and studying. Then they are more likely to work together, sharing common experiences to create play scenes of their own design.

Frequently Asked Questions About Dramatic Play

Sometimes children's play makes me uncomfortable. How should I respond?

Children's dramatic play often reflects what they see around them. For many children violence, sex, and drugs are everyday experiences—either in real life or what they see on TV or in the movies. By taking on a pretend role, you can address children's interest in the topic and redirect behaviors that are not constructive. Here are some examples:

Two children are sitting on the couch and pretending to use drugs. You can take on a role and say, "You know some kinds of drugs are very good for you and some are very bad. I want to be sure you are safe. If you are sick, the doctor can give you medicine to make you better. Is someone sick? Should we call the doctor?"

Three children are playing house and eating dinner. One child hits the doll and says, "Shut up, baby. Stop your crying. No more food for you." Rather than criticizing the "mother" for this behavior, you can ask, "What do you think would make the baby stop crying?" If the child doesn't offer any ideas you might say, "Some babies stop crying when you hold them on your lap and rock them gently."

You notice that two children are lying on each other as if they are having sex. Realizing that they are replaying roles they can't really understand, you can redirect this play by saying, "I just got home from work. Is dinner ready? What should we have?"

What should I do about superhero play that is overly aggressive?

Increasingly, teachers report that children's dramatic play is heavily influenced by television. Play based on TV shows usually involves a lot of action—jumping, leaping, and fighting. For this reason, some teachers limit this kind of play to the outdoors. Others forbid any superhero play because of its aggressive nature. Because banning this type of play often escalates it, we advocate taking a problem-solving approach and helping children to develop more constructive ways to play. (See Chapter 2 [pp. 114–115], where we show how a teacher led children in a discussion to resolve this kind of problem.)

If you are seeing a lot of this kind of play in your classroom, consider that children may be trying to deal with very real fears about violence they have experienced or seen on the news. For example, after the Pentagon was hit and the World Trade Center destroyed by hijacked planes, preschool children were seen building towers in the block area and then taking a toy plane and destroying them. Teachers were very aware of what children were worried about and used the opportunity to talk with them. They asked questions such as, "Is anyone in those buildings? We better get the firefighters and ambulance to come and help save the people."

What do I say to parents who do not want their sons to use dress-up clothes or play with dolls or their daughters to play with tools?

First, reassure parents that this kind of play is entirely normal during the preschool years. This is the time when children use dramatic play to better understand their world and the different roles people play, both men and women. They enjoy dressing up in clothes they normally wouldn't wear and trying out roles of the people who are important to them, especially mothers and fathers. The classroom is a safe place to explore and learn. At the same time, be sure you have included dress-up clothes and props used by men and women in a variety of roles in your Dramatic Play Area.

A LETTER TO FAMILIES ABOUT DRAMATIC PLAY

Dear Families,

In the Dramatic Play Area children take on different roles and recreate real-life experiences. They use props and make-believe to deepen their understanding about the world they live in.

The ability to pretend is very important to your child's development. Children who know how to make believe develop a good vocabulary, which is important for reading. They learn to cooperate with others and solve problems, and are able to think abstractly—all important skills for success in school. When children pretend, they have to recall experiences and re-create them. To do this, they need to picture their experiences in their minds. For example, to play the role of a doctor, children have to remember what tools a doctor uses, how a doctor examines a patient, and what a doctor says. In playing the doctor or other roles, children learn to cooperate with others and to share their ideas.

When children make believe, we might ask:

> *Is your baby sick? What are you going to do?*
> *Are you the storekeeper here? I need to buy some food.*
> *What are you cooking for dinner tonight? It smells so good.*

We talk with children and participate in their play to extend their thinking.

What You Can Do at Home

You can encourage the same kind of pretend play at home that we do at school simply by playing with your child and providing some simple props. A sheet over a table creates a house or a hideout. A large empty cardboard box can become almost anything—a pirate ship, a doghouse, a castle, or a train. The nice thing about dramatic play is that it requires only your imagination. Here are some simple ways to encourage your child's learning through dramatic play:

- During bath time, include plastic boats, cups, and rubber dolls and play pretend.

- Save food cartons, make some play money, and play store with your child.

- Read stories together and involve your child in acting out different parts of the story.

- Collect some old clothes your child can use to dress up and make believe.

- Say to your child, "Let's pretend we're going on a train ride. What do we need? Tickets? Suitcases? Do you want to collect the tickets?"

When you engage in pretend play with your child, you are teaching important learning skills, and you are spending valuable time together.

inside this chapter

295 How Playing With Toys and Games Promotes Development
296 Connecting Toys and Games With Curriculum Objectives

298 Creating an Environment for Toys and Games
299 Selecting Materials
303 Displaying and Caring for Toys and Games

304 What Children Learn in the Toys and Games Area

306 The Teacher's Role
306 Observing and Responding to Individual Children
310 Interacting With Children in the Toys and Games Area
313 Frequently Asked Questions About Toys and Games

315 A Letter to Families About Toys and Games

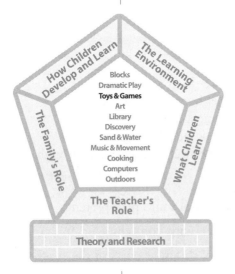

Toys and Games

How Playing With Toys and Games Promotes Development

The Toys and Games Area includes manipulatives, puzzles, collectibles, matching games, and other games that children can play at a table, on the floor, or on top of a divider shelf. These materials offer children a quiet activity that they can do alone, with a friend, with a teacher or a parent volunteer, or with a small group. Children strengthen all areas of their development as they play with toys and games.

Social/emotional development. Children learn to cooperate with one another by sharing and taking turns as they play a game or build an intricate design. They develop confidence when they complete a task successfully using self-correcting toys such as puzzles, sorting boards, and stacking rings.

Physical development. Children practice eye-hand coordination while lacing cards or placing pegs in a pegboard. When children string beads or construct with interlocking cubes, they refine small muscle skills.

Cognitive development. As children build with table blocks or make designs with pattern blocks and parquetry blocks, they experiment with construction and invention and use creative problem-solving skills. They also expand their emerging math skills such as counting, seriation, matching, patterning, and classification. In fact, the Toys and Games Area often serves as the math hub in your classroom.

Language development. Children use words to describe how they are putting together a puzzle or sorting a collection of objects. They compare the size, shape, and color of objects as they play. While using beads, pegboards, puzzles, dominoes, and collectibles, they develop reading skills such as left-to-right progression, visual discrimination, and matching similar objects. As they use magnetic letters and alphabet blocks, children explore letters, then arrange and rearrange them to form words.

Connecting Toys and Games With Curriculum Objectives

The *Creative Curriculum* goals and objectives give you a focus for thinking about children's development as they play in the Toys and Games Area. For example, you might work on objectives related to learning about patterns for a child who consistently makes repetitive designs with pegs or pattern blocks. Or you might focus on objectives related to self-direction and independence or use of classroom materials if certain children seem tentative in their approach to using materials. The following chart shows how children in the Toys and Games Area demonstrate their growing abilities in relation to selected *Creative Curriculum* objectives.

Selected Curriculum Objectives	What a Child Might Do in the Toys and Games Area
Social/Emotional Development	
3. Recognizes own feelings and manages them appropriately	Says, "You took the Lego I wanted! Can you help me find another one just like it?"
4. Stands up for rights	Says, "I'm using this puzzle right now. I'll give it to you when I'm finished."
5. Demonstrates self-direction and independence	Strings beads and, when finished, returns them to the proper place on the shelf.
7. Respects and cares for classroom environment and materials	Asks teacher for tape to repair the game box.
8. Follows classroom routines	Begins to put away puzzle when clean-up song is played.
9. Follows classroom rules	Tells friend, "You aren't supposed to make a gun with Tinkertoys."
10. Plays well with other children	Takes turns while playing a board game.
11. Recognizes the feelings of others and responds appropriately	Sees a child being rejected by others and says, "That's OK. You can play with us."
12. Shares and respects the rights of others	Says, "It's your turn to be first."
13. Uses thinking skills to resolve conflicts	Finds another car when a friend wants the same one.
Physical Development	
19. Controls small muscles in hands	Uses tweezers or tongs to pick up objects; pinches clothespins on matching game.
20. Coordinates eye-hand movements	Strings beads, places pegs in holes, and laces sewing cards.
21. Uses tools for writing and drawing	Uses toys such as Magnadoodle or Etch-a-Sketch for writing and drawing.

Selected Curriculum Objectives	What a Child Might Do in the Toys and Games Area
Cognitive Development	
23. Approaches problems flexibly	Puts together puzzle by looking at shapes of the pieces as well as the pictures printed on them.
24. Shows persistence in approaching tasks	Tries putting several different shapes in the hole of a sort toy before finding the right one.
25. Explores cause and effect	Says, "If you stack these blocks too high, they will crash."
26. Applies knowledge or experience to new context	Creates a fence for toy animals after visiting the farm.
27. Classifies objects	Groups teddy bear counters by color.
28. Compares/measures	Holds a chain of interlocking links up and says, "This is as tall as I am."
30. Recognizes patterns and can repeat them	Strings beads in a pattern—red circle, blue square, red circle, blue square, etc.
31. Shows awareness of time concepts and sequence	Places sequence cards of a plant growing in order—seed, sprout, plant.
33. Uses one-to-one correspondence	Systematically fits one peg in each hole of a pegboard.
34. Uses numbers and counting	Counts collection of buttons.
36. Makes believe with objects	Pretends to conduct a band with a Tinkertoy stick.
37. Makes and interprets representations	Makes a helicopter with Bristle Blocks.
Language Development	
39. Expresses self using words and expanded sentences	Says, "I put these rocks together because they are rough and these together because they are shiny."
41. Answers questions	Answers "The red one" when asked, "Which bead will you put on next?" while making a pattern with beads.
42. Asks questions	Asks, "Where did all of these keys come from?"
43. Actively participates in conversations	Talks with friend about Lego structure as they build it.
45. Demonstrates understanding of print concepts	Lines up alphabet blocks from left to right.
46. Demonstrates knowledge of the alphabet	Names letters while moving them around on magnetic board.

Creating an Environment for Toys and Games

Children will enjoy using toys and games and will get maximum benefits from these materials when the area where they are kept is arranged carefully and thoughtfully. Both the location of the Toys and Games Area and how toys are displayed affect the way children use these materials, learn from them, and take care of them.

Materials are labeled with both a picture and words. Labels are laminated first, then attached with clear tape.

The shelves are neatly arranged so that children can see the available choices.

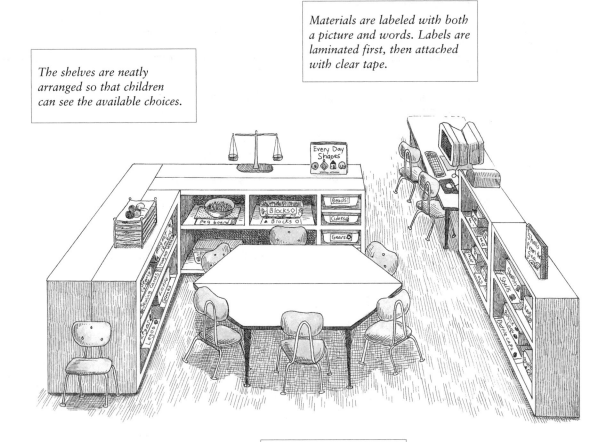

The tables can be separated so children can use toys and games on the floor if they choose.

Setting up the Toys and Games Area	Suggested Materials
	Puzzles: with knobs and without, large-piece jigsaw, racks for puzzles
Location:	
Near other quiet areas such as the Library and Art areas	Stacking cubes, nesting cubes, attribute blocks, Unifix cubes, hardwood table blocks, geoboards, stacking, interlocking toys, stringing beads, Legos, dominoes
Set up:	Self-help frames for buttoning and zipping
Low shelves to hold materials in labeled containers	Magnetic boards and felt boards with shapes
One or two tables with chairs	Small props: animals, trucks, cars, boats, wagons, etc., for sorting
	Templates for tracing
	Lotto and other board games
	Collections of objects (plastic bottle caps, keys, shells, etc.)

Selecting Materials

Look through any catalog of early childhood materials and you will see a wide range of toys and games. To make good choices for your children, think about variety and complexity as well as safety, durability, and price. Select toys that do not convey stereotypes. At the end of this section we discuss types of toys to avoid.

 Types of Toys and Games

Toys and games can be grouped into four categories: self-correcting, structured toys; open-ended toys; collectibles; and cooperative games.

Self-correcting, structured toys are those that fit together in a specific way—for example, a puzzle. A child using this type of toy can determine readily if the toy has been put together correctly. Self-correcting toys include the following:

- puzzles: wooden, rubber inset, durable cardboard, and large floor puzzles
- self-help skill frames (buttoning, zipping, tying)
- graded circles that fit on a cylinder
- nesting boxes, cups, racks, poles
- geometric shape sorters

Open-ended toys have no right or wrong way to be used. They can be put together in a variety of ways, depending entirely on the child's creativity and level of development. They promote problem solving and initiative. Many are excellent for developing motor skills and eye-hand coordination. These toys are also natural tools for developing mathematical skills and concepts. Open-ended toys include the following:

In selecting toys and games, pick a few from each category to offer children a variety of choices.

- felt boards
- Lego blocks, people and props
- colored cubes, wooden or plastic
- beads and sewing cards with yarn or string for stringing
- pegs and pegboards

- Cuisenaire rods
- parquetry blocks
- magnetic letters and numbers
- geoboards
- wooden geometric shapes
- interlocking links and cubes

Collectibles, like open-ended toys, can be put together in a variety of unspecified ways. The difference is that collectibles contain sets of like objects. Attractive collections encourage children to sort, match, and compare in many inventive ways. Examples of collectibles include:

- bottle caps
- buttons
- keys
- plastic coffee scoops
- small boxes
- small toys

- erasers
- sample paint chips
- nuts and bolts
- plastic fasteners (e. g., from bread bags)
- lids

Cooperative games encourage children to work together to match pictures, numbers, symbols, and objects. Rather than winning or losing, these games give children opportunities to develop social skills while improving visual discrimination skills. Games in this category include:

- lotto
- dominoes
- concentration

- matching games
- card games
- board games

Because some toys and games can be used in different ways, they fall into more than one category. To illustrate, parquetry blocks are a structured toy when used with pattern cards—that is, when the child chooses to replicate the design on the card. However, they are open-ended when children create their own patterns.

Criteria for Selecting Toys and Games

As you make plans to select and purchase materials for the Toys and Games Area of your classroom, keep the following criteria in mind.

Safety. The most basic requirement is that all toys should be safe to use and in accordance with standards outlined by the U.S. Consumer Product Safety Commission, a federal agency that sets safety standards. (These standards as well as other toy safety information, can be obtained from the CPSC web site at http://www.cpsc.gov or by calling 1-800-638-CPSC.) Avoid toys with sharp points or edges, pieces small enough to be swallowed, and pieces that can be used as projectiles.

Durability. Because of their constant use, materials in a program for young children need to be more durable than those purchased for home use. For example, wood or rubber puzzles last longer than cardboard ones.

Construction. Toys should be well made and work as intended. All pieces of a puzzle or interlocking toy should actually fit together, and all the pieces of a lotto game or domino set should be intact. Toys made from different kinds of materials—plastic, wood, metal, fabric, or rubber—give children a variety of sensory experiences.

Flexibility. Interlocking and manipulative toys work in many ways. The more flexible a toy is, the more varied its uses are, and the longer it will hold children's attention as they develop new interests and skills.

Price. The cost of a table toy should be balanced against its flexibility. Some expensive toys may be good investments because they can be used in many ways and will last a long time. Before purchasing, consider these questions: Can the toy be used in many different ways? Can it be used in more complex ways as children's skills develop? Can it be used in different ways by children of different ages?

Values (multicultural/non-sexist/non-violent). Toys convey values to children. The pictures and photographs on the toys and games, therefore, should be non-stereotypical and should reflect a diversity of roles and experiences. For example, a puzzle of community helpers might depict women as firefighters or doctors. We strongly recommend that you select toys that do not promote violence.

Levels of Complexity

Toys have varying levels of complexity. At the beginning of the year you may need to have more simple toys. Gradually, you can include more complex materials as the children in your program become more skilled. The toys and games in the area should be challenging but not frustrating. On the following chart you can see examples of how materials vary in complexity.

Keep issues such as safety, durability, flexibility, and values in mind when you select toys and games.

Toy or Game	Simple	⟶	Complex
Puzzles	4-10 large pieces, knobbed	10-20 pieces, no knobs	20-30+ pieces
Legos or similar construction toys	Large pieces (2-4 inches)	Smaller pieces, but limited number	Full range of pieces and accessories
Beads and pegs	Large beads with stiff string; large pegs	Intermediate size beads or pegs	Small beads with different types of string and yarn; small pegs
Card and lotto games	Simple games matching colors or pictures	Memory or concentration games	Bingo or lotto games developing letter and number concepts
Board games	Simple board games with few rules	Games following a simple plan of action and/or having simple scoring	Games with more rules and requiring some strategy

Some toys can have a harmful effect on children's development and should be avoided.

Toys and Games to Avoid

Toys and games impact play. When carefully selected, toys can facilitate creative and imaginative play. On the other hand, some toys can have a harmful effect on children's development. In the TRUCE (Teachers Resisting Unhealthy Children's Entertainment) Toy Action Guide, author Diane Levin (2001-2002) suggests avoiding toys such as these:

Toys that make electronic technology the focus of play. These toys tend to control and limit children's play. Examples include toys that talk and walk.

Toys that lure young girls into focusing on appearances. These toys tend to focus on physical appearance, promoting sexual and stereotyped behaviors. Examples include teen dolls with makeup and tattoos.

Toys that emphasize violent, sexualized language or behavior. These toys will undermine your efforts to create a respectful, caring classroom environment. Examples include wrestling or science fiction action figures.

Toys that are linked to commercial products and advertisements. These toys become instant advertisements, for fast food restaurants and chain stores.

Toys that are linked to TV programs, movies, and video games rated for teens or adults. These toys are inappropriate for preschool children. Examples include any products linked to PG-13 or R-rated movies.

Toys that link play to candy or unhealthy foods. These toys encourage poor nutrition. Examples are toys linked to fast food restaurants.

Displaying and Caring for Toys and Games

Children will be drawn to the Toys and Games Area if it is attractive and uncluttered. Random piles of toys are likely to go unused if children cannot find what they want easily. Thus, your method for displaying and storing these materials is important.

Guidelines for Displaying Toys and Games

Label toys and games so children can find what they need and return it to the right place when they are finished with it. You can make labels in several ways. For example, take a photograph of each toy, draw its picture, or cut the picture of the toy from a catalog or from the box. Then laminate it and attach it to the shelf where the toys are to be stored.

Write the name of the toy or game below the picture on each label. Use initial capitals and lowercase letters just as you might see in a book. If you have bilingual children in your class, also include the word written in their first language.

Place toys and games at children's eye level so they can easily see what materials are available.

Group materials by type: puzzles in one area, pegboard and pegs in another area, and so on.

Remove broken toys or those with missing pieces until they can be repaired or replaced.

Store extra toys (for replenishing the area) outside the Toys and Games Area in a teacher cabinet or on high shelves.

Use bins or plastic tubs to maximize storage space for collectibles, table blocks, and other toys with multiple pieces, and puzzle racks so children can see each one.

Avoid stacking game boxes too high. If you stack three or more, games often fall on the floor when a child pulls the bottom game from a tall pile.

Toys and games inevitably suffer from wear and tear. You can preserve cardboard pieces by laminating them or covering them with clear Contact paper. Try replacing puzzle pieces by laying a piece of plastic over the empty space and filling it with wood putty. When the homemade piece dries, you can paint it to resemble the missing piece. An occasional routine cleaning with soap and water for plastic and wooden toys will increase their attractiveness and, in some cases, help them last longer. Finally, keep a lost and found basket in the Toys and Games Area for stray parts. Over time, you can recycle these odds and ends and use them as collectibles for sorting, classifying, and graphing, or decorating block structures.

What Children Learn in the Toys and Games Area

Toys and games can cultivate children's emerging math, science, social studies, and literacy skills and develop their problem-solving skills and creativity. For very young children, skills begin to form as they handle materials repeatedly. As children get older, their skills sharpen and they can begin to make patterns, sort, and classify. Here are some examples of what children learn in this area when teachers are knowledgable about content.

Literacy

Enhance children's **vocabulary and language** by talking with them as they play with toys and games. Discuss, for example, the pictures on the puzzles or the truck they are building with Legos. Introduce new descriptive words like *shiny, dull, pointed, curved, rough,* and *smooth* as children play with collections.

Help children learn about **letters and words** by talking with them as they manipulate magnetic letters, letter blocks, and letter tiles. Describe what you see happening as children arrange and rearrange letters, (e.g., "You made a word! You put an *m*, an *a*, and a *t* together and spelled *mat!*")

Strengthen children's **knowledge of print** by encouraging them to draw and write (using scribbles or transitional spelling) about the designs and constructions they make.

Mathematics

Help children to develop **problem-solving skills** as they construct, design, and assemble materials. Encourage them to put puzzles together, make designs with parquetry and pattern blocks, sort and classify collections, or construct a building with Lego blocks.

Help children to develop **number concepts** as they count beads, blocks, and teddy bear counters. Use mathematical terminology as you compare quantities—more than, less than, the same as.

Encourage children to explore **patterns and relationships** by providing collectibles such as keys, buttons, or small cars so children can copy, extend, or create their own patterns. Offer open-ended materials such as interlocking blocks or links, pegs, colored cubes or tiles, and magnetic shapes and figures to develop patterning skills.

Teach children about **geometry** while working with two- and three-dimensional shapes. Point out how all triangles don't look alike by showing them triangles with parquetry blocks, shape puzzles, and geoboards.

Develop children's **spatial sense** by describing how the needle is going in and out as they work with a sewing card. Include board games to help them learn about directionality and use terms like *forward, backward, beginning,* and *end.*

Use collections to develop an understanding of **data collection, organization, and representation.** Show children how to create graphs by organizing collections of rocks, leaves, or toy cars. Encourage children to compare the collections on their graph.

Science

Teach concepts about **physical science,** such as balance, strength, and gravity, by encouraging children to build with Legos and other small construction toys. Encourage exploration with their creations ("I wonder what would happen if you put larger wheels on your Lego car.").

Use puzzles and games that feature plants and animals as an opportunity to talk about **life science.** Comment for example, when children sort a collection of plastic animals according to where the animals live—the farm, the zoo, or the ocean.

Social Studies

Teach children about **people and how they live** by encouraging them to work cooperatively and solve problems together. Give children positive feedback for following the rules of a game, sharing, and taking turns.

Encourage children to play board games such as "Candyland" or "Chutes and Ladders" to learn about **spaces and geography.**

The Arts

Encourage development in the **visual arts** by including open-ended construction toys so children can represent their thoughts, ideas, and feelings in a concrete way.

Technology

Promote an **awareness of technology** by including toys with moving parts such as gears, hinges, or wheels. Help children make a connection between these toys and objects they see in their surroundings.

We have described only a few of the ways that toys and games can be integrated into your program. You will be able to think of many more ideas as you observe and interact with children in the Toys and Games Area.

The Teacher's Role

Young children's play with toys and games varies widely. When given high-quality toys, children will experiment, explore, discover, and create. They need toys and games that allow for both solitary play and cooperative play, and adults who value the work they are doing as they play in this Area.

Observing and Responding to Individual Children

Children approach toys and games in fairly predictable ways. Depending on their previous experiences with these materials and their physical skills, children generally move from simple to more complex and integrated play.

 ### How Children Approach Toys and Games

Functional play. Children approach a new toy by getting to know its characteristics. Their exploration helps them answer questions such as these:

- How does this object/toy look?

- How does it feel? What kind of texture does it have?

- How big or small is it? How heavy or light?

- What shape is it?

- What color is it?

The purpose of functional play is to investigate the physical properties of the toy.

The purpose of functional play is to investigate the physical properties of the toy. This type of free exploration is necessary before any purposeful or structured use of toys occurs.

Constructive play. In constructive play, children use toys creatively to make something. They may build a tower with colored inch cubes, construct a fence with construction toys like Legos, create a design with parquetry blocks, or use pegs and pegboards to make a birthday cake. Before using collectibles such as bottle caps or buttons to sort and compare, children may use them to create patterns or complex designs. In constructive play, children ask themselves questions such as the following:

Children use toys creatively in constructive play.

- What can I do with this toy?

- Can I make somehing new with these shapes?

- Can I use these blocks to build something big?

- How high can I build before it falls down?

- What kind of design can I make with these materials?

Dramatic or pretend play. The next type of play after exploring and constructing is using toys and games for pretend play. After children have explored the materials using their senses (functional play) or created something new (constructive play), they often begin to use them in their pretend play. They may fill a pegboard with pegs to make a cake and carry it to you as they sing "Happy Birthday." They may string beads, wear them as a necklace, and tell you or a friend they are going to a party. They will also work together to build a construction site with Legos and then take on roles such as the worker or the boss as they play with their creation.

Games with rules. Board and card games offer the opportunity to master the skills of understanding and accepting the limits of rules. Remember that learning about rules is difficult for most 3- to 4-year-olds. Very often, children create and invent their own games with rules. They determine each person's role, devise a system for taking turns, and decide who will go first, second, or third. This development can precede or occur simultaneously with learning to play by conventional rules.

As children experiment with toys and games, they invent more and more ways to use these materials, gaining new skills as they play. A child's development in this interest area is enhanced when teachers make good decisions about when and how to introduce new and increasingly complex materials. After first observing how children use toys and games, you can then decide how to respond.

Responding to Each Child

The teacher's role is to provide encouragement, help children get involved with materials, introduce new skills, challenge them to take the next step in their learning, and talk to them about their efforts and accomplishments. You'll know how to respond after observing what children say and do as they work. Your role is to be a detective of sorts, trying to figure out what interests children and how they approach materials. Based on what you learn you can build on children's interests and address their individual needs. Notice whether a child

- selects and cares for materials independently

- explores the physical properties of the materials (functional play), builds and creates (constructive play), roleplays (sociodramatic play), or follows the rules of a game

- is developing increased eye-hand coordination and fine muscle skills

- uses logical thinking skills to work with the materials (e.g., classifying, patterning, measuring, comparing, counting)

- communicates what he is doing while playing with the toys and games

The information you gain from focused observation enables you to respond appropriately. It also can guide you in the kinds of questions you ask, the comments you make, and the materials you provide.

Careful observation lets you know which toys and materials the children select and how they use those materials. Observation also gives you insight on the different ways children use the materials and how they apply literacy, math, science, and other content area skills. Based on what you see, you can plan ways to enhance each child's development in this interest area.

Observation	Reflection	Response
Leo moves a "Candyland" marker around the board like a race car. He ignores a friend's request to take turns.	Leo is engaged in functional play. He is playing alongside other children, but is not taking turns in the game. *(Objective 12, Shares and respects the rights of others)* Leo is pretending with the race car. *(Objective 36, Makes believe with objects)* Does he have the skills necessary to play games with rules?	Follow his interest in race cars and offer him blocks to use as ramps and roads. Play with him in a game he has created and talk about what you are doing as you take turns ("I'm finished my turn. Now it's your turn.").
Malik lifts up his T-shirt, pulls from his belt a toy gun made from Legos, and says "This is just like Daddy's."	Malik uses Legos to represent a real object. *(Objective 36, Makes believe with objects; and 37, Makes and interprets representations)* How can I redirect his attention from gun making? How can I help Malik use his creativity in a more constructive way?	Play alongside Malik suggesting other kinds of constructions. Offer props and pictures that inspire different ways to use Legos.
Jonetta places blue and yellow pegs in an alternating pattern around the edge of a pegboard.	Jonetta is creating a simple pattern. *(Objective 30, Recognizes patterns and can repeat them)* She is showing coordination and control as she places the pegs in the holes. *(Objective 19, Controls small muscles in hands)* How can I challenge Jonetta to work on more complicated patterns?	Say, "I see you've made a pattern: blue, yellow, blue, yellow." Draw Jonetta's attention to patterns in the environment throughout the day. Create a three-color pattern with pegs and invite her to continue it.
Dallas connects three interlocking cubes and counts them saying, "One, two, three, four, five."	Dallas can count five objects accurately. *(Objective 34, Uses numbers and counting)* He connected the cubes with ease. *(Objective 20, Coordinates eye-hand movement)* Does Dallas connect number names with quantities in other situations (e.g., brings two cookies when asked)?	Invite Dallas to do simple tasks that will reinforce one-to-one correspondence (e.g., pass out cups, put one seed in each container, place one note in each cubby). Show him how to touch each object as he counts. Encourage Dallas to use numbers and counting throughout the day.

Interacting With Children in the Toys and Games Area

As you observe the children in your program, you will probably discover many different ways to interact with them in the Toys and Games Area. The teacher's presence and the promise of personal attention for a few minutes can be a powerful incentive for children to remain in the area and engage with materials. Here is an example of how this might happen.

Sonya, Carlos, and Tasheen have each assembled a pile of buttons. Mr. Alvarez asks if he can join them. He begins arranging his buttons as he observes the children's play.

Sonya: *My mommy made a dress that had a button that looked just like this one.*

Carlos: *Hey . . . I've got one like that! And here's another . . . and another . . . and another.*

Mr. Alvarez: *You've found four buttons that are just alike . . . one, two, three, four. [Carlos joins in touching and counting the buttons.]*

Tasheen: *I've found more than that. I've got 42. [Tasheen lines up 10 buttons.]*

Carlos: *No you don't. Count them.*

Tasheen touches and counts her buttons, although she counts faster than she touches.

Mr. Alvarez: *May I count them with you? [Both Tasheen and Mr. Alvarez begin counting the buttons.]*

Sonya is still exploring her buttons, examining the colors, lines, sizes, and designs. She begins to create piles of like buttons.

Mr. Alvarez: *Sonya, do you have more big buttons or more small ones?*

Sonya: *I have the mostest buttons that look like these.*

Mr. Alvarez: *You certainly do have the most big buttons. And you even have some buttons with a scalloped edge like this.*

By talking with children about their play with toys and games, you show you value what they are doing and acknowledge their increasing skills and competence. Your involvement also supports their learning:

- You introduce new vocabulary, model correct grammar, and encourage conversation.

- You help children to become more aware of what they are doing, what they are discovering, and what they are thinking and feeling by talking with them.

- You help them identify concepts and label them: "These are the smaller blocks" or "You have the red pegs."

At times, for some children, you may need to teach specific skills necessary to work with, for example, certain toys and games. A child who has had little experience with puzzles may need to be shown, step by step, that to complete a puzzle one has to

- spill out the pieces

- turn them all over so that the painted side is up

- start by putting the outside pieces in first

- find the corner pieces

- put in the pieces next to one another until the whole picture is made

- either do the puzzle a second time or return it to the designated place on the shelf

When you talk with children about their play, first ask them to describe what they are doing. For children who have difficulty expressing themselves, you can take the lead by providing non-judgmental observations about their work:

Tell me about the puzzle you put together.

You seem to like the red and yellow pegs today.

You matched the two elephants. Here's a picture of a giraffe. Can you find the other giraffe?

I see you've put all the circles in one pile and all the squares in another pile.

You used the parquetry blocks to make your own design.

Given opportunities to gain experience, even reluctant children can begin to express themselves and describe their efforts. By focusing on the process—what they are doing and how they are doing it—rather than the product, you help children to develop thinking, planning, and organizing skills.

Frequently Asked Questions About Toys and Games

Each time I introduce a new material in the Toys and Games Area, all the children want to do is mess around. How can I be sure they are acquiring skills?

Messing around is a first step. Children need time to explore materials and learn about their properties. Carefully observe them as they play with the materials and you will be able to figure out how to help them learn new skills and concepts. Use the *Developmental Continuum* to guide you in taking the appropriate next steps. For example, if a child has connected a long row of interlocking cubes, you might say "Wow. Those blocks are as long as you are!" This comment could lead this child into making other comparisons, a skill that is part of objective 28, Compares/measures.

The children in my class have such a wide range of abilities. How can I possibly include enough materials to meet all of their individual needs?

Include many open-ended materials in your Toys and Games Area. Because there are no right or wrong ways to use these materials, they can serve different purposes for different children. While one child may experiment with snapping together interlocking cubes, another child may use them to create complicated patterns or even solve an addition problem.

Make sure, though, that the materials you have available meet their developmental needs. A child whose fine motor skills have not developed fully might need larger beads to string or larger pegs and pegboards. A child who is very proficient at working puzzles might enjoy trying simple jigsaw puzzles.

How often should I rotate materials in the Toys and Games Area?

Observe and assess how children use the area. Is one toy very popular? Then leave it in the area as long as children are interested in it. Are there other toys and games in which children are not interested? Take them away for a period of time. As children's abilities change, so should your materials. At the beginning of the year, you may include puzzles with fewer pieces and large beads and pegs. As children's small muscle skills develop, you can add more complex materials. Don't forget, however, always to leave some familiar, favorite toys available even as children's skills grow.

I have a child in my class who hoards toys! She will dump an entire tub of Legos on the floor and guard them. She doesn't really play with the Legos, she just makes sure no one else will. What should I do?

As we learned in Chapter 1, many children before the age of 3 1/2 to 4 are not developmentally ready to share. In addition to hoarding materials, some children may refuse to take turns, leave the area if asked to share, or take toys that other children are using. Learning to share takes time, practice, and guidance from you.

First of all, make sure you have ample materials in the classroom with duplicates of popular toys. If the child always tends to take the entire bucket of Legos, you might try dividing the collection into smaller containers. Find opportunities to play with this child and emphasize taking turns. Use language such as "Now it's your turn" and "Now it's my turn" when tossing a beanbag, playing a computer game, or talking on a toy telephone. Practice this new skill by playing a simple board game in the Toys and Games Area.

A Letter to Families About Toys and Games

Dear Families,

Toys and games include puzzles, various table blocks, small construction materials such as Legos, board games, and collections of objects (including shells, bottle caps, and buttons). When children use toys and games, they explore how things work; learn to be creative and use their imaginations; strengthen and control the small muscles in their hands; work cooperatively and solve problems; and learn math ideas and concepts.

When children use toys and games in the classroom, we encourage them to talk about what they are doing. For example, we might say:

> *Tell me about the design you made.*
>
> *How did you get those rings to fit together?*
>
> *You've picked out all blocks that look the same. Can you tell me how they are the same?*

These questions and comments are designed to help children develop their thinking skills.

What You Can Do at Home

You play an important role in selecting toys and games that are safe, interesting, and appropriate for your child's abilities. More importantly, research shows that the most creative children are those who have had adults involved in their play. Here are a few ways that you can be involved in your child's play with toys and games:

- **Observe.** Watch as your child plays and notice his abilities and his interests.

- **Play.** Follow your child's lead and join in his play.

- **Imagine.** Keep in mind that there's more than one way to play with a toy. Be creative!

- **Enjoy.** This isn't a time to drill your child or test him on what he knows. Just have fun being together, talking, and playing.

Good toys do not have to be expensive. You might collect various small objects such as buttons, seashells, rocks, and plastic bottle tops. Make suggestions such as sort all the buttons that are the same color or all the beads that are the same size. Encourage your child to tell you about the design he or she is making or to explain why things belong together.

Playing with toys and games at home promotes a child's development in many ways. We welcome you to help us out in the classroom by playing in our Toys and Games Area with the children. In this way you can see for yourself how much your child is learning there.

inside this chapter

317   **How Art Promotes Development**
     318   Connecting Art With Curriculum Objectives

320   **Creating an Environment for Art**
     322   Selecting Materials
     332   Displaying and Storing Art Materials

334   **What Children Learn in the Art Area**

336   **The Teacher's Role**
     337   Observing and Responding to Individual Children
     341   Interacting With Children in the Art Area
     347   Frequently Asked Questions About Art

349   **A Letter to Families About Art**

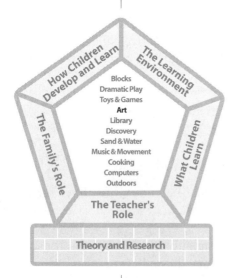

Art

How Art Promotes Development

The Art Area is a place filled with materials that children can enjoy on a purely sensory level. Here children can create and represent their ideas in a visual form. On a table or the floor, at an easel or a workbench, children draw, paint, knead, cut, glue, and make things of their own choosing. Sometimes they simply explore the materials and enjoy the process. At other times they create designs or make something that represents a real object, place, or living thing. Creative art is another language children use to express what they know and what they feel. The Art Area is a studio for children's development and learning.

Social/emotional development. Art is a natural vehicle for children to express their feelings. Children reflect their thoughts and emotions through their choices of color, texture, and media. For example, when happy or excited, a child might use bright colors. When sad or upset, a child may choose darker tones. Children also express their originality and individuality in their art. Who says the pumpkins they paint have to be orange? A child may prefer having a purple one simply because it will stand out better in a patch.

Physical development. As children tear paper for a collage or use scissors to cut, they refine small muscle movements. Making lines and shapes with markers and crayons or hitting a nail on the head with a hammer are activities that help children develop the fine motor control they need for writing. Art is all about fine motor skills.

Cognitive development. Children draw, paint, and sculpt what they know. As they translate their ideas and feelings into art, they use thinking skills to plan, organize, select media, and represent their impressions. When children draw, paint, and make collages, they experiment with color, line, shape, and size. Using paints, fabrics, and woodworking tools they make choices, try out ideas, plan, and experiment. They learn about cause and effect when they mix colors. Through trial and error, they learn how to balance a mobile and weave yarn.

Language development. Children often talk about what they are doing and respond to questions about their creations as they engage in art. Teachers can write down what children say about their artwork as a permanent record of the experience. Art also fosters vocabulary development as children learn and use related technical vocabulary: sculpture, palette, and clamp, to name just a few terms.

Connecting Art With Curriculum Objectives

A glance at the *Creative Curriculum* goals and objectives underscores the many ways that children demonstrate what they know and can do as they engage in art experiences. In the chart below, we give examples of what a child might do or say that would indicate progress on selected objectives.

Selected Curriculum Objectives	What A Child Might Do in the Art Area
Social/Emotional Development	
1. Shows ability to adjust to new situations	Draws picture of family members after saying goodbye to mother.
3. Recognizes own feelings and manages them appropriately	Gets angry at a classmate and uses a hammer at a woodworking bench to pound nails into wood scraps instead of hitting.
5. Demonstrates self-direction and independence	Goes over to shelf, takes out paper bag, scissors, glue, and felt, brings it over to the table, and makes a puppet.
6. Takes responsibility for own well-being; and 9. Follows classroom rules	Goes to the woodworking area, puts on safety goggles, and then gets teacher so he can use the saw.
8. Follows classroom routines	Takes finished artwork to cubby and stores it there to take home at the end of the day.
10. Plays well with other children	Stays in assigned space while painting an outdoor mural of ocean life, and talks with other painters about which colors to use first.
Physical Development	
19. Controls small muscles in hands	Pounds and rolls clay to form snakes.
20. Coordinates eye-hand movement	After tightening a piece of wood in a vise, places both hands around the saw handle and slides saw back and forth across the wood with determination.
21. Uses tools for writing and drawing	Tries out a variety of painting tools: brushes, cotton swabs, string, and sponges.

Selected Curriculum Objectives	What A Child Might Do in the Art Area
Cognitive Development	
22. Observes objects and events with curiosity	Picks up objects from nature walk displayed on art table (leaves, pods, acorns, stones) and places them in different positions before getting glue to make an assemblage.
24. Shows persistence in approaching tasks	Asks the teacher if she can continue working on her weaving during the next choice time.
25. Explores cause and effect	Experiments at the easel to see how many different colors she can make by combining blue, red, yellow, white, and black paint.
30. Recognizes patterns and can repeat them	Paints a series of rainbows, all with stripes of red, orange, and green.
32. Shows awareness of position in space	Looks at landscape hung on the wall and says, "The reason the cows look so small is because they are far away."
Language Development	
39. Expresses self using words and expanded sentences	Describes his drawing: "It stopped raining. Here's the sun making everyone happy because they can go out to play."
42. Asks questions	Asks another child painting on the fence outside next to him: "How come my paper is blowing away and yours isn't?"
43. Actively participates in conversations	Talks with a parent volunteer who is helping out at the woodworking table about how to tighten the wood in a vise.
49. Understands the purpose of writing	Gets pencil and scribbles her name on the bottom of the painting, imitating teacher.
50. Writes letters and words	Signs her name to the bottom right side of drawing.

Creating an Environment for Art

The organization of the Art Area is directly related to its effectiveness in inspiring children's creativity and self-expression. If the area is inviting, children will be drawn to the art materials kept there. But if the Art Area looks messy, overwhelming, or barren, children are not likely to be attracted to it. Children's creativity flourishes in an environment that is both appealing and well-organized.

Easels can be used as room dividers.

A moveable cart for art supplies can work well if shelf storage is limited.

Materials are displayed attractively on low shelves and labeled clearly so children can find what they need.

Setting up the Art Area

Location:

Near a sink, if possible, or provide buckets of water

Protected from traffic

Set up:

Washable floor covering or protect the floor with a shower curtain or vinyl table cloth

Table and 4–6 chairs

Double-sided easel (1 or 2)

Sturdy workbench with a vise

Suggested Materials

Plain and assorted papers for drawing and painting

Colored pencils, markers, crayons

Child-size scissors

Assorted paintbrushes and paints

Playdough, clay

Collage materials

Clay hammers, cookie cutters, rolling pins

Washable ink stamp pads and assorted stamps

Glue, glue sticks, paste, tape

Real woodworking tools (hammers, saws, hand drills) of a size to fit children's small hands

Safety goggles

Soft wood and assorted objects for woodworking: nails, knobs, wooden wheels, leather scraps

Selecting Materials

Art materials can be as diverse as your creativity and funds allow. Before gathering exotic or highly challenging materials, however, teachers should stock the Art Area with the basics, materials that children can

- **paint on** (an easel with paper, washable surfaces such as exterior walls or blacktop)

- **paint with** (brushes, tempera, finger paint, dyes, water)

- **draw on** (a variety of papers, chalkboard, whiteboard, sidewalks)

- **draw with** (crayons, markers, pencils, chalk)

- **put things together with** (paste, glue, wire, nails, rubber bands, paper clips, staples, tape)

- **cut with** (scissors, saw, pumpkin carving knife)

- **mold** (clay, playdough, other doughs, soap bars, plaster of Paris, putty)

- **construct** (wood, papier-mâché, crepe paper, foil, wire)

- **clean up with** (soap, detergent, mops, sponges, brooms, paper towels)

For discussion purposes, we have grouped these basic art materials into five categories: (1) painting, (2) drawing, (3) cutting and pasting, (4) molding, and (5) three-dimensional art and woodworking.

Painting Materials

Painting requires easels and other flat surfaces as well as different kinds of brushes, paints, and paper. When everything children need is easy to reach, children can paint and clean up independently with little help from their teachers.

Easels typically are double- or three-sided, freestanding, and adjusted to the children's height.

Try to have two easels in the Art Area to promote socializing.

If no standing easels are available, home-made tabletop easels can be constructed out of a cardboard box. The sides of large wallpaper sample books also can be fashioned into two-sided table easels. Clothespins or binder clips can substitute for easel clips. Although painting is essentially an individual activity, children like to see what other children are doing and sometimes enjoy talking to each other while they paint. Therefore, try to have two easels in the Art Area to promote socializing and reduce the amount of time children have to wait their turn for this popular activity.

Wall easels are another alternative. Commercially made wall easels can be attached permanently to the wall or hung over a bookcase or fence. Or you can make your own wall easel. Tack a large piece of plastic or a drop cloth to the wall at an appropriate height for the children. Then attach chart paper or butcher paper to this protective backdrop. Place newspaper or plastic on the floor to catch drips. While easels allow children to throw their whole bodies into the painting process, some children get frustrated that the easel's slant causes paint to drip. For these children, you can set up painting at a table or cover the floor with newspapers and let them paint there.

A lapboard is appropriate for painters who wish to paint sitting on the floor, on a bench, or on the ground. Pieces of Formica or linoleum, cookie sheets, and trays all can make improvised lapboards if you don't want to purchase them.

Don't forget, too, that painting outdoors brings a fresh perspective. The sun's natural light and shade are themselves artistic elements. Freestanding easels can be carried outside. Outdoor easels with hooks can be hung on fences where children can get a view beyond their playground. Children also can paint standing or seated at outdoor picnic tables or seated on the ground using lapboards.

The best brushes for preschool children are those with metal bands and no seams. Brushes come with either flat or round bristles, and are known, accordingly as "flats" or "rounds." Flat one-inch bristle brushes are suggested for younger preschoolers; older preschoolers can use both flats and rounds for variety. If some children have trouble holding a paintbrush, insert the handle into a wad of clay to give the child a broader grasping surface. Long-handled brushes are best for painting at easels. Shorter brushes work best when children paint at a table or on the floor.

Children also enjoy trying out other kinds of brushes. These include anything from pastry brushes, makeup and powder brushes, bath or nail brushes, scrub brushes or vegetable brushes, hairbrushes, foam brushes, shaving brushes, toothbrushes, and whisk brooms to household paintbrushes, watercolor, or varnish bushes.

In addition to brushes, children can experiment with paint rollers, plastic squeeze bottles, sponges, cotton tips, balloons, eyedroppers, popsicle sticks, powder puffs, shoe polish or liquid makeup applicators, straws, marbles, string, and yarn. Each of these implements gives children a different type of painting experience. A final alternative to the traditional paintbrush is the human body. Hands and feet make attractive prints when covered with paint.

You can set up painting at a table or cover the floor with newspapers and let the children paint there.

Painting outdoors brings a fresh perspective.

Flat one-inch bristle brushes are suggested for younger preschoolers; older preschoolers can use both flats and rounds for variety.

Types of Paints

Liquid tempera lasts a long time and produces vibrant colors; however, it is costly. Detergent will improve the consistency of tempera (that is, keep it from cracking) and make it easier to remove from clothes. Bentonite (available in art stores) will thicken tempera paint and keep it from dripping while painting at an easel. Liquid laundry starch will make tempera paint creamy. Corn syrup or liquid glue gives tempera a glossy sheen. Glitter makes it sparkle. Shaving cream gives it volume. School glue makes it stringy.

Water-based paints, which include poster paint and watercolors, are good to use at a table. Smaller brushes are better.

Finger paints offer a completely different kind of painting experience. Children can control the paint by using their whole hand, the back of their hands, their fists, their fingertips, fingernails, or knuckles to produce differing effects. Trays, tabletops, and glossy paper all can be used as painting surfaces.

Dyes that are water-based can be used with textiles. Using string or rubber bands, children can tie-dye fabric for collages or make tie-dyed T-shirts. Water mixed with food coloring also can be used to paint. Vegetable-based dyes made by boiling beets, berries, beans, or onion skins are good for printmaking, stamp art, or coloring eggs.

Water, right from the tap, can be used as a type of paint. Children love to paint the side of a building, blacktop, or the sidewalk with water and watch it disappear.

Manila paper and newsprint are the most commonly used papers for painting in preschools.
Manila paper is of high quality and substantial weight, but quite expensive. Newsprint is less expensive and ideal for easel painting. Younger children need a large space on which to paint. Offer them paper that is 24" x 36". Older preschoolers can use smaller paper, 18" x 24", and also may appreciate using the higher-quality manila or white drawing papers. Always try to buy the largest size paper, then cut it down to meet different children's needs and uses.

For finger painting, glazed paper specifically meant for finger painting is preferable, but can be expensive. An alternative is to let children finger paint on a tabletop. The table surface gives children a lot of room to move and opens up possibilities for experimenting with paint rather than making a picture. Or you can use cafeteria trays or a large piece of heavy-duty plastic (such as a shower curtain) stretched over a table and taped in place. If children want a copy of their finger paintings, any type of paper can be placed on top of their picture and pressed down to create a reverse imprint.

In addition to these standard papers, here are some variations:

- butcher paper or grocery bags
- cardboard (flat, corrugated, boxes, or tubes)
- coffee filters or doilies
- computer printer paper
- construction paper or fadeless art paper (only one side is colored)
- molded paper or cardboard (e.g., egg cartons)
- oaktag or poster board

- onionskin, typing, or tracing paper
- paper plates
- shelf paper
- Styrofoam packing pieces or egg cartons
- tissue paper
- wrapping paper and recycled greeting cards

Smocks can be purchased, but using old adult-size shirts is more economical. Trim the sleeves of long-sleeved shirts and have the children put them on backwards for maximum protection. Make art sleeves by putting elastic on the tops and bottoms of shirt sleeves. Alternatively, you can use part of an old sheet or bath towel by cutting a hole in the center large enough for a child's head. An adult's T-shirt usually can be used as a smock without any alterations.

Drawing Materials

For drawing, children need paper and tools. These are basic drawing materials for the Art Area:

- **Markers**—water-based—in a variety of colors

- **Crayons**—jumbo crayons for younger children

- **Chalk**—white and colored, jumbo and narrow

- **Chalkboards**—wall-mounted, easel-style, or laptop

- **Paper**—all colors, sizes, and textures

Cutting and Pasting Materials

The materials you need are straightforward: scissors, glue, and paste. Be sure to have scissors for both left- and right-handed children. Provide safety scissors and the squeezable "snip loop" variety for preschoolers who are just beginning to learn how to cut. You'll need to get school paste and white glue, which is water-based. Glue sticks give children easy control over the pasting process.

In addition to cutting and pasting tools, think about assembling the materials that children will want to use for making collages. Here are suggestions:

• acorns, nuts, and seeds	• glitter
• beads	• netting and lace
• bottle caps	• old costume jewelry
• cheesecloth or gauze	• paper clips, binder clips, rubber bands
• clock and watch parts	
• coffee grounds	• paper lamb frills
• computer-related junk ("chip jewelry")	• pipe cleaners
	• ribbons
• confetti	• sequins
• cotton balls	• shells
• doilies	• shoelaces
• drink umbrellas	• string, yarn, and twine
• eggshell pieces	• toothpicks
• fabric/felt scraps	• wallpaper samples
• feathers	• zippers, hook and eyes, snaps, thread
• flowers	

Through experimentation, children learn that paste works when attaching paper to paper, but glue is needed to hold wood scraps together or to attach pieces of felt to cardboard. Glue can be watered down (half glue/half water) to make a kind of starch. This mixture is good for fabric or yarn collages. Children can put the fabric into the mixture, place it on a cardboard surface, and let it dry in that form.

Collages can be created on a variety of papers, including cardboard, heavy corrugated paper, or construction paper and poster board. Newsprint isn't recommended because it is too thin. Computer paper can be used as long as the children are just attaching paper scraps. Once children have developed skills in using scissors, they can cut pieces of paper or thin materials, such as wallpaper samples or ribbon, to the size and shape they want.

Collages can be created on a variety of papers.

Molding Materials
Children enjoy manipulating and creating with clay, playdough, and other dough-like materials. Each offers a different type of art experience, and each can be made in the classroom. Making these homemade art supplies using recipe cards provides children with valuable literacy experiences.

Clay is viewed by many preschool educators as an ideal medium.
Whole books have been written on this one subject. Researchers such as Sara Smilansky view clay as a central experience in the preschool classroom. As Smilansky et al. (1988) write:

> *Here, in one of humankind's oldest mediums of expression, is a way in which children can be helped to learn. Clay, found in the earth, shaped and molded by young hands, also helps to shape and mold the mind, allowing the young child an additional way in which to discover and make sense of the world (p. 20).*

Two types of clay are appropriate for preschool children: modeling clay (soft clay) and baking clay that can be baked in a kiln or left to harden on its own. Older preschoolers, with stronger hand muscles, also may enjoy playing with plasticene, an oil-based clay.

Modeling clay can be manipulated easily and made into balls, snakes, or different shapes. This soft clay is also fun to use with rolling pins, plastic knives, or tongue depressors. Clay that hardens can be painted, and the final products children make can be saved. Plasticene does not stick to surfaces, nor will it dry out. It cannot be baked or painted, however. It also takes concerted effort to knead plasticene to the point where it can be readily shaped and molded. Some children do not like its texture as much as they like the feel of real clay.

If you're fortunate, you can get clay from its natural source—the earth. You may need to clean out the sand that backyard clay usually contains, however. The sand in backyard clay feels scratchy and typically makes the clay crack as it hardens. To remove the sand, place backyard clay in a large tub of water. After approximately 15 minutes, the clay will float and the sand will sink to the bottom. Using a large slotted spoon, remove the clay. Then dry the clay to the right consistency and store it in an airtight container.

Many recipes are available for homemade clays that will not harm a child if swallowed accidentally. Two are listed on the following page.

Two types of clay are appropriate for preschool children: modeling clay and baking clay.

Older preschoolers also may enjoy playing with plasticene.

Quick Modeling Clay

Ingredients:	1 cup salt, 2 tsp. oil, 1 cup cold water, 3 cups flour, 2 T cornstarch, 1 T food coloring
Equipment:	Clay board (piece of formica, marble, Corian, or ceramic tile), storage container
Method:	**1.** Put salt, oil, water, and food coloring onto clay board. Work mixture into a ball. **2.** Gradually add and knead in flour and cornstarch. **3.** Continue kneading until mixture feels like bread dough. **4.** Store in airtight container.

Baker's Clay

Ingredients:	4 cups flour, 1 cup salt, 1-1/2 cups warm water
Equipment:	Bowl, spoon, storage container
Method:	**1.** Add salt to warm water and mix in a bowl. **2.** Add flour and stir in. **3.** Form mixture into a ball and knead for 5–10 minutes. **4.** Store in airtight container. (Clay products can be placed on cookie sheet, baked at 300 degrees for 1 hour, then painted and varnished.)

Playdough is another molding material.

Although playdough can be purchased readily, homemade playdough saves money and allows the children to vary its texture, color, and vibrancy. Here are two recipes.

Easy, No-Cook Playdough

Ingredients:	3 cups flour, 1-1/2 cups salt, 1/4 cup oil, 1 cup water, 1 T food coloring
Equipment:	Bowl, wooden spoon, storage container
Method:	**1.** Mix all ingredients together in a bowl. **2.** Form mixture into a ball and knead the dough. **3.** Add more flour if dough is too sticky. **4.** Store in airtight container.

Bouncy, Cooked Playdough

Ingredients:	2 cups flour, 1 cup salt, 2 T cream of tartar, 2 T oil, 1 cup water, 1 T food coloring
Equipment:	Saucepan, wooden spoon, storage container
Method:	**1.** Mix all ingredients together in a saucepan. **2.** Cook over medium heat, stirring constantly until the dough pulls away from the sides of the pan. **3.** Knead the dough into a ball. **4.** Store in airtight container.

Children's hands are the chief tool for playing with clay and playdough. You can introduce any number of accessories as well during the year to extend the children's art experience. These accessories include:

- alphabet and cookie cutters
- clay board and hammer
- clay rolling pins
- meat tenderizing mallet
- melon baller

- pastry bag and tips
- pie crimper
- plastic knife and fork
- plastic pizza cutter
- potato masher and ricer

There are other doughs to use as well.
They are silly putty, goop, oobleck, gak, glarch, glerch, slime, or flubber. These doughs have very strange properties not found in other types of materials. Most are slimy; many are unstable—hard one minute, flowing another. The disparities between the way these materials look and the way they feel offer lessons in both science and art. Here are recipes for some of these intriguing art materials. Because these materials break down easily and can get dirty, it's best to make them fresh each time you use them.

Gak

Ingredients:	1 cup white glue, 1 cup liquid starch, 3 drops food coloring
Equipment:	Plastic mixing bowl, wooden spoon, storage container
Method:	**1.** Pour glue and food coloring into bowl. **2.** Stir to mix in color. **3.** Add starch gradually, mixing vigorously. **4.** Stir until mixture is consistency of putty.

Oobleck (also known as cornstarch and water)

Ingredients:	4 parts cornstarch, 1 part warm water
Equipment:	Bowl
Method:	Mix ingredients together with hands until satiny smooth.

Glorax (also known as flubber)

Ingredients:	3 T water, 1 T white glue, 2 heaping T Borax
Equipment:	Ziploc bag
Method:	**1.** Pour all ingredients into Ziploc bag. **2.** Squish ingredients together into a ball. **3.** Remove and stretch.

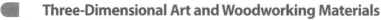

Three-Dimensional Art and Woodworking Materials

Three-dimensional art has great appeal to young children, adding an exciting perspective for children who want to recreate what they see and experience. In this category, we discuss assemblages, mobiles, stabiles, and woodworking.

Assemblages are three-dimensional collages.

Assemblages may be put together in many creative ways.

All of the materials listed for collage also can be used to make assemblages. While collage materials are glued or pasted to a flat surface, assemblages may be put together in many creative ways. A visit to an office supply store will give you many ideas for assemblage fasteners. Here are a few examples:

- brads
- binder and paper clips
- clothespins
- pipe cleaners
- ribbon
- rubber bands
- staples
- string, yarn, or twine
- tape
- twisties, wire

There are two types of assemblages. Mobiles are hanging sculptures that move and stabiles are freestanding mobiles.

Mobiles are constructed by suspending the moving parts from a stationary overhead base.

Mobiles are hanging sculptures.

Coat hangers—because of their shape and built-in hanging top—are natural supports for mobiles. Other materials that can be used as an overhead base include:

- driftwood or tree branches
- dowels
- rulers
- yardsticks

These platforms must be tied to the ceiling or a door frame with string, yarn, ribbon or wire using tacks or a hook. For young children, most mobiles are only one level—more than one level involves balancing skills that are beyond the typical preschooler's abilities.

Stabiles are mobiles that are freestanding.

Stabiles are more difficult for children.

They can be made using any of the assemblage materials we suggested. Stabiles are more difficult for children to make than mobiles because they tip easily. The key to constructing a stabile is using a large enough base to support the suspended items.

Woodworking is an exciting art experience for preschoolers.
Whether indoors or out, the first thing you need is a sturdy workbench. This can be purchased or home-made by cutting down a wooden kitchen table, by using a door and sawhorses, or by using a butcher block and wooden telephone cable spools. It should be child-size (24" high), made of strong wood, and secured well. Benches should not wobble and must be able to withstand constant pounding by children, who throw their whole bodies into hammering and sawing.

Like most materials in the classroom, introduce woodworking tools a few at a time. Bring out the basic ones first. Real tools provide a more authentic experience and are actually safer than toy tools that break and leave children vulnerable to injury. Before letting children use any woodworking tools, make sure they know and can demonstrate safe handling procedures. Basic tools and materials include:

> Real tools provide a more authentic experience and are actually safer than toy tools.

- backsaw with 10–14 teeth per inch
- miter box
- lightweight hammer (8 to 12 oz.)
- roofing nails
- C-clamp or vise
- soft wood
- yellow wood glue
- sandpaper (different grades)
- sandpaper block

Younger children may enjoy hammering golf tees or drywall screws into burlap-covered Styrofoam sheets, acoustic ceiling tile, or layered cardboard. Over time, children will enjoy using screwdrivers (both slotted and Phillips) with various screws, nuts, washers, and bolts. Older preschoolers can use an eggbeater-style hand drill with two or three different size bits. Rug samples, plastic bottle caps, tongue depressors, and metal juice lids add variety to constructions. Wood can be painted or stained with dyes. Pliers, rulers, and tape measures will enrich the experience further.

There is no end to the types of art experiences and materials you can provide. Once children are comfortable with the basics, introduce other art techniques that you think will trigger their creativity and provide them with fulfillment. Some of your many options are etching and printing, stitchery and weaving, and puppet making.

Displaying and Storing Art Materials

As in all activity areas, children will become fully engaged with their play when the shelves are orderly and inviting. Here are some practical suggestions:

Egg cartons with the edges taped together can be used to hold scissors.

Ice cream containers make good paper holders. They also can be used to store collage materials. Several containers stapled or bolted together can house a variety of small art items.

Six-pack cardboard beverage carriers can be made into paint caddies. Place a clean orange juice can lined with Contact paper in each of the six slots. Or use clear squeeze bottles so children can see the paint colors inside. Children can pick up the caddy and a brush, an advantage when easels don't have a paint drawer attached or when a wall easel is used.

A plaster of Paris holder can store markers upside down in their caps. Place the caps upside down in the wet plaster. Once the plaster hardens, the caps will stay in place and markers can be removed and returned to them.

Airtight containers can hold clay, playdough, and other doughs. Use either plastic with a tight-fitting lid or metal with a plastic liner.

Empty yogurt containers with plastic lids make good glue or paste containers, as do squeeze bottles used for ketchup or mustard. It is a good idea to have enough glue and paste containers for each child in the art area to have one to use himself.

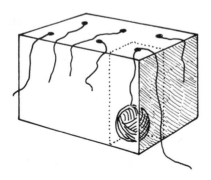

Yarn, ribbon, or twine dispensers can be made from a cardboard box with corrugated cardboard dividers. The divided areas make convenient spaces for individual balls of yarn/ribbon/string and prevent tangling. Punch a hole in the top of the box over each space and draw the strands through the holes.

A pegboard with hooks can be used to hang smocks or woodworking tools. Shadows of the objects can be cut out of colored Contact paper to show children where tools should be returned.

Displaying Children's Artwork

Children's drawings and paintings, prominently displayed, enhance the charm and warmth of any classroom. They also provide concrete documentation of what children have learned.

Selecting which pieces of artwork to display is often a challenge. Most teachers want to give all of the children in the classroom a chance to see their work on the walls or displayed on shelves. Too often, teachers assume responsibility for making this decision. A better alternative is to ask the children to make that choice. Give them the opportunity to decide which art they want displayed and which they would like to take home. This practice conveys respect for their judgment.

When hanging children's artwork, treat it as if it were on display in a museum. A simple construction paper backing can be used as a frame to give children's art a professional look. Framing shops sometimes will donate mats for this purpose. Some teachers work with children to make frames using cardboard, Styrofoam, or wood from the woodworking area or a piece of construction paper rolled up like a scroll.

What Children Learn in the Art Area

Work in the Art Area provides many opportunities to learn academic content as described in Chapter 3. Consider these natural linkages to literacy, math, science, social studies, the arts, and technology.

Literacy

To help children expand their **vocabulary and language** through art, introduce them to words describing art elements such as color (warm, cool, bright, dull), line (straight, zigzag, wavy, curly), shape (round, square, oval, diamond), space (near, far, inside, on top of), and texture (smooth, rough, bumpy, prickly). Ask questions that encourage children to express their thoughts and feelings through art.

Teach **knowledge of print** by having children sign their names to their pictures or post their names next to sculptures, mobiles, and assemblages. With their permission, write children's descriptions of their work directly on their artwork or on an accompanying sentence strip.

Expose children to some of the many wonderful children's **books and other texts** on art that call attention to artists and their styles of painting, such as *Camille and the Sunflowers* (Laurence Anholt) about impressionist Vincent Van Gogh; *Once Upon a Lily Pad: Froggy Love in Monet's Garden* (Joan Sweeney) about Claude Monet's paintings at Giverny; *Picasso and the Girl with a Ponytail* (Laurence Anholt) about painter/sculptor Pablo Picasso.

Mathematics

Introduce children to **number concepts** by pointing out that many artists both sign and number their prints. Help children develop an understanding of one-to-one correspondence as they place one paintbrush in each paint pot or replace a cap on each marker.

Encourage children to observe **patterns** in art such as stripes or alternating shapes. Challenge children to make patterns as they use stencils or sponge paint a border.

Invite children to explore **geometry and spatial sense** as they use three-dimensional shapes in sculpting and constructing. Talk about the shapes children use in their paintings. Use positional words—over, under, inside, next to—as you talk to children about their creations.

Give children practice with **measurement** by having them tear paper "as long as this shelf." Involve children in making art materials. They can measure ingredients as they follow the recipes.

Science

Introduce children to **physical science** by conducting experiments with different art media. As they add water to clay or mix paints together, encourage children to observe changes. Teach them about balance while building a sculpture or creating a mobile. Ask questions to help them explore the physical properties of materials ("What can we use to hold these wooden pieces together?").

Teach children about **life science** by having them incorporate leaves and flowers collected on a nature walk into their art. Bring in living things—plants and animals—to the Art Area for children to observe and draw.

Increase children's awareness of **earth and the environment** by having them observe the use of shadow in fine art and then trace their friends' shadows in chalk while playing outdoors. Create art using various items from the earth such as clay, sand, dirt, or water.

Social Studies

Encourage children to learn about **people and how they live** by drawing, painting, and sculpting the people and things in their world. Invite a parent or local artist to demonstrate pottery, weaving, basket making, or other works of art from their culture.

Promote children's knowledge of **people and the environment** by creating art that will beautify the environment at school. Encourage children to conserve materials by reusing clay, drawing on the backs of used paper, and keeping tops on markers.

The Arts

Tie **music** to art activities by playing background music that sets a tone and tempo for creativity. Have the children draw, paint, or sculpt in the manner that the music makes them feel.

Link art to **drama** by providing children with art supplies they can use to make backdrops and costumes for a puppet show or dramatic play.

Technology

Help children to develop an **awareness of technology** by teaching them how to use woodworking tools such as hammers, saws, and drills. Point out how carpenters use these same tools to build everything from houses, to outdoor decks, to picture frames.

Expand children's experiences with **technology tools** by giving them art programs such as *Magic Crayon* or *Kid Pix Deluxe 3*. Hang their computer-generated art alongside their other creations.

The Teacher's Role

Art materials, like blocks, have the potential for stimulating a broad range of creative endeavors. Teachers who understand the value and potential of art materials take an interest in children's pleasure as they apply paint to paper, glue wood scraps together, and pound a lump of clay. They appreciate that for preschool children, what they make is often less important than the creative process itself. And they know that art is a vehicle for children to express what they know and what they feel.

In addition to encouraging children to create with art materials, teachers can help children learn to appreciate art. As children observe their creations, the art of their peers, and the art of recognized painters and sculptors in their community and in museums, they develop an aesthetic sense. Fine art can both inspire and please them.

The teacher's role in *The Creative Curriculum* is based on this holistic view of art. Our philosophy has been influenced by the Reggio Emilia approach to art. Reggio teachers—like *Creative Curriculum* teachers—value children as both creators and "meaning makers." You play a vital role in making art a joyful learning experience.

Observing and Responding to Individual Children

Your first step in using the Art Area to promote children's learning is to observe what children do so you can determine how best to respond to each child. We suggest that you begin this task by observing where each child is developmentally. Children go through distinct stages that will give you clues to how they are developing and the skills they have mastered.

Stages in Painting and Drawing

The development of drawing and painting skills are very much like writing. Children need to scribble before they learn to write letters or draw realistically.

Stage I: Scribbling and Making Marks

In this first stage, children manipulate different media and enjoy the effect they have. They use crayons, pencils, or paintbrushes to make marks. Because their fine motor control and eye-hand coordination are still developing, they go through a long period of experimenting. The random marks and scribbles they make are a form of sensory exploration.

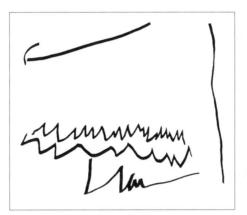

Stage II: Making Shapes, Outlines, Designs, and Symbols that Have Personal Meaning

In the second stage children become purposeful in their scribbling. Through continued drawing and painting, they begin to make patterns, to repeat patterns, and to create designs in their scribblings. A circle with lines in it may be Mommy's face, or actually represent Mommy's entire essence.

While adults may not recognize these patterns as being anything specific, they indicate an attempt to organize the children's world. At this stage, being able to create is more important than making something recognizable to adults.

Stage III: Pictorial Art that Is Becoming Recognizable to Others

Once children gain mastery of crayons, markers, and paintbrushes, they want to create something. Though they don't always plan their pictures beforehand, what shows up on the paper once they start to draw or paint makes them think of something.

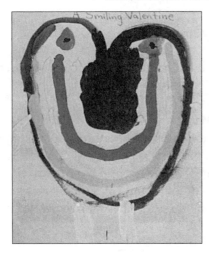 

With experience, older preschoolers will begin to plan in advance what they will draw or paint. The self-portrait is a typical favorite subject. Children may experiment with size, proportion, and placement on the paper. Many children will focus their drawing around a large circular head and tiny stick-like arms and legs.

Another benchmark of this developmental stage is "X-ray" art—depicting interiors and exteriors all at the same time. You might see a child's drawing of a firetruck that shows both the outside of the vehicle and the passengers and hose inside.

Stage IV: Realistic Art

By the time they are 4 and 5, most children are interested in doing art that looks real. As much as we want to avoid stereotypes, many boys like making drawings of superheroes, transportation vehicles, and war-like scenes. Girls frequently are interested in drawing people, rainbows, and floral vistas. Both boys and girls seem to like drawing the important people in their lives.

Stages in Using Other Art Materials

Although the stages children go through in other media aren't as clear-cut as the stages in drawing and painting, children's use of these media is nonetheless developmental. They move from a stage of exploration (functional play) to one of experimentation (constructive play).

Initially, children familiarize themselves with the medium: What does clay feel like? How do you hammer nails? What makes the collage items stick? How does a loom work? Children like to use all of their senses to learn about a particular medium before they begin to use it purposefully. Gradually, as they become familiar with the new medium, they experiment with it. They roll clay into worms. They pound roofing nails into a tree stump. They paste pictures on cardboard to see how they look when glued to a surface.

Increasing skills enable children to become ever more creative and purposeful in their art.

With experience, children's experiments become purposeful and more skilled. Eventually, they are able to turn clay into an animal, make a sculpture out of wood, make a balanced design in a collage, and weave scraps of ribbons on a loom. Increasing skills enable children to become ever more creative and purposeful in their art.

Responding to Each Child

From your observations of children using the Art Area, you can plan experiences that will further children's growth. As you carefully observe a child in action, reflect on what you have seen and heard, so that your response will help the child develop and refine skills. Think about whether a child

Observe carefully to learn how a child uses art materials.

- is able to effectively hold and use a scissors, paintbrush, crayons, chalk, and other art materials

- comes up with her own ideas or looks to others for inspiration

- represents her ideas and feelings in different art forms

- is able to describe what he likes about his own and others' art

- takes risks in creating art that looks different

- enjoys using art to illustrate stories and to make books

Based on your observations, you can determine each child's developmental strengths and challenges. Use the *Developmental Continuum* to guide your reflections and responses. The chart that follows gives examples of how this might work.

Observation	Reflection	Response
While gluing wood pieces together, Ben keeps trying to glue a round knob to a flat board without success. As he picks up the knob for the third time, he says, "Round things are hard to build with."	Despite encountering difficulties, Ben keeps trying to glue the knob to a board. *(Objective 24, Shows persistence in approaching tasks)* How can I help him maintain his interest in completing this task and experiencing success?	Encourage Ben to observe why round objects are hard to glue: "What do you think makes those round pieces so hard to build with?" Talk with Ben about how he might approach the task to ensure success: "Do you think it might help if we tape the round piece in place until the glue dries?"
Crystal rolls clay into four balls and sticks a pipe cleaner into each one. As she lifts one up she says, "I made you four cupcakes."	Crystal is able to use clay and pipe cleaners to construct and name real objects. *(Objective 37, Makes and interprets representations)* What can I do to encourage her to use the cupcakes to pretend? *(Objective 36, Makes believe with objects)* She matches one pipe cleaner for each lump of clay. *(Objective 33, Uses one-to-one correspondence)* How can I build on her skills to make math comparisons?	Use the child's words as an introduction to make-believe play, asking, "Oh what kind of cupcakes are they? I can't wait to eat one!" Tell Crystal: "Let's count to see if we have enough cupcakes so that everyone sitting at the art table can have one."
At the easel, Jonetta begins to paint a picture. As paint starts to drip down the paper, she complains loudly, "I can't make it stop!"	Jonetta notices the dripping paint but doesn't seem to know what the problem is. *(Objective 25, Explores cause and effect)* How can I help her wonder about this and test out some solutions *(Objective 25, explores cause and effect)* and think of this as a problem to be solved? *(Objective 23, Approaches problems flexibly)*	Say, "I wonder why the paint drips. What do you think?" If she is clearly frustrated offer some possible solutions, e.g,. wiping the brush or painting on a flat surface.
Juwan makes a sculpture of clay, twigs, yarn, and Styrofoam peanuts. After completing it, he announces, "I made a grasshopper."	Juwan manipulates objects with increasing control. *(Objective 19, Controls small muscles in hands)* He knows about grasshoppers and is able to construct a model that represents something specific. *(Objective 37, Makes and interprets representations)* How can I build on his interest in grasshoppers?	Comment on what he has done: "Tell me about your grasshopper. How did you know how to make one?" Suggest looking in a book to learn more about grasshoppers. Offer an idea: "Does your grasshopper need a home? What materials would you need?"

Interacting With Children in the Art Area

The Art Area is a place for children to explore and create. Your interest in what they are doing and producing is a very important factor in children's enjoyment of art and their developing sense of competence. In addition, because children express their ideas and feelings through art, teachers need to be attuned to what children are trying to communicate and thoughtful about their interactions with each child.

Introducing Children to New Art Experiences

For the most part, teachers need do no more than provide children with basic art materials and they will explore and experiment in the ways described above. Put a container of gak out on the art table and children will begin pounding it, dropping it, and nestling it in their hands to observe how this unstable substance reacts to different conditions.

Likewise, you can put out a tray of sponges, cotton swabs, or netting balls and challenge children to paint with these nontraditional brushes. Because art is a creative experience, you want children to experiment with materials without the constraint of preconceived notions of what they should be doing. Let children take artistic risks and the results will delight everyone.

Woodworking is one area where teachers need to impose rules and structure. Because woodworking involves tools that have the potential to be dangerous, you can never just let children explore them on their own. Therefore, first familiarize yourself with the woodworking tools. You cannot work comfortably with children if you feel unsure of how to use saws and drills safely. Some teachers who are anxious about incorporating woodworking into their program prefer to introduce woodworking Outdoors before trying it in the Art Area. You can bring out a workbench or use a tree stump.

Develop a set of safety procedures for woodworking, including some simple rules the children can follow. Write them down and review them with the children often. In this way, children will appreciate the reasons behind the rules and the importance of following them. Here are some rules that we suggest:

- Use woodworking tools only when an adult is present.

- No more than three children can be at the workbench at one time.

- Always wear safety goggles.

- Use only one tool at a time.

- Hold all materials in your hands; never in your mouth.

- Sweep up any sawdust on the floor so no one slips.

With most art materials, teachers can let children explore and experiment.

Once children learn the rules and develop skills in using the woodworking tools, you will feel more relaxed about including this valuable activity in your Art Area.

Talking With Children About Their Art

When you talk with children engaged in art activities, you make them aware of what they are doing and help them reflect on their work. You can use art as a time for vocabulary development (e.g., learning such words as texture, pastel, collage); concept development (e.g., learning shapes, colors, thick versus thin); and problem solving (e.g., learning about what happens if..., what goes first, what do we need). Conversation also helps children learn to appreciate art.

When you comment or ask children about their work with art materials, you convey the following messages:

- I am aware of what you are doing.

- I am interested in your efforts and therefore in you.

- I will help you look closely at your own work.

- I appreciate your growing confidence.

Because so much of children's art is experimentation—seeing what mixed colors look like or how water affects clay—it's not always easy to know what to say. For example, when presented with a painting of lines and squiggles, some adults might automatically say, "That's pretty!" or ask "What is this a picture of?" A much better approach, however, is to ask such questions as "Can you tell me about your picture?" or "What did you enjoy about doing this?" These questions encourage children to talk about their creations without feeling judged. Keep in mind that many young children have no idea what they've painted or drawn. And those who do may be insulted that their fish or tree is apparently not obvious to you.

When you talk to children engaged in art activities, you can do the following to support their efforts.

 Describe what you see: *I see you used all the colors on the easel today. You were very careful about what materials you used in your collage and where you wanted to put them.*

We suggest that you focus your comments on the basic elements of design, which include color, space, line, texture, mass or volume, balance, pattern, composition, and shape.

Talk about children's actions: *You really are pounding that playdough. Look how fast your arm is moving when you finger paint.*

Ask children about the process: *How did you make that new color? What part did you enjoy most? How did you make these tiny circles?*

 Ask open-ended questions that encourage children to think and respond: *What are some ways that we can use these scraps of wood? What will happen if you mix these two colors together? How is this collage different from the first one you made? What do you think you might want to do differently the next time you make something with clay?*

Use words that encourage and support the children's efforts: *You sure made a lot of paintings today. Which one should we hang up on the wall? You thought of so many different ways to use the loom. Perhaps you'll want to share these with the other children.*

Keep in mind that many young children have no idea what they've painted or drawn.

As noted in Part 1, rote praise tends to make children want to please adults rather than themselves. In developing an appreciation for art, children should learn to value the way art makes them—not others—feel.

Sometimes children get stuck or seem uninspired in the Art Area. By observing and analyzing the problem, you can respond appropriately. Here are some ideas:

When a child...	Try saying...
Tears up a drawing he just made	"I can see you are not happy with that drawing you made. Let's take a look together and see what bothers you so you can do one you like better next time."
Avoids materials that are messy	"You can put on a smock if you're worried about getting your outfit dirty. We'll be sure to clean up everything when you're done."
Ends an activity abruptly without finishing	"Is there anything else you would like to add to your collage?"
Seems unsure of what to do	"What do you think will happen if you dip the colored chalk in the starch first?"
Wants you to make a drawing for him	"Let's see what you have in mind. What's the biggest part of the cat? Can you draw that first?"
Doesn't know what to make and asks you for an idea	"Let's look through some books to get ideas. Maybe that will help."

In each of these examples, the teacher tries to build the child's confidence and foster a positive view of art activities. So many of us have had our creativity drained by negative art experiences in which our efforts were misdirected, ignored, discouraged, or dismissed. But you can give the children you teach two lifelong gifts: the confidence to try many different art activities and the ability to enjoy the process, regardless of the outcome.

Nurturing Children's Appreciation of Art

Your art program can also include art appreciation. As one educator has noted, "Few people continue to be art producers beyond childhood. But being an art appreciator is a skill and pleasure that can last a lifetime" (Epstein, 2001, p. 43).

Children of preschool age can readily learn to develop what museum educators term "art criticism" skills. Art criticism involves learning to enjoy different types of art. Use guided discussions to focus children's attention on the process of art and what it means to them as individuals. This concept may seem sophisticated, but even young preschoolers can begin to develop an aesthetic sense. Here are some suggestions.

Surround children with art—both theirs and the works of the masters—so they become aware of the presence of art in their everyday life. Integrate art into all areas of the classroom—not just the Art Area. Renoir's portrait of a young girl with a watering can might hang in the Discovery Area near growing plants. Framed covers of children's books might grace the wall in the Library Area. Van Gogh's painting of the potato pickers or Cezanne's bowls of fruit might inspire chefs in the Cooking Area. Fine art provides a subtle atmosphere of beauty. Hanging children's work among these masterpieces shows children that their art is honored.

Take the lead in introducing the topic. Ask questions that lead children to reflect on how art makes them feel and what it brings to mind:

> *How does this sculpture make you feel?*

> *Close your eyes and tell me what you remember about this picture.*

> *Are the colors in this painting friendly?*

> *What do you suppose the artist was thinking when he painted this picture?*

Encourage children to evaluate their own art. Children can learn to be critics of their own work if you give them a reason to reflect on what they have produced. For example, you can ask them to select which drawings they want to put in their portfolio or hang on the wall. Ask them to tell you why they choose those items and write down what they say.

Help children evaluate the work of other artists. Encourage them to guess at the artist's intention in creating a particular work of art. Why does one artist make paintings with splotches and lines and another artist do paintings that look like photographs?

Including All Children in Art

The Art Area can present special challenges for some children, in part because it involves relatively unstructured activities and abstract thinking. Depending on the problem, you can make modifications to help all children be involved in and benefit from art experiences.

If a child..	Try these strategies...
Has trouble finding and using art materials	Separate materials into containers by attributes or function. For example, markers might be arranged by color or size.
	Provide visual cues (for example, a strip of tape on the floor in front of an easel) to indicate where to stand.
	Define children's work space for drawing, sculpting, or collage material by marking a large area on the table with tape or providing cookie sheets to hold their artwork.
	Give children large sheets of paper to draw or paint on, to accommodate the broad arm movements typical of less mature development.
	Place brightly colored tape around paintbrushes and woodworking tools to show the child where to place his hand.
Has difficulty handling or seeing materials	Use modified items as needed, such as double-handled scissors (adult's fingers go outside of child's) or squeeze scissors; large-grip crayons or markers; squeeze bottles with handles for paints, etc. (such as an old syrup bottle). Children who do not have the use of their hands can paint with brushes secured to the head by Velcro headbands.
	Tape the top end of a large sheet of paper to the wall for cutting practice. (In cutting vertically from the bottom up, the child is forced to have the correct orientation for easy cutting.)
	Give children colorful, textured, and fragrant materials to enhance their art. Offer high-contrast (bright or dark colors) paints and markers and pastel papers, which reduce glare.
	Secure drawing paper to the art table and easel paper to the easel.
	Offer children opportunities to do art on the computer; for children with severe manual dexterity, voice-activated art programs are available.
Is easily frustrated	Help the child plan her project before she gets started, accessing and arranging all materials, and even deciding where she will display the artwork at the end of the session.
	Provide alternatives to gluing and pasting such as using Contact paper as a base for a collage or offering children precut pieces of tape.
	Limit the available choices—for example, provide only 2–3 paint colors, three or four collage materials, one or two props for playdough.

Ask a special education consultant for specific assistance to meet the individual needs of children in your class. Art is such an important part of the early childhood curriculum that you will want to find ways to involve and include all children in art experiences every day.

Frequently Asked Questions About Art

What is wrong with coloring books and precut patterns? The children love them.

Because art is another language for children to express themselves, coloring books, predrawn patterns, and adult-made models do not belong in a *Creative Curriculum* classroom. They leave little room for imagination, experimentation, individuality, or discovery—the true benefits of art. Moreover, many of these materials are frustrating to 3-, 4-, and 5-year-olds who don't have the manual dexterity or eye-hand coordination to color within the lines or to cut along predrawn lines.

When children are given coloring books rather than pieces of paper on which to draw, they receive a subtle but powerful message: "We don't think you can draw as well on your own." The same holds true for teacher-made models. Holding up a model of a teddy bear made from three circles as an example for children to follow is not an art experience for the child. The child's model will never be done as skillfully as the adult's. Besides, where is the creativity in producing a wall full of nearly identical teddy bears? As some observers might put it, these are examples of craft projects masquerading as art experiences.

Some people defend using coloring books or cutting out predrawn patterns on the grounds that such activities are good for developing fine motor skills. However, there are many other more developmentally appropriate ways for children to develop these same skills through art, for instance, by cutting out their own designs or learning to use a hammer, glue, tape, a stapler, or a hole punch. Others will tell you, "Children love coloring books." But many children also love sweets, violent superheroes, and staying up all night. Everything children like is not always what is best for them. It is up to us to provide children with experiences that will be most beneficial to them. A coloring book is not one of these.

Are there any art materials that are dangerous to use with young children?

Yes, there are. Many teachers use powdered tempera instead of the premixed, liquid kind. It is so much less expensive that it would seem a wise choice. It is not, however. When mixed with water, powdered tempera produces dust that children can inhale. It also contains pigments and preservatives that may be toxic to young children. We do not recommend powdered tempera for use with children under 12 because young children's growing bodies absorb toxic substances more quickly than do older children's and adults'. It also takes less of a potentially harmful substance to affect a younger child.

In addition to powdered tempera, all of the following materials may be toxic to young children and should be avoided:

- anything that is lead-based or contains asbestos
- permanent and dry erase markers

- epoxy or rubber cement
- powdered clay

- instant glue
- solvent-bond glue

- instant papier-mâché
- spray paint

- pottery glaze
- wheat wallpaper paste

Is there any reason I shouldn't use food as an art material?

In contrast to commercially available art supplies, food products make inexpensive art materials—either by themselves (e.g., macaroni strung as necklace beads or beans pasted into a collage) or as ingredients in an art-related recipe (such as clay or playdough). However, some teachers and families believe it is inappropriate to use food or food products for anything other than nutrition. Others think that as long as food is used for educational purposes, it is not being wasted. Still others believe it is acceptable to use food as an ingredient in art supplies, but not by itself. We suggest that you discuss this issue with your colleagues and the children's families. In most cases, if anyone objects, honor that person's viewpoint.

What about holiday art?

Holidays clearly pose a special challenge for teachers. Some teachers have a holiday-oriented curriculum, moving with the calendar from one holiday to the next. At the other extreme are programs that ban holiday celebrations altogether so as not to offend anyone who may not partake in a particular holiday. We suggest that at the start of your program year, you discuss this topic with the children's families and decide how you will approach the celebration of holidays. How important are these celebrations to the family's values? Do some families not celebrate any holidays?

Holidays can be celebrated in a respectful and developmentally appropriate way, exposing children to differing customs. For example, you can feature the value of a holiday— the "thankful" element of Thanksgiving and the celebration of love and friendship at Valentine's Day. Keep in mind that anything that you do for a holiday should allow the children to express themselves individually, in ways of their own choosing. What you don't want children to be doing is coloring pumpkin cutouts at Halloween or having everyone in the class dipping their hands in paint at Thanksgiving to make a print of a turkey's tail. The artwork needs to reflect the children's ideas and feelings—not yours or those in an activity book.

A Letter to Families About Art

Dear Families,

Art is an important part of our curriculum. Every day, children find a variety of art materials available on our shelves. Drawing, painting, pasting, molding and constructing are not only enjoyable but also provide important opportunities for learning. Children express original ideas and feelings, improve their coordination, learn to recognize colors and textures, and develop creativity and pride in their accomplishments by exploring and using art materials.

When children are engaged in art activities, we talk with them about what they are doing and ask questions that encourage them to think about their ideas and express feelings.

We are just as interested in the creative process as we are in what children make. We say things that will encourage children to be creative and confident, such as:

> *Tell me about your picture* instead of *Is that a house you made?*

> *It looks like the playdough is sticking to your fingers. What could we do to make it less sticky?*

What You Can Do at Home

Art is a very easy way to bring your child's school life into your home. Children love to bring home their art products to share with the most important people in their lives. Take time to talk with your child. Here are some things you might say:

> *Tell me about your picture.*

> *How did you decide which colors to use?*

> *What do you like best about it?*

> *Should we hang it up in a special place so we can all enjoy your work?*

You can help your child appreciate art right in your home. When you look at books together, talk about the illustrations with your child. Discuss the art on the walls in your home.

Art is something your child can do at home in almost any room. You might designate a drawer in the kitchen or living room as an art drawer, or use a bookshelf or sturdy cardboard box. In this space include crayons, marking pens, paper, a pair of child-sized, blunt-edged scissors, glue, and a separate box for collage materials. A child's mind is much more creative and artistic than any coloring book allows.

inside this chapter

351 How the Library Area Promotes Development

352 Connecting Play in the Library Area With Curriculum Objectives

354 Creating an Environment for the Library Area

355 Selecting Materials

360 Displaying and Caring for Materials

362 What Children Learn in the Library Area

365 The Teacher's Role

365 Observing and Responding to Individual Children

370 Interacting With Children in the Library Area

376 Frequently Asked Questions About the Library Area

379 A Letter to Families About the Library Area

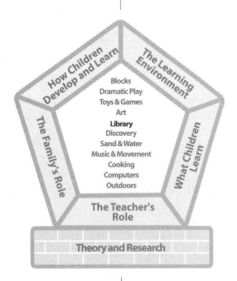

How Children Develop and Learn

The Learning Environment

Blocks
Dramatic Play
Toys & Games
Art
Library
Discovery
Sand & Water
Music & Movement
Cooking
Computers
Outdoors

The Family's Role

What Children Learn

The Teacher's Role

Theory and Research

Library

How the Library Area Promotes Development

An attractive space with soft furniture, beautiful picture books, and writing materials can be an oasis in the classroom—a place to get away from more active interest areas and relax. In the Library Area children develop the motivation and skills necessary to read and write. As they hear stories read aloud every day, look through books on their own, listen to story tapes, retell familiar stories, and make up their own stories, they also have many opportunities to grow in all areas of development.

Social/emotional development. From books, children learn about people who are like them and who are different. They feel comforted learning that others have had experiences or fears similar to their own and managed them. They develop empathy for those who have challenges and struggles that make life difficult. Children develop social skills when they share books together, re-enact a story, and write a card to a sick friend.

Physical development. Children strengthen the small muscles in their hands when they use tools for writing and illustrating. They use their eye muscles as they follow the pictures and words in a book.

Cognitive development. Books help children gain a better understanding of the world around them. They develop an understanding of symbols (relating the picture of a boy to the written word "boy"). They learn to make predictions and think about cause and effect ("If the pig builds his house of straw, the wolf will blow it down."). When they hear a story, children make connections between the story and things they already know. When they retell stories, they learn to sequence as they relate the events in a story in order. Children also can learn basic skills such as counting, number recognition, colors, and shapes through books.

Language development. All aspects of literacy—reading, writing, listening, and speaking—can be strengthened in the Library Area. When children hear stories, they learn new words and their meaning, and their comprehension grows. Children develop phonological awareness when they hear and explore the sounds and rhythms of language in books. They learn how to follow the flow of print on a page, left to right and top to bottom. Children use writing in a meaningful way in the Library Area when they create a message for a friend or a letter to Mom.

Since a love for books is a powerful incentive for children to become readers, every *Creative Curriculum* classroom includes an attractive Library Area filled with beautiful books and writing materials.

Connecting Play in the Library Area With Curriculum Objectives

Teachers who are familiar with the *Creative Curriculum* goals and objectives and the steps outlined in the *Developmental Continuum* can see how literacy crosses all developmental areas. They can use the Library Area to reach a wide range of learning objectives as shown in the examples on the following chart.

Selected Curriculum Objectives	What a Child Might Do in the Library Area
Social/Emotional Development	
3. Recognizes own feelings and manages them appropriately	Says, "I'm not scared of giants" after hearing *Jack and the Beanstalk*.
5. Demonstrates self-direction and independence	Selects a book and turns pages from left to right.
7. Respects and cares for classroom environment and materials	Notes a page is torn in a book and asks teacher for tape to fix it.
10. Plays well with other children	Invites another child to take part in dramatizing a story.
11. Recognizes the feelings of others and responds appropriately	After hearing Ira Sleeps Over (Waber), says, "He was scared to be away from his Mom and Dad."
12. Shares and respects the rights of others	Says, "When I finish using this puppet, I'll give it to you."
Physical Development	
19. Controls small muscles in hands	Uses hole puncher and stapler when making a book.
20. Coordinates eye-hand movement	Places disc in CD player and presses the "play" button.
21. Uses tools for writing and drawing	Writes messages, greeting cards, and signs during play.

Selected Curriculum Objectives	What a Child Might Do in the Library Area
Cognitive Development	
25. Explores cause and effect	While reading *Where the Wild Things Are* (Sendak) says, "If Max doesn't go home, he won't get any supper."
26. Applies knowledge or experience to a new context	After hearing the story of *The Rainbow Fish* (Pfister), talks about being a good friend.
27. Classifies objects	Gathers props for Baby Bear, Mama Bear, and Papa Bear.
30. Recognizes patterns and can repeat them	Joins in saying, "and he was still hungry" while listening to *The Very Hungry Caterpillar* (Carle).
31. Shows awareness of time concepts and sequence	Puts events in the plot in order when retelling a story, for instance, *The Napping House* (Wood).
Language Development	
38. Hears and discriminates the sounds of language	Says, "There's a ned on my head!" after hearing the story *There's a Wocket in My Pocket!* (Seuss).
39. Expresses self using words and expanded sentences	Dictates story for teacher to write under a drawing.
41. Answers questions	Responds when asked "What do you think this story is about?"
42. Asks questions	Asks, "How can the man wear so many caps?" while listening to *Caps for Sale* (Slobodkina).
43. Actively participates in conversations	Has conversation with friend about what kind of bread is served at school after reading *Bread, Bread, Bread* (Morris).
44. Enjoys and values reading	Asks for favorite book to be read at story time.
45. Demonstrates understanding of print concepts	"Writes" message to friend from top to bottom and left to right.
46. Demonstrates knowledge of the alphabet	Points and says letters while reading *Chicka Chicka Boom, Boom* (Martin).
47. Uses emerging reading skills to make meaning from print	Uses pictures as cues when "reading" *Rosie's Walk* (Hutchins).
48. Comprehends and interprets meaning from books and other texts	Dramatizes the story, *The Mitten* (Brett).
49. Understands the purpose of writing	Writes name on a card to "check out" a book in the Library Area.
50. Writes letters and words	Writes "I LV U" on card to mother and signs name.

Creating an Environment for the Library Area

An effective Library Area is inviting so children will want to spend time there. Such an area conveys the message that exciting things can happen in a quiet atmosphere. While children learn about reading and writing, listening and speaking in all interest areas, the Library Area is the hub of literacy learning. It should include spaces for looking at books, listening to recordings, writing, retelling familiar stories, and perhaps, a computer.

The books are displayed on open shelves with the covers facing out to spark children's interests. A wide variety of books are available that reflect children's interests and backgrounds.

A cozy area offers a place for both physical and emotional comfort. Add softness such as beanbag chairs, pillows, stuffed animals, and dolls.

Paper, pencil, and markers are easily accessible on a writing table. The alphabet and children's names are displayed.

Setting up the Library Area	Suggested Materials
Location:	Wide variety of children's books (e.g., story books, nursery rhymes, informational, predictable, alphabet, and number books) reflecting all cultures and backgrounds, displayed with covers facing out
In a quiet area of the classroom, away from traffic	
Carpeted floor with good lighting	A selection of big books
Near electrical outlets (for lamps, computers, and tape recorders)	Displays on walls, including book jackets, posters, a job chart, schedule, and the alphabet
Set up:	Tape or CD players and two headsets (or individual Walkman-type players)
Comfortable places to sit and look at books or listen to tapes	Computer word processing software
A table and chairs for writing	Hand puppets, flannel board, magnetic board, and other props for retelling stories
Computer stand and chairs	
Bookshelf to display books facing out	Assorted paper, lined and unlined
Big book stand	Assorted writing pens, paper, markers
Shelf for writing materials	Alphabet strips, name cards, letter and number stamps

Selecting Materials

The Library Area can be one of the most popular places in the classroom when teachers stock it carefully. Consider the books, tapes, writing materials, and storytelling props that are most appropriate and appealing for the children in your classroom.

 **Selecting Books**

With so many wonderful and appropriate books for young children, how do you go about choosing the best ones for your children? As with all materials, keep the ages and interests of children in mind when you select books. In general, younger preschoolers like books with a simple plot about familiar experiences; colorful and bold illustrations that are clear and filled with detail; lots of repetition in the plot; and rich language (rhymes, nonsense words, and repetition). Older preschoolers have a longer attention span and like books with a plot they can follow. They can appreciate humor and fantasy, and are beginning to enjoy stories about faraway places.

Put out a manageable number of books and rotate them regularly.

It isn't necessary to gather or to display your entire inventory of books at one time. It isn't even a good idea because stacking books defeats the goal of displaying covers. Put out a manageable number of books and rotate them regularly. In this way, children have the feeling of seeing new books or they are excited by old favorites they haven't seen for a while. As new interests emerge, you can add relevant books. In selecting books for your classroom, keep variety in mind. Here are some key features to consider.

Select books that relate to the interests and life experiences of children.
The "here and now" is a good starting point because it allows children to make connections to something meaningful in their lives. Young children's attention centers on themselves, their families, their homes, and their friends. They like stories about characters they can identify with easily. If a child has a new baby at home, choose a book for your Library Area such as *The Baby Sister* by Tomie dePaola. If a child has a particular interest in trucks, books like *Truck* by Donald Crews will inspire an interest in learning through reading.

Also include books that take children beyond the here and now to broaden their knowledge of the world. A child who is interested in a cat as a pet might enjoy books that have animals as the main characters, such as *Puss in Boots*, or picture books featuring cats. If a child is fascinated by airplanes, she might enjoy browsing through books about rockets and space shuttles.

Include books describing the cultures of the children represented in your classroom.

Multicultural books are another way of broadening children's experiences. Most important, include books describing the cultures of the children represented in your classroom. Listening to stories, folktales, and experiences of children from other cultures helps develop sensitivity and appreciation for other groups of people. The Library Area is a place for all children to gain information, ask questions, and express their feelings.

Select predictable books in which children can actively participate.
Books that encourage children to join in a story, repeating a phrase or refrain, are called predictable books. These books have the following characteristics: lot of repetition, rhyming, and refrains; cumulative text where one sentence is added on each page and the text is repeated (such as *The House that Jack Built* by Rodney Peppe); illustrations that exactly match the text; and text on each page that relates to only one idea or thought (Schickedanz, 1999). After a few readings of these types of books, children learn to retell the story word-for-word as they look at the book independently or read to a doll. These activities help children view themselves as readers and give them opportunities to practice reading.

After a few readings of predictable books, children learn to retell the story word-for-word.

Select books that enrich children's language development.
Exposing children to complex language and vocabulary advances their comprehension. The language in children's non-predictable books, which is typically more formal than our spoken language, challenges children's understanding. For instance, listen to the complex language in Jan Brett's book, *The Mitten*:

> *A waft of warm steam rose in the air, and a fox trotting by stopped to investigate. Just the sight of the cozy mitten made him feel drowsy.*

Books such as *The Mitten* that are rich in language help to build children's vocabularies.

Select books that help children gain knowledge of the alphabet and phonological awareness.
Research shows that children who know about the alphabet and who understand that words are made up of separate sounds are more likely to experience success when they are learning to read. As children look at alphabet books, such as Bill Martin's *Chicka Chicka Boom, Boom*, they begin to point out and talk about the letters they see. To encourage children to play with language, read aloud Dr. Seuss books such as *There's A Wocket in My Pocket!* or Bernard Most's *Cock-a-Doodle-Moo!*

Select books that reflect diversity and promote inclusion.
Books for all children should challenge prejudice, bias, and stereotyping and convey positive messages about differences of all kinds. Therefore, select books with the following characteristics:

- Men and women are seen in a variety of roles, displaying the ability to make decisions, solve problems, care for family members, and work outside the home.

- Family configurations are varied (e.g., a father and child, two children and a grandmother, etc.).

- Illustrations portray people accurately (e.g., mothers who wear clothing other than aprons and people of various ethnic origins portrayed realistically, not stereotypically).

- People of all ethnic backgrounds are seen to be assertive, have and solve problems, make decisions, take on a variety of family roles, and display a wide range of emotions.

- Adults and children with disabilities participate in all aspects of life, including mainstreamed schooling, an active family life, and sports and other recreational activities.

Books that are rich in language help to build children's vocabularies.

Children who know about the alphabet are more likely to experience success when they are learning to read.

Books should convey positive messages about differences of all kinds.

For children in your program whose home language is not English, provide books in their primary language. This practice conveys to children and their families that their primary language is honored and respected.

On the Teaching Strategies web site (www.TeachingStrategies.com), you will find a list of recommended children's books. You can use this list to build and supplement your own selection of books for your classroom.

Materials for Story Retelling

> Retelling stories is important for building comprehension skills, language structure, and a sense of story.

Retelling stories is important for building comprehension skills, language structure, and a sense of story. After children have heard a story several times and have seen the story retold using props, they will want to retell it independently. For retelling, select books that have story lines that are easy to follow, such as *The Napping House* (Audrey Wood), *Caps for Sale* (Esphyr Slobodkina), or *Mrs. Wishy-Washy* (Joy Cowley). In addition, look for books that:

- have repetitive phrases, e.g., *Mrs. Wishy-Washy*

- contain familiar sequences, e.g., *The Very Hungry Caterpillar*

- include conversation, e.g., *Who Sank the Boat?*

- are popular and familiar to the children, e.g., *Caps for Sale*

Include materials in the Library Area that encourage children to tell their own stories and dramatize stories they have heard. Props such as flannel boards and puppets stimulate storytelling and engage children's active learning. Here are some suggested materials:

- story clothesline (children use clothespins to hang pictures from a story in the correct sequence on a clothesline)

- flannel board

- Velcro board

- magnetic board

- storytelling apron

- puppets (made from cloth, popsicle sticks, paper bags, or wooden spoons)

- props from the Dramatic Play Area

Materials for Listening

Children can practice following a story in a book, turning the pages at the appropriate time, and matching the story with the pictures when you include tapes or familiar stories. If possible, the Library Area should include two or three small cassette players and a variety of tapes (or CD players and CDs) for children to select. Headphones allow children to listen to tapes without disturbing others.

The same general guidelines noted for books also apply to selecting story tapes. The best tapes are

- short, because children's attention spans are limited

- lively in their presentation, because nothing is more boring than a dry, monotonous voice

- high quality, without static and hisses

- anti-bias in content

- narrated by both men and women

In selecting story tapes, begin with stories that are familiar to children or that accompany books you have in the classroom.

In selecting story tapes, begin with stories that are familiar to children or that accompany books you have in the classroom. You can make tapes yourself, recording books that the children particularly love and know well. As you record the story, you might wish to include sound effects or put in cues to let children know when to turn the page while reading along with the tape. You can also pause for a few moments while recording the story to encourage the children to respond interactively. Invite family members or community volunteers to help you make tapes for the children.

Materials for Writing

When you include writing tools in the Library Area children can explore the world of print. A place for writing offers children an opportunity to use writing for a purpose—to create a greeting card or write a message to a friend. Include a table and chairs as well as a shelf for storing writing materials. On the following page is a list of suggested materials to include in this space.

Materials for Writing

Writing tools

- variety of pencils — "chubby" and regular
- magic markers—thick and thin, water-based, variety of colors
- chalk and chalkboards
- magic slates or "magnadoodle" boards
- crayons
- lap pads
- clipboards

Printing tools

- letter and design stencils
- alphabet letter stamps and ink pad

Paper

- computer printer paper
- magazines
- index cards
- envelopes and stationery
- unlined and lined paper
- construction paper
- carbon paper
- small blank books

Other tools and materials

- hole punch
- stapler
- paste or glue stick
- old wallpaper samples to use as book covers
- scissors
- paper clips
- pencil sharpener
- typewriter or computer with word processor
- small alphabet strips

Displaying and Caring for Materials

The way materials are displayed in the Library Area can affect how often and how effectively children use them. Books should be in good repair and attractively arranged on shelves so that children will be drawn to them. They need to be freestanding, with their covers in view, so children can pick out titles readily by themselves.

Tapes and writing materials can be stored on shelves or grouped in storage containers such as bins, cans, folders, and boxes. Draw pictures of objects contained inside a folder or box to let children know exactly where particular items are stored.

Include the written word on labels as well as a picture of the object. By adding words to the picture, you can help children use written language while they seek out and clean up library materials.

If books are torn and marked up, pencils have no points, and markers are dried out, children soon get the idea that the Library Area is not a very important place to be. Check periodically to see that all books, tapes, and equipment are in good repair. Torn materials, nonfunctional cassette players, and worn-out supplies should all be replaced as soon as possible.

Ask children for help in caring for library materials. Books in particular should be checked routinely and mended with the children's help. Preschoolers can learn to tape torn pages and erase pencil marks in books. To facilitate this effort, a book repair kit can be kept in the Library Area. A shoebox or plastic container works well to house the repair items, which might include

- transparent tape to repair torn pages

- cloth tape to repair the spines of books

- gum erasers to remove pencil marks

- correction tape to cover ink and crayon marks

- a pair of scissors

Keeping a book repair kit in the library, using it yourself, and encouraging children to use it conveys the message that books are to be respected and cared for by everyone in the classroom.

What Children Learn in the Library Area

In Chapter 3, we identified the key components of standards in each content area—literacy, math, science, social studies, the arts, and technology. Because reading and writing serve as vehicles to learn about all content areas, the Library Area offers a wealth of opportunities to connect content, teaching, and learning. Here are some of the many ways that content is addressed in the Library Area.

Literacy

Expand children's **vocabulary and language** as you introduce them to new words in books. Relate the words they are learning to their own experiences. Help children expand their general knowledge by offering them a wide variety of books on different topics.

Develop children's **phonological awareness** by reading stories that play with language such as Dr. Seuss books and other rhyming books. As children begin to write, help them think about the sounds of words, e.g., "Milk. . . that starts the same way your name, Mikey, does."

Enhance children's **understanding of books and other texts** by drawing their attention to the different forms of print in their environment. Include a variety of materials to read in the Library Area, such as magazines, information books, story books, and alphabet and number books.

Increase their **knowledge of print** by sweeping your hand under the words as you read, or demonstrating writing top-to-bottom and left-to-right on a chart. Offer children opportunities to use print by setting up a message board or mailboxes. Teach children about letters and words by talking about them as they read and write.

Develop their **comprehension** skills by using open-ended questions during storybook reading. Encourage children to retell familiar stories using props to gain a sense of story.

Encourage children to view **literacy as a source of enjoyment** by reading and re-reading favorite stories. Put expression in your voice and show your passion for good books.

Mathematics

Guide children's understanding of **number concepts** by including counting books in the Library Area. Gather a collection of books focusing on a number, such as *The Three Little Pigs*, *The Three Billy Goats Gruff*, and *The Three Wishes* to help children conceptualize the number three. Talk about and compare quantities in your story time discussions. For example, in Pat Hutchins's book, *The Doorbell Rang*, Ma bakes 12 cookies that have to be divided differently in order to be shared each time more children ring the doorbell. Talk about big numbers as you read books such as *How Much Is a Million?* by David Schwartz and Stephen Kellogg.

Call children's attention to the various **patterns and relationships** found in books. Point out visual patterns and help children discover language patterns in predictable books.

Teach children about **geometry and spatial sense** in their world by talking about the photographs of everyday surroundings in Tana Hoban's books such as *Shapes, Shapes, Shapes* or *Over, Under, & Through*.

Promote an understanding of **measurement** by pointing out comparative words in books, such as an "enormous turnip" or a "teeny tiny woman." Emphasize time concepts by stressing words such as "a long, long time ago," "tomorrow," "in a little while," or "many days later." A book such as *The Tortoise and the Hare* will talk about fast, slow, and the passage of time.

Science

Encourage children to use informational books in the Library Area to learn more about plants and animals, core topics of **life science**. You can incorporate all areas of science into a cooking activity after reading *Stone Soup*. Children learn about healthy foods for the body (life sciences), how to boil water and use kitchen tools (physical science), and about stones (earth and the environment).

Help children learn about **physical science** by sharing informational books about how things work or fiction books featuring gadgets such as *The Cat in the Hat*.

Support children in using what they have learned about the **earth and the environment** by having them dictate a letter urging the school not to cut down the trees near the playground.

Social Studies

Promote an understanding of **people and how they live** by reading stories from other lands or about different occupations. Share books that will help children deal with their feelings and emotions and that show them examples of friendships. Books can help illustrate how people are alike and different. Provide opportunities for children to write a letter or a get-well card or a thank-you note to a parent.

Use children's books as tools to support understanding of **spaces and geography**. Children learn about directionality as they hear vocabulary words such as above, below, around, forward, backward. Help them learn beginning mapping concepts by exploring books like *Me on the Map* (Joan Sweeney) or *As the Crow Flies: A First Book of Map*s (Gail Hartman).

Show children how they can use writing to advocate for a better **environment**. Children can create signs urging others to recycle.

Enhance children's understanding of **people and the past** by sharing books about life long ago. Invite a grandparent to share a favorite childhood story or rhyme with your class.

The Arts

Develop appreciation for the **visual arts** by talking about the illustrations in books. Point out the name of the illustrator on the cover each time you read a book. Compare the techniques the artists use, for example Leo Lionni's torn-paper pictures or Alexandra Day's watercolors of Carl the Dog.

Nourish a child's interest in **music** by reading picture books based on songs such as "This Land Is Your Land" or "Down by the Bay." Encourage children to explore **drama** and **dance** by dramatizing familiar stories.

Technology

Help children develop an **awareness of technology** by pointing out computers, phones, faxes, and other technology tools in stories. Provide opportunities for children to use tape recorders to listen to stories.

Encourage children to experiment with **basic operations and concepts** of technology as they use simple word processors or computers to read interactive stories such as the *Living Book* series.

These are just a few of the ways you can address content in the Library Area. In the next section we show how teachers purposefully plan experiences with books and writing materials to help children acquire critical skills in reading and writing.

The Teacher's Role

By observing what children do in the library and reflecting on what you see, you can learn a lot about what each child knows and can do. When you spend time in the Library Area talking with children about what they are doing, commenting on what interests them, and asking open-ended questions, you promote their learning.

Observing and Responding to Individual Children

Some children have had many experiences with books at home and come to school with early reading and writing skills. Others are being introduced to literacy skills for the first time. In the library, all children—no matter where they start—are led along the path to reading and writing. Teachers who know what specific skills children are acquiring in using books and the developmental stages in writing can guide children's learning in the Library Area.

 Skills for Engaging With Books

When you encourage children to develop a love of books, you are helping them to explore new worlds. If they love stories, they will be eager to read on their own, practice reading, and ultimately read for their own information or pleasure. Once they become readers, their world is enriched forever.

Learning to read is a complex process that involves many skills that develop simultaneously rather than in a set sequence. Look for and encourage children's skills as they progress on the road to reading.

Listening for understanding.
Listening and reading are closely related. As children listen to stories, they learn the meaning of new words. They try to make sense of these words by connecting them to their own experiences. Later, when children begin reading, they have an easier time recognizing a word when they know its meaning. Listening to stories improves children's ear for grammar and the structure of language. This skill helps to pave the way for figuring out what sounds right and makes sense in a sentence.

Exploring books.
Copying adults and older children, young children like to play at reading. Even though a child may not be actually reading, he will display many reading-like behaviors. He will hold the book correctly and turn the pages appropriately. Children also want to have books read to them, frequently asking for the same picture book over and over again at one sitting. Often it's adults who tire—long before the child—of hearing the same story read many times. Children enjoy repetition because they love to anticipate what happens next and feel powerful knowing the answer.

> Learning to read is a complex process that involves many skills that develop simultaneously rather than in a set sequence.

Understanding how stories work.
Children gradually recognize that stories have a beginning, middle, and end. They use pictures as cues to remember the details of their favorite stories. You might hear children use book language such as "Once upon a time..." or "and that's the end of our story." After repeated readings of a picture book, children call on their comprehension and verbal skills to retell the story.

Understanding the function and value of print.
Readers understand why and how print is used. Throughout the classroom, from a menu, a daily schedule, or a name on a cubby, children learn that print gives us information. Children use books as a source of information to locate a picture of a bug they found on the playground or a truck they saw passing on the street.

Recognizing that written words are symbols.
When children are first introduced to books, they often believe that it is the picture on the page that is read. Gradually, they start to relate the stories contained in books to both the pictures and the words on the page. They realize that printed words function differently from pictures and that words are symbols that stand for ideas and thoughts.

Connecting written symbols with sounds.
As children explore the sounds and rhythms of language, they begin to understand that spoken words are made of individual sounds that are represented by the letters of the alphabet. When they listen to the story of Ping, a child may say, "That starts the same way as my name!"

Matching words with the printed text.
You may see children run their fingers along the text or point to individual words as a book is being read. They may begin matching spoken with printed words by pointing. These behaviors indicate that they are beginning to understand the concept of a word although they cannot necessarily read words correctly.

Children may notice words from a favorite book and excitedly point them out in less familiar books or real-life settings.

Recognizing printed words.
Children who have learned this skill take an active interest in the text and demonstrate curiosity about the meaning of words. They may ask questions such as: "What does this say?" or "Where does it say that?" Children develop a sight vocabulary. They may notice words from a favorite book and excitedly point them out in less familiar books or real-life settings.

Developmental Steps in Writing

Long before children come to school, they have seen writing displayed and used in their environment. When children have opportunities to write in the context of everyday activities, they learn many important literacy skills such as concepts of print, functions of print, and phonological awareness.

The *Developmental Continuum* maps the stages of writing in objective 50, "Writes letters and words." We have given you more information on each of the steps below to guide you as you analyze children's writing.

Forerunner: Scribbling. Young children love to use pencils, pens, crayons, and other writing implements to imitate adult writing. These early attempts at writing mark the first developmental stage. Although writing at this stage looks more like scribbling than anything else, it takes on definite form. In the child's mind, beginning attempts at writing are quite different from beginning attempts at drawing. The illustration at right shows how a child organized scribbles horizontally on the page.

Step I: Scribble Writing and Letter-Like Forms. In the second stage of development, scribbles gradually transform into little marks. Many times, a recognizable letter will suddenly emerge from a row of little marks. The first letter of a child's name is usually one of the first to emerge. With practice, though, recognizable letters begin to outnumber unrecognizable marks.

Step II: Writes Recognizable Letters. In this stage you will see recognizable letters. Sometimes a child will fill a whole page with one letter he has learned to write. Or, every letter he knows will be written randomly on a page. Usually the first letters to emerge are the ones that are most important to a child—those in his own name. In the illustration at right, a child wrote a shopping list of five items and read it to the teacher—eggs, ice cream, cherries, potato chips, and bubble gum. As you can see, she writes many letters, but has not yet begun to associate each letter with a sound.

Step III: Uses Letters that Represent Sounds in Words. By the end of preschool years and early in kindergarten, children's writing generally shows increased organization. Children learn that letters are not just placed randomly on a page. Often they will sit and write rows and rows of letters, sometimes in alphabetical order. Next, children attempt to write words by writing the sounds they hear. For example, in the illustration at right, a child drew a picture of a brontosaurus and wrote "Brtsrs." When children spell this way, they are grasping the concept that a word is made up of a series of sounds—an important skill in learning to read.

Responding to Each Child

Children using the library materials tend to be quiet, so there is a temptation for busy teachers to turn their attention to more active and noisy areas where children demand their immediate assistance. Yet the Library Area offers so many opportunities for learning that it's important to make time during every work period to visit the area and talk with children.

You can gain many insights into a child's language development and emerging literacy skills by focusing your observations. An appropriate starting point for your observations is to look for the reading behaviors and developmental stages of writing described earlier. In observing a child's use of the Library Area, notice if the child

- shows a preference for certain topics or books and often connects them to familiar experiences

- talks about the story, pretends to read it, and points out words in the text

- handles a book appropriately and follows print from left-to-right and top-to-bottom

- retells stories in his own words or by using props

- writes or scribbles messages to communicate meaning

These kinds of focused observations can provide a picture of each child's interests and skills in library-related activities. Your assessment then can be used to plan specific activities to extend each child's learning and growth. As you observe children in the Library Area, keep *The Creative Curriculum Developmental Continuum* in mind. This framework will help you to determine where a child stands on a continuum of learning and what you can do to help her progress. Look at the examples on the following chart to see how you might respond to promote learning.

An appropriate starting point for your observations is to look for the reading behaviors and developmental stages of writing described earlier.

Observation	Reflection	Response
Zack holds a pencil in his fist when he is attempting to write.	Zack is making attempts at writing and seems to be in the scribbling stage. *(Objective 21, Uses tools for writing and drawing; and 50, Writes letters and words)* Are the small muscles in his hands developed enough to hold and control a pencil correctly? *(Objective 19, Controls small muscles in hands)* Has Zack had many opportunities to write?	Offer Zack writing tools in different sizes—chubby and regular—and have him choose which one is most comfortable. Show him how to hold it. Encourage him to build the small muscles in his hands by using small manipulatives and playdough.
Kate points to the pictures in a book and pretends to read to a baby doll.	Kate chooses to read a book over the other classroom activities. *(Objective 44, Enjoys and values reading)* She imitates beginning reading behaviors. *(Objective 48, Comprehends and interprets meaning from books and other print)* Does Kate realize that it is the words on the page that are read and not the pictures? *(Objective 47, Uses emerging reading skills to make meaning from print)*	Invite Kate to choose a book for story time. When reading a story to Kate, occasionally sweep your hand under the words. Provide her with props and encourage her to dramatize a story.
Derek asks how to spell "Pappy" when creating a get-well card for his grandfather.	Derek writes to convey meaning. *(Objective 49, Understands the purpose of writing)* He is able to write recognizable letters and copy letters that I form. *(Objective 50, Writes letters and words)* Is he able to hear any letter-sound connections? Do I have appropriate materials to support his interest in writing?	As you write the word, "Pappy," on a piece of paper, talk about the letters as you write them and what other words start with the same sound. Include interesting stationery, markers, and stickers to encourage card-making. Share books such as *First One Foot, Then the Other* by Tomie dePaola to help him talk about his feelings.
Tasheen pretends to walk through tall grass and then chants, "Swishy swashy! Swishy swashy!" while joining others in dramatizing *We're Going on a Bear Hunt*.	Tasheen participates interactively in story time and acts out main events. *(Objective 44, Enjoys and values reading; and 48, Comprehends and interprets meaning from books and other texts)* She often plays with words in stories and rhymes. *(Objective 38, Hears and discriminates the sounds of language)* Are there similar stories and rhymes I can share with Tasheen to strengthen her phonological awareness? I wonder if Tasheen is able to retell this story in the correct sequence.	Invite Tasheen to lead others in chanting words to this story during group time. Introduce her to Dr. Seuss books and similar stories that play with words. Offer Tasheen props to help her retell the story. Help her learn the meaning of the words in the story such as "cave" or "stream."

Interacting With Children in the Library Area

Teachers are role models for young children. If you show children how much you enjoy books, and they see you writing often and for a purpose, children will want to imitate you. The Library Area is a place where teachers actively read books to children, tell stories, enjoy listening to tapes, and promote children's writing.

Reading Books to Children

There are two things to keep in mind about reading books to children. First, reading aloud is the very best way to inspire a love for reading and promote language and literacy skills. Second, it's how you read a story that makes a difference. Research has shown that children's language development is positively influenced when adults encourage them to become involved in the story by asking open-ended questions, adding information, and prompting them to make a connection to their prior experiences (Whitehurst, 1992).

The following chart shows the kinds of questions and comments you might think about.

Interactive Story Reading	
Kind of Question or Comment	**Example**
Completion—Leave off a word at the end of a sentence and let the children fill it in.	"Run, run, as fast as you can. You can't catch me. I'm the Gingerbread _____."
Open-ended—Ask the children a question that will make them think of several different answers.	"What do you think the Gingerbread Man is doing in this picture?" "I wonder why the Gingerbread Man wanted to run away. What do you think?" "How would you feel if you were a Gingerbread Man?"
Who, What, When, Where, Why, and How—Ask the children these kinds of questions about the story and the pictures.	"What did the baker use to make the Gingerbread Man?" "What did the little old man say when the Gingerbread Man ran away?" "Where did the fox want the Gingerbread Man to go?" "Why do you think the fox wanted the Gingerbread Man to ride on his head across the river?" "How did the fox trick the Gingerbread Man?"
Connections—Help the children see how the story relates to something familiar.	"Have any of you ever eaten gingerbread?" "Did anyone ever try to trick you?"

There should be at least one time, and preferably more, every day when you read aloud to a group of children. Reading to a group of preschoolers makes it a social experience as well as a learning event. These strategies will make for successful story reading with a group of preschoolers.

Strategies for Reading Stories to Children

Carefully select books for reading aloud. Choose books that you enjoy and you think the children will enjoy. Repeat familiar, well-loved books. Make sure all books are an appropriate length and will capture children's interest.

Prepare before you actually read aloud. Practice reading the story aloud before you read it to the group. If you plan to use props, gather them ahead of time. Think about the questions you will ask or prompts to involve children in the story.

Transition into story time. When you want children to move from an activity into a group for reading, sing a transition song to signal that you are beginning. You can even make up a song to a familiar tune, "Do You Know the Muffin Man?": "Do you know it's story time? It's story time. It's story time. Do you know it's story time . . . In our preschool today?"

Set the stage for story time. Make sure the children are comfortable and can see the book you are reading. Do something to capture children's interest when introducing the story, such as wearing the same or a similar hat as one of the characters in the story.

Use expression while reading. Change your voice to match the character. Use body language while reading such as making a fist and frowning when a character is mad.

Take your time as you read. Slow your pace so children can form a mental picture of what is happening in the story.

Show the pictures. Draw children's attention to the pictures to help them understand the story and predict what will happen next.

Occasionally run your fingers under the text. Help children learn that it's the words, not the pictures, that are read. This technique also shows children you are reading from left to right and top to bottom on a page.

Involve children in the story. Pause and wait so children can join in a predictable phrase or complete a sentence. Stop to ask thinking questions like, "Where did he go?" or "What do you think will happen next?"

Showcase the book after reading. Display the book on the top of a shelf in the Library Area after reading so that children will want to re-read it during choice time. Add props so that children can retell the story.

In addition to reading aloud to a group of children, there will be times when you, or other adults, will read a book to just one child. At these times you can focus on specific skills with that child. Here are some strategies.

Before reading:
Have the child sit comfortably beside you or in your lap.

Note a child's preferences: *This must be your favorite book. You've picked it out every morning this week. Tell me what you like best about it.*

Look at and discuss the book's cover: *I wonder what this story is about.*

Take a "picture walk" with the child by talking about the illustrations in the story and asking the child to predict what might happen: *I wonder why the insects are hiding in the grass in that picture.*

During reading:

Reinforce how the child handles books: *I can see from the careful way you are turning the pages that you really know how to take care of our books.*

Encourage the child to think critically: *What would you do if you were Andrew? Why do you think Peter's mother said, "No"?*

Help the child come up with new ideas and solutions: *That glue on her shoes really slowed her down, didn't it? What else would you do?*

Anticipate the storyline as you read: *What do you think will happen next?*

Explore feelings: *Have you ever felt like Francis? I bet you know just how Ira felt about sleeping at a friend's house. Have you ever stayed overnight at a friend's house?*

Relate what is happening in the story to the child's own life: *The little boy in this story has a new baby brother, just like you do, Tasheen.*

Encourage the child to point to words: *Can you find where it says "Dog"? It starts like your name, Derek.*

After reading:

Discuss the completed story with the child: *What did you like about this story? Who was your favorite character?*

Encourage the child to retell or act out the story: *Would you like to use flannel board pieces to tell the story?*

Retelling Stories With Children

Retelling stories helps children to grasp the structure of the story and to understand its meaning.

Like reading books, storytelling inspires children's interest in reading. When done in an animated way and with props, storytelling can fascinate children as much as their favorite picture books. Children also can retell stories they know or make up stories. In this way, they gain a greater understanding of the relationship of the written and spoken word.

Retelling stories, either in the same way they were told originally, or in a new and different way, increases children's enjoyment of a story. Retelling helps children to grasp the structure of the story (beginning, middle, and end) and to understand its meaning. The best stories for retelling are predictable books that have a simple story line, few characters, and a recurring pattern. To encourage children to retell stories, consider the following suggestions:

- Reread favorite stories during group-time activities.

- Gather a few simple props to use in the retelling.

- Model retelling the story in your own words using the props.

- Display the props and the book in the Library Area so children can retell the story during choice time.

You may take on one of many roles during retellings.

- **Narrator**—Children may want you to narrate the story as they act it out.

- **Player**—Children may invite you to assume a role in the story.

- **Resource Person**—Children may ask you for assistance in finding props.

- **Observer**—Children retell the story using props independently as you observe the action.

Carefully follow the lead of the children during a retelling and determine when children need additional support.

Take the time to join one or two children in listening to a taped story.

Listening to Tapes With Children

To promote learning, take the time to join one or two children in listening to a taped story. For some children, you may need to turn the pages of the book to keep up with the recorded voice. Other children may be able to do this on their own.

Some children may be reluctant to select a tape on their own, or they may be unsure about how to operate the tape recorder. Sometimes the assistance of another child is all that's needed. Once children learn to operate the equipment, they can listen to tapes independently.

Promoting Children's Writing

Keep writing tools and paper readily available and show an interest in what children do. Try these approaches.

Comment on the child's work: *I see you've been busy writing. Would you like to read what you've written to me?*

Describe what you see: *You made a whole row of* As *and then a row of* Ms.

Help a child use the equipment: *Let me help you find a way to make the marker caps fit.*

Ask questions or make statements that help a child solve a problem: *You want to know how to write Alexa's name? I wonder if we can find her name on something in the classroom.*

One way to promote writing is to create blank journals for each child. Simply staple blank paper together with a construction paper or wallpaper cover. Encourage children to use the journals to record their ideas, thoughts, and observations. Though they may just scribble or draw, the point is to use the journal in a purposeful way.

A teacher's genuine interest and involvement in the Library Area can go a long way to reinforce children's budding interests in writing and reading.

Including All Children in the Library Area

Children who experience fine motor difficulties in manipulating small items, and children who have trouble attending to language, may not seem to be particularly interested in library activities. The following suggestions can help children with special challenges participate actively in the Library Area with their peers, and access the curriculum to the best of their ability.

If a child...	Try these strategies...
Shows variable attention during listening/reading activities	Encourage the child's involvement in stories with hands-on experiences. For example, adapt pop-up or flap books by cutting off the flaps, laminating them for long-term use, then re-attaching to the book with Velcro. The child can interact with the book by pulling each item off, or putting it on, during the reading of the story. Use related props with every story, so that the child has something to hold and manipulate (e.g., a spider ring for the *Itsy-Bitsy Spider* book). Use books that repeat phrases over and over, to encourage the child's learning and participation. Allow a child to play the role of lead storyteller to encourage attention and participation.
Has difficulty hearing, understanding, or seeing books read orally	Have the child with hearing, language, or vision problems sit close to you. Repeat words to allow extra time for comprehension. Use exaggerated facial expressions, voice tones, and non-verbal gestures. Encourage the use of a magnifying glass, binoculars, or "third eye" magnifying lens for a child with vision problems. Use reader buddies/peers to provide individualized support to the child in looking at books.
Has trouble holding and manipulating reading materials	Use adaptive equipment such as book trays or holders. Use peer buddies as page turners. Attach Velcro tabs on page edges to make page turning easier for children with fine motor difficulties.
Avoids writing	Include large-size writing tools in many interest areas. Encourage the child who is interested in playing with magnetic letters and numbers to trace those items, and to make words with them.
Has difficulty holding and manipulating writing materials	Use adaptive equipment to encourage writing, such as pencil grips, very large crayons, velcro straps around hand or wrist to hold writing utensils, etc. Consult with an assistive technology professional for the latest tools available to support children with fine and visual motor problems.

Frequently Asked Questions About the Library Area

Children rarely go to the Library Area during choice time. Should I be concerned?

The Library Area is the hub of learning about reading, writing, listening, and speaking. However, it is not the only place children can learn these skills. Each interest area in the classroom should engage children in reading and writing during play. Children in the Block Area might look at a book on skyscrapers to build a tower. In the Dramatic Play Area, they may use paper and pencil to write phone messages or read a book to a baby doll.

Literacy learning happens throughout the day. At group time, you can read a story, invite children to act out a story, write an experience story on a chart, or engage in discussions. During daily routines, you can display a recipe card to make a snack, provide books for children to read while resting on a cot, or post picture-word directions for hand washing.

Since literacy is a part of all interest areas, daily routines, group times, and studies, you don't need to be too concerned if a child rarely visits the Library Area. However, make sure the area is attractive and inviting. Stock it with a collection of books that will interest the children in your class, and spend time yourself in the Library Area each day. After reading a book to the group, display the book prominently in the area. Use props when you re-read a story, then leave them in the Library Area for children to use during choice time.

Should I be teaching children to read?

Just as all children don't learn to walk or talk on the same day, they don't learn to read on the same day. As you incorporate the key components of literacy (see Chapter 3) into your daily activities, you are teaching children to read. By reading stories, engaging in conversations, playing with language, retelling stories, drawing attention to print in the environment, and incorporating reading and writing in play, you are paving the way for children to become competent, independent readers and writers. Research tells us that the children who are most at risk for reading difficulties are those who have limited vocabularies, less phonological awareness, less knowledge of letters and words, less knowledge of how print works, and less knowledge of the purposes of reading and writing. Given the proper support in the early years to remove these stumbling blocks, most children become good readers by first or second grade.

In each interest area chapter of this book, we have given you ideas about how to link literacy to children's play. You must intentionally support children as they acquire beginning literacy skills. To do this, you create a literacy-rich environment as we have described and thoughtfully and purposefully interact with children with the literacy goals in mind.

We don't recommend that preschool teachers try to replicate formal reading instruction like you might see in elementary school. What is good for a 6- or 7-year-old is not necessarily good for a preschool child. Your job is to help children to develop basic knowledge of language and literacy and the motivation they need to learn.

I have a child in my class who is already reading and is only 4-years-old! What should I do so he won't be bored?

A small percentage of children break the code and learn to read with little or no formal reading instruction. Such children are entitled to instruction that meets their needs. Include in your Library Area some early reading books that are interesting, colorful, and have a controlled vocabulary appropriate for his reading ability. Let him read to you or to friends. While you work with him on additional decoding and comprehension strategies, remember that he is still a 4-year-old, and choose books accordingly.

Should formal handwriting instruction be taught in preschool?

We do not recommend formal handwriting instruction for preschool children. By formal handwriting instruction, we mean structured drill and skill lessons on how to form letters. Even those with a good understanding of how letters are formed often can be frustrated because they lack the necessary fine motor skills to write. They may notice that their writing attempts do not match the model. If you rush into formal handwriting instruction too soon and place unreasonable expectations on children, they may become frustrated, and their interest in writing may be undermined.

Take advantage of "teachable moments" to demonstrate writing in authentic ways and help individual children as needed. Authentic handwriting instruction can take place every day. You can help children learn about the form of letters by providing lots of alphabet materials— magnetic letters, alphabet puzzles, and alphabet books. Talk about letters in familiar words, such as their names. Demonstrate writing, for instance, when your class dictates a thank-you note or composes a story after a field trip. Talk about how you are forming the letters. This authentic handwriting instruction helps children not only learn about how to form letters, but also the nature and purpose of writing.

Should labels be in all capital letters or with the first letter capitalized only?

Most children begin writing with all capital letters because they are easier to form. However, we recommend that the labels you create in your classroom be made with lowercase letters and initial capital letters only. In this way, you help children to begin making a connection between the print they see in the environment and the print in books.

What's the story on the alphabet. . . should I be teaching it or not? Are there particular letters to concentrate on? Is it better to teach some letters before others?

Yes, you should be helping children learn the alphabet. However, what is most important is how you teach it. The letters children learn first are the ones that are in their hearts and in their heads. They usually learn the letters in their name first, followed by letters in words that are important to them, such as Mom, Dad, or Fido the dog. Start there. Children also should have opportunities to use all of their senses to learn about the alphabet: through books, songs, environmental print, puzzles, magnetic letters, sandpaper letters, alphabet cookie cutters, and writing. You also can draw children's attention to the alphabet and the sounds of letters and words during read-aloud activities. Post the alphabet at the children's eye level so they can see a model. Include samples of the alphabet written on cards or strips of paper in the writing area so children can hold them in their hands and refer to them as needed.

A Letter to Families About the Library Area

Dear Families,

The Library Area is a very important part of our classroom and of your child's life. It's where children gain the foundation for reading and writing. It's also a place where children can relax and enjoy the wonderful world of children's books.

We encourage children to look at books, to listen to taped stories, to retell stories, and to scribble and "write" throughout the day. Sometimes children dictate stories to us, which we record in books."

We read stories to the children every day. Reading introduces new ideas, helps children learn how to handle problems that come up in life, and mostly encourages them to develop a love for books. As children listen to us read, their own reading skills begin to develop. Here are some of the things we do as we read.

- We look at pictures and ask: "What do you see?"
- We encourage children to predict what will happen next: "What do you suppose will happen now?"
- We encourage children to repeat words, rhymes, and phrases they've memorized.

What You Can Do at Home

Research has shown us the important role families play in helping children learn to read and write. The single most important thing you can do is to read to your child every day. When your child sits next to you as you read, he begins to connect books with good feelings. Here are a few more things you can do with your child.

- Encourage your child to talk about the stories you read.
- Ask questions like, "I wonder what will happen next?" or "I wonder why . . ."
- Try to relate the story to something in your child's life ("That dog looks just like Grandpa's").
- Visit the library and check out books that interest your child.
- Give your child paper and pencils, pens, or markers and let him experiment with writing. Don't worry if his writing isn't perfect!

If you'd like some help choosing books—or guidance on how to read with your child—please come see us. To keep your child's home library well stocked, you can draw on the resources of your local public library. When you take time to read to your child every day, you are doing the very best thing to help your child grow up to be a successful reader.

inside this chapter

381 How the Discovery Area Promotes Development
382 Connecting the Discovery Area With Curriculum Objectives

384 Creating an Environment for Discovery
385 Selecting Materials
387 Displaying Materials

391 What Children Learn in the Discovery Area

394 The Teacher's Role
394 Observing and Responding to Individual Children
397 Interacting With Children in the Discovery Area
400 Frequently Asked Questions About the Discovery Area

401 A Letter to Families About the Discovery Area

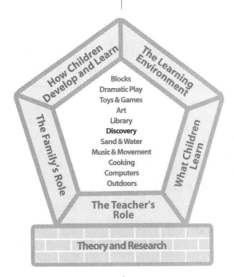

11 The Discovery Area

How the Discovery Area Promotes Development

Young children wonder about the world around them. They think to themselves:

- I wonder what will happen if I push this button.

- I wonder what the bunny feels like.

- I wonder why my plant died.

- I wonder how I can make a bigger bubble.

The Discovery Area is a place to find the answers to these kinds of questions with few right or wrong answers. It is a place to spark curiosity and wonder using new and interesting materials. In the Discovery Area, children can use their senses to touch, feel, taste, smell, and see. They can *act* on objects and *observe* what happens next. You can help nurture children's curiosity. When you join children in the Discovery Area and pose questions or wonder aloud, children respond by using their thinking skills to investigate and explore. In the Discovery Area, all areas of development can be enhanced.

Social/emotional development. Children learn to work together as they explore, make discoveries, and solve problems. They take care of living things such as classroom pets and plants, and they learn classroom rules for using materials safely and responsibly.

Physical development. Children develop their fine motor skills when they use eyedroppers to squeeze colored water onto wax paper or pick up a dead insect with tweezers. They develop dexterity and eye-hand coordination as they turn gears, take apart a broken toy, and pick up paper clips with a magnet. When they measure ingredients to make Silly Putty and then squeeze, pull, stretch, and bounce it, children practice many different fine motor skills. They strengthen their gross motor skills as they pull the rope on a pulley, create shadows on the wall using their bodies, or run in place to feel their pulse.

Cognitive development. Children use all the process skills when they observe and ask questions about the world around them. They watch plants and animals with great curiosity and make predictions about how they change, move, and react to different conditions. Children organize their thoughts by classifying, comparing, measuring, counting, and graphing objects. They represent their findings in drawing, writing, and by creating models.

Language development. When children make discoveries, they are eager to share their excitement with others. They want to talk about their investigations, ask questions, and share experiences. They use new words to describe how things look, touch, taste, smell, and sound. Using books and other texts, children find out about topics that are beyond the classroom walls.

Connecting the Discovery Area With Curriculum Objectives

A good understanding of the goals and objectives of *The Creative Curriculum* helps you to guide children's learning in the Discovery Area. In the chart that follows are examples of how children demonstrate their progress in each area of development while making discoveries.

Selected Curriculum Objectives	What a Child Might Do in the Discovery Area
Social/Emotional Development	
5. Demonstrates self-direction and independence	Finds insect on playground and places it in a "bug house" for others to see.
7. Respects and cares for classroom environment and materials	Waters classroom plants and helps feed fish when asked.
9. Follows classroom rules	Says, "You can't open the door to the cage because the bird might fly away."
10. Plays well with other children	Says "Will you hold the mirror while I shine the flashlight on it?"
11. Recognizes feelings of others and responds appropriately	Asks, "Are you scared to touch the bunny? Don't worry. He won't hurt you."
13. Uses thinking skills to resolve conflicts	Gives a child who tries to take away his magnifying glass another one.
Physical Development	
14. Demonstrates basic locomotor skills (running, jumping, hopping, galloping)	Runs in place, then listens to heart with stethoscope.
19. Controls small muscles in hands	Uses small screwdriver to take apart broken clock.
20. Coordinates eye-hand movement	Uses tweezers to pick up seeds and sort them into egg carton.

Selected Curriculum Objectives	What a Child Might Do in the Discovery Area
Cognitive Development	
22. Observes objects and events with curiosity	Asks, "How can our fish sleep if they can't close their eyes?"
23. Approaches problems flexibly	Uses different magnets to lift a spoon.
24. Shows persistence in approaching tasks	Continues adding objects to pan scale until it balances.
25. Explores cause and effect	Says, "If you water the plant too much, it might die."
26. Applies knowledge or experience to new context	Looks at a displayed apple that has rotted and says, "Our pumpkin at home rotted and it was yucky!"
27. Classifies objects	Sorts collection into leaves, rocks, and shells.
28. Compares/measures	Uses balance scale and says, "These blocks weigh more than the shells."
31. Shows awareness of time concepts and sequence	Says, "A long time ago our butterfly used to be a caterpillar."
37. Makes and interprets representations	Creates graph of different kinds of rocks and says, "We have more shiny rocks than anything else."
Language Development	
39. Expresses self using words and expanded sentences	Uses words such as *prickly, soft, furry, scratchy,* and *sticky* to describe how things feel when touched.
41. Answers questions	Says, "It doesn't get enough water" when asked why the plant died.
42. Asks questions	Asks, "Why won't my magnet pick up the pencil?"
48. Comprehends and interprets meaning from books and other texts	Uses books, charts, and CD-ROMs to find the name of the butterfly.
50. Writes letters and words	Writes "BNE" on a label and places it by the bunny's cage.

Creating an Environment for Discovery

A Discovery Area stocked with interesting materials invites children to explore and investigate. It should include some basic tools as well as objects and materials from the natural world. The best materials are those that are open-ended and can be used in a variety of ways, such as balls, objects from nature, and mirrors.

Children's ages and experiences affect how they use materials. A young preschooler may delight in listening to the ocean in a seashell, while an older preschooler might explore more deeply by looking for a picture of the shell in a book or by sorting a collection of shells by type or by weighing the shells.

Tools—such as magnifying glasses, balance scales, and magnets—further children's discoveries.

The Discovery Area is located near a window where children can observe nature and have natural light for growing plants and exploring shadows and reflections.

A computer is nearby so children can use it to access information or record their discoveries.

Collections of interesting objects to explore are stored in bins or trays.

Setting up the Discovery Area	Setting up the Discovery Area
Location	Animal(s) and food
Near natural light	Animal houses (cages, aquarium, ant farms, etc.)
Set up:	Balance scales
Table to hold displays and collections	Discovery tools (e.g., magnifying lenses, eyedroppers, tweezers, tongs)
Shelf to store discovery materials	Containers for sorting, classifying, mixing, and measuring
Trays to hold related materials	Seeds/plants for growing
	Magnets and assorted objects
	Collections (e.g., shells, seeds, rocks, leaves)
	Paper and writing tools
	Books, magazines, and posters related to displays

Think about the best location for your Discovery Area. If possible, locate it near a window so you can take advantage of sunlight for planting seeds or for exploring light and shadows. A computer nearby is helpful for locating information and recording discoveries. If the Sand and Water Area is nearby, children can borrow materials such as sieves, funnels, and plastic tubing. Because exploration can be messy at times, a floor covering that is easy to clean is helpful. Some materials can be stored away until needed, but other basic materials should be easily accessible.

Selecting Materials

To create interest and encourage discovery and exploration, include a wide variety of materials in the Discovery Area and change the materials periodically. Keep the area stocked with basic tools for scientific exploration—magnifying glasses, balance scales, magnets, containers for sorting and classifying objects. Take note of children's interests as you decide what to put out and when. One child may have a strong interest in animals while another child may be fascinated by finding out how things work. Children eventually will help you stock this area by bringing in treasures they have discovered—an X ray of a broken arm, a seashell found on the beach, an abandoned wasp nest, or a collection of wildflowers or rocks.

Basic Materials for Scientific Exploration

Because the list of possible materials is limitless, the Discovery Area may look very different in each classroom. To help you get started, we offer a range of ideas. Pick and choose considering what you think will inspire your children and what materials are readily available to you. Children would be overwhelmed to have *all* of these materials accessible at one time. So provide selected materials and rotate them periodically to keep children interested and engaged.

The following list of materials is grouped according to the broad content areas of science: life science, physical science, and earth and the environment.

Exploring Science

Life Science

- animal housing—cages, aquariums, bug catchers, ant farms
- plants (non-toxic)
- seeds and bulbs
- pets
- stethoscope
- old X rays of bones or teeth donated by doctor, dentist, or veterinarian
- collections such as leaves, twigs, shells, bones, feathers, pinecones

Physical Science

- magnets of all shapes and sizes
- collection of metal and non-metal items
- prisms or "sun catchers"
- "discovery bottles" (filled with different liquids and floating objects)
- broken toys or small objects to take apart
- balls (all sizes, densities, weights, and surface materials)
- mirrors of different shapes and sizes
- lenses
- kaleidoscopes
- flashlights
- tubing (plastic tubing, cardboard tubing of various lengths and widths)
- thermometers
- pulleys, gears, wheels
- boxes (variety of shapes and sizes)

Earth and the Environment

- soil
- rocks
- funnels, sieves, pitchers, colanders
- water
- clear plastic tubing
- straws
- shells

Acquiring Materials

Since the content of science discoveries in preschool is the surrounding world, materials are easy to obtain. Children might bring an interesting object to display, such as a large seashell found on a trip to the beach or an abandoned bird's nest. Parents often are willing to donate items for a Discovery Area. Businesses are also good sources for donations. A simple way to ask for donations is to send home a paper bag with a request for one item at a time.

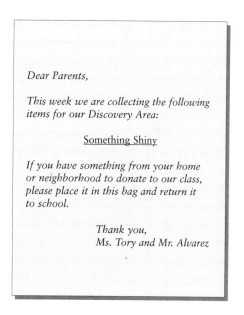

Dear Parents,

This week we are collecting the following items for our Discovery Area:

<u>*Something Shiny*</u>

If you have something from your home or neighborhood to donate to our class, please place it in this bag and return it to school.

Thank you,
Ms. Tory and Mr. Alvarez

Displaying Materials

In addition to the basic materials in the Discovery Area, you can create and rotate materials such as discovery trays, sensory tables, or take-aparts for special activities.

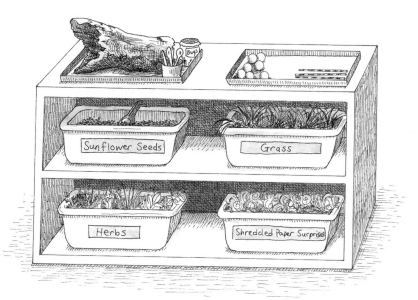

Discovery Trays

One way to focus children's observations on a particular science concept is to set up a collection of materials on a tray. Discovery trays offer structured areas of exploration.

Ideas for discovery trays include:

• a collection of wind-up toys	• broken toys to take apart
• magnets with metallic and non-metallic items	• collection of things to spin
• bowl of soil with sifters and colanders	• "loose parts" to build and create
• assortment of seeds, tweezers, and egg carton for sorting	• small boxes (all shapes and sizes) for building and nesting
• pairs of film canisters with objects inside (marbles, rice, pennies, etc.) to shake and match	• rotted-out log with popsicle sticks or spoons for digging, magnifying glass, bug container
• texture matching cards or "feely" board	• separate containers with baking soda, flour, salt, vinegar, oil, red water, blue water, yellow water, and empty containers for mixing
• collection of shiny things (e.g., mirrors, CDs) and flashlights	• magnetic marbles, cookie sheet, magnetic wands
• collection of metal toy cars and a variety of magnets	• collection of things to look through (e.g., sunglasses, binoculars, bottles of colored water, kaleidoscope, lenses)
• drinking straws and Ping-Pong balls	

Discovery trays can focus children's explorations on different science concepts.

For example, if you are interested in having children learn more about mixing colors, you could set up a tray with a sheet of waxed paper, three containers of water colored red, blue, and yellow, and an eyedropper. Children can experiment by placing drops of colored water on the wax paper and watching them merge to form new colors. You may want to put out one new discovery tray a week. Observe children's interest to decide how long to keep a particular discovery tray out.

Sensory Table or Sensory Tubs

A sensory table can be an exciting part of the Discovery Area. Commercial sensory tables can be purchased, or you can fill a plastic dishpan with materials that children can explore.

Use your imagination and think of things that children handle and explore using all use their senses. Examples of items that can be placed in a sensory table periodically include:

You can fill a plastic dishpan to create sensory tubs.

- foam packing (biodegradable)
- shredded paper with things hidden inside
- fish tank pebbles
- potting soil
- dried, unhusked corn to shuck (feed to animals later)
- shredded paper, confetti
- coffee grounds mixed with potting soil
- seeds
- "oobleck" (cornstarch and water mixture)
- grass clumps with roots attached
- fresh herbs
- ingredients to make playdough

- bird seed with funnels and cups
- sand with metallic objects hidden and a magnet
- different kinds of ice (e.g., shaved, cubed, crushed, blocks) with eyedroppers and warm, colored water
- shaving cream and food coloring
- mud pie-making materials—dirt, water, pie tins, leaves, twigs
- snow
- flower petals
- block of ice with salt used as "glue" for sculpting (gloves are helpful!)
- pumpkin insides

Take-Aparts

A table of take-aparts appeals to children's sense of wonder about how things work and what's inside. Use a take-apart table as a special activity.

Taking apart broken mechanical objects or small appliances gives children a chance to investigate gears, springs, magnets, levers, and moving parts. Take-apart items can be donated by parents and friends or found at a garage sale. Use some WD-40 to loosen screws a bit before children begin; it will make disassembling items easier.

The materials you need are:

- telephones, toasters, record players, stereos, tape players, VCRs, answering machines, cameras, clocks, radios, sewing machines—all things that can be taken apart

- safety goggles

- tweezers

- screwdrivers (short, stubby ones that fit children's hands)

- containers to put parts in

- paper and markers to draw what's inside

Keep safety in mind when you set up a take-apart activity.

Keep these safety considerations in mind:

- Do not take apart computers or televisions.

- Always cut cords and remove batteries.

- Remove any glass, tubes, or bulbs.

- Always have an adult close by.

What Children Learn in the Discovery Area

In Chapter 3 we talked about how academic content can be addressed in every interest area in *The Creative Curriculum*. The Discovery Area offers many opportunities to promote children's learning. Here are some examples.

Literacy

Build children's **vocabulary and language** by talking with them about their discoveries. Use every opportunity to introduce new vocabulary as they touch, feel, taste, hear, and observe objects and living things (e.g., "The caterpillar has spun a cocoon." "This sap from the wood is very sticky."). Encourage them to describe what they are doing, for example, "I can make the Ping-Pong ball move fast when I blow into the straw really hard."

Help children gain a **knowledge of print** by recording their experiences and their discoveries on charts. Draw their attention to **letters and words** used in the Discovery Area (e.g., "Puffy's name starts with a 'P,' just like yours.").

Strengthen their understanding of **books and other texts** by using books to find information (e.g., "Let's see if we can find the name of this bug in our book about insects.").

Help children learn to use **literacy as a source of enjoyment** as they read and hear stories related to discovery topics such as *The Very Hungry Caterpillar* or *The Enormous Turnip*.

Mathematics

Strengthen children's **number concepts** by guiding them in counting objects such as leaves, pets, rocks, and shells. Help them develop one-to-one correspondence skills by planting one seed in each container or feeding each rabbit one carrot. Make comparisons of quantities (e.g., "You have more small rocks than big ones."). Introduce estimating—making a good guess—to help children gain a sense of numbers (e.g., "Do you think four more shells will make the scale even?").

Help children discover **patterns and relationships** as they observe the life cycle of a butterfly. Encourage them to find patterns in nature items placed in the Discovery Area such as the scalloped edges of a leaf or the lines on a seashell. Children can create patterns with items (e.g., feather, leaf, feather, leaf) or line up rocks from the smallest to the largest.

Develop **measurement** skills by providing tools such as measuring cups, kitchen timers, measuring spoons, tape measures, and balance scales for children to use in their exploration.

Enhance **geometry** skills by providing many three-dimensional shapes for children to explore. Ask probing questions as they explore whether a ball will roll down a ramp more easily than an egg shape. Describe how the gerbil runs *around* the cage, hides *in* the nesting, or scampers *out* of the cage to increase their **spatial sense**.

Guide children to use **data collection, organization, and representation** to make sense of the world around them. Encourage them to sort and classify items from nature, things that are magnetic and non-magnetic, living and non-living. Invite them to record their findings by drawing, constructing, molding, and graphing.

Science

Guide children in using **process skills** as they make discoveries. Help them learn how to observe, collect information, make a prediction, and then experiment.

Teach children about **life science** by including plants and animals in the Discovery Area. Discuss how plants and animals live, how they grow, and how they move. Help children develop an understanding of the difference between living and non-living things. Lead them to discover more about their own bodies by looking at a cut finger under a magnifying glass or by listening to a heartbeat with a stethoscope.

Introduce concepts about **physical science** by including balls, ramps, pulleys, and magnets. Ask questions to stimulate thinking about how things move. Encourage them to experiment with mixing different combinations of things (water, flour, salt, sugar, baking soda) so they can learn about the physical properties of objects.

Introduce children to concepts about **earth and the environment** by including rocks, shells, and other items from the earth's surface. Ask children to bring a cup of dirt from their backyard and place it in the Discovery Area for exploration. Ask how they are the same, how they are different. Use recycled items for experimentation.

Social Studies

Encourage learning about **spaces and geography** by using positional words when children are making discoveries (e.g., "You've rolled the car *down* the ramp." "Try standing *behind* the screen to make a shadow." "You're letting the ball roll *through* the paper towel roll.").

Teach children about **people and how they live** by helping them to work cooperatively to solve problems and involving them in developing rules for using materials safely. Relate their experiences in the Discovery Area to the world of work (e.g., "A tow truck uses a pulley just like the one you are using, only bigger." "A dentist uses a tiny mirror just like this to look at your teeth.").

The Arts

Encourage children to explore the elements of the **visual arts** by mixing colors and feeling textures. Talk about the beauty of nature—the patterns in the leaves or the design on a butterfly's wing. Provide drawing tools, clay or wire for children to use the arts to represent their discoveries.

Teach children how **music** is made by providing materials that make sounds. For instance, stretching different sizes of rubber bands over a shoe box creates different sounds when plucked. Blowing into a soda bottle partially filled with water sheds light on the mechanics of musical instruments.

Technology

Enhance children's **awareness of technology** by relating their experiences in the Discovery Area to the world around them.

Introduce the **basic operations and concepts** of technology by providing broken toys or small appliances. Children can take these apart and see how they work. Select a software program so children can learn more about living creatures, like ants or birds.

Use **technology tools** for discovery. Take pictures at different times in the life cycle of the butterfly or as a bean buds and becomes a plant.

In a *Creative Curriculum* classroom, children make discoveries in all interest areas—they mix paint to create a new color, note the different sounds they can make playing a xylophone, and shake cream until it turns to butter. Even so, we recommend having a separate area set aside for discovery where children can engage in extended, in-depth investigations. The Discovery Area is a place where children can explore materials freely. It serves as storage for particular science tools. In the next section we will discuss your role in building on children's natural sense of wonder and helping them to explore important scientific concepts.

The Teacher's Role

The Discovery Area is a place where children can learn new concepts and practice the process skills used in everyday situations. Your role in this area is to focus both on *how* children learn (process skills) as well as *what* they learn (content knowledge). As we discussed in Chapter 3, scientists use *process skills* when they study and investigate. Process skills are used to gather information and develop concepts. Observing, asking questions, making predictions, experimenting, forming conclusions are all process skills. *Content knowledge* is what children learn. In the Discovery Area, children are introduced to life science, physical science, and the earth and environment. Some of the topics in each of these sciences are as follows:

Life Science	Physical Science	Earth and the Environment
plants	how things change	rocks
growing seeds	magnets	water
animals	how things work	air
senses	how things move	recycling
your body	hot and cold	soil
health	light	day and night
	shadows	weather

Observing and Responding to Individual Children

As children explore the materials in the Discovery Area they go through different stages of learning (Bredekamp and Rosegrant, 1992):

Awareness. They notice what is in the Discovery Area.

Exploration. They explore the physical properties of the materials in the Discovery Area (e.g., feel feathers, pet animals, bounce and roll balls, run hands through shaving cream, spin tops).

Inquiry. They seek answers to questions (e.g., "How can I make the car go down the ramp faster?" "Why does the gerbil sleep all day?").

Utilization. They use the information they have for specific purposes (e.g., pick up spilled paper clips with magnet; use magnifying glass to count the number of legs on a beetle).

In the Discovery Area, more than in any other interest area, your attitude about scientific discovery makes learning come alive. Think of the Discovery Area as a place to learn and discover together. Adopt a "let's find out" attitude and model important qualities for scientific inquiry—curiosity, risk-taking, perseverance, and imagination. If a child brings in an insect in a jar and wants to know its name, use your available resources to help him find the answer. Make the words "I wonder" part of your daily vocabulary. Soon children will incorporate these scientific attitudes into their everyday life.

Responding to Each Child

Observing children in the Discovery Area will give you insight about their level of understanding and their interests. Observing is the basis for deciding how and when to offer guidance.

As you observe children using the materials or making observations, consider what you can do to challenge their thinking. Ask yourself:

> Are there materials that I can offer?
>
> Are there questions I can ask?
>
> Are there problems I can pose?

When you observe children in the Discovery Area, think of yourself as a detective trying to figure out what children are thinking. As you observe, notice whether a child

- explores the physical properties of the materials to figure out how they work

- is curious about how things work and comes up with different ways to find answers

- communicates about discoveries

- works with other children in exploring objects and living things

- connects discoveries with experiences

To support children's learning in the Discovery Area, observe carefully as children use the materials and interact with other children. Document what you see happening by writing or taking photographs. Reflect on how a child's thoughts and skills are developing using the *Developmental Continuum*. Ask yourself what you can do to help this child progress. The following chart shows examples of what you might see children doing in the Discovery Area and how you might respond.

Observation	Reflection	Response
Tyrone repeatedly rolls a truck down a block ramp. He tilts the ramp and says, "Wow! Look at this! It's going faster!" He then tries tilting it at different angles.	Tyrone wonders "what will happen if" and tests out the possibility. *(Objective 25, Explores cause and effect)* He was engaged in his task and continued to work even when he encountered difficulties. *(Objective 24, Shows persistence in approaching tasks)* What other materials can I offer to help him explore motion? What kinds of questions can I ask that will help him understand these concepts?	Offer other materials to try rolling down the ramp, such as balls of various sizes, spools, etc. Ask, "What do you think would happen if we used a longer ramp?" Show him how he might create different ramps in the Block Area and let him leave his experiment up for several days. On a walk in the community or around the school, point out ramps to Tyrone and talk about how they make work easier.
Alexa uses a feather to tickle others in the Discovery Area even though they are annoyed.	Alexa knows that feathers can be used to tickle. *(Objective 22, Observes objects and events with curiosity; and 25, Explores cause and effect)* Her focus is on the tickling rather than on the feelings of others. *(Objective 11, Recognizes the feelings of others and responds appropriately)* How can I help her respect the feelings of others? Are there other sensory experiences I can provide for her?	Say, "Tasheen doesn't like it when you tickle her." Provide more sensory experiences such as shaving cream, finger painting, etc. Suggest different ways to explore feathers (e.g., letting them float to the ground, blowing to keep them in the air).
Setsuko observes the rabbit at a distance and imitates his movements saying, "I'm hopping like the rabbit." She will not go near the rabbit to pet or feed it.	Has Setsuko had a bad experience with animals in the past? *(Objective 3, Recognizes own feelings and manages them appropriately)* Setsuko notices details about the rabbit and imitates his movements. *(Objective 22, Observes objects and events with curiosity, and 14, Demonstrates basic locomotor skills)* How can I ease her into feeling safe and secure around the classroom pets?	Read books about children and their pets to Setsuko. Encourage her to express her fear. Give her time to observe others touching and caring for the pets. Hold the rabbit and invite (but don't force) her to touch it.
Ben works with Janelle for long periods of time taking apart a broken VCR. He says, "If you move this thing, that other thing will move. You try it."	Ben and Janelle play well together. *(Objective 10, Plays well with other children)* Ben notices and comments on what happens when you move one wheel. *(Objective 25, Explores cause and effect)* How can I give him more opportunities to experiment and test possibilities?	Include other small appliances in the Discovery Area for him to take apart. Ask open-ended questions such as "I wonder what will happen if you moved this." Describe what you see Ben doing: "When you moved this small gear, the larger one moved too."

Interacting With Children in the Discovery Area

Good teaching involves knowing how and when to ask questions, make suggestions, or to say nothing. If you notice that a child is stuck, a thoughtful question might move him along. However, if a child is trying to figure something out and is close to drawing a conclusion, a question or comment might interrupt the process and cause him to change his focus or walk away from the activity. Always ask yourself if your question will support or inhibit a child's exploration. Questions and comments are helpful when they are related to what the child is experiencing.

Open-ended questions lead to problem solving. They help children consider another point of view. You can pose open-ended questions such as these in the Discovery Area to focus children's observations and thinking:

What do you think will happen if. . . ?

I wonder why. . .

How do you think that happened?

What do you know about. . . ?

How do you think we can find out. . . ?

Can you tell me about. . . ?

How many ways can you. . . ?

How do you think ____ and ____ are alike?

Do you have some ideas about. . . ?

Can you think of a way to. . . ?

How do you feel about. . . ?

Open-ended questions focus children's observations and thinking.

A question such as, "What did you notice happening in the gerbil's cage today?" will draw children's attention to something that might have been ignored. Children will compare and contrast objects if you ask, "Which balls roll down the ramp the fastest?"

Asking open-ended questions that lead to understanding takes time and practice on your part. It's worth the effort because the kinds of questions you ask and comments you make will lead children to more complex scientific thinking.

Sometimes you might want to try a non-verbal interaction. For example, if a child is trying to blow a Ping-Pong ball across a table and appears frustrated, you might casually place a drinking straw in sight without saying a word. The child might use it to channel the air toward the ball rather than blowing in its general direction.

The following scenario shows how a teacher can successfully guide children's learning in the Discovery Area.

Mr. Alvarez gives each child a paper bag and asks him or her to bring something shiny from home to explore in the Discovery Area. As children arrive the next day, he invites them to remove the shiny things from their bags and place them on a tray. He has extra bags of shiny objects for those who are unable to bring them. During group time, Mr. Alvarez talks about the new things that will be placed in the area.

Mr. Alvarez:	*Today in the Discovery Area you will find this collection of shiny things that many of you brought from home.*
Juwan:	*I brought a shiny penny.*
Zack:	*I brought an old CD. If you wiggle it, you can see a rainbow.*
Tasheen:	*My uncle fixes bikes. He gave me a circle mirror. If you look in it, it makes your face look fat!*
Mr. Alvarez:	*I wonder what you could do with all these shiny things.*
Dallas:	*We could make funny faces in the mirrors.*
Mr. Alvarez:	*Yes, you could look at your reflection in the mirror.*
Alexa:	*If we had a flashlight, we could shine it on the shiny stuff.*
Shawn:	*You could spin the CD 'round and 'round on the table.*

Mr. Alvarez asks Kate to place the tray of shiny things on top of the shelf in the Discovery Area.

Mr. Alvarez: Our collection of shiny things will be one of your choices in the Discovery Area. When you finish exploring the shiny things, please put them back on the tray and then put the tray on the shelf for someone else to use.

During work time Carlos looks at his reflection in one of the mirrors sitting on the table. He notices that he can see the mobile hanging from the ceiling and motions for other children to see what he discovered.

Mr. Alvarez: I wonder how you could look in the mirror and see lights that are on our ceiling.

Carlos and Zack pick up the mirrors, but hold them vertically.

Carlos: I can't see the lights, but I can see Jonetta in the Block Corner!

Zack: Turn your mirror this way, then you can see the lights.

Carlos: Watch this, Zack. I'm going to walk on the lights! [Carlos holds the mirror parallel to the ground and walks around the room pretending to step over lights on the ceiling.]

Mr. Alvarez builds on Carlos and Zack's interest in mirrors in the following days. He gives them a flashlight and asks them how they can use it with the mirrors. They soon discover how they can make light "turn the corner" by shining it into the mirror. He shows them how they can hold the mirror at different angles on a picture in a book to change the images. Carlos draws a picture of himself, stands the mirror next to it, and says, "Look. I'm a twin!"

When teachers are involved in children's play, opportunities for learning are rich and plentiful.

In this example, Mr. Alvarez was successful in involving children and families in collecting objects he wanted to put in the Discovery Area. Anticipating that some children might not bring anything from home, he made sure to bring in extra materials. He introduced the new materials to the group and invited the children to talk about them and think of ways to use them. During choice time, he showed an interest in children's discoveries, asked questions to invite further explorations, and offered new materials to extend their learning. When teachers are involved in children's play, opportunities for learning are rich and plentiful.

Frequently Asked Questions About the Discovery Area

I have a mental block about science. How can I teach about topics that I know so little about?

Remember that the essence of science is discovery. Think about how you use science in your everyday life. Do you know how to grow plants? Do you know how to play with shadows? Do you know about your classroom pet? If a child asks you a question you can't answer, use it as an opportunity to learn. Be a risk-taker. Experiment with the child. Look at reference and guidebooks from the library with children. Remember that your attitude about science will have an impact on the children!

Should I conduct science experiments for the class?

Children may be amazed with your science "tricks." However, they begin to form explanations for why things happen when they are actively involved in exploring and using their senses. Therefore, instead of conducting the science experiment yourself, let the children get their hands on the materials and make their own discoveries. Refer to the questions in the Teacher's Role section of this chapter to help you guide their learning as they investigate.

My principal and some parents want me to teach topics like the solar system or animals of the rainforest. Should I?

Part of your job as an early childhood educator is to explain to parents, administrators, and colleagues how young children learn science topics best. They learn through hands-on, minds-on exploration with their senses. Some topics are too remote for young children to explore firsthand. When visitors come in your classroom, explain *what* children are learning as they play with materials in the Discovery Area. Take pictures of children engaged in science experiences and write down what they are learning. Post the pictures. Include information about science learning in your newsletters to parents. Show your administrator the charts in Chapter 3 that connect the components of national science standards to *The Creative Curriculum*.

Sometimes an entire school may be exploring a topic, with each grade level learning different concepts. You can take part in this too. Just remember to begin with what children already know. For example, if a school is focused on outer space, then you could explore what is most relevant and real to preschoolers—shadows or day and night.

Think about hosting a Family Science Night. Set up the classroom with materials to explore. Invite parents to come *with their children* and work with the materials. Close the evening by discussing what the parents and the children learned.

A Letter to Families About the Discovery Area

Dear Families,

Young children have many questions about the world around them. They ask: *"Where did the puddle go?" "What do worms eat?" "How can I make my truck go faster?" "Do fish go to sleep?"*

In our classroom, the Discovery Area is a place where children can explore and investigate to answer their questions. They observe, experiment, measure, solve problems, take things apart, and explore the materials and living things we put out. They guess what will happen as a result.

In the Discovery Area children *do* what scientists do—ask questions, plan and conduct investigations, gather information, construct an explanation, and communicate findings. They also learn important concepts in science as they study plants, animals, magnets, properties of materials, light, shadows, how things work, rainbows, our body, our senses, how things move and change, and more. In addition to learning science content, they learn how to solve problems together and how to communicate with others.

What You Can Do at Home

Young children are curious and love to investigate. You don't need to be an expert to help your child learn about science. Science is all around us—from making bubbles in the bathtub to boiling water on the stove. Your enthusiasm and positive attitude about science will be contagious. Get in the habit of wondering out loud ("I wonder how that ant can carry that big piece of food." "I wonder why your shadow is sometimes small and sometimes big.").

The kinds of questions you ask and statements you make when your child is exploring will help develop his scientific thinking skills. Here are some examples:

> *What do you think will happen if. . . ?*
>
> *I wonder why. . .*
>
> *How do think we can find out. . . ?*

Look for opportunities to develop your child's scientific thinking during everyday activities: while playing with toys, taking a bath, helping to bake cookies, playing in the backyard, or going on an outing. Remember, you don't need to know all the answers! It's a good sign if your child is curious, wants to discover everything, asks lots of questions, and wants more answers. We welcome you to come and visit our Discovery Area with your child.

inside this chapter

403 How Sand and Water Play Promote Development
404 Connecting Sand and Water Play With Curriculum Objectives

406 Creating an Environment for Sand and Water Play
407 Selecting Equipment and Materials
410 Displaying Materials

411 What Children Learn in the Sand and Water Area

413 The Teacher's Role
413 Observing and Responding to Individual Children
416 Interacting With Children in the Sand and Water Area
419 Frequently Asked Questions About Sand and Water Play

421 A Letter to Families About Sand and Water Play

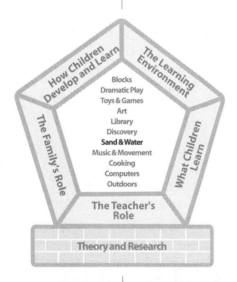

12

Sand and Water

How Sand and Water Play Promote Development

Play with sand and water involves sensory experiences that appeal to young children. They need little introduction to playing with these materials. While sand and water play can delight the senses, it also can challenge children's minds and promote all areas of development.

Social/emotional development. Sand and water inspire children to work together to construct a sand village, wash a baby doll in water, or chase a giant bubble as it sails through the air. The fact that play with these materials can calm a child who is agitated or upset has been well documented. When children play with sand and water they often express their thoughts and feelings.

Physical development. Children strengthen their small muscles as they mold wet sand and scoop water. They develop fine motor skills and eye-hand coordination working with props as they pour water through a funnel, sift sand through a sieve, and squeeze a baster full of water. They build gross motor skills as they carry buckets of sand or water outdoors.

Cognitive development. Sand and water are natural companions in scientific explorations and engage children in making careful observations and in classification, comparison, measurement, and problem-solving activities. Children discover that as a liquid, water can be splashed, poured, and frozen. As a dry solid, sand can be sifted, raked, and shoveled. When children combine the two, the properties of both change: the dry sand becomes firm and the water becomes cloudy. The texture of sand changes, too. Wet sand can be molded. It also feels cooler to the touch than dry sand. Children learn about volume and capacity as they fill empty containers. They explore cause and effect when they observe which objects sink and which float. And they discover that the amount of sand or water remains the same whether the container is thin and tall or short and wide.

Language development. While playing with sand and water, children expand their vocabularies as they learn words like *grainy, sprinkle, shallow,* and *sieve.* They build emerging literacy skills as they write letters in the sand or use alphabet molds. Equally important, as children perform experiments in the Sand and Water Area, they routinely ask and answer questions.

Connecting Sand and Water Play With Curriculum Objectives

Your familiarity with *The Creative Curriculum* goals and objectives will give you a perspective on just how much children are learning as they engage in sand and water play. This information enables you to document children's progress on the *Developmental Continuum*, and also helps you to determine when to intervene to support a child's learning. In the chart below, we give examples of what children might do to demonstrate their progress on selected objectives.

Selected Curriculum Objectives	What a Child Might Do in the Sand and Water Area
Social/Emotional Development	
4. Stands up for rights	Tells a child next to him at the water table, "You're getting me wet."
5. Demonstrates self-direction and independence	Asks teacher if she can take paintbrushes and a pail of water outside to paint the fence.
9. Follows classroom rules	When done playing at sand table, gets broom and dustpan and sweeps up sand that has fallen on the floor.
12. Shares and respects the rights of others	Lets a friend use the funnel while he picks up another water prop to use.
13. Uses thinking skills to resolve conflicts	When friend grabs at sieve she's using, she says, "There's another one on the pegboard you can have."
Physical Development	
15. Shows balance while moving	Carries pail of water over to water table without spilling.
19. Controls small muscles in hand	Uses tongs to find the plastic animals the teacher has buried in the sand tray.
20. Coordinates eye-hand movement	Pours water onto waterwheel to set it in motion.
21. Uses tools for writing and drawing	Uses a twig branch to write name in the wet sand.

Selected Curriculum Objectives	What a Child Might Do in the Sand and Water Area
Cognitive Development	
24. Shows persistence in approaching tasks	When she has difficulty bending wire with her hands to make a bubble-blowing form, gets a wrench from the workbench to assist her in the task.
25. Explores cause and effect	Figures out how high to hold the plastic tubing to make water run into the tub.
27. Classifies objects	Separates objects into two piles: things that float and things that sink.
33. Uses one-to-one correspondence	Gets a smock off the hook for each child at the water table to wear.
36. Makes believe with objects	Makes a mound out of wet sand and announces, "I made a cake for your birthday."
Language Development	
39. Expresses self using words and expanded sentences	Notes aloud, "The water makes everything wet and slippery."
41. Answers questions	When asked what she's doing, replies, "I'm burying the trucks in the sand so they'll be hard to find."
42. Asks questions	Asks the teacher, "How can I make big bubbles like hers?"
43. Actively participates in conversations	Discusses with a friend how to go about building tunnels in the wet sand.
46. Demonstrates knowledge of the alphabet	Exclaims, "Look, I made a *D* in the sand!"

Creating an Environment for Sand and Water Play

Even those programs that have outdoor sand and water play areas should have sand and water play inside the classroom as an interest area. An indoor sand and water interest area gives children more time to use these soothing materials. Also, some children may be more comfortable exploring sand and water in a controlled indoor environment than in the less structured outdoor area.

While sand and water play are two distinct activities, we recommend setting them up near one another, as one interest area. This arrangement allows children to play with sand and water separately and to have wet sand play with a minimum of confusion and mess.

The number of available smocks and a board where children place their names both indicate the number of children the area can accommodate at one time.

Note that you don't need to fill the tables high with either sand or water.

Play props are stored beneath the table in a plastic tub and labeled with words and a picture.

Setting up the Sand and Water Area	Suggested Materials
Location: Near a water source On washable floors or flooring that can be protected **Set up:** Tables specifically designed for sand and water use or sizeable rubber tubs Props and storage space	Sterilized white sand Water Plastic smocks Buckets, measuring cups and spoons, molds, scoops Funnels, squirt bottles, basters, whisks, eggbeaters Collectibles such as shells, leaves, plastic insects, feathers Eyedroppers, tongs, tweezers Cleaning supplies: sponges, mop, broom and dustpan

Selecting Equipment and Materials

To equip the Sand and Water Area, you need sturdy tables or tubs, which can be purchased or constructed. If you purchase commercial tables, look for ones that have sturdy covers, locking wheels, and a built-in shelf for storing props. A strong cover is helpful so the table can be used for other purposes when it's not in use. Wheels enable you to move the table easily from the classroom to the outdoors.

As an alternative you can use a variety of containers to hold sand and water. For example, you can purchase two flat containers such as plastic under-the-bed storage containers, baby bath tubs, plastic laundry sinks, or cement-mixing tubs. These containers are available at hardware stores, lumber suppliers, or department stores.

The size of the tub you select can vary, although a capacity of 20 to 25 gallons is probably the most comfortable size for preschoolers. We suggest a depth of at least 9 inches so the tubs can be filled with enough water or sand to engage children in play. To use the water tub, fill it with warm water to a height of about 3–4 inches. At the end of the day, be sure to empty the tub, because water left overnight can grow bacteria.

Fill the sand tub with dry, finely textured white sand. Bags of sterilized white play sand can be purchased at lumber or building supply stores. (Dirt or coarse-grain sand are not as good for construction as fine-grain sand, which holds together better.) Fill the sand tub only about halfway so children have room to use props, and so that the sand can dry out overnight.

Individual Sand and Water Tables

As a variation, you can provide children with their own miniature-size individual sand and water tubs. A dishpan makes an ideal individual sand or water container, particularly for younger preschool children who are in the beginning stages of sand and water play and may want to explore the properties of these materials quietly on their own.

Tubs can also be ideal containers for artistic and scientific activities that older preschoolers might enjoy, such as making a beach scene or watching a beetle make tracks across a smooth layer of sand. Consider setting up two of these individual containers side by side on a small table or on the floor where children can play together if they wish.

Whether you have group or individual tubs, sand and water play require that the floor and the children be protected. If you have carpeting in the Sand and Water Area, protect it by placing a vinyl tablecloth, oilcloth, drop cloth, shower curtain, or tarp under the tables. (Taping the edges down with masking tape will prevent children from tripping.)

Children can wear plastic/vinyl smocks or aprons. You can purchase these or make them from a piece of oilcloth and Velcro fasteners. While aprons and smocks keep children dry and clean, you also may want to keep an extra set of clean clothes in the children's cubbies.

Materials for Sand and Water Play

Initially, children enjoy exploring sand with very few toys, tools, or equipment. Take note of which materials they seem to use most and start with just a few simple props, such as plastic bottles or dolls to wash.

Gradually add props, such as measuring cups, funnels, and floating toys for water play, to introduce a range of new possibilities. For the sand table, digging and sifting tools do the same. In selecting props, look for ones that are versatile, but don't limit your selection to props that can be used in both areas. Below are some ideas for stocking your Sand and Water Area:

- acrylic tubing
- bottle brushes
- bubble wands and frames
- buckets/pails
- bulb basters
- cardboard signs and billboards attached to straws
- colander
- combs
- cookie cutters
- cookie press
- corks
- eggbeater/wire whisks
- eyedropper
- feathers
- fishing bobbers
- fishnets
- fizzy bath balls
- flags
- foam or rubber alphabet letters
- food coloring/ vegetable dye
- funnels
- gardening tools
- gutters

- ladles
- magnetic wands
- magnifying glass
- marbles
- measuring cups, spoons
- molds
- muffin tins
- paintbrushes
- pebbles and rocks
- pinecones
- Ping Pong balls
- plastic ants and other insects
- plastic counting bears
- plastic doll dishes/ non-breakable dishes
- plastic fish
- plastic flowers
- plastic squeeze bottles
- plastic tubing
- potato mashers
- pulleys
- PVC 1/2-inch pipes and T-connectors
- rakes and shovels (small)

- rolling pin
- rubber animals and people
- rubber or all-plastic baby dolls
- scales
- scoops
- screening
- shakers with large holes
- shells
- sifter
- soap: liquid, solid, flaked
- sponges
- spray bottles
- sticks/driftwood
- strainer
- straws
- toothbrushes
- toy boats, cars, or trucks
- tweezers or tongs
- waterwheels
- wheel and chute toys (also called gravity gears)
- whisk broom

Pick and choose items from this list that will excite children's curiosity and further their exploration. Start out slowly with four or five different types of props. Add a few others and rotate the selection to keep children's interest. Remember, though, to have only a few of these props out at any one time. Too many props in the sand or water table at once interfere with play.

> ### Alternative Sand and Water Settings
>
> You can set up specialized sand or water tables as well.
>
> **The Ocean:** fill table with aquarium rocks, white sand, and water; add seaweed, a variety of plastic fish, and other ocean life; provide fishnets and art supplies.
>
> **Dishwashing:** fill table with water and dishwashing soap; provide plastic dishes, sponges, rubber gloves, dish rack, and towels.
>
> **Rock Garden:** fill tub with 1-1/2 inches of water; add different types of rocks; provide scrub brushes and towels, scoops, rakes, and magnifying glasses.
>
> **Bubble Factory:** fill table with 2 gallons of water, 2 cups of liquid soap (Joy, green Dawn, or clear Ivory are recommended), and 1/4 cup of glycerin (available at drugstores). Play with the proportions to get a formula you like. On clear, dry days you may use as much as 50 percent more water if you're making bubbles outdoors. In addition to standard blowing wands, offer children bubble-blowing frames made from eyeglass frames, plastic rings from a six-pack of soda, coat hangers, electrical wire fashioned into shapes, plastic lids with shapes cut into them, plastic berry boxes, or canning jar rings.
>
> **Snow Table:** fill table with snow or ice balls; provide shovels, scoops, and pails.

Displaying Materials

Materials should be accessible so children can select the ones they want. The key to displaying props is to keep the area attractive and uncluttered.

Place props at children's eye level so they can readily select what is available.

Use a pegboard with hooks to store many of the kitchen-related items used in sand and water play, such as ladles, sieves, and measuring cups.

Use narrow drawers or boxes to hold collectible props such as seashells, marbles, or feathers.

Store props in plastic dish bins to maximize storage space. We recommend bins for props that may remain damp from water play when they are put away. Alternatively, you can hang damp props in nylon or string bags to air dry.

Group props in boxes or tubs by function, such as filling, floating, or measuring. A bubble-blowing box might contain bubble solution, bubble pipes/wands, plastic berry boxes, straws, plastic rings from a six-pack of soda, and other homemade bubble frames. You also might include children's books on blowing bubbles such as Mary Packard's *Bubble Trouble*.

A functional and attractive Sand and Water Area sets the stage for children to have fun, follow the rules you establish for using the materials safely, and for learning.

What Children Learn in the Sand and Water Area

Because sand and water play are so much fun, we sometimes lose sight of what great learning laboratories they can be. Consider the many ways you help children learn academic content in the Sand and Water Area.

Literacy

Expand children's **vocabulary and language** by introducing them to terms such as *water pressure, gritty, funnel,* or *siphon.* Ask open-ended questions that not only encourage children to experiment, but also provide opportunities to express the way they feel when playing with sand and water.

Read **books and other texts** about sand and water play. Some recommended titles are: *Better Not Get Wet, Jesse Bear* by Nancy White Carlstrom; *Bubble Bubble* by Mercer Mayer; *In the Middle of the Puddle* by Mike Thaler; *The Quicksand Book* by Tomie de Paola; *The Sand Castle* by Shannon Brenda Yee, Thea Kliros, and Brenda Shannon Yee.

Include logos and signs from the community as props to help children gain a **knowledge of print.**

Add alphabet cookie cutters and molds to create **letters and words.**

Mathematics

Teach **number concepts** by having children count how many measuring cups of sand are needed to fill a pail. Reinforce one-to-one correspondence by helping children to develop a rule for using the water table: there can be only as many children at the water table as there are smocks hanging on the coatrack. Use words such as *more, less,* and *same* to describe quantities.

Encourage children to make **patterns** in damp sand using objects like shells or cookie cutters.

Help children to explore the concept of **geometry** by providing them with bubble blowers in a variety of shapes. Encourage children to observe that regardless of the shape of the frame, bubbles come out round. Offer cylinders, cones, and boxes for building sand castles.

Teach **measurement** by having children observe how many teaspoons of sand or water are needed to fill measuring cups of varying sizes.

Science

Introduce children to firsthand explorations of **physical science** by giving them props such as ramps, gutters, funnels, and sieves that they can explore with sand or water.

Offer children varied opportunities to learn about the **earth and the environment** through their everyday observations of sand and water in the outdoors.

Social Studies

Promote children's understanding of **people and the environment** by replicating what they have seen people do in the environment. For example, they might recreate how farmers irrigate fields, how engineers make dams, and how people at the seashore clean the beach.

Help children gain an understanding of **people and how they live** by encouraging them to role play with dump trucks, bulldozers, and rakes at the sand table.

The Arts

Encourage children to use water to make **music** by showing them how to blow air over a partially filled bottle of water. Play soothing nature music, such as sounds from the ocean, near the water table.

Bring the **visual arts** into children's sand play by taking pictures of the children's sand creations and displaying the photos. Display photos of artists' sand sculptures.

Technology

Expose children to basic **technology tools** they can use with sand or water: waterwheels, gravity gears, pulleys, and the like.

Guide children to think about **people and technology** by talking about how they move sand and water (bulldozers, waterwheels, paddleboats) and provide similar props for play.

Keeping the components of each content area in mind as children play with sand and water will help you uncover many opportunities to promote their learning of content.

The Teacher's Role

Sometimes so much group activity takes place in the Sand and Water Area that you may find it challenging to focus on what each child is doing and experiencing. This interest area, however, is no different from any other and you play the same critical role in facilitating children's learning. You start by observing to see where children are developmentally and what interests them. Your observations lay the groundwork for building a relationship with each child in your program and planning your interactions.

Observing and Responding to Individual Children

Children typically approach new materials in similar ways. They start by using their senses to explore the materials and then begin to manipulate sand and water in purposeful ways. The addition of props encourages children to engage in more advanced play.

Developmental Stages in Sand and Water Play

Functional play is the first developmental stage for both sand and water play. Children use their senses of touch, sight, sound, smell, and occasionally even taste to become familiar with the properties of sand and water. What does sand feel like when it is sifted through one's fingers? What does water feel like when it is splashed? What happens to water when soap is added? Do individual grains of sand disappear after being sifted through a strainer? As children sift, pour, poke, splash, and combine sand and water, they acquire information about these materials and how they can be used.

As children sift, pour, poke, splash, and combine sand and water, they learn about these materials and how they can be used.

Constructive play follows the exploratory stage. During this stage children apply what they have learned about the properties of sand and water. For example, instead of simply scooping wet sand in and out of pails, they now use these skills to create a sand structure. Starting with an undifferentiated sand mound, they create a building and give that building a name. Activity during this stage is more intentional and often includes a series of experiments.

Dramatic play is an extension of the preceding stage. Children may experiment with building moats around castles or creating tunnels. Water play may involve sociodramatic elements that rely on children's imaginations when they give the baby a bath or dive for buried treasures in the water tub.

Play activities in this last stage also require a higher degree of cooperation than before. In the early stages, children are often content to explore sand and water by themselves. As they begin to apply what they know, their play reflects team efforts to build and experiment in shared projects.

Responding to Each Child

To guide children's learning, begin by observing children at play. Make your observations meaningful by providing a focus. This, in turn, will give you a pool of information that you can reflect upon and use to decide how best to respond. Think about whether a child

- uses the sand or water props for dramatic play or to conduct experiments

- plays on his own or joins another child in an activity

- plays with sand and water both indoors and outdoors

- selects the props he wants to play with or uses those that are already out

By observing children with the *Creative Curriculum* goals and objectives in mind, you can determine what skills they have and what support they need. Your observations will lead you to ask questions so you can determine how best to respond to each child. The chart that follows illustrates how this process might work in the Sand and Water Area.

Observation	Reflection	Response
Malik spends most of choice time at the water table playing by himself with the rubber dinosaurs.	Malik is content playing alone, and may need help in involving other children in his play. *(Objective 10, Plays well with other children)* How can I encourage Malik to play cooperatively with another child? How can I build on his interest in dinosaurs?	Invite both Malik and another child to wash the dinosaurs and all of our rubber animals at the water table. Show him books on dinosaurs to see if he is interested in learning more.
Tasheen goes to the shelf and brings the measuring cups and pitchers to the water table. As she pours water from a measuring cup into a quart pitcher, she announces to no one in particular, "It takes lots of cups to fill this."	Tasheen chooses and gets involved in one activity out of several options. *(Objective 5, Demonstrates self-direction and independence)* She seems to be exploring the comparative size of objects. *(Objective 28, Compares/measures)* How can I build on her interest in measuring things so she can learn some measurement words?	Talk with Tasheen about different objects she might like to compare. Ask, "How many cups do you need to fill that pitcher?" Make a suggestion: "What else can you use to measure? Let's look through the props we have and see what might work for measuring."
While at the sand table, Sonia tries to make a ball out of sand. When the sand keeps falling through her fingers, she proclaims, "I want to make a meatball, but I can't."	Sonia seems to have forgotten how she solved this problem when she played with sand outdoors. *(Objective 26, Applies knowledge or experience to a new context)* How can I extend her interest in pretending? *(Objective 36, Makes believe with objects)*	Help Sonia recall how she molded with sand in the past. "Do you remember what you did last time you wanted to make the sand stick together?" Encourage Sonia to get the spray bottle and dampen the soil. Then ask, "Can you make enough meatballs so everyone at the sand table can have one?"
Derek uses a rubber band to fasten a rock to a toy boat at the water table. When the boat capsizes and sinks to the bottom, he shouts with glee, "Did you see how the boat sinked?"	Derek comes up with an idea and experiments to find out what will happen. *(Objective 23, Approaches problems flexibly)* He notices and comments on the effect when the boat, weighed down with a rock, sinks. *(Objective 25, Explores cause and effect)* How can I help him apply what he is learning about sinking the boat to other experiments?	Take note of what he has done: "You found a way to make the boat sink. How did you figure that out?" Pose a new challenge: "Is there anything you could do to make the rock float?" Offer new materials for experiments: "We have some other things that float in the water. I wonder if you could find a way to make them sink like the boat."

Interacting With Children in the Sand and Water Area

You can build on children's natural interest in sand and water play by responding in ways that will encourage them to learn more. Simply by talking with children about what they are doing, you help them become aware of their actions and you give children the message that their activities are important and valued.

Ask children to describe what they are doing. You may need to ask specific questions such as these:

What sound does water make when you pour it?

Do your two pitchers of water hold the same amounts of water?

What does the sand feel like?

What did you discover when you used the sieve?

Open-ended questions will encourage children to reflect on their actions.

Once children have described their actions to you, focus their attention on what they have done. Open-ended questions will encourage them to reflect on their actions:

What do you notice about the design you made with the comb in the sand?

Why do you think the tunnel collapsed?

You really made that waterwheel go fast. What can you do to make it turn slowly?

I see you're having a hard time getting the sand into that little opening. Is there anything you can use to help you pour the sand into the bottle without spilling so much of it?

Can you think of some ways to use these cookie cutters in the sand tub?

Encourage children to come up with their own ideas about how to experiment with these materials. In this way, they become scientists and problem solvers with a thirst for learning.

Facilitating Children's Investigations

One way to support children's learning in the Sand and Water Area is to encourage them to investigate the many properties of sand and water. Using props, children can explore concepts such as gravity as they watch water run downhill; friction as sand travels down a gutter; and water pressure as they draw water into a baster. Their experiences using materials in the Sand and Water Area will lead them to begin to construct understandings of scientific knowledge. Later, when they are older they will learn scientific concepts such as buoyancy and density. The purpose of engaging children in explorations now is to help them learn to raise questions and become involved in the process of scientific investigations.

Children can explore **sinking and floating** if you collect a number of objects that float (e.g., a piece of wood, a cork, a plastic bottle with a tight cap, a leaf, an acorn) and a number of objects that don't float (e.g., a marble, a nail, a clay ball, washers, a stone). Encourage children to make predictions, test them out, and talk about their discoveries by wondering aloud and asking questions:

I wonder why this big boat floats and this little penny sinks.

Is there a way to make this piece of wood sink?

I wonder what will happen if you hold this empty water bottle underwater. Do you think something different will happen if you take the cap off?

What do you notice about the things that float and the things that sink?

Children can explore **water pressure in action** with a homemade water fountain. You can drill three small holes in the bottom of a 1-liter plastic soda bottle and fill the bottle with water. Encourage children to experiment with the bottle. They will find that when they loosen the cap, water runs out. When they tighten the cap, water pressure traps the water in the bottle.

Once they have observed the fountain in action, provide them with plastic tubing, a funnel, and straws to encourage children to experiment further. Children can put their thumbs across the top of submerged tubing and watch water climb upward. They can make bubbles in the water by blowing through straws.

Encourage children to make predictions, test them out, and talk about their discoveries.

To encourage their investigations, ask questions such as these:

> *How can you make the water travel through the tube?*
>
> *How can you keep the water from coming out of the holes in the bottle?*
>
> *What happens when you blow through the straw?*

When children **compare fine-grain white sand to the dirt** they may dig with outdoors, they learn about different properties of materials. White sand is best for molding. Dirt grains are small, but water does not go through them easily. However, the substances in dirt—such as twigs and stones—strengthen constructions. Have children experiment with each type of material, first dry and then when wetted down. Encourage children to talk about their observations by asking questions such as the following:

> *What did you notice?*
>
> *I wonder what happens when you add water to each material.*
>
> *Which would you want to use for making a castle?*
>
> *Which would work better in our sand table?*

Encourage children to talk about their observations by asking questions.

Children can compare the sand and dirt using a magnifying glass or a microscope (if available). A clear marble also can serve as a magnifying glass, or a water lens can be constructed using a clear plastic bottle filled with water.

Frequently Asked Questions About Sand and Water Play

Some of the children in my class hate to get messy. How can I get them to play in the Sand and Water Area?

Here are some suggestions for encouraging these children to enjoy sand and water play:

- Let children know that it is okay to get messy. That's why they wear smocks and the floor is protected. If need be, reassure them that they have a change of clothing in their cubbies.

- Start by introducing children to basic props and then gradually add others as appropriate (e.g., when children are experimenting with how to fill a bottle, introduce a funnel).

- Offer materials to children sequentially (e.g., first dry sand, then wet; first clear water, then colored water or soapy water).

With strategies such as these, you can create an environment in which children can take their time getting used to the area.

Are there any health and safety concerns I should know about?

Yes, there are some specific guidelines you should follow. If you have a permanent outdoor sand area, it needs to be covered with a secure lid when it's not in use. However, to allow natural cleansing of the sand, the cover must allow light and air to circulate through the sand. A loose-fitting plywood cover on hinges works well.

Outdoor sand needs to be turned over to a depth of 18 inches annually. It should be entirely replaced every two years. On a regular basis, both indoor and outdoor sand tables should be cleaned of foreign matter and disinfected. For procedures on preparing and using disinfectant, see *Caring for Our Children: National Health and Safety Performance Standards: Guidelines for Out-of-Home Child Care Programs*, 2nd ed. (American Academy of Pediatrics, American Public Health Association, and National Resource Center for Health and Safety in Child Care, 2002, p. 95 and pp. 417-418).

Water tables should be drained and replaced with water daily for health reasons. Floors need to be covered to prevent children from slipping. Children also need to wear protective smocks. All props used in sand and water play should be made of sturdy, durable materials and disinfected with bleach solution weekly. No glass objects other than marbles should be permitted. Sponges, mops, brooms, and dustpans should be located nearby so that spills can be cleaned up quickly. Children should get into the habit of cleaning up after themselves.

How do I keep sand and water play from getting too rough and out of hand?

Often this is a problem if the table is overcrowded. With overcrowding, children tend to be unable to concentrate on an individual activity, so they gravitate toward a group effort—which often turns to roughhousing. See the suggestions for limiting the number of children who can play at one time. You also might check to see if there are too many props in the table. If these strategies don't work, try discussing the problem with children at a group meeting and have them brainstorm some solutions. You might try modeling appropriate water play behavior or redirecting inappropriate behaviors. Invite a typically rowdy child to join you at the water table in conducting science experiments that will appeal to him. Involve the children in making rules for the area. If, for instance, water (like sand) needs to stay in its table, ask them how they can work to do this.

What can I do when the custodian complains about how messy the sand table is and asks me to confine sand to outdoor play?

Yours is not an uncommon problem. The first thing to do is to acknowledge that the concern has merit and you want to address the problem. Explain why sand play is so important to children's development. You might share this chapter to illustrate the many benefits of enthusiastic, albeit messy, play. Then offer some suggestions for addressing the problem and making the situation more manageable. One solution might be to use a drop cloth, even if your floor is tiled or covered with linoleum or wood. This will contain the sand so that it can be taken outside and poured into the trash. You also might offer to get some small brooms and dustpans so the children can help clean up any spills. The miniature sand trays we discussed are another way to contain the sand. As a last resort, offer to take the sand table outside. Sand play is too vital to the curriculum to drop it because it's inconvenient.

A Letter to Families About Sand and Water Play

Dear Families,

Although you're probably used to seeing your children splash in the bathtub and dig in a sandbox at the playground, you may be surprised to know that the Sand and Water Area is an important part of our school program. Both sand and water are natural materials for learning.

When children pour water into measuring cups, they are exploring math concepts. When they drop corks, stones, feathers, and marbles into a tub of water, they are scientists exploring which objects float and which sink. When they comb sand into patterns, they learn about both math and art.

We encourage children to experiment with these materials. As they do, we ask questions to focus their thinking on their discoveries:

> *Now that we've turned the water blue, what should we do with it?*
>
> *How did the water change when we added the soap flakes?*
>
> *What can wet sand do that dry sand can't? What can dry sand do that wet sand can't?*
>
> *How many of these measuring cups of water do you suppose it will it take to fill this quart pitcher?*

What You Can Do at Home

If your child particularly enjoys playing with water and sand, you may want to set up some play areas for these activities in your home. Water play can be set up at the bathroom or kitchen sink. Lay a large towel on the floor, and if the sink is too high for the child, provide a stool or stepladder. Outdoors, you can use a small wading pool, tub, or old baby bathtub. Give your child a baster, plastic measuring spoons and cups, a funnel, and plastic or rubber animals and boats. Or for a novel experience, add soap flakes or food coloring to the water. And don't forget about blowing bubbles with your child. Try using different kinds of bubble blowing frames. Plastic six-pack rings, empty berry containers, or an eyeglass frame without the lenses make interesting bubble wands.

If a sandbox is not available outdoors, you might use a small dishpan as a miniature sandbox. All you need is a few inches of fine white sand. Collect small items such as shells, rubber animals, a very small rake, coffee scoops, measuring cups and spoons, sieves, and funnels and offer them to your child, a few at a time. These props will lead to many hours of enjoyment for your child.

The opportunity to play with sand and water on a regular basis helps children to develop their minds and bodies in relaxing and thoroughly enjoyable ways.

inside this chapter

423   **How Music and Movement Promote Development**
      424 Connecting Music and Movement With Curriculum Objectives

426   **Creating an Environment for Music and Movement**
      427 Selecting and Displaying Materials

428   **What Children Learn From Music and Movement**

430   **The Teacher's Role**
      430 Observing and Responding to Individual Children
      434 Interacting With Children During Music and Movement Activities
      440 Frequently Asked Questions About Music and Movement

441   **A Letter to Families About Music and Movement**

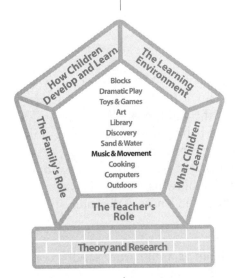

13

Music and Movement

How Music and Movement Promote Development

Music naturally delights and interests children. An early childhood program that includes time for music and movement provides an outlet for children's high spirits and creative energy. Music and movement experiences help develop both sides of the brain—an important finding in recent brain research—and contribute to children's social/emotional, physical, cognitive, and language development.

Social/emotional development. Music and movement activities can be shared experiences that make children feel part of a group. Different kinds of music evoke different feelings and actions in children. Lively music can lift children's spirits and make them want to get up and move their bodies. Quiet, soothing music calms and relaxes children. Children use their bodies to express different kinds of emotions—excitement, anger, sadness. Sharing a song or a dance learned at home helps children to feel good about themselves and their culture. They develop social skills playing musical games requiring simple cooperation such as "Ring Around the Rosy," or progress to those requiring more complex cooperation such as "Farmer in the Dell."

Physical development. Children work on gross motor development (moving to the music and participating in other movement activities) and explore the many ways their bodies can move (finding different ways to get to the other side of a line without stepping on it). Through movement activities (playing "Follow the Leader"), they can improve large muscle skills, balance, and coordination. They strengthen small muscle skills as they learn fingerplays and play musical instruments.

Cognitive development. Children solve problems while engaged in music and movement activities. They use logic and reasoning to figure out how to make a scarf fly like the wind or which instrument can be used to make a sound like thunder. They create patterns with the words they sing or chant, with the motions they make with their bodies, and with musical instruments. Children learn about number concepts as they clap their hands and stomp their feet four times or as they sing number songs. They think symbolically when they pretend to walk like an elephant or hop like a bunny.

Language development. Children develop and refine their listening skills as they notice changes in tempo or pitch of music and adapt their dancing or clapping accordingly. They learn new words (and concepts) through songs and movement (singing "Head, Shoulders, Knees, and Toes," or "I'm Being Swallowed by a Boa Constrictor"). Responding to chants and songs, they practice following directions ("balance a beanbag on your head and walk around the circle"). They develop phonological awareness as they play with the sounds and rhythms of language ("Fe-Fi-Fiddly-I-O" or "Bibbity-Bobbity-Boo") and learn concepts about print as they look at the words of their favorite song on a chart or in a book.

Connecting Music and Movement With Curriculum Objectives

Music and movement are part of everyday life in a *Creative Curriculum* classroom. Your knowledge of the Curriculum objectives will help you see that children can enjoy and learn from music and movement experiences.

Selected Curriculum Objectives	What a Child Might Do in Music and Movement
Social/Emotional Development	
3. Recognizes own feelings and manages them appropriately	Says, "This music makes me feel happy."
4. Stands up for rights	Tells others, "Please be quiet! I can't hear the music."
5. Demonstrates self-direction and independence	Uses tape recorder and headphones independently.
6. Takes responsibility for own well-being	Moves away during a movement activity to avoid getting bumped.
7. Respects and cares for classroom environment and materials	Uses rhythm instruments carefully and returns them to the shelf.
9. Follows classroom rules	Stops playing instruments when a signal is given.
10. Plays well with other children	Asks, "Will you be my partner?" while dancing to music.
12. Shares and respects the rights of others	Says, "You can use the purple scarf 'cause it's your favorite color."
13. Uses thinking skills to resolve conflicts	Gets ready to play a drum and finds one for a friend so they can play together.

Selected Curriculum Objectives	What a Child Might Do in Music and Movement
Physical Development	
14. Demonstrates basic locomotor skills (running, jumping, hopping, galloping)	Imitates movement of animals (e.g., hops like bunny, jumps like a frog, gallops like a horse).
15. Shows balance while moving	Walks across balance beam.
18. Demonstrates throwing, kicking, and catching skills	Throws and catches beanbag.
19. Controls small muscles in hands	Responds with appropriate movements to songs such as "Open, Shut Them."
20. Coordinates eye-hand movement	Coordinates finger movements while singing "The Itsy Bitsy Spider."
Cognitive Development	
23. Approaches problems flexibly	Experiments with different instruments to find one that sounds like a galloping horse.
25. Explores cause and effect	Holds scarf up in air, and then runs to make it flutter.
28. Compares/measures	Uses comparative words such as high/low, loud/soft, short/long, fast/slow.
30. Recognizes patterns and can repeat them	Repeats musical patterns by clapping or using rhythm instruments (e.g., clap, clap, snap; clap, clap, snap).
31. Shows awareness of time concepts and sequence	Sings sequential songs such as "Farmer in the Dell" or "I Know an Old Lady Who Swallowed a Fly."
32. Shows awareness of position in space	Understands directions to move *around, in, through, beside, between,* etc.
34. Uses numbers and counting	Sings counting songs and rhymes.
35. Takes on pretend roles and situations	Pretends to be a feather floating from the sky or a great, big grizzly bear looking for food.
Language Development	
38. Hears and discriminates the sounds of language	Changes words in the song "Fee Fi Fiddley I O" to "Me Mi Middley I O."
39. Expresses self using words and expanded sentences	Says, "Let's sing the song about the boa constrictor."
40. Understands and follows oral directions	Plays instrument when music begins and stops when it is over.
45. Demonstrates understanding of print concepts	Points to the words on a song chart and sings them.
46. Demonstrates knowledge of the alphabet	Uses magnetic letters to spell "BINGO" while singing the song.

Creating an Environment for Music and Movement

Music and movement involve children in listening activities, joining in group experiences, and experimenting with materials on their own. The environment, therefore, must include a specific location where you store musical instruments, a tape recorder, and a variety of props. In this place, children can be free to make or listen to music and dance to the music if they wish. Group music and movement activities may occur wherever space permits. When the weather is good, take music and movement materials outdoors for a very different kind of experience.

Display those instruments that children may explore during choice time. Have instruments available such as xylophones or melody bells so children can create melodies.

Provide a variety of props for children to use while moving to music.

Make floor space available for movement activities.

Setting up Space for Music and Movement	Suggested Materials
Location:	Easy-to-operate tape recorder, CD player, and/or record player
Open area with carpeting, if possible	Headphones
Set up:	Children's songs, albums/CDs/tapes, including music that is fast, or slow and soothing; diverse in style and tradition (e.g., folk, classical, country, jazz, rock, reggae, bluegrass, ragtime); representative of the children's cultural backgrounds.
Storage for musical instruments: a shelf, pegboard, or box	
Storage for tapes and CDs	Streamers/scarves
Tumbling mats	Rhythm instruments

Selecting and Displaying Materials

While it's desirable to have a wide selection of musical instruments available to children, you wouldn't want to put them all out at the same time. Here is a list of instruments preschool children can use and enjoy.

- drums, tambourines
- kazoos
- rhythm sticks
- bells/bell bands
- triangles, cymbals
- xylophones
- melody bells
- maracas, shakers, rattles

Of the instruments listed above, you may want to purchase triangles, bells, and a xylophone. You can make drums from oatmeal boxes, cymbals from tin pie plates, and rattles from containers with dry food. Some of these instruments, like drums, have many different versions. Children's families might help you locate some samples and bring them in to share with the children. To encourage creative movement, include some props such as paper streamers, colorful scarves, large pieces of fabric, hats, costumes from different cultures, pom-poms, and feathers. Here are some suggestions for displaying instruments and props.

Hang musical instruments on a pegboard. Make labels by cutting out silhouettes of the instruments on construction paper or solid Contact paper and taping them on the pegboard.

Place instruments such as keyboards, xylophones, and melody bells where children can reach them easily.

Make labels to identify tapes and CDs (e.g., pictures of children dancing, marching, resting, etc., to match the music, or colors or symbols to identify types of music such as bluegrass, classical, or rap).

Sort props into boxes and label each one with a picture and words.

What Children Learn From Music and Movement

Both music and movement have natural connections to the content areas.

Literacy

Expand children's **vocabulary and language** as you introduce new words, such as *banjo, waterspout, weasel,* or *stream,* in a song. Talk about what the words mean and act them out.

Strengthen their **phonological awareness** by singing songs that are full of rhymes and repetition.

Help children gain an **understanding of books and other texts** by reading story songs (e.g., "Down by the Bay" by Raffi).

Facilitate children's **knowledge of print** and understanding of **letters and words** by writing songs on a chart so they can follow along as they sing or listen.

Encourage children's **comprehension** skills by dramatizing a story using body movements.

Mathematics

Help children learn **number concepts** by singing number songs, rhymes, and chants.

Strengthen children's ability to recognize **patterns and relationships** by clapping and repeating rhythmic patterns to music.

Explore **geometry** by marching around a circle. Develop children's **spatial sense** by having them move around, in, out, through, or hold a streamer in different positions—above, below, high, or low.

Teach concepts of **measurement**, especially time, as you or the children in your group move quickly and slowly, or hold a note for a long time. Make comparisons in movement activities, for instance, by taking long steps, short steps, or making yourself as tiny as a bug and as big as a giant.

Science

Explore **physical science** by experimenting with rhythm instruments or found objects to make sounds. Encourage children to find ways of making high and low sounds, loud and soft sounds.

Investigate the **earth and environment** by creating musical instruments from objects found in nature. Use streamers during movement activities to see how things move in the wind.

Social Studies

Learn about **spaces and geography** as children participate in movement activities (e.g., go forward, backward, to the side).

Teach about **people and how they live** by inviting a professional musician or dancer to your class. Draw children's attention to the part music and dance play in people's lives. Explore music and dance from other cultures.

Enhance an understanding of **people and the environment** by creating musical instruments from recyclable materials.

Help children to develop an appreciation of **people and the past** by introducing music and movement from different eras—ragtime, blues, waltz, and rock and roll. Show children dances that were popular when you were growing up.

The Arts

Introduce **dance** by having children move in different ways to music. Play different types of music and explore movements that go with each.

Explore **music** by providing opportunities to listen to and appreciate a variety of musical styles. Provide musical instruments for creative self-expression. Include music throughout the day so children can join in group singing.

Introduce children to **drama** by providing props to re-enact familiar stories. Read stories to children that lend themselves to creative dramatics.

Technology

Help children develop an **awareness of technology** by learning how different instruments make sounds. Learn from a local musician how sounds can be changed or distorted using technology such as a mixer on an electronic keyboard or how the sounds of an electric guitar and an acoustic guitar are different.

Teach children to learn **basic operations and concepts** of technology by having them operate a tape recorder or CD player and using the on/off, volume, forward, reverse, and pause buttons. Navigate through software games that include musical components, such as *Thinkin' Things I* by Edmark.

Learn about **people and technology** by observing all the ways a musician or technician creates sound.

The Teacher's Role

Think for a moment of a favorite song from your childhood. Where were you when you were singing that song? What were you doing? Who taught you the song? What about that song makes it memorable to this day? Was there a story associated with the song? Experiences with music, which often involve movement as well, are memorable because they are not restricted to the intellect but also touch the emotions and involve the senses. Both are ways to communicate thoughts, ideas, feelings, and stories. Equally important, music and movement help people form relationships and bond with one another.

As a teacher, you select music for children's enjoyment and to introduce songs, action games, and other music and movement activities. But your primary role, as in other areas of *The Creative Curriculum,* is to facilitate children's development by observing them as they respond to music, talking to them about what they are doing, reacting to and reinforcing their explorations, and asking open-ended questions.

Observing and Responding to Individual Children

Most preschoolers are quite at home with movement. They learn about the world by acting on objects and people, and they think with their bodies well before they think with words. They learn that movement can communicate messages and represent actions; for example, a thumbs-up sign means everything's okay. For these reasons, body movement is fun for young children and presents a good opportunity for them to solve problems.

When you ask questions that call for verbal responses ("Can you think of some other ways that Pooh could get up to the honey tree?" or "What did we do to make applesauce yesterday?"), some children may have difficulty responding in words. But when questions call for movement ("How many different ways can you think of to get from this side of the mat to the other?"), children are not limited by their verbal abilities. Problems that can be solved with movement offer different kinds of challenges to all children and a way for less verbal children to demonstrate their abilities.

How Children Engage in Music and Movement

Children engage in music and movement activities in many different ways. Their style depends, in large part, on their interests, temperament, and experiences.

Listening. From early infancy, children attend to music and are able to recognize snatches of familiar tunes. With time children get better at noticing variations in musical selections, such as changes in tempo (fast-slow), pitch (high-low), and volume (loud-soft). Older children begin to listen to their own singing or playing with sounds to match the tones of music they have heard.

Singing. At first, children are able to sing along with others, but not always in time or in tune. Next, they are able to match tones as they sing with others. Then comes the ability to sing alone, and finally, to sing in tune.

Moving to music. At first, children move to their own beat rather than the beat of the music. It is especially difficult for young children to follow a slow tempo. However, by the age of 3 or 4, they typically can keep time to a regular beat. They begin to adjust their body movements with changes in the music, adapting to contrasts such as slow and fast or light and heavy.

Playing instruments. In the first stage, children manipulate and experiment with instruments. They become aware of differences related to instrument families (wind, percussion, brass), and they learn to recognize the sounds of each. In the second stage, children use instruments to accompany their movements. Although they may not match the rhythm to their steps, they beat sticks while marching. Next, most children can play a simple percussion or rhythm instrument, keeping the tempo of another instrument or a recording being played simultaneously.

Imitating/representing movement. Infants can imitate simple movements they see at the moment. They smile back when you smile at them, and when you open your mouth, they do the same. By the second year, most children can reproduce human actions they've seen before. Representing the movements of objects is more difficult. For instance, children find it harder to represent the motion of a seesaw, windshield wipers, or a falling feather than to reproduce the motion of someone kicking a ball or washing his or her hands. That ability develops gradually, along with the ability to communicate words or concepts through movement ("Show me angry faces" or "How do you pick up something heavy?").

Children can listen, sing, move to music, play instruments, and imitiate movements.

Responding to Each Child

Observation helps you see how a child is progressing in relation to the *Creative Curriculum* goals and objectives. As you observe, you make choices. Do you step into the action and join in the play or do you simply observe and reflect? Obviously, if children are engaged in spontaneous music and movement activities, stepping in and offering suggestions might stifle their creativity. But if a child is frustrated by trying to remember the words to a favorite song, joining in can be helpful. Knowing children's basic patterns of development in music and movement (described above) will help you to intervene effectively.

During music and movement activities, notice if a child

- enjoys listening to music and is able to follow the beat

- experiments with different instruments and identifies the different sounds of each one

- enjoys singing and can make up new words to songs

- is able to create movements to go with your directions (e.g., flying like a butterfly, walking like an elephant, picking apples off a tree)

- interacts with others in music and movement activities

The purpose of these focused observations is to give you factual information. Use *The Creative Curriculum Developmental Continuum* as a lens to focus your observations. Your observations provide a picture of each child's interests and skills in relation to music and movement. With this information, you can respond to each child's interests, abilities, and needs.

On the following page we offer some short observations and examples of what you might think about and how you might respond.

Purposeful observations help you respond appropriately.

Observation	Reflection	Response
Carlos constantly drums different rhythms on tables when he's happy.	Carlos expresses his feelings through rhythm. *(Objective 3, Recognizes own feelings and manages them appropriately)* The rhythms he creates have a simple pattern and require increasing hand conrol. *(Objective 30, Recognizes patterns and can repeat them and 19, Controls small muscles in hands)* Does he have a talent that I should nurture? Am I providing enough opportunities for rhythmic activities? Is he able to describe feelings and their causes?	Give Carlos the label for his feeling: "I can tell you're happy. You're smiling and tapping to the music." Include recordings with a strong drumbeat and provide rhythm instruments. Draw Carlos' attention to sounds and rhythms in the environment (a faucet dripping, a clock ticking) and encourage him to copy them using musical instruments.
Tyrone skips and then gallops around the circle.	Tyrone attempts to skip, but often reverts to galloping. *(Objective 14, Demonstrates basic locomotor skills [running, jumping, hopping, and galloping])* How can I break down this skill to make it easier for him to learn it? Is he progressing as expected in other areas of gross motor development?	Work on skipping by practicing hopping on one foot and then the other. Hold his hand and join in skipping around the circle.
Susie makes up silly words to a familiar tune. She sings "Twinkle, twinkle, little car…"	Susie recognizes and invents rhymes. *(Objective 38, Hears and discriminates the sounds of language)* How can I encourage her creative singing without interfering? Is she able to substitute the first sound in words (for example, "Miss Berry Back" instead of "Miss Mary Mack")?	Offer her a tape recorder to record her songs and share them with others. Ask her to teach you the song she created. Teach her songs that play with words such as "Michael Finnegan" or "Willoughby, Wallaby, Woo."
Setsuko moves spontaneously to music, but prefers not to be noticed.	Setsuko stops moving when attention is drawn to her. *(Objective 3, Recognizes own feelings and manages them appropriately)* When she moves to music, she does so with rhythm and balance. *(Objective 15, Shows balance while moving)* What type of music does she enjoy? Does she feel safe and secure in expressing herself in other ways?	Observe how Setsuko moves to music without calling attention to her. Ask family members for suggestions of music she likes and add them to your collection. In whole-group activities, give her other ways to participate, e.g., passing out instruments, turning on the music.

Interacting With Children During Music and Movement Activities

One of the best ways to reinforce children's explorations, problem solving, and creativity in music and movement is to pick up on their spontaneous involvement. As you respond to what children do, you not only validate their actions, you increase their awareness of what they can do. As a result, they begin to see themselves as people who can make and enjoy music and moving to it.

Describing What Children Are Doing

In interacting with children during music and movement activities, begin with where they are. Sometimes you may simply describe what you see the child doing. Suppose, for example, that you hear a child making up a song as she squishes clay through her fingers. You might comment, "That clay makes you think of a song," and then sing along with her. Such a response can make the child more aware of her actions and how much you value what she is doing.

Your descriptions of what you see or hear children doing also expand their music and movement vocabulary. When listening to music or exploring movement with children, you can introduce words such as *smooth, jerky, gliding,* or *bouncy.* You can help children make connections between music and movement: "The way you're moving is called 'gliding'—do you think the music sounds like gliding?" Movement often helps children notice musical qualities better than words can. For example, hearing higher and lower notes played, children can stand up high on tiptoes and stoop down low.

Your descriptions of what you see or hear children doing also expand their music and movement vocabulary.

Asking Open-Ended Questions

Asking open-ended questions about what a child is doing or perceiving helps you discover what interests the child at the moment. One child playing a xylophone might be focusing on how each color sounds, while another might be experimenting with volume or pretending he is playing the piano like his father. When you understand exactly what interests a child, your questions and comments are more likely to elicit a positive response and promote learning. Here are some open-ended questions you might ask:

How does it sound?

Have you ever heard that before?

Does it sound the same when you hit each drum (or each note on the xylophone)?

What would happen if. . . ?

What else could you do. . . ?

Are you making music that's loud or quiet?

How would you make the drum sound very quiet?

While open-ended questions encourage children to think about what they are doing, be sensitive to what a child is experiencing before you ask a lot of questions. Sometimes the best approach is to watch and listen because the child is obviously happily engaged.

Joining in Music and Movement Activities

Another way to enrich a child's experience with moving to music is simply to join in when the child is dancing—children love to have adults follow their lead—and then add a variation. For instance, Carlos was bouncing his body to a lively song. The teacher bounced with him for a while and then began moving her head from side to side along with the beat. Soon Carlos was moving his head from side to side and rotating his body as he bounced. Without saying a word, the teacher sparked the child's desire to explore new possibilities.

As you interact with children, take care not to interrupt their spontaneity. When you see that children are caught up in dancing, for instance, it's better to stand back and not ask a lot of questions. Questions and comments are better timed just after the child finishes dancing, or perhaps between tapes. ("You were dancing a special way to that music. I wonder if this next tape will make you want to dance the same way or differently.")

Enjoying Music Together

Music experiences don't always have to include movement. Sometimes you may want to play music and enjoy a quiet time with the children. You might ask them to listen for certain sounds, such as the sound of a drum or bells. Or say, "Close your eyes and tell me what you think about when you hear this sound."

Add new recordings and new musical instruments, periodically. If you have access to the technology, you can download favorite songs from the Internet and create your own CDs. Also, invite parents to share their musical talents with the group—singing or playing instruments that are favorites of their family/culture (e.g., accordions, guitars, violins).

One teacher started a "sound table" with a few small boxes and an assortment of objects such as buttons and paper clips and suggested that the children add to the collection. The children brought objects they found elsewhere in the room (beads, small blocks) and outdoors (rocks, wood chips, gravel). From time to time, the teacher added new materials, including rice, marbles, tiny bells, and boxes of varied sizes, from Band-Aid boxes to coffee cans. Encouraged to try different combinations of boxes and objects, the children became more aware of sound and more interested in exploring the sound-making possibilities. They used some of the sound boxes (with the tops glued or taped shut) to accompany their songs and as sound effects for stories and dramatic play.

Children love to have adults follow their lead.

Sometimes you may want to play music and just enjoy a quiet time with the children.

Try to use music selectively by reserving it for certain times of the day. If you play it in the background throughout a work time, children will regard it as noise and tune it out. Rather, music experiences should teach children to enjoy, appreciate, and notice music.

Group Singing and Movement Activities

Singing and moving together is an enjoyable activity for children that helps everyone feel a part of the group. Even shy children tend to feel a little more at home when singing with others. Group singing and action games also help children learn to cooperate with others, including singing when the group is singing and being quiet when everyone else is quiet.

Here are the types of songs and related activities that are popular with young children.

Simple songs with lots of repetition (a repeated line or refrain). Children love songs such as "Yellow Submarine," "Old McDonald Had a Farm," and "Skip to My Lou" because they are based on easy, repetitive refrains. Even if children cannot remember the verses, they can always join in on the refrain, which they can learn more easily.

Songs with fingerplay. "The Wheels on the Bus," "Where Is Thumbkin?" and "The Eensy Weensy Spider" are examples of songs with finger movements. Children love the combination of action, words, and music. Some children may participate by moving their hands and fingers before they actually sing.

Singing games and action songs. Games such as "Farmer in the Dell," "Go In and Out the Window," "Hokey-Pokey," and "You Sing a Song" combine music, movement, and group cooperation. You can encourage children to make up new verses to these familiar songs ("this is the way we swing our arms") and invent original games. For instance, set up a series of hula hoops on the floor and challenge each child to move through them in a different way. A simple chant ("Jenny is spinning, spinning, spinning") adds to the fun.

Songs with funny sounds or silly lyrics. Nursery rhymes have lots of funny sounds, like "higgledy, piggledy," "hey-diddle-diddle," and "rub-a-dub-dub." Many folk songs have silly lyrics too. Children like songs that play around with familiar words, particularly with their own names ("Annie, Annie, Bo-Bannie"). These songs contribute to the development of phonological awareness.

Songs and dances of different cultures. You may already know some songs and dances you can teach to children. Better still, invite parents to share the songs, music, and instruments of their cultures.

Movement games without music. Older children can play charade-style games such as "What Animal Am I?" or "What Am I Doing?" Usually they are more proficient at guessing than at acting out, but both sides of the game encourage children to attend closely to specific movements.

Strategies for Introducing a New Song

- Select a song that is relatively short, has simple words, and a melody that is easy to remember.

- Make sure that you have practiced the song and know it by heart.

- Tell the children a story about the song.

- Sing the song to the children. Be animated and sing with a smile!

- Sing the song again and again, if you wish. Invite the children to join in or clap along.

- Use props, such as puppets, flannel board figures, or pictures, to help children remember the words of the song.

- Add motions to the song.

Simple Songs for Preschoolers

Traditional songs are a good starting point for teaching words and melodies.

While there are hundreds of songs for preschoolers, traditional songs (mostly folk songs and popular music of previous eras) are a good starting point for teaching words and melodies. The advantage of these songs is their familiarity to many families and teachers. When children sing them at home, family members recognize them and can join in. You also may have learned these songs when you were growing up, or sung them with your family. Or perhaps you learned them when you became a teacher.

"Baa Baa Black Sheep"	"Mary Had a Little Lamb"
"B-I-N-G-O"	"Old MacDonald Had a Farm"
"She'll Be Comin' Round the Mountain"	"Pop Goes the Weasel"
"Did You Ever See a Lassie"	"Ring around the Rosie"
"The Eensy Weensy Spider"	"Row, Row, Row Your Boat"
"Green Grass Grows All Around"	"Skip to My Lou"
"Here We Go 'Round the Mulberry Bush"	"Three Blind Mice"
"There's a Hole in the Bucket"	"A Tisket, A Tasket"
"If You're Happy and You Know It"	"Twinkle, Twinkle, Little Star"
"I've Been Working on the Railroad"	"The Wheels on the Bus"
	"You Are My Sunshine"

In addition to these familiar songs, take the time to learn and teach some songs and dances of the cultures that are represented in your classroom. Your best resource is the families themselves. Invite them to teach a song to the class if they feel comfortable doing so. But more important, continue the tradition of passing their culture from one generation to the next by having them share the stories behind their song or dance.

Inviting Children to Participate in Group Movement Activities

Most children delight in exploring the many ways their bodies can move. Movement can be done with or without music. Open-ended prompts for children to move creatively may begin like this:

Can you. . .   *What can. . .*   *How. . .*

How can. . .   *Show me. . .*   *Be. . .*

Using Movement to Explore Body Awareness
Can you. . .

touch your ear to your shoulder? Touch your nose to your knee?

bounce like a ball?

keep a balloon in the air using different parts of your body?

move both legs at the same time? Sway like a tree in the wind?

walk on your hands and feet like a monkey? like a crab?

Using Movement to Explore Space
Can you. . .

move around the room without touching anyone?

move around the room in slow motion?

move around the room as if you were in a hurry?

pretend to be a feather and float around the room?

pretend to be driving a car around the room?

Using Movement to Explore How Your Body Moves
Can you. . .

move as if you were carrying a very heavy box?

walk like a big giant? Run like a deer? Hop like a bunny?

pretend to be an ice cream cone that melts in the sunshine?

move like a robot? like a rag doll?

make an interesting shape with your body?

Music and movement should be part of every day, from the time children first arrive until they go home. Music and movement can ease children through transitions and routines: coming to sit down for snack, calming down for rest or naptime, cleaning up the room, putting on clothes to go outside, or transitioning to the next activity (e.g., "Float like a cloud to the circle for story time."). Music and movement are also natural activities for times when the whole group is gathered. And children—individually and in small groups, on their own or with a teacher—can enjoy music or movement activities.

Frequently Asked Questions About Music and Movement

I cannot carry a tune or play an instrument. What should I do?

Don't despair! The important thing to remember is that your responsibility is to expose children to music and movement and create an environment where children can explore. For group singing, you may feel more confident using CDs or tapes. Children can explore music spontaneously without your singing to them. Preschoolers don't focus on the voice quality of their teachers—they just want to sing!

How do I encourage all children to participate in music or movement activities?

Some children have a natural inclination toward music and movement. They sing or hum throughout the day as they work and play. They notice the rhythm of a ticking clock or water dripping from a faucet. They experiment with their bodies by clapping, slapping their thighs, and making popping sounds with their mouths. They move and sway as they work a puzzle or draw a picture. Turn on music and they move to the beat.

Other children may be reluctant to participate. They may not be performers or simply not like the music being played. Whatever the reason, don't force a child to sing or dance. Remember that even if they are not participating, children are still hearing the music and feeling the rhythm. Hesitant children may want to explore the materials on their own, pass out musical instruments, or help out with props.

Do I have to have a separate music and movement area in my classroom? It's just not big enough.

A separate music and movement interest area can be small and used for individual, independent activities. Larger-group music and movement activities can take place in your circle area or whatever is the largest space in your room.

A LETTER TO FAMILIES ABOUT MUSIC AND MOVEMENT

Dear Families,

We do a lot of singing and creative movement in our program. Singing and moving to music give the children a chance to hear and appreciate different kinds of music, express themselves through their movement, and practice new skills. The children love our daily time for singing together, and it helps them learn to cooperate in a group. Here are some of the things we do to encourage a love for music and movement.

- We listen to all different kinds of music.

- We play instruments to make our own music.

- We give the children colored scarves and paper streamers to use as they move to the music.

- We use chants to help us get through the daily routines, such as clean-up time.

- Sometimes we take a tape recorder outside and play jazz or folk music, and the children dance and act out songs.

What You Can Do at Home

You don't have to play an instrument or sing on key to enjoy music with your child. Taking a few minutes to sit together and listen to music can provide a welcome break for both of you. Also, the music you share with your child doesn't have to be "kid's music" only. It can be reggae, country, jazz, classical, rap, or any other music you like. Here are some ideas for enjoying music and movement with your child.

- Children love a song or chant about what they are doing at the moment, especially when it uses their name. While pushing your child on a swing, you might chant, "Swing high, swing low, this is the way that [your child's name] goes."

- Songs and fingerplays help keep children occupied at challenging times, for instance, during long car trips, while waiting in line, or when grocery shopping.

- Songs can ease your child into tasks like picking up toys, getting ready to go outside, undressing for a bath, and so on. You might try making up a chant to the tune of "Here We Go 'round the Mulberry Bush" such as, "water is filling up the tub, up the tub, up the tub. . . " or "Pick up a toy and put it on the shelf, put it on the shelf. . . ."

- Musical instruments can be made or improvised at home easily. You (or your child) already may have discovered that cooking pots and lids make wonderful instruments.

Sharing music with your child is a wonderful way to build a warm, loving relationship. It's a gift that will last forever.

inside this chapter

443 How Cooking Experiences Promote Development
444 Connecting Cooking With Curriculum Objectives

446 Creating an Environment for Cooking
447 Selecting Materials
449 Displaying Cooking Equipment and Tools
450 Special Health and Safety Considerations

453 What Children Learn in the Cooking Area

456 The Teacher's Role
456 Observing and Responding to Individual Children
459 Interacting With Children in the Cooking Area
468 Frequently Asked Questions About Cooking

469 A Letter to Families About Cooking

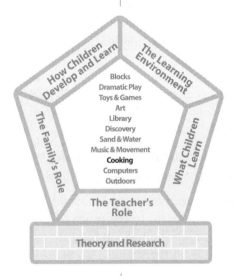

Cooking

How Cooking Experiences Promote Development

Cooking is fun. It's also a natural laboratory for helping children to develop and learn. When children participate in cooking activities, they learn how food is prepared and how it contributes to their health and well-being. They also form eating patterns that can last a lifetime.

Social/emotional development. Children show pride in their ability to produce a snack that they and others can enjoy. They develop independence as they follow a recipe on their own or work cooperatively on a common task.

Physical development. Chopping celery, squeezing a lemon, and spreading apple butter are actions that develop children's small muscle control and eye-hand coordination. In fact, children cannot cook without working on their physical development.

Cognitive development. Cooking activities inspire children's curiosity and thinking. They learn comparative words as they measure items for a recipe and fill a gallon pitcher with four quarts of water. They develop problem-solving skills through experimentation and observe cause and effect when they watch bread dough rise once yeast is added to it. Cooking is also an outlet for creativity. Pretzel dough can be made just as effectively into letters, numbers, or snakes, as well as its characteristic looped shape.

For children with learning disabilities, cooking can be a valuable activity because it provides hands-on experiences with cognitive concepts that are often difficult to master. While cooking, children can organize ingredients, follow the sequence of a recipe, and carry out multiple directions.

Language development. Cooking has its own terminology. Food names and basic cooking-related words like *ingredients, recipe, gadget, grate, knead, simmer, grease*, and *dice* all may be new additions to children's vocabularies. Moreover, as children match pictures to the written words in recipes, they learn to read and follow recipes on their own.

Connecting Cooking With Curriculum Objectives

In the Cooking Area, children have the rare treat of doing the same things that grown-ups do. As children become familiar with cooking procedures, they develop skills and knowledge. Your familiarity with the *Developmental Continuum* will help you pinpoint each child's development. In the chart that follows, we give examples of how cooking experiences help children reach many *Creative Curriculum* learning objectives.

Selected Curriculum Objectives	What a Child Might Do in the Cooking Area
Social/Emotional Development	
5. Demonstrates self-direction and independence	Looks at recipe cards for making Waldorf salad and collects the ingredients needed.
6. Takes responsibility for own well-being.	Helps herself to crackers with peanut butter and then signs name on list, indicating that she has eaten her morning snack.
7. Respects and cares for classroom environment and materials	Cleans up before sitting down to eat prepared snack.
8. Follows classroom routines	Washes hands before and after working with food.
9. Follows classroom rules	Puts peeled cucumber skin in the trash during cleanup.
12. Shares and respects the rights of others	Gives child who has been waiting to use the vegetable peeler a turn, even though he still has other carrots he wants to peel.
13. Uses thinking skills to resolve conflicts	Decides to use a whisk to beat eggs so that another child can have the eggbeater.
Physical Development	
19. Controls small muscles in hands	Pounds and turns bread dough to prepare it for rising stage.
20. Coordinates eye-hand movement	Pours unused oil into a bottle using a funnel.
21. Uses tools for writing and drawing	Helps make recipe cards for the Cooking Area.

Selected Curriculum Objectives	What a Child Might Do in the Cooking Area
Cognitive Development	
22. Observes objects and events with curiosity	Says, "A kiwi has fuzzy brown skin and a lime has smooth skin, but they're both round and green inside."
23. Approaches problems flexibly	Suggests frosting muffins with cream cheese after the dentist warns the class about eating sweets like sugary icing.
24. Shows persistence in approaching tasks	When having difficulty folding wet ingredients into flour, moves the bowl off of the table and onto a chair and continues using wooden spoon to mix the batter.
25. Explores cause and effect	Observes that putting popcorn in the microwave makes the bag puff up.
26. Applies knowledge or experience to a new context	Suggests adding more flour to biscuit dough, so it won't be so sticky—just as the group did when making playdough.
27. Classifies objects	Sorts recipe cards into foods for snacks, food for lunch, and special treats.
28. Compares/measures	Fills measuring cups with flour, sugar, and water for baking project.
33. Uses one-to-one correspondence	Sets table for snack by putting out one plate, napkin, and glass for each chair at the table.
34. Uses numbers and counting	While cooking, counts out 3 tablespoons of lemon juice as indicated in a recipe for lemonade.
Language Development	
40. Understands and follows oral directions	Picks up the wooden spoon and starts to stir everything in the bowl when teacher tells her to "mix all of the ingredients together."
41. Answers questions	Replies, "It gets smushy" when asked what happens to the cheese when it's heated.
42. Asks questions	Asks teacher, "Why doesn't corn on the cob pop when we put it in the microwave?"
47. Uses emerging reading skills to make meaning from print	Follows picture recipe cards to make "meat loaf muffins."
50. Writes letters and words	Attempts to write a menu announcing "Today's Snack."

Creating an Environment for Cooking

Most preschool teachers cook with children. Cooking is typically a special activity—for example, baking bread together or inviting parents to share a treasured family recipe.

While special activities of this type are a welcome part of your program, they do not tap the full potential for learning through cooking. In *The Creative Curriculum*, we view the Cooking Area as a place where, on a daily basis, children can explore, experiment, and create on their own, in small groups, or working one-on-one with a teacher, parent volunteer, or another child. The Cooking Area is as active and well developed as all of the other interest areas in your classroom.

Children wear aprons to protect their clothing.

Safe cooking tools are within the children's reach.

Recipe cards guide the cooking activities. It is set up for self-serve snack so children can prepare and eat their snack whenever they wish.

Water is close at hand to assist both cooking activities and cleanup.

Setting up the Cooking Area	Suggested Materials
Location: Preferably near a water source and electrical outlet(s) but away from computers Optional: Access to refrigerator, oven, or microwave **Set up:** Child-size table and chairs Materials stored in boxes on low shelves and/or hung on pegboards	Plastic/metal bowls, of various sizes Plastic/metal measuring cups and spoons Pyrex measuring cups Wooden spoons, funnels, whisk, eggbeater, potato masher, knives, spatulas, cutting boards, peelers, corers, juicers, cookie cutters, tongs, large spoons, small pitchers Pot holders, aprons, dish towels Can openers, cooking shears, grater Cake pans, saucepans Place mats, dishes, flatware Recipe cards with pictures and words, laminated or covered in clear Contact paper

Selecting Materials

It isn't necessary to spend a lot of money on cooking equipment and tools. Used materials can be donated or bought inexpensively at secondhand stores. Instead of a conventional oven or a microwave, you can use a toaster oven, electric wok, electric frying pan, or electric Dutch oven. Place saucepans on plug-in electric coils and use sandwich makers to make more than sandwiches. You can even use an iron to make a foil-wrapped grilled cheese sandwich. Some teachers rely on alternative resources, such as light bulbs, for baking. Easy-Bake ovens, which sometimes can be picked up at flea markets for only a dollar or two, can be used to bake portions for one. A refrigerator, although nice to have, isn't necessary; you can store perishables in a cooler, insulated picnic bags, thermoses, or in the school's refrigerator (if one is available).

You may want to begin with just a few essential items and then add materials over the course of the year.

The following inventory is offered to guide your thinking. You can add or omit items from this list to reflect your preferences and resources and your children's tastes. You may want to begin with just a few essential items and then add materials over the course of the year, as children experiment more with food. Note that we recommend real knives over plastic ones because their weight makes them more stable. We recommend a chef's knife because children can wrap their hands around the handle, which is at a safe distance from the blade.

Cooking Equipment Inventory Suggestions

Measuring

- plastic/metal measuring spoons
- pitchers
- plastic/metal measuring cups (for dry ingredients)
- Pyrex measuring cups (for liquids)

Baking/cooking

- aluminum foil
- biscuit/cookie cutters
- cake pans (round or square, metal and Pyrex)
- cookie or jelly roll sheet
- cooling rack
- griddle
- loaf pan (metal and Pyrex)
- muffin tin and liners
- nesting mixing bowls
- plastic mixing bowls of various sizes
- pastry brush
- pie plates
- plastic wrap
- rolling pin
- saucepans with lids, including a double boiler

Gadgets/appliances

- blender
- candy thermometer
- can openers
- electric frying pan
- graters
- hand mixer
- hullers
- ice-cream freezer
- manual juicer (citrus reamer)
- mortar and pestle
- soft-grip vegetable peelers
- ice cream or cookie dough scoop/melon baller
- timer

Utensils

- butter/table knives
- colander
- eggbeater
- funnel
- chef's knives (sharp ones with soft-grip handles)
- ladle
- large slotted spoon
- potato masher or ricer
- pumpkin carving knife (child-size)
- rubber scraper
- safety scissors or cooking shears
- sandwich spreader
- sifter or strainer
- small and large rubber spatulas
- soft-grip wire whisks
- tongs
- vegetable brush
- wooden spoons

Accessories

- aprons
- wooden cutting boards
- pastry bag with coupler and tips
- potholders or oven mitts
- trivets

We encourage you to allow children to use real kitchen equipment, as they may become frustrated trying to make toy utensils work. Select materials made of rubber or unbreakable plastic to protect children from being hurt by broken bowls, glasses, or utensils. Soft-grip handles are easy for small hands to hold firmly. In some specific cases, Pyrex utensils are recommended, because they allow children to see what's inside and understand the measuring or baking process. Some cooking activities involve the use of sharp objects such as knives, grinders, graters, or corers. Their use should always be under close adult supervision.

Allow children to use real kitchen equipment.

Displaying Cooking Equipment and Tools

The key to making the Cooking Area both functional and attractive is to store and display equipment and supplies neatly and in a way that children can get at them independently. Use open shelving at the children's eye level. Group items by function, such as mixing, baking, rolling dough, and so on. Just as you label blocks and props, you can trace outlines of cooking items on colored contact paper, cut them out, and place them on appropriate locations on the shelf. Written labels will help the children learn to associate the utensil with its name.

Small items such as a pastry bag and tips can be placed in cardboard or plastic boxes or large juice cans and stored on the shelves.

Utensils such as wooden spoons or spatulas can be stored in a large food can covered with Contact paper or coated wallpaper and placed on a counter. Alternatively, large plastic vases or canisters can be used for storage. Frequently used items, such as measuring cups, spoons, and pot holders, can be hung on hooks near the area where children actually cook. Or, place these items in hanging baskets within the children's reach.

Consider using a system of portable cooking boxes.

If space is an issue in your classroom, think about how you can cut back on the space needed for cooking. For example, baking requires more equipment than making soup or blending a smoothie. Consider using a system of portable cooking boxes, similar to the prop box system used in dramatic play. Label several portable cooking boxes: one for baking; one for making soups, pudding, and other activities that require saucepans; and one for cooking activities that don't require baking or heating. Then, when children need this equipment, you can grab the appropriate box and take it to a table.

Smocks or aprons made of old shirts, oversize T-shirts, or oilcloth can be hung from a children's coat tree or on a pegboard hook placed near the entrance to the activity area.

Clean-up supplies, such as a dishpan and drainer, paper towels, and mops, should be stored at or near the sink area and accessible to children.

Sharp items, such as knives, grinders, and graters, should be stored out of the children's reach. Bleach and other cleaning solvents should be locked away.

The walls in the Cooking Area can be decorated in many creative ways. Invite children to draw or paint pictures of foods they've made. You also might choose to hang reproductions of fine art such as still life paintings of fruits and vegetables or impressionist drawings of picnic scenes. Relevant health and safety posters can also be displayed. For instance, hang a poster of the food pyramid to emphasize the need to eat healthy meals. If any of the children in your group or their families are vegetarians, you could hang the vegetarian food pyramid as well. Next to the sink area you might post a sign reminding children to wash their hands before and after handling food.

Special Health and Safety Considerations

Health and safety regulations are very important in creating a Cooking Area. If you and the children follow some basic guidelines, you can proceed with confidence.

First of all, do a safety check of the area. Make sure that outlets are not overloaded and that those not in use have safety caps. Sharp knives and potentially dangerous equipment like graters, grinders, and blenders should be stored out of the children's reach and brought out only when you can supervise the use of this equipment. Cleaning agents, as always, need to be stored in locked cupboards or closets.

Before children use the Cooking Area, discuss safety rules with them.

Before children use the Cooking Area, discuss safety rules with them. Just as they need to be introduced to the proper way to use computers and woodworking tools, they need to know about cooking safety. While we review the major precautions here, we recommend that you also get a copy of *Caring for Our Children: National Health and Safety Performance Standards: Guidelines for Out-of-Home Child Care Programs*, 2nd ed. This document, published in 2002 by the American Academy of Pediatrics, American Public Health Association, and the National Resource Center for Health and Safety in Child Care, provides detailed information on food health and safety (as well as guidance and standards for all areas of out-of-home child care).

Good Practices Related to Burns and Cuts

To prevent/treat burns/fire:

- Use dry potholders to handle hot pots and pans or foods.

- Use dry hands when plugging in an appliance.

- Use only wooden spoons in pots or pans (metal utensils get very hot).

- Keep pot holders, aprons, and dish towels away from heating elements.

- When using a stove top, turn pot handles toward the center of the stove.

- When lifting lids off heating pots or pans, lift the lid toward the back of the stove.

- Keep an open box of baking soda on the counter. If a fire should break out, teach children to smother it with baking soda—not water. If an oven or microwave should break out in flames, shut the door.

- To treat skin burns, place the burned area under cold, running water. Butter should not be used, it's bad for burns.

To prevent cuts:

- First introduce children to spreaders and butter knives (limiting cooking activities to those that do not require a sharp knife). Then move to serrated table knives. Older preschoolers can learn to use a chef's knife safely.

- Grip knives, graters, and peelers by handles only.

- Keep knives sharp; dull knives are dangerous.

- Place unused knives flat side down on a cutting board, not the counter.

- Never let a child use knives and other sharp utensils unsupervised.

- Never let children cut food in their hands.

- Demonstrate how to hold onto foods when grating or peeling so one's fingers are not exposed to sharp edges.

- Teach children to make their fingers into a "claw" when holding foods to be cut to keep fingertips out of harm's way.

Good Food Preparation Practices

To prevent food-borne illnesses:

- Post pictures of proper hand-washing procedures and remind everyone to wash hands before and after handling foods. Twenty seconds of washing with soap is recommended to get hands clean. You may wish to put out a timer or have children sing a prearranged song to make sure they spend this long washing.

- Teach children to sneeze or cough into their elbows or towards the floor. After blowing their noses, they should wash their hands.

- Use separate wood cutting boards for raw and cooked foods.

- Wash all utensils—including cutting boards—after using raw foods.

- Cook foods thoroughly.

- Don't let foods that need refrigeration sit out for more than two hours.

Safeguard children from eating something that might be harmful to them.

Before you begin cooking with children, find out if any of them have food allergies. Some preschoolers are allergic to peanuts, which are obviously present in peanut butter but also less obviously present in foods containing peanut oil, like M&M's. Some children are so allergic that even a trace amount of peanuts can be life-threatening. Other children are lactose intolerant and have difficulty digesting milk products. Be sure to consult children's records and talk with their families before undertaking any food-related activities. Plan so that you safeguard children from eating something that might be harmful to them, but find a way to allow all children to be able to participate in cooking activities.

To help you keep current with best practices, there are several Internet web sites that provide up-to-date information on food safety. Two of the best are: www.foodsafety.gov and www.fightbac.org. In addition, you might want to post your emergency health and safety plans and phone numbers in a set place. Should an emergency arise, you don't want to have to rely on your memory about how to put out a kitchen fire. While safety information is both necessary and important, try not to lose perspective. Cooking is a fun, light-hearted activity. Keeping health and safety in mind is like taking an umbrella with you on a cloudy day. Even if you never need to put your knowledge to use, you can feel confident that you're prepared.

What Children Learn in the Cooking Area

Cooking is a natural laboratory for teaching academic content. When children are engaged in preparing food, all of the key components of the content areas discussed in Chapter 3—literacy, math, science, social studies, the arts, and technology—can be explored. Here are some examples of how you can make this connection among content, teaching, and learning.

Literacy

Go over recipes cards with children to expand their **vocabulary and language**. As children learn how to knead bread, grind peanuts, and flip pancakes, they learn new words as well as skills.

Stock the Cooking Area with wonderful children's books that feature eating and cooking to enhance children's **understanding of books and other texts**. Many books—such as *Storybook Stew* (Suzanne I. Barchers and Peter J. Rauen) and *Cooking Up a Story* (Carol Elaine Catron and Barbara Catron Parks)—can enhance children's enjoyment of literature and cooking. Include cookbooks, recipe cards, store coupons, and recipes from newspapers and magazines to demonstrate different kinds of print.

Expand children's **knowledge of print and letters and words** by developing and using recipe charts and cards and picture cookbooks with children. Point to the words as you read the chart from left to right and top to bottom. Draw children's attention to the words on food containers and boxes. Offer children alphabet cookie cutters or show them how to form dough in the shape of letters.

Mathematics

Involve children in solving problems about **number concepts** by posing challenges for them to solve. For example, ask children how they could divide the bowl of dip they made so that everyone in the group can have some. Give children practice in developing one-to-one correspondence by having them set the table for the same number of children as there are chairs at the table.

Help children to gain knowledge of **geometry and spatial sense** by giving them shape cutters for making sandwiches, and having them select the best place to position a rack for baking in the oven.

Develop **patterning** skills by showing children how to create a layered salad or lasagna.

Provide children with recipes to follow to give them experiences with **measurement**. Have children observe how many teaspoons are in a tablespoon and how many cups are in a quart.

Encourage children to use **data collection, organization,** and **representation** skills in the Cooking Area by recording how many people want to cook different recipes, such as pancakes or waffles.

Science
Pose questions that will encourage children to conduct **physical science** investigations. For example, have them test an egg's freshness by seeing whether it sinks or floats in a glass of water. (Spoiled eggs will float to the top.) Encourage children to use their senses to observe what the gelatin looks like as it sets, how the dough feels when flour is added, or what the lemonade tastes like without sweetener in it. Help children to understand why food changes form—why ice cream freezes, chocolate melts, or pudding thickens.

Have children plant radish, pea, and cucumber seeds that can be grown for cooking activities to see **life science** in action. Children can suspend sweet potatoes or avocado seeds in jars of water until they root and give off branches. Make every cooking activity a lesson in nutrition and good eating habits. Set out carrots, celery, and sprouts for children to prepare and eat; encourage children to prepare recipes with fruits instead of sweets.

Social Studies
Ask parents to share their family recipes to expose children to **people and how they live**. Supplement these family treasures with recipes that you have collected reflecting varied cultures and customs, regions of the United States, and climates.

Focus children's attention on **people and the past** by having them keep a weekly picture food diary of everything they eat at school. Use these diaries as you discuss nutrition. Parents can learn about their children's diets, too.

Begin a classroom recycling program to learn about **people and the environment**. Start by collecting whatever food containers—steel cans, glass jars, plastic jugs—are recycled in your community. If you're ambitious, you might even set up a compost. To do this, collect vegetable and fruit wastes that can be added to the soil for enrichment. As children clean up in the Cooking Area they can separate out their paper, metal, glass, plastic, and food trash. (Most of your recycled newspapers and office paper will probably come from other activity areas.)

The Arts

Decorate the walls and backs of dividers with children's paintings and drawings of foods they have cooked to expose children to the **visual arts**. Develop a class cookbook that children can illustrate.

Promote **drama** by pantomiming the movements of various cooking activities such as moving legs like an eggbeater, being a kernel of corn popping, or a piece of bread in a toaster.

Technology

Talk with children about the appliances they use in the Cooking Area to make them **aware of technology**.

Challenge children to explore gadgets and other **technology tools**. Pose questions such as, "How would you open cans without a can opener?" or "How are an egg beater, a wire whisk, and an electric hand mixer alike and different?"

On field trips to a farm or hatchery, encourage children to explore how **people use technology**. Request that the guide show children the machines that are used to milk cows, plant seeds, harvest plants, feed fish, and the like.

The examples we give of cooking experiences that engage children in learning important content can happen in any Cooking Area when teachers are purposeful about what they plan. In the next section we explore the teacher's role in more depth.

The Teacher's Role

In the Cooking Area, like all activity areas, you are a leader, facilitator, and support system for children working there. While there are health and safety concerns that require adult supervision, children can still use this area independently and with one or a few friends. Your primary job is to respond to children's cues so that all children make the connection between cooking and learning.

Observing and Responding to Individual Children

When children first interact with food in the Cooking Area, they start by exploring. In this early stage, they use all their senses to find out what food is like. Feeling the texture of a pineapple's skin, smelling bread as it bakes, watching pudding thicken, hearing popcorn kernels pop, and tasting the tartness of lime juice, they learn the properties of different foods. Tasting and seeing how food reacts to being cooked, sliced, and mashed, they learn about differences in raw and cooked states.

Once children have a feel for what food is like, they experiment with it. In this stage they want to see what happens to bread dough that has been kneaded and then punched down. They want to see how the dough then rises again when left to sit in a warm place. During this experimentation phase, children's actions are purposeful. Their curiosity leads them to ask how food reacts to their manipulations, and they delight in creating finished products that can be eaten. Cooking also provides an opportunity for children to learn how to follow rules. Cooking with recipes requires that children understand directions and carry out activities in a preset sequence. These are skills that will serve children well throughout their lives.

Learning Basic Techniques

In planning cooking activities for preschool children, you need to be sure that children have knowledge of basic techniques. Once they have these skills, cooking will be both easier and more sophisticated. Many of the techniques can best be introduced by direct instruction. Once learned, most of these skills can then be used by children independently. Those skills that may pose a safety danger (slicing, grating, and coring, for example) should only be done under adult supervision.

Techniques that 3- to 5-Year-Olds Can Learn:

- basting
- cracking
- cutting
- dipping
- dredging (as with flour)
- forming shapes
- greasing
- kneading
- marinating

- measuring dry ingredients
- measuring liquids
- melting
- mixing
- peeling with fingers
- pouring
- rolling with hands
- rolling with rolling pin

- scrubbing
- shaking
- shredding
- sifting
- slicing
- spreading
- squeezing
- stirring

Techniques to Introduce to Older Preschoolers:

- beating
- coring
- dicing
- draining

- grating
- grinding
- hulling
- juicing

- mashing
- peeling with vegetable peeler
- pitting

Responding to Each Child

By observing children participating in cooking activities, you can plan an approach that will enhance their experiences. As you observe, look to see what skills a child has acquired and how the child responds to cooking activities. Notice if the child

- helps herself to snack or waits until she is reminded

- chooses a particular job or waits to be assigned a task

- can follow a recipe card or chart

- is able to handle and control tools safely

- sees a cooking activity through to completion

- is able to cook cooperatively with other children

Your focused observations will give you insight into a child's development and enable you to make decisions on what to do next. Using the *Developmental Continuum* as a guide, reflect on what you learn and consider how best to respond. In the chart that follows, we provide examples of how this process works in the Cooking Area.

Look to see what skills a child has acquired and how the child responds to cooking activities.

Observation	Reflection	Response
After watching Ben throw a strawberry huller on the floor, Juwan picks up the huller, rinses it off, and hands it back to Ben.	Juwan understands and follows rules without being reminded. (*Objective 9, Follows classroom rules*) He recognizes what Ben might need and tries to help him. (*Objective 11, Recognizes the feelings of others and responds appropriately*) How can I encourage his tendency to help others?	Acknowledge Juwan's behavior with appropriate praise: "Thank you for remembering how to take care of our cooking tools." Make a suggestion: "Maybe you can help Ben learn how to use the strawberry huller."
After watching Ben throw a strawberry huller on the floor, Juwan picks up the huller, rinses it off, and hands it back to Ben.	Ben seems to be frustrated and is not able to express his feelings in words. (*Objective 3, Recognizes own feelings and manages them appropriately*) I wonder if he has the small muscle control to use the strawberry huller. (*Objective 19, Controls small muscles in hands*)	Help Ben learn to better manage his feelings by encouraging him to use words: "Ben, I can tell that you got upset trying to use the huller. However, if you throw it on the floor, you might break it. Could you tell me what the problem is so we can try to solve it?" Suggest that he use his hands to remove the stems and offer him other activities to develop his small muscle skills such as picking up objects with tongs and playing with clay.
On her own, Jonetta rolls out cookie dough and uses cookie cutters. When Derek asks for the rolling pin, Jonetta says, "Why don't you use this can to roll your dough. Then you can use it to make circles in the dough."	Jonetta is able to think of different uses for classroom objects. (*Objective 23, Approaches problems flexibly*) How can I extend her ability to apply what she's learned to new contexts? (*Objective 26, Applies knowledge or experience to a new context*)	Acknowledge how she solved a problem: "You thought of a new way for Derek to roll out his dough." Challenge her: "I wonder what other objects we might use to roll out dough. Maybe Derek has a new idea."
While making pretzels with Zack's mom, Crystal points to her pretzel and says, "Look, I made a C pretzel."	Crystal recognizes and can make the first letter in her name. (*Objective 46, Demonstrates knowledge of the alphabet*) What can I do to build on her growing interest in letters?	Say, "Yes, you made a C, the first letter in your name. What other letters can you make with the pretzel dough?" Introduce her to the pastry bag and tips and let her experiment squeezing dough, soft cheese, or pudding through the various tips to make letters.

Interacting With Children in the Cooking Area

One of the best ways to promote learning while children are cooking is to engage them in conversation. By doing so, you also help children develop critical thinking skills and expand their vocabulary.

As a starting point, **describe** what you see children doing:

> *You've put all the banana peels together in one bowl. That will make cleanup very easy.*
>
> *It takes hard work to mix the peanut butter and corn syrup together. The peanut butter balls are going to come out nice and smooth.*
>
> *You've been over to the tasting table twice this morning. I noticed that you especially liked peeling and tasting the orange.*

When you describe what they've done, children review their actions in their own minds. The re-run helps to develop self-awareness. Next, you can encourage children to **think about and articulate their actions**, skills that are fundamental to language development:

> *You've been shaking that jar of cream for a long time. Is anything happening?*
>
> *I see you've taken the potato masher off the shelf. What will you be doing with it?*
>
> *What have you discovered at the tasting table?*

Talk with children and pose questions to help them develop critical thinking skills and expand their vocabulary.

Once you have helped children to reflect on their actions, you can facilitate their learning further by encouraging them to think about their activities in deeper ways. In this step you are **posing questions for children to analyze and solve**. Here are some examples of questions to extend children's learning:

> *What happened to the raisins when you soaked them in water? Why do you think the banana turned brown?*
>
> *Do you suppose we could do something with the orange halves after we've squeezed the juice out of them?*
>
> *How does the strainer keep the lemon's seeds from falling into the juice?*
>
> *How could you make a triangle out of this cheese? Which part of the recipe did you like doing the best?*

Small-Group Cooking Activities

Group activities are most effective when limited to three or four children at a time. Some 3-year-olds may have difficulty doing advanced tasks, so it's important to match activities to children's skills. In a mixed-age group, older children can assist younger ones. Here are some suggestions for introducing recipes to be used by several children at once.

Introducing Recipes to Children

Prepare simple recipe charts illustrating each step.

Have all necessary equipment and ingredients available.

Read the entire recipe aloud, reading and discussing each step.

Involve the entire group in doing each step in the cooking activity so no one is just standing around and watching.

Help children think about the activity as they work. Begin by making "here and now" statements to describe what you see them doing: "You're cracking the egg on the edge of the bowl." Then pose questions to help them reflect on the process: "Why do we use a vegetable peeler to peel the apples instead of using our fingers, as we do for a hard-boiled egg?" "What did you add to the applesauce that made it turn brown?"

Have the children serve and eat their handiwork as the final step in the cooking process.

Include all children in the clean-up process. Children can take turns washing and drying utensils, mopping counters, wiping the eating area, and putting supplies away.

On the following pages are some recipes to start you off.

Solar Tea

Food:
Teabags (2)
Honey (1 T)
Water (4 cups)
Lemon (1)
Ice cubes

Equipment:
Large glass jar (at least
1 gallon) with lid
4-cup Pyrex measuring cup
Cutting board
Knife

Method:
1. Measure 4 cups of cold water.
2. Pour water into jar.
3. Add teabags and honey.
4. Place jar in sun for 3 to 6 hours. Tea is done when it turns a hearty brown color.
5. Let jar sit at room temperature 1 hour. Refrigerate.
6. Using cutting board and knife, cut lemon into wedges.
7. Fill drinking glasses with ice and lemon. Pour tea.

Measure 4 cups water

Pour water

Add tea and honey

Put jar in sun. (3 to 6 hours)

Let sit for 1 hour Refrigerate

Cut lemon

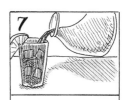
Fill glasses

Alfalfa Sprouts

Food:
Alfalfa seeds (1 T)
Water

Equipment:
32-oz. jar
Cheesecloth
Rubber band

Method:
1. Place seeds in jar.
2. Cover with warm water.
3. Let seeds soak for 24 hours in warm, dark place.
4. Cover the top of jar with cheesecloth. Secure with rubber band.
5. Pour out water. Rinse and drain twice.
6. Repeat for 5 days.
7. On last day, place sprouts in window to turn green.
8. Store in refrigerator.

I ♥ Peanut Butter

Food:
Peanuts (1 lb.)
Peanut oil (2 T)

Equipment:
Hand grinder *(on which a cardboard collar has been placed to make it safer)*
Bowl
Measuring spoons
Wooden spoon

Method:
1. Secure grinder to table or counter. Place bowl near grinder's spout. Shell peanuts.
2. Place handful of peanuts in grinder.
3. Gradually add oil so grinder turns smoothly.
4. Grind all peanuts.
5. Stir ground peanuts in bowl with spoon.

1 — Shell peanuts

2 — Put peanuts in grinder

3 — Add oil

4 — Grind peanuts

5 — Stir

Using the Cooking Area Independently

If you set out foods that require only minimal preparation, children can learn to use the Cooking Area independently. Begin by making a recipe chart and recipe cards. For example, if you plan to have children prepare a snack of stuffed celery, the recipe chart would illustrate four activities, using pictures and simple wording: (1) rinse the celery in the sink; (2) dry the celery with paper towels; (3) use a spreader to put cottage cheese in the celery; and (4) eat the stuffed celery.

When you prepare individual recipe cards, children learn sequencing as they put the cards in order. To make recipe cards, use 5" x 8" index cards or pieces of cardboard. Gather or make as many cards as there are steps. On each card write one step in the recipe. Laminate these cards to protect them from dirty hands and spills. Then children can handle them while they cook.

For independent cooking experiences, look for recipes that can be prepared without electrical equipment or sharp tools so that children don't need constant adult supervision. Introduce the cards to the children to be sure they know what to do and how to use them. Make sure that all needed equipment and ingredients are accessible to the children and let them know you are available if they need help.

Here are foods that can be prepared by children working independently.

- ants on a log*
- apple, banana, cheese, peanut butter, cream cheese and jelly, or bologna sandwiches
- bean dip and tortilla chips
- bologna and cheese roll-ups
- celery and carrot sticks with dip
- cereal and milk
- cheese shapies (cutouts of cheese made with cookie cutters)
- cottage cheese with raisins or sunflower seeds
- lettuce "roll-ups" stuffed with bologna slices, peanut butter, or cottage cheese
- freshly squeezed orange juice
- green or Waldorf salad*
- peanut butter-covered crackers or rice cakes
- pineapple and cheese tidbits
- pita pockets filled with fruit, cheese, bologna, or peanut butter and jelly
- ring-around-the-peanut-butter*
- sliced fruit and nuts with yogurt
- trail mix or granola
- under the sea snack (gummy fish in blueberry Jello)
- watermelon zipper sipper (crushed watermelon in a bag)

Recipes for the foods with an * after them are provided below.

Ants on a Log

Food:	1 stalk celery, cottage cheese or peanut butter, raisins
Equipment:	knife, cutting board, spoon
Method:	**1.** Pull off one stalk of celery (the log). **2.** Wash stalk. **3.** Trim celery ends. **4.** Spoon cottage cheese or peanut butter into center of celery. **5.** Decorate with raisins (ants).

Waldorf Salad

Food:	1 apple, 1 celery stalk, about 10 raisins, walnuts, 1 T mayonnaise
Equipment:	cutting board, bowl, plastic knife, nutcracker, wooden spoon
Method:	**1.** Slice apple and cut into bite-size pieces. Place in mixing bowl. **2.** Slice celery and cut into bite-size pieces. Place in mixing bowl. **3.** Add raisins to bowl. **4.** Crack walnuts. Remove shells. Break up pieces. Place in bowl. **5.** Add mayonnaise. 6. Stir all ingredients.

Ring-around-the-Peanut-Butter

Food:	1 apple, jar of peanut butter
Equipment:	corer, metal spoon or thin spatula
Method:	**1.** Wash apple. **2.** Dry apple. **3.** Working around the stem, use corer to remove the center of the apple. **4.** Fill inside of apple with peanut butter. **5.** Slice crosswise to make apple circles with peanut butter in the middle.

Tasting Tables

Teachers set up tasting tables to give children the opportunity to explore unfamiliar and interesting foods. Depending on the children's backgrounds, the definition of unfamiliar will vary from group to group. Fennel, crystallized ginger, or star fruit will be a surprise for most children. Familiar foods also can be paired with unfamiliar ones for children to compare and contrast: brussels sprouts with cabbage, green peas with black-eyed peas, and spaghetti with cooked spaghetti squash. If you are using perishable foods, be sure to keep them stored in a refrigerator or cooler when not being used.

Be careful about children's allergies. If you know a child is allergic to certain foods, either don't use them or provide alternatives. To extend children's learning, try asking questions such as these:

If you know a child is allergic to certain foods, either don't use them or provide alternatives.

> *In what ways are bananas and plantains alike? In what ways are they different?*
>
> *You just tasted the cooked cabbage. How do you expect the brussels sprouts to taste?*
>
> *What did the crystallized ginger taste like?*
>
> *Does the fennel smell like anything else you've ever eaten?*
>
> *How does a sliced star fruit look different from an unsliced one?*
>
> *Which food did you most enjoy tasting today? Why?*

Using the Cooking Area With Adult Supervision

Any time children use heat, knives, or plug-in appliances, you'll need to be nearby to provide safety advice and model careful cooking practices. Try to support children rather than being the inspector who swoops down to correct mistakes.

Here are two recipes that children can prepare on their own with an adult present to supervise.

For an easy experience: Yogurt Drink

Food:	milk, plain yogurt, banana, strawberries or blueberries
Equipment:	blender, drinking glass
Method:	**1.** Peel 1 banana. **2.** Wash strawberries or blueberries. **3.** (If using strawberries), hull strawberries. **4.** Place fruit in blender. **5.** Add 1/2 cup of milk. **6.** Add 1/2 cup of yogurt. **7.** With grown-up's assistance "blend" ingredients. **8.** Pour into glass.

For a more challenging experience: Baba Ghanouj (Eggplant Dip)

Food:	1 eggplant, parsley, 1/2 lemon, garlic powder, salt, pepper, pita bread
Equipment:	toaster oven, fork, spoon, cutting board, chef's knife, bowl, citrus reamer, masher, measuring spoons
Method:	**1.** Pierce eggplant with fork. **2.** Place on tray in toaster oven, preheated to 300 degrees. Bake until eggplant collapses (about 30–35 minutes). **3.** Using pot holders, move eggplant to cutting board on counter. Let sit until cool to the touch. **4.** Slice eggplant in half lengthwise. **5.** Using spoon, scoop filling out into bowl. **6.** Sprinkle in two shakes each of garlic powder, salt, and pepper. **7.** Using reamer, squeeze 1 T of lemon juice. Add to bowl. **8.** Tear pieces of parsley leaves. Add to bowl. **9.** Use masher to combine ingredients. **10.** Stir mixture. Scoop onto pita bread slices.

Introducing Children to New Recipes

To keep cooking experiences interesting, add new recipes for children to make on their own and as part of the group. Keep familiar ones around, however, because children like to repeat old favorites.

In selecting recipes, take into consideration

- the ages and developmental levels of the children (can they successfully use corers, graters, peelers, juicers, etc.?)

- the appliances you have and the adequacy of supervision that can be arranged

- the children's interests and other class activities (can a recipe be tied to a project being studied or a field trip the group is taking?)

- healthy food choices you'd like to promote

- cultural relevance to family backgrounds and local and regional cooking styles and tastes

- cost (making use of seasonal fruits and vegetables is a cost-effective approach)

Although it's a little more challenging, try to find recipes that involve making something from scratch. Handling ingredients provides for a more satisfying experience—one in which children can learn about food as they cook and not simply focus on the finished product. Like the art process, the act of cooking is most important.

Children's families are a good resource for new recipes. By inviting families to share recipes, you foster a home-school connection and provide opportunities for multicultural experiences.

By inviting families to share recipes, you foster a home-school connection.

To locate additional resources for recipes and cooking activities, combine your own experiences with other information resources. All kinds of cookbooks—some written specifically for cooking with children—are available at bookstores and at public libraries. Almost any style of cooking can be adapted for classroom use. The children will enjoy the experience of cooking and eating different ingredients: chopping and stir-frying vegetables, rolling tortillas around refried beans, blending cucumber and yogurt into *raita*, or frying potato pancakes and covering them with applesauce.

For additional ideas, you might ask your state or county U.S. Department of Agriculture Cooperative Extension Agent for some recipes and safety tips. The Web is a rich source of information, whether you search specifically for information on children and cooking, or explore the ideas of other professional individuals, organizations, and businesses working with young children.

Frequently Asked Questions About Cooking

Can I use my center's kitchen for my Cooking Area?

We do not recommend this option. First, you need to check to determine if health regulations even permit children to be in the kitchen. Assuming children are allowed, you need to consider what the benefits and disadvantages would be. On the positive side, children will have access to appliances. On the negative side, this area is not one that children can use on their own. In addition to the safety factor, the counter and work space sizes are not suited to use by children. If you choose to have children cook in the kitchen, you will need an adult stationed there at all times. And because children cannot cook on their own, there is a strong likelihood that cooking will turn into an adult demonstration of cooking—not the participatory activity intended for this activity area.

Is it okay to let the children make cakes and other sweets for special occasions?

While the occasional sweet isn't harmful, we do not recommend associating celebrations with eating sweets. The association is like using food as a reward, a practice that almost everyone agrees is neither a good behavior modification strategy nor a healthy eating practice. So try to think of a healthier way to eat something special for celebrations.

What if children want to cook the same thing all the time?

Don't be too concerned. First, we know that children find comfort in doing the familiar. Just as they may ask you to read the same storybook or sing the same song over and over, they enjoy making the same recipe day after day. The repetition helps to reinforce learning. Second, children go through periods in which they want the same food every day. It's common for a young child to eat peanut butter and jelly or slices of cheese with gusto every single day. Still, if you think a child is not stretching his skills as much as you'd like, you can introduce him to other recipes. Begin by using ingredients you know the child favors.

What if children want to make up their own recipes?

Great! You certainly want to encourage children to be creative in the Cooking Area and everywhere else. Respond as if a child were telling you a story that you wanted to record. Write down the ingredients the child uses and procedures that he follows. When he is finished, review what he did. Is there anything he might want to try differently next time? Afterward, together with the child, make up a recipe chart and cards for the new recipe. Let all of the children know that a cheese and cucumber recipe is now available for everyone in the Cooking Area. You may even have a future professional chef in your class!

A Letter to Families About Cooking

Dear Families,

Cooking is an important part of our Curriculum. When children cook, they have an opportunity to learn about nutrition, to be creative, and to prepare their own healthy snacks. Cooking teaches a lot of academic skills too. When children learn to follow picture recipe cards, they develop skills they need to read and write. Measuring 1 cup of flour and pouring 1/4 teaspoon of lemon juice into batter gives them a lesson in math. Whipping egg whites into meringue and melting cheese under a broiler are lessons in science.

When children cook, we talk a lot about what they are doing and why. They are scientists, observing what happens to flour when we add water to it and predicting how high we should fill a muffin tin so the batter doesn't overflow.

When we prepare the special foods of each family, your child learns to appreciate the cultures of everyone in our class. Perhaps you have some favorite family recipes that you would like to share with us. Please give them to us at any time. We'd like it, too, if you could come to our Cooking Area and introduce the class to your child's favorite foods.

Cooking is a very special part of our program. It is one of the few activities children get to do that is also done by adults. Children pretend to be grown-ups making meals in their dramatic play. They can read books and sing songs about food. But in cooking, children can actually behave as grown-ups.

What You Can Do at Home

Since cooking is already a part of your home life, think about involving your child. Including your child may take extra time, and there may be more of a mess than if you cooked alone, but there are many rewards. Your child will be learning literacy, math, and science skills just by helping you. In addition, cooking sets the stage for lifelong healthy eating habits. When children help prepare their meals, they tend to eat better.

Start your child on simple tasks like stirring batter, squeezing lemons, adding spices, or shaping meatballs. Discuss what you are doing together while cooking. Ask questions like these.

> *What happened to the butter when we put it in the microwave?*
>
> *How should we get the flour into this cup?*
>
> *Did we get all the juice out of that lemon? Let's push down on the lemon together and see what happens?*

The beauty of cooking with children is that they learn skills and have fun at the same time you are attending to a household chore. What could be better than that!

inside this chapter

471 How Computer Play Promotes Development
472 Connecting Computer Play With Curriculum Objectives

474 Creating an Environment for Using Computers
475 Selecting Materials

482 What Children Learn From Using Computers

484 The Teacher's Role
484 Observing and Responding to Individual Children
487 Interacting With Children in the Computer Area
489 Frequently Asked Questions About Computers

491 A Letter to Families About Computers

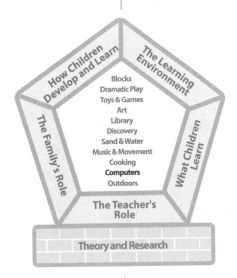

Computers

How Computer Play Promotes Development

The Computer Area is a place where children can have fun while exploring the many exciting things that computers do. Children use computers to investigate questions, solve problems, and explore and manipulate objects on a screen. This work supports development in all areas.

Social/emotional development. Computers are a way for children to demonstrate self-direction and independence. At the same time, they offer children opportunities to work with other children to solve problems, as they jointly maneuver their way through a program. For some children, becoming computer "experts" provides them with a valued leadership role in the classroom they might not have otherwise.

Physical development. Children work on fine motor skills as they use a keyboard, put a CD-ROM in the drive, and coordinate the cursor with the movement of the mouse. In fact, every action on a computer involves fine motor development and eye-hand coordination.

Cognitive development. Computers contribute to children's intellectual development, and bridge the gap between concrete and abstract thinking. As children explore cause and effect, create patterns, solve problems, and discover solutions, they learn to do on a screen what they already have mastered through hands-on learning. Creativity flourishes, too, as children create art, arrange objects in unique ways, and experiment with graphics.

Language development. As children learn to identify and use computer-related terms such as *icon, cursor,* or *CD-ROM,* they gain a technical vocabulary. With practice, they begin to identify the letters of the alphabet on the keyboard and in programs. As they use software that can read and highlight spoken text, they make connections between speech and print.

Connecting Computer Play With Curriculum Objectives

As you become familiar with the many ways computers can be used effectively in your classroom, children's learning opportunities will multiply. Your knowledge of the *Creative Curriculum* goals and objectives will help you to think about how best to support development. In the chart below, we offer some examples of what children might do that would indicate their developmental progress on selected objectives.

Selected Curriculum Objectives	What a Child Might Do in the Computer Area
Social/Emotional Development	
4. Stands up for rights	Tells classmate who joins him at the computer, "I was working on this program. You can help me play, but I don't want to switch programs."
5. Demonstrates self-direction and independence	Navigates through a software program using picture icons as guide.
7. Respects and cares for classroom environment and materials	Makes sure that CDs are returned to their cases before leaving the Computer Area.
9. Follows classroom rules	After eating snack, washes hands before using the computer.
10. Plays well with other children	When child asks friend if she can join him at the computer, he replies, "You can be in charge of the mouse since your chair is close to it."
12. Shares and respects the rights of others	Lets child sitting with him at the computer finish scanning in a drawing before asking for a turn to do the same.
Physical Development	
19. Controls small muscles in hands	Uses trackball or mouse to move the cursor on the screen.
20. Coordinates eye-hand movement	Moves cursor onto picture of a box, and clicks trackball or mouse to open the box.
21. Uses tools for writing and drawing	Uses paintbrush tool on drawing program to make a self-portrait.

Selected Curriculum Objectives	What a Child Might Do in the Computer Area
Cognitive Development	
22. Observes objects and events with curiosity	Looks at butterfly emerging from a cocoon on Internet site bookmarked by teacher.
24. Shows persistence in approaching tasks	Asks the teacher for help in locating the program she was using earlier in the day because she's not yet done using it.
25. Explores cause and effect	Comments on the fact that clicking on the tube of paint changes the color of the lines on the screen.
27. Classifies objects	Using a touch screen, puts all of the red eggs in the red basket, blue eggs in a blue basket, and yellow eggs in a yellow basket.
33. Uses one-to-one correspondence	Using a mixed body parts program, finds one head, one torso, and one pair of legs for each person.
34. Uses numbers and counting	Touches each object in a scavenger hunt program to make sure that the right number of objects are visible on the screen.
37. Makes and interprets representations	Uses drawing program to construct an airport like the one he built out of blocks.
Language Development	
40. Understands and follows oral directions	Responds to computer's spoken command to click on the object she thinks is biggest.
42. Asks questions	Asks teacher how to make the images on the screen appear larger.
43. Actively participates in conversations	Debates with a friend the best way to work through the maze on the screen.
46. Demonstrates knowledge of the alphabet	Types the letter "*D*" repeatedly and says, "See, there's a *D* for Derek."
47. Uses emerging reading skills to make meaning from print	Clicks on the EXIT icon, with the word EXIT written on it, to leave the program.

Creating an Environment for Using Computers

Successful experiences with computers depend on how the computer is integrated into the classroom. The setup of the Computer Area, and the software and web sites you make available, influence whether children's experiences are successful or frustrating, and whether computers are used appropriately or inappropriately. Obviously, the location of outlets, phone jacks, and Internet connections will influence the placement of computers.

If possible, locate your Computer Area either adjacent to or within the Library Area. Much of what the children will do with the computer—problem solving, communication, and gathering information—are tasks that children naturally do in the Library Area. If you have additional computers, consider putting one in the Toys and Games Area, where children can use patterning and classification software to reinforce the activities they do with puzzles, toys, and games, or in the Discovery Area, where children can use a computer to find answers to questions about their explorations or to look at pictures that help them understand what they are seeing.

Children should sit no closer than 18" from the screen, with the monitor angled so they do NOT have to look up.

Keyboard is at a child's elbow level.

Software is organized and labeled with pictures and words.

Setting up the Computer Area	Sugested Materials
Location:	One or more computers and a printer set up against a wall or back to back
Next to or part of the Library Area	Printer (ideally color)
Near electrical outlets, and other necessary connections, with cords placed out of children's reach	Adaptive devices for children with special needs
Good lighting that does not cause glare on computer screens	Software stored on the computer or within children's reach
Set up:	Paper for printing
Child-size table (or computer stand)	Blank diskettes labeled with each child's name
Screw the power strip/surge protector into the bottom of the computer table. Plug all equipment (speakers, printer, etc.) into the power strip so that it is easy to turn everything on and off at one time.	Additional computer accessories such as speakers, scanner, digital camera, or computer microscope
Place eye screws on bottom or back of table to gather wires. Use twist ties to keep the wires away from children's feet.	
Two chairs at each computer	

Selecting Materials

There are many options for both computers and the software you will use. Sometimes the choices can be overwhelming. To help you get started, we offer the best advice we could find. You may also want to consult the web sites we recommend as well as knowledgeable colleagues and specialists.

 ### Selecting Hardware

Computer hardware refers to the physical equipment itself. A hardware setup that works well in a preschool setting is shown on the previous page. In selecting a computer for your classroom, find one that has enough hard disk space (the place inside your computer that stores the majority of software and information) and memory to run today's CD-ROM software and store digital images. Specifications for hardware are being improved constantly, making the standards for the field ever higher.

Additional Computer Hardware

Mouse. The mouse, a hand held hardware attachment, passes instructions to the computer. For many younger children, a mouse is easier to use than keyboard keys. An alternative to a traditional mouse—an optical mouse—offers children better control, eliminates the use of a mouse pad, and does not accumulate grime and dirt.

Keyboard modifications. Templates and keypads help young children maneuver and master the keyboard before they are able to recognize and read letters.

Disk drive for floppy disks. Floppy disks are used to store information, such as a child's writing samples and documents (older computers used floppy disks to load software also). All software applications now come on CDs, and today's computers increasingly use CDs for storing large amounts of data that won't fit on floppy disks. Due to their small storage capacity, floppy disks are used less often.

CD-ROM drive. Nearly all computers now have trays for inserting software in the form of CDs or DVDs. (DVDs—digital video discs—look like CDs but hold more information.) CDs and DVDs store huge amounts of data.

Modem. There are different ways to get connected to the Internet. A modem is a connection between a computer and the other computers that are on the Internet. Modems use telephone, cable, or fiber optic-based connections. Some classrooms have direct high-speed connections via cable-modems or DSL (digital subscription lines) on schoolwide networks.

Network. A network is a group of computers that are connected via cables, telephone wires, or wireless signals.

Wish list accessories. If you have the resources, you may wish to invest in alternative input devices, such as a touchpad or a trackball, which some children find easier to use than a mouse. A scanner, a Zip drive (for high-capacity storage), or a CD-writer for storing large files such as photos or scanned children's work can enhance your computer's capabilities. Other accessories you might wish to investigate include computer microscopes, digital cameras, sound morphers, tape recorders, and musical keyboards.

Here are a few additional considerations in picking a suitable computer.

Available software. Not all software runs on all computers. In general, early childhood software has been developed for use on two different types of computers: PCs or MACs.

Repairability. If something goes wrong, you don't want to be in the position of having your computer in the shop for weeks or finding out that the needed parts are obsolete. You'll also want to know if the machine can be repaired on-site or at a local repair shop, or if it will need to be shipped out.

Selecting Software

Much of the software you will use is already preloaded onto the computer. In addition, there are literally hundreds of programs marketed as appropriate for preschoolers. Be cautious. Only about 20 percent of the software on the market is truly developmentally appropriate (Haugland and Wright, 1997). While some software offers children exciting choices and experiences, other software is merely a watered-down version of ones developed for school-age children or an electronic version of work sheets. Graphics and sound are not enough to make software appropriate. As you begin to examine software, think first about how children will interact with it. One authority describes a software based on a continuum of child involvement (Bowman, 1997). The following diagram illustrates this continuum. The materials in columns two, three, and four allow the child increasing degrees of involvement.

> Only about 20 percent of the software on the market is truly developmentally appropriate.

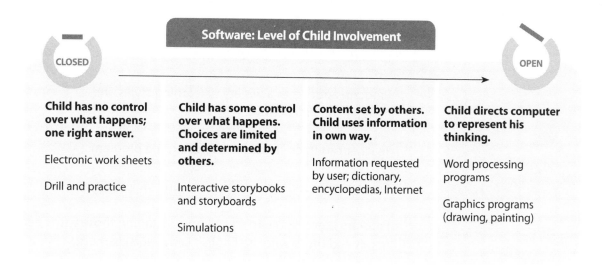

Software: Level of Child Involvement

CLOSED → OPEN

Child has no control over what happens; one right answer.	**Child has some control over what happens. Choices are limited and determined by others.**	**Content set by others. Child uses information in own way.**	**Child directs computer to represent his thinking.**
Electronic work sheets		Information requested by user; dictionary, encyclopedias, Internet	Word processing programs
Drill and practice	Interactive storybooks and storyboards		Graphics programs (drawing, painting)
	Simulations		

The Creative Curriculum® Checklist for
Selecting Developmentally Appropriate Software

☐ Program has age-appropriate content and approach with realistic expectations for children's skill levels. Children experience success and feel competent using it.

☐ Child can use and adjust control features independently, without adult assistance.

☐ Program makes use of intrinsic motivation, not rewards, and is paced so children don't have to wait a long time for the program to load or for graphics or feedback to appear.

☐ Program offers choices that child can control.

☐ Content is meaningful and interesting and can be expanded. The software is open-ended and engages children in exploration and problem-solving activities.

☐ Child can set the pace for movement through the program and exit at any time.

☐ Child and/or teacher can set the level of difficulty.

☐ Feedback uses meaningful graphics/sound and can be individualized.

☐ Instructions are clear and simple and not dependent on the ability to read.

☐ Program appeals to a variety of learning styles and multiple intelligences.

☐ Teacher can track child's history using the program.

☐ Content and feedback are bias-free and violence-free.

☐ Program is accessible to all children, including those with special needs and those who are English Language Learners.

☐ Program offers good value for the cost.

Rather than having a large inventory of software, as you would for example, with books, we recommend that you limit children's choices to no more than 10–12 good ones. Children tend to get more out of the experience when they learn to explore a program's options in depth, rather than jumping from one program to the next. In addition, as children develop skills, they learn to use a program in different ways or at a more advanced level. Here are some recommended resources for selecting appropriate software:

Limit children's choices to no more than 10–12 good ones.

- *Children's Technology Review*
  www.childrenssoftware.com
  Educators review interactive media for ages zero to 16 years.

- *Tech Learning: The Resource for Education Technology Leaders*
  www.techlearning.com
  "Resources" page has reviews of children's software programs.

- *SuperKids® Educational Software Review*
  www.superkids.com
  Reviews children's software. Offers buyer's guides, arranged by topics and children's ages, comparing prices and features.

Storing Software

Children need to access software independently. In many centers and schools, software is stored directly on the computer's desktop. In addition, some software programs allow teachers to create a personalized desktop for each child with access to specific programs. This arrangement keeps children from tampering with your important files.

Some software programs allow teachers to create a personalized desktop for each child.

Even if your classroom computer is set up to allow children to access software directly, there will be instances when children will need to use a CD for particular software. This means that you need to devise a storage system. Because CDs need to be handled carefully, they should be stored in CD pockets or jewel cases. The picture labels on the cases and the CD itself will help children identify the one they want to use.

Selecting Appropriate Web Sites

The Internet, with its incredible resources, has changed the way teachers, families, and children approach education. Even children of preschool age can benefit from its richness. Its vastness, though, is both its chief benefit and its chief drawback. The sheer number of sites can make it seem unmanageable. The quality of web sites also varies widely. Many, many sites are neither appropriate nor desirable for young learners.

Many of the sites developed for teachers and parents of preschoolers maintain logs of approved or award-winning sites.

We suggest that you view the Internet as you would children's software. You need to guide children in using those sites that will be of benefit to them. Many of the sites developed for teachers and parents of preschoolers maintain logs of approved or award-winning sites. These lists are updated frequently, as new ones appear and old ones are abandoned. Most teacher-oriented web sites also include links to web resources that have been categorized by subject area. Some have searchable databases of these links. You can then go to these links and check them out yourself.

Because preschool children should not be using the Internet without guidance, you will need to preview any site that you want children to use. You can use many of the items on the checklist to evaluate software (p. 478). In addition, look for sites that have no advertisements.

One very effective way to make use of the Internet is to post children's work. The Internet provides exposure and opportunities to learn that children might never imagine. One teacher reports that when a child in her class posted a photo of a bee they were studying, they heard from an entomologist (an expert on insects) that the photo was actually of a wasp. In an e-mail to the children, he explained how they could tell the difference between bees and wasps. Those children not only see insects in a whole new light, they understand the power of the Internet as a research tool.

Probably the most effective way to publish children's work is to create your own web site. You can do this for your classroom or as part of your school or center's web site. If your program is part of a public school system or is affiliated with a university, your district or host institution most likely has its own server (a special computer that is designated for hosting web sites). Alternatively, you can do this on your own using web authoring software. It's no longer necessary to master complicated programming languages or to hire a specialist in web site design. You can be your own webmaster.

Adapting Computers for Children With Special Needs

Because computers can be used to present small bits of information in a planned sequence and offer repetition, individualized instruction, and immediate feedback, they are ideally suited to many children with special needs. Studies of children with developmental delays show that they enjoy and learn from computer experiences. Moreover, preschool children with attention-related problems seem to respond to computers in the same ways that children without disabilities do. Both groups of children can be happily engaged at computer activities for 15 minutes or more.

For children with mild developmental delays—the most common type of disability in young children—you don't have to alter your approach to the Computer Area. The benefit of the computer is its ability to respond to individual children's timetables. Children with developmental delays can get the repetition and reinforcement they need simply by using the program as any other user would. You might consider pairing a child with developmental delays with a child who is not disabled. The more skilled child will be able to encourage and boost the confidence of the other child. Both children can be enriched by their time at the computer.

> The benefit of the computer is its ability to respond to individual children's timetables.

For children who have vision-related or physical disabilities, there are innovative adaptive devices that can be added to a computer station to make computers accessible. The chart below lists some adaptive devices, the disability they address, and information on what they do.

Computer Assistive Devices

Device	Problem Addressed	What Device Does
Large-size monitor	Vision impairment	Enlarges everything on the screen
Software magnification lenses	Vision impairment	Enlarges screen images
Speech synthesizer	Blindness/severe vision impairment	When combined with speakers, can be used to read text on a screen
Voice-recognition system	Physical disabilities (manual dexterity problems)	Accepts voice commands as input
Headpointer and mouth stick	Physical disabilities (manual dexterity problems)	Provides an alternative for children with good head control
Keyguards	Physical disabilities (manual dexterity problems)	Prevents user from accidentally pushing wrong keys
Expanded keyboard	Physical disabilities (manual dexterity problems)	Provides more space for keys and can be positioned in an accessible location
Head-controlled mouse	Physical disabilities (manual dexterity problems)	Mouse controlled by movements of the head

This list is a sample of the many exciting developments in this field. If you wish to make use of adaptive devices in your classroom or are interested in learning more about including children with disabilities there are many information resources and organizations you can investigate. For more information, consult your local library, network with other early childhood professionals, or search on the Internet.

What Children Learn From Using Computers

The Computer Area offers many opportunities to integrate learning across content areas.

Literacy

Expand children's **vocabulary and language development** by introducing them to software that labels vocabulary with pictures, written words, and the spoken word. A program such as the *Let's Explore . . .* series (Humongous Entertainment) verbally identifies an object when the child clicks on it.

Help children develop **phonological awareness** with interactive software that plays with language. *Bailey's Book House* (Riverdeep) lets children create silly rhymes and pay attention to the sounds of language.

Increase children's **understanding of books** by exposing them to electronic books. After hearing Janell Cannon's *Stellaluna* in the Library Area, children can explore the electronic version (*Living Books® Library*, Riverdeep). They can have the story read to them or use the "Let me play" feature and go directly to their favorite pages.

Enhance children's **knowledge of print** by recording their responses on a word processing/reading program. Some programs give children hints on reading words and use pictures to show how words combine to form sentences.

Offer children practice in learning about **letters and words** with a program that matches pictures to their beginning letters.

Develop children's **enjoyment of literacy** by letting them explore electronic storybooks.

Mathematics

Teach children **number concepts** by using a program like *Millie's Math House* (Riverdeep). They can create monsters by adding the right number of body parts.

Let children discover **patterns and relationships** through a program such as *Stuart Little: His Adventures in Numberland* (SuperMentor.com).

Promote children's understanding of **measurement** using programs such as *Richard Scarry's Best Math Program Ever* (Simon & Schuster Interactive). Here, children use measurement to determine who won a sledding race.

Science

Teach children **physical science** by letting them explore how things work. *Sammy's Science House* (Riverdeep) offers a construction Workshop.

Introduce children to **life science** on the computer. Children can use Internet web sites to learn about plants and animals. Some zoos and aquariums have live web cams that allow children to view animals in real time.

Programs that have children report on the day's weather can help children learn about **earth and the environment** by checking weather web sites.

Social Studies

Children can learn about **people and how they live** by using e-mail to communicate with other classes around the world. Children can dictate questions to you to ask their e-mail pals.

Help children to understand the concept of history—**people and the past**—by asking them to bring in their baby pictures. These can be scanned and shown in a PowerPoint slide show alongside current photos of the children.

The Arts

Expose children to the basics of **music** (melody and rhythm) by letting them experiment with a smart toy such as *Music Blocks* (Neurosmith).

Use the computer as a medium for children to experiment with color, shape, and design. Children can use the tools available in a graphics program such as *Kid Pix Deluxe 3* (The Learning Company) to create **visual arts**.

Technology

Make children **aware of technology** by including computers in your everyday classroom life, so children start regarding them as natural tools.

Children learn the **basic operations and concepts** of technology when you show them how to use computers. Children's literature such as *Patrick's Dinosaurs on the Internet* (Carol Carrick) give children insight into the working of this technology.

Encourage children to try out and use **technology tools** such as computers, printers, CD-ROMs, scanners, and digital cameras.

The Teacher's Role

They way you support children's use of computers will influence whether their experiences are successful or frustrating and whether computers are used appropriately or inappropriately. Your role is to help children learn to use computers as tools for problem solving, research, creativity, and fun.

In general, the best way to introduce children to computers is in small groups. Sit with the children at one monitor and talk about how the computer operates. As you discuss the parts of the computer and how they work, encourage children to explore the computer under your guidance. You can comment on their actions. Once they've mastered the basics, you can work together on an exploratory program such as *Fisher-Price Dream Doll House* (Knowledge Adventure), which is specially designed to familiarize children with using computers and software. As children work on the program, you can comment on

> *Once children have mastered the basics, you can work together on exploratory programs.*

- the way to hold a disk or CD-ROM at the edges and insert it into the disk drive

- the location of keys needed to operate the program

- how a mouse moves items on the screen or points to objects

- what happens when children click on the icons, props, and people

- how to advance through the program, going from room to room

- sounds that tell you that the printer is working

- how to exit the program

Observing and Responding to Individual Children

To support children's learning in the Computer Area, take time to observe each child. You are likely to see a wide range of skills based on whether a child has used computers before.

How Children Use Computers
As with all learning, children use computers in a developmental progression. The stages presented here are based on those described by Haugland and Wright (1997).

At the **investigation** stage, children explore the computer with an adult, on their own, or with peers. They explore the sights, sounds, and feel of the computer. They see what happens to the screen when the power switch is turned on. They listen to the motor and see how the light flickers. They feel what it's like to press a key and to click a mouse. They learn how to put a CD in the disk drive. They also discover what software is, and realize that what they do with computer hardware affects what happens on the screen.

At the next stage—**involvement**—children become creative and purposeful in their interactions. They look for answers to questions such as these: What happens when I click on the icon of a house? What happens when I click the mouse? What happens if the Enter/Return key is hit? By seeing that every action has an effect, children learn how to operate a program.

Self-confidence follows involvement. Children start using the computer to accomplish a task. They know what computers can do for them and they use them accordingly. They may search out a drawing program to illustrate a story or scan in and post a photo of a block building they've created.

The last stage—**creativity and original thinking**—is the long-range goal of children's use of computers. In preschool, children and teachers work together to find answers to questions that come up, scan pictures, or use programs that promote literacy. Children begin to view computers as exciting tools for learning, not just tools for playing games.

Children use computers in a developmental progression.

Responding to Each Child

As you observe children's use of computers, think about how you might enrich their experiences. Notice whether the child

- uses the computer independently or relies on adult assistance

- stays engaged with a program

- shows initiative in using the computer or relies on others for ideas

- makes printouts of his work, if applicable

Based on your observations, you can plan to address each child's needs. If you also keep in mind the *Creative Curriculum* objectives, you can watch what a child does and consider which objectives are most relevant to what you have observed. As you think about your observations you can plan interactions and experiences that will help a child proceed to the next step on the *Developmental Continuum*. The chart that follows gives examples of how you might do this.

Observation	Reflection	Response
While working on the computer, Crystal calls over Leo and says, "Look, I made a picture of the truck you brought to school today. I'm going to drive it off the screen now."	Crystal is using the computer to make a representation of a real object and names it. *(Objective 21, Uses tools for writing and drawing; and 37, Makes and interprets representations)* How else can I encourage Crystal to make increasingly elaborate representations using the computer?	Show Crystal how to use a variety of drawing tools in paint programs so that she can continue experimenting with computer art. Encourage her to write and illustrate stories on the computer that she can then act out.
Alexa sits down in an empty chair next to Kate, who is in the middle of using a program. Alexa studies the screen for a few seconds, and then asks, "Is it OK if I do the mouse?" "Sure," says Kate, turning over the mouse.	Alexa and Kate are interacting very well, successfully entering a group and sharing in response to a request. *(Objective 10, Plays well with other children; and 12, Shares and respects the rights of others)* How can I encourage these social skills?	Comment on how well the children are working together, "You shared the mouse so you both can stay in the Computer Area this morning." Pair these children together on other team tasks.
Setsuko puts a CD of animals in the computer and clicks on the picture of a seal, causing the program to say, "Seal." "*Seal* starts with the same letter as *Setsuko*," she announces, "with an S."	Setsuko notices words that begin the same way and recognizes letters by name. *(Objective 38, Hears and discriminates the sounds of language; and 46, Demonstrates knowledge of the alphabet)* How should I reinforce her interest in letters?	Engage her in conversation: "Are there any other animals that start with the same letter as seal and Setsuko?" Suggest that Setsuko print out the picture of the seal and put it in the alphabet book she's been making with cutouts from magazines and catalogues.
Susie takes a milkweed leaf that had been collected on a nature walk from the Discovery Area and places it under the computer microscope. With great excitement she exclaims, "Those white things are bugs!"	Susie takes an interest in nature and wants to learn more. *(Objective 22, Observes objects and events with curiosity)* She knows how to use the computer microscope to investigate answers to questions she has. *(Objective 26, Applies knowledge or experience to a new context)* How can I involve other children and build on Susie's discovery?	Engage Susie in conversation, letting her know that you value her observations: "What a great discovery, Susie!" "How did you find out that those dots are really bugs?" "What was it you saw through the microscope?" Invite others in the class to come to the microscope and take a look. Place a basket of other collected items near the microscope to encourage children to observe them and notice similarities and differences.

Interacting With Children in the Computer Area

Your interactions with children as they use computers provide opportunities for learning. You set the stage for whether children truly learn to use the computer as a tool for problem solving and investigations or as something they just dabble with. Thoughtful interactions with children stretch their minds and extend learning.

Talking With Children About Computers

One of the most important ways of encouraging children's computer use is to talk with them about their experiences. This helps them reflect on what they are doing and why. As a first step, you can describe what you see a child doing. For example, you could discuss the child's

> **interactions with the computer:** *When you pressed the* Enter *key, the screen changed,* or *Clicking the mouse made the dollhouse light up.*

> **use of the computer:** *You were able to put the CD in the right way the first time you tried.*

> **reactions to feedback:** *I see you figured out how to make the stars jump out of the hat.*

> **social interactions:** *What a good idea you had, to work together to create a thank-you card.*

> **accomplishments:** *That's an interesting grouping you made of the animals at the farm. Let's print a copy so we can look at it more clearly.*

Comment on what children do and ask questions.

Your descriptions of what they are doing let children know you are interested in their work. By encouraging children to use the computer in their own ways, you allow them to be in control of their learning.

After children hear you describe what they've done, they develop confidence in their ability to use computers. Now encourage children to put their actions into words by asking questions such as the following:

> *How did you and Carlos decide what program you would work on?*

> *How did you figure out what to do?*

> *What part of the program was the most fun to do?*

> *What printouts did you make?*

These questions help children see that you think their computer experiences are valuable. As you further question children, focus on open-ended questions that promote process skills.

> **Observation:** *What do you think might happen when you put in a CD-ROM?*
>
> **Cause and effect:** *What happens to the screen when you press the* Enter *key?*
>
> **Comparison:** *Which programs let you change colors?*
>
> **Problem solving:** *How do we get back from the castle to the playroom?*
>
> **Application:** *In the last program we clicked on the picture of the house if we wanted to return to the beginning of the program. What should we click on here to get back to the main menu?*
>
> **Prediction:** *What do you guess will happen if we touch this* Escape *key?*

Through your observations and conversations with children, you can promote each child's learning in the Computer Area.

Frequently Asked Questions About Computers

Do computers really belong in preschools?

Some early childhood educators (see the report *Fool's Gold: A Critical Look at Children and Computers*, 2000, for example) feel that computers are not developmentally appropriate for young children. They would prefer that children build with blocks, explore manipulatives, and engage in art activities and dramatic play. They fear that children working alone at computers are isolated and will lack social skills. They are concerned about health problems and stunted imagination, creativity, and intellectual growth.

These are valid concerns. We believe, however, that proper computer use does not lead to these consequences. Research has demonstrated that computers can provide effective learning opportunities for children when used appropriately. Susan Haugland (2000) notes that 3- and 4-year-old children who use computers as part of their learning show strong gains in intelligence, non-verbal skills, structural knowledge, long-term memory, manual dexterity, verbal skills, problem solving, abstract thinking, and conceptual skills when compared to peers who have not used computers.

The Computer Area can be a very social place. Studies have shown that children working on a computer have nine times the number of conversations as children doing a puzzle together. Moreover, 95 percent of these conversations are task-related (Clements and Swaminathan, 1995).

We wholeheartedly agree with those educators who say that the question to ask isn't, "Should I be using computers in my preschool classroom?" but rather, "How can I make best use of computers in my preschool classroom to help children achieve higher levels?" (Fouts, 2000).

I'm eager to set up a Computer Area. However, I'm very uneasy about my own abilities. What can I do to make sure I'm doing a good job in this area?

Computers are new to many teachers. Even if you have a home computer, you may not know how best to use this technology to help children learn. As one expert has noted, "A school can have the newest hardware, the best software ever designed, and Internet access on every computer. But differences in student learning won't emerge unless . . . teachers know how to use the technology effectively with children" (Totter, 1999).

The first thing to do is seek training. We hope that your school or center will support you. Look for training through your county, state, college, an open university continuing education system, or even online.

Many teachers form study groups or mentoring programs. Experienced users help novices with guidance, validation, and "hand holding." You can also join user groups and listservs for support and advice. The Technology Caucus of the National Association for the Education of Young Children (NAEYC) listserv is geared toward teachers of young children. Join the listserv at http://www.techandyoungchildren.org/listserv.html.

How much time should children spend at the computer?

Extended time at computers (several hours a day) can lead to repetitive stress injuries, visual strain, and childhood obesity due to a sedentary lifestyle. However, with all that goes on in your classroom every day, including plenty of time for outdoor play and music and movement activities, it is unlikely that preschool children will be at computers long enough to experience these health problems.

Treat the Computer Area as you would every other interest area. Children need time to explore, to reflect on their actions, and to feel challenged and competent enough to move on to the next level. This takes time and interest. Children who spend a lot of time in this area do so because they are having successful experiences and finding comfort in the familiarity of what they know well. Some children shine at the computer and derive satisfaction from being able to help their peers learn to use the computer. This is a role that enhances a child's self-esteem and one that you should nourish.

However, if you feel that a child is in the Computer Area to the exclusion of other activities, you may want to limit time in this area. Use your judgment. If a child is clicking aimlessly, intervene.

Parents tell me that their children know more about computers than they do. How can I involve families so they gain skills too?

Many programs sponsor family computer literacy events, to which families are invited to join their children in learning about technology. There is probably no better learning environment for children than to sit side-by-side at the computer with their parents and explore together how computers, software, and the Internet work. Using preschool children as instructors can be a good way to teach adults who have computer anxiety.

A Letter to Families About Computers

Dear Families,

In our program we are delighted to have computers as learning tools for the children. Here are some of the things children learn when they use computers:

- to be comfortable with technology
- beginning reading and writing skills
- math skills and concepts such as counting and numerical relationships
- how to express themselves creatively
- how to solve problems and begin to do research

We encourage children to work at the computer in pairs or small groups. This helps them learn from each other and develops their social skills at the same time. While the children are working at the computer, we ask them questions to help them think about what they're doing:

"What made you decide to choose this program to work on?"

"How can we use the computer to send a copy of your painting to your grandparents?"

"What would you like to do with the printouts you made today?"

By working with children in these ways, we not only encourage their growth and development but also help prepare them for a future in which they will need to know how to work with computers.

What You Can Do at Home

You may or may not have a computer in your home. It is certainly not necessary that you do for your child to benefit from our program's Computer Area. If you do have a home computer and would like to know some things that you can do with your child, please ask. We will be glad to provide you with assistance, including how to judge which programs and Internet sites are appropriate for use with young children. We have some good information on this topic that we'd like to share with you.

You may be interested in visiting our program to observe how children use computers. If you'd like to volunteer to work with children in the Computer Area, we'd be delighted to have your help. You may even enjoy learning more about computers yourself!

inside this chapter

493 How Outdoor Play Promotes Development
    494 Connecting Outdoor Play With Curriculum Objectives

496 Creating and Using the Outdoor Environment
    496 Basic Outdoor Spaces and Equipment
    505 Playground Structures
    509 Special Considerations

511 What Children Learn Outdoors

514 The Teacher's Role
    514 Observing and Responding to Individual Children
    517 Interacting With Children Outdoors
    521 Frequently Asked Questions About Outdoor Play

522 A Letter to Families About Outdoor Play

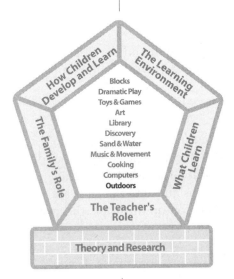

16 Outdoors

How Outdoor Play Promotes Development

Outdoor play is essential for children's health and well-being. The sense of peace and pleasure children experience when they take in fresh air, feel the warmth of the sun on their backs, and watch a butterfly land gently on a flower is immeasurable. What is very evident is how much children enjoy running, jumping, climbing, and playing outdoors. The time children spend outdoors every day is just as important to their learning as the time they spend in the classroom. For teachers, the outdoors offers many ways to enrich the curriculum and support children's development and learning.

Social/emotional development. Children experience a sense of accomplishment and growing competence when they spend time outdoors every day engaged in purposeful activities. You can see the sense of pride a child feels when she can keep a swing going on her own, climb to new heights, throw and catch a ball, and complete an obstacle course. Social skills grow as children share equipment such as tricycles and shovels, work together to build a tunnel in the sandbox, and follow safety rules.

Physical development. Many reports suggest that the number of children who are overweight is increasing steadily. One factor contributing to the problem is that children do not get the large muscle activity essential for their healthy development. Part of the problem is that in many places it is not safe for children to play outdoors and children spend too much time watching TV. Thus, it's even more important to make the most of outdoor time while children are at school. Children develop their gross motor skills as they run, leap, hop, jump, swing, slide, and climb. These activities allow children to take risks and try out new skills. Children also use their fine motor skills outdoors to weed a garden, collect bugs, and pour sand through a funnel.

Cognitive development. The outdoors is a natural laboratory for scientific explorations as children observe and explore nature firsthand. They find and study bugs and butterflies, plant seeds and watch vegetables grow, observe leaves change color, taste snow, touch the bark of a tree, hear crickets, and smell the air after a rain shower. They count the seeds they plant and the number of petals on a flower; measure how tall a sunflower grows and calculate how long it takes for a flower to appear; note patterns on the bodies of caterpillars and butterflies; and solve problems, for instance, how to make water or sand run through a plastic rain gutter.

Language development. Children expand their vocabularies when they learn the names of insects and plants and use words to describe the characteristics of each—*fuzzy, fast, shiny, hard, colorful, striped, slimy*. They learn to read traffic signs and use field guides to identify the leaves, birds, or spiders they find.

Connecting Outdoor Play With Curriculum Objectives

Almost every *Creative Curriculum* objective can be addressed during outdoor time. Your observations of children will enable you to identify where each child is on the *Developmental Continuum* so you can determine the child's progress and next steps. The following chart lists just a sample of objectives and shows what a child might do that indicates progress in meeting each one.

Selected Curriculum Objectives	What a Child Might Do in Outdoor Play
Social/Emotional Development	
1. Shows ability to adjust to new situations	On a field trip taking a walk through the woods, tells teacher, "I never was in this place before. It's cool!"
3. Recognizes own feelings and manages them appropriately	Says to teacher, "I don't like being up so high. Can you help me get down?"
4. Stands up for rights	When another child grabs the watering can he was holding, says, "I was using it!"
9. Follows classroom rules	Says, "You're standing too close to the swings. Get back of the line or you could get hit."
10. Plays well with other children	Invites a peer to work with her on connecting the plastic pipes and elbows.
Physical Development	
14. Demonstrates basic locomotor skills (running, jumping, hopping, galloping)	Hops across the playground and then gallops back in a relay race organized by the teacher.
15. Shows balance while moving	After creating a bridge with boards and boxes, walks across the board with arms extended.
17. Pedals and steers a tricycle (or other wheeled vehicle)	Gets on tricycle and steers it around an obstacle course the teachers set up.
18. Demonstrates throwing, kicking, and catching skills	Participates in a game of kickball.
19. Controls small muscles in hands	Washes doll clothes and hangs them on a clothesline using clothespins.
20. Coordinates eye-hand movement	Scoops up dry sand and pours it into a bottle.

Selected Curriculum Objectives	What a Child Might Do in Outdoor Play
Cognitive Development	
22. Observes objects and events with curiosity	Discovering an anthill, runs to get magnifying glass and says to a peer, "Hey, come see what I found!"
23. Approaches problems flexibly	When sand castle keeps falling, adds water to make the sand stick together.
25. Explores cause and effect	Watches bubbles floating in the wind and says, "They pop when they hit something dry, but not if it's wet."
26. Applies knowledge or experience to a new context	Announces, "Yesterday, the worms ate lettuce. I bet they'll like this spinach too."
30. Recognizes patterns and can repeat them	Sees butterflies and takes out the field guide to compare the different patterns on their wings.
32. Shows an awareness of position in space	Tells a friend, "You go on top of the tunnel and I'll go through it. We'll meet at the other end."
34. Uses numbers and counting	Announces, "I'm going to see how many times I can hop without stopping. 1, 2, 3, 5, 6. I did it six times."
Language Development	
38. Hears and discriminates the sounds of language	Says, "Listen to the bees. They're going z-z-z-z-z-z."
39. Expresses self using words and expanded sentences	Tells teacher, "I'm sweaty because I ran so fast."
42. Asks questions	Asks, "What happened to the snowman we made yesterday?"
43. Actively participates in conversations	Discusses with another child how they will use the plastic pipes and elbows to build a water tunnel.
47. Uses emerging reading skills to make meaning from print	Takes stop sign from shed and says, "This says 'stop'. You have to stop when you see this sign."

Creating and Using the Outdoor Environment

Probably no other aspect of an early childhood environment varies as much from one program to another as the layout and appearance of the Outdoor Area. Some programs have natural environments with lots of grass, trees, plants, and playground equipment designed specifically for preschool-age children. Others have only asphalt with very little equipment. No matter what kind of outdoor environment you have, you can create a setting where children can enjoy the outdoors.

In this section we describe the basic outdoor spaces and equipment and ways you can take full advantage of what you have. We offer suggestions to enhance your outdoor space with moveable materials and to use places in your neighborhood and community. We also address safety considerations.

Basic Outdoor Spaces and Equipment

The best way to start planning your outdoor space is to inventory the existing space and equipment. Ideally, there should be enough space to accommodate all the children who will be using it at the same time (e.g., 80 to 100 square feet per child). You want a safe place, protected from street traffic and free from debris, electric wires, and hazardous equipment. Assess whether the space you have includes the following:

Assessing Your Outdoor Space

Does your space have

- an unobstructed view of the children at all times

- easy access to and from the indoor space used by the program and to bathrooms

- a drinking fountain and water spigot for attaching a hose

- age-appropriate equipment for climbing, swinging, and building

- a storage shed

- soft materials such as sawdust, sand, or bark under swings, slides, and climbers

- sunny as well as shady areas

- a paved or hard-surfaced area for riding, skating, chalk drawings, and games

- a covered area for use in wet weather

- places to be alone or with one or two friends (boxes, tents, an old wooden rowboat, tractor tires, a porch swing that seats two or three, mats or blankets for reading, doll play, or picnics)

- open, grassy spaces for walking, tumbling, running, kicking, throwing, and catching balls

- an area for digging

An inviting outdoor environment offers children a variety of clear choices for very different kinds of experiences and challenges.

Once you have assessed what you have, consider what you need to add. An inviting outdoor environment offers children a variety of clear choices for very different kinds of experiences and challenges. We recommend creating spaces for:

- sand and water play
- wheeled toys
- indoor materials that can be brought outdoors
- playing games, building, and pretend play
- planting a garden
- caring for living things

The key to making these different areas work is to define each space, create easy-to-follow traffic patterns, and equip them well. With clearly designated areas and interesting materials, you can minimize injuries and maximize learning and fun.

 ### Sand and Water Play

Sand and water are ideal materials to use outdoors where mess is not a problem. A good sand area is large enough for several children to play in without feeling crowded. If you don't have a sandbox, you can bring the sand table outdoors or use tubs. Locate the sand area close to a water supply, such as outdoor faucets or water fountains, if possible, so children can experiment with both wet and dry sand and explore the properties of water. Use pails, pitchers, or spray bottles to transport water and offer water play in tubs or wading pools if you don't have an outdoor water supply.

Many items can enhance digging, pouring, constructing, and dramatic play with sand and water.

Here are some suggestions for items to add to enhance digging, pouring, constructing, and dramatic play with sand and water:

- buckets, mixing bowls, and pails with handles
- plastic rain gutters
- shovels, spoons, and scoops of all sizes
- funnels and sifters
- pots, pans, and molds
- cups and saucers
- measuring spoons and cups
- muffin tins
- plastic pitchers and jugs
- sand or water pumps and wheels
- small wheelbarrows
- old trucks, cars, fire engines, and trains
- plastic people and animals
- popsicle sticks
- small cardboard boxes and plastic blocks
- natural objects such as shells, sticks, stones, or leaves

If you have a sand area, be aware of sanitation concerns. Use only sanitized play sand. Keep in mind that cats and other animals will use the sandbox as a litter box if the area is unprotected. This health problem can be prevented by using a hinged top or plastic tarp to cover the sandbox when it's not in use.

A Track for Wheeled Toys

Outdoors is the perfect place for using tricycles, big wheels, scooters, and wagons. These wheeled toys build large muscle strength while promoting balance and coordination.

Wheeled toys build large muscle strength while promoting balance and coordination.

The area for using wheeled toys needs a hard surface. Pulling and pushing wheeled toys and skills such as peddling, maintaining balance, starting, and stopping are all mastered more easily on a hard surface. Be sure to provide helmets for the children.

You can enhance children's use of this area by adding signs, chalk, road markers, directional arrows, and big orange cones to control traffic. Prop boxes or play crates can extend play activities, and they can transform a wheeled toy into an ambulance, fire truck, or a mail truck. Similarly, you can introduce materials that will inspire children to create a gas station or car wash.

Creating a Garden Outdoors

If you have space, you can create a garden to grow flowers or vegetables for children to enjoy. Try to locate the garden area away from more active outdoor areas and out of the way of play traffic. If space is limited, and you only have asphalt outdoors, plant your garden in containers—a yard cart with two wheels, wagon, tractor tire, or large pots. The advantage of using a two-wheeled cart or wagon is that you can move it around to control the amount of sun the garden gets or to clear a space for a game.

Planting, caring for, and harvesting a garden is an ongoing project that involves children in planning and laying out a space, selecting seeds and plants, arranging them in the soil, and watering and tending them as they grow. Seeds will grow and thrive if the soil is fertile and they get plenty of sun and water. Tending a garden is enjoyable as well as educational and also teaches patience and perseverance.

Suggested materials for the garden area include:

- several shovels, rakes and hoes with short handles
- child-size garden gloves
- a wheelbarrow
- seeds or plants
- bags of dirt
- watering cans and a hose
- string to mark off the rows and tongue depressors for signs

You want to avoid planting a garden with children and having few plants grow. A little care can prevent this disappointment. First, pick your plants carefully. If you are in a location with cool temperatures, plant petunias, pansies, flowering cabbage, collards, broccoli, peas, onion, and potatoes. Plants that do well in warm climates include zinnias, okra, peanuts, tomatoes, and sunflowers. (If a child has an allergy to peanuts, avoid them.) If your growing area is mostly shady, add lots of color with impatiens. Gardens also can attract insects and birds. Do some research before planting to find out which plants attract butterflies and hummingbirds, for example (Clemens, 1996).

Even if you know little about plants yourself, you can be successful in offering a gardening experience to children. Seek guidance from the staff at a local nursery or the Agricultural Extension office near you. You can also check out web sites that provide information and links to other sites.

Tending a garden is enjoyable as well as educational and also teaches patience and perseverance.

Pick your plants carefully.

Caring for Living Things

Outdoors can be the perfect place to observe and care for living things. Some pets can live outdoors, and even the most urban environments contain insects, birds, and squirrels.

Keeping pets gives children the opportunity to care for animals and to be responsible for them. They also can observe growth, change, and the habits of animals. They can learn about birth, different lifestyles, and sometimes death. Even very young children can learn to care for pets. They may need your guidance, however, in learning how to handle, hold, and pet animals without injuring them.

Rabbits, hamsters, gerbils, and guinea pigs are common pets in early childhood programs. Be cautious about the more exotic pets such as lizards and snakes which can carry salmonella, and birds which are a problem for children with asthma. Be sure to check licensing requirements before bringing pets into your room. Administrators, boards, and leasing agents also should be consulted ahead of time to ensure that there are no problems.

Cages for pets should be large enough for them to move around without getting hurt, and should be cleaned frequently. The location of the cage is important, because animals must be protected from weather and other animals if they are left out all night. In some cases, taking pets inside at night may be best. Keep in mind that pets can get sick if given food that isn't in their diets. Labeled cans for pet food help children learn what their pets can eat.

Keeping pets gives children the opportunity to care for animals and to be responsible for them.

While worms are not exactly considered "pets," children can learn to care for and observe them outdoors if you create a worm farm. (See pp. 194–197, where we describe a study of worms.) A simple way to make a worm farm is to put a wire fence around a pile of compost where worms can live and be observed easily. If you have only hard surfaces outdoors, a large old aquarium will do nicely as a home for worms. In either case, children can feed the worms with their leftover fruits and vegetables and see firsthand how worms transform them into fertile soil.

In many settings, nature provides just about everything you need outdoors. You can build on what is there and take steps to woo living things to your playground. For example, here's what you might do to attract birds to your Outdoor Area:

- Hang bird feeders outside, some near the classroom window if possible so children can observe them closely indoors and outside. Be sure to keep them stocked with birdseed.

- Put up birdhouses.

- Create a birdbath by turning a large flowerpot upside down and putting a large saucer on top for the water.

- Plant bushes that will attract birds (ones with berries).

- Put out materials birds can use to build nests: twigs, straw, string, ribbons.

Once birds start coming to the play area, children can observe and learn about them. They will see the materials they put out become part of a bird's nest. If you provide pictures and field guides, children can identify the birds that visit and learn about them. Later, in the classroom, they can learn more about the birds on the Internet.

Children also can use the tools provided for investigations in the Discovery Area outdoors to explore nature: magnifying glasses, binoculars, yardsticks, and clipboards with paper and writing tools to document discoveries. Self-locking plastic bags are great for holding collections.

In many settings, nature provides just about everything you need outdoors.

Open Spaces for Games, Building, and Pretend Play

Reserve some space outdoors where children can just run and have fun. Ideally, the area you choose should be grassy with large shade trees. However, if all you have is asphalt and tarps for shade, you can still offer a range of exciting and challenging experiences for children.

Balls of all sizes should always be available outdoors. Sometimes you might organize group games such as kick ball, jump rope, "Red Light/Green Light," "Hopscotch." Another day bring out bubble solution so children can blow bubbles outdoors and watch them float in the wind. If you give several children a parachute and have them hold it in different places, they can make it float up and down with large movements of their arms. Children can fly kites on a windy day, paint on easels, color with chalk, or jump through hula hoops. Bring out musical instruments and hold a parade. Take scarves and streamers and a tape recorder outdoors where children can move freely. The ways you can use this space are unlimited.

You can turn an open area into a construction site or a challenging obstacle course (Griffin and Rinn, 1998). You can gather inexpensive materials to offer children adventure and a chance to develop gross motor skills and self-confidence in open spaces.

- Plastic trash cans with the bottoms cut out are a cheap way to create tunnels. You can use duct tape to secure several cans together and extend the tunnel.

- Planks of wood, plastic milk cartons, or wooden boxes offer children a chance to build their own constructions and obstacle courses. Provide carpet samples or scraps to add softness and more texture.

- Cable spools, 4-1/2 feet in diameter, are often available from television or telephone companies. They can be used with planks and tires for construction projects, or simply as tables for art projects or places to sort collections.

- A plastic swimming pool can be filled with assorted balls or beanbags and—on a hot day—water.

- Large cardboard boxes from appliance stores can be used to create a maze for children. A single box can be transformed into a school bus or a rocket ship for dramatic play.

- Plastic pipes and elbows from a plumbing supply store can be used for construction projects and scientific experiments involving water and sand.

Turn an open area into a construction site or a challenging obstacle course.

Once you begin thinking about the creative use of materials, you may surprise yourself with the number of throw-away objects that can transform your Outdoor Area and delight children.

Indoor Materials That Can Be Brought Outdoors

Many indoor activities can be brought outside, where they create different kinds of experiences. Three examples are music and movement, art, and library materials.

Music and movement activities outdoors can enjoy more space and higher sound levels than possible in most classrooms. Bring a boom box outside to provide music and encourage dancing on the grass or hardtop surfaces. Bring out musical instruments and have a marching band parade around the Outdoor Area. Streamers, big pieces of fabric, parachutes, or scarves add to the fun.

Art activities that are fun, messy, large, and imaginative can take place outdoors. The large space, different textures and objects, and ease of cleaning up all contribute to the success of these activities. Painting is a popular outdoor art activity. For easel painting, you might tape paper on a storage shed or use clothespins to attach paper to a fence. (See the Art chapter for a description of hanging easels designed to go on fences.) Tables and the ground are also adequate and interesting surfaces for working on paper. Outside painting should involve a variety of types and sizes of brushes and paper. On a warm day, children might like to try foot and toe painting on butcher paper. (Mix the paint with liquid soap to make it easier to remove.) Finger painting can be more expansive outside where children don't have to be as careful about making a mess. On another day, bring drawing paper, pencils, markers, and crayons outdoors for a quiet activity, or large colored chalk for drawing on the sidewalk or making outlines around shadows.

Dramatic play props can be brought outdoors to encourage children's pretend play. A simple firefighter hat can inspire a child to zoom across the area on his tricycle, arriving just in time to put out a fire. Children who want to have a picnic can bring dishes, pots and pans, and a towel outdoors. A blanket hung over a clothesline or play structure can become a fort or spaceship.

Books can be enjoyed outdoors, and they are especially appealing in the shade on a hot day. You can select books that relate to children's outside play and learning. When gardening is a current activity, you might read a story about children planting a garden. If children collected shells on a recent beach walk, you can read a story about a child's trip to the ocean.

Many indoor activities can be brought outside where they create different kinds of experiences.

Tools for investigations such as magnifying glasses, measuring instruments, prisms, water catchers, and binoculars help children explore outdoors. Bring out field guides and nature magazines so children can identify their discoveries. Keep a supply of writing materials and paper so children can make signs and record information and observations.

Play Crates

Just as you provide prop boxes to enhance dramatic play, you can collect and store outdoor materials in "play crates" (Odoy & Foster, 1997). These boxes hold and transport items that connect activities and materials to a theme. Plastic milk crates, wooden boxes with handles, or plastic laundry baskets all can serve as play crates. Here are some ideas for play crates you can create with materials that are easily gathered:

Camping crate—tent, blanket, firewood, metal dishes, blankets

Laundry crate—clothesline, clothespins, liquid soap, basins

Building crate—PVC pipes and elbows in all sizes including some clear tubing so children can observe water and sand as they flow through

Painting crate—buckets, large paintbrushes, painter's hats

Digging crate—shovels, funnels, pails, scoops, molds, rakes

Gardening crate—watering cans, small rakes and hoes, child-size gardening gloves, tongue depressors to make signs, seeds

Woodworking crate—wood scraps, hammers, nails, hand drill, sandpaper, glue, wooden spools and dowels. Children can hammer nails into a tree stump outdoors, or you could bring out the workbench occasionally.

Moveable equipment and materials that augment your outdoor space must be stored conveniently. If you don't have to worry about vandalism or theft, a covered area for equipment such as tricycles and wagons and for materials may be sufficient. Otherwise, you need a locked shed or storage place to keep materials and equipment when not in use. Other materials can be stored indoors and brought outside in wagons, baskets, or large laundry bags.

Playground Structures

Most children love playing on large playground structures. They especially enjoy opportunities to climb, slide, swing, jump, and hang. Playground equipment that is enjoyable and safe includes:

- balance beams and a log structure
- slides
- ramps
- stairways and stepladders
- platforms

- suspension bridges
- tire climbers and tire swings
- swings
- tunnels
- spring rockers

Playground equipment should be challenging enough to invite use but not so challenging that it becomes dangerous. Safety considerations are paramount when it comes to playground structures.

Preventing Injuries on Playground Equipment

The playground is where most injuries occur.

Young children are experimenters by nature; they're eager to explore the many ways in which playground equipment can provide fun and excitement. Although they often refer to playground equipment as "the most fun," the Outdoor Area is also where most injuries occur. Therefore, you need to consider developmental factors besides physical skill in providing for children's safety while using outdoor equipment. Some of these developmental factors include the following:

- **A tendency to focus on only one aspect of a situation.** Intent on climbing to the top of a playground structure, a child may not see the danger he might be creating for another child by pushing him out of the way.

- **Difficulty judging distances.** Young children may estimate incorrectly the height of a piece of equipment and injure themselves jumping.

- **Lack of attention to what is going on around them.** Preschool children may not notice a nearby moving swing or another child sliding their way.

- **Loose clothing.** Children may be unaware that loose jackets, shirts, pants, strings on hoods, or scarves can get caught on equipment.

These factors can lead preschool children into dangerous situations. Careful adult supervision—including reminders of major hazards and rules for safe play—is essential to prevent injuries. In addition, most states have licensing laws and regulations that define minimum requirements for an outdoor play space, including the number of square feet of area needed, access to the play area, cushioning materials, fencing, basic safety regulations, and specifications for playground equipment.

Protective Surfacing

The best impact-absorbing materials are wood mulch, sand, and pea gravel.

Since most equipment-related injuries involve falls to the surface below play equipment, protective surfacing material is essential. Asphalt and grass or soil do not provide adequate protection against falls. Impact-absorbing surfaces can minimize both the frequency and severity of injuries. The best materials are wood mulch, sand, and pea gravel. These materials should be installed at a depth of at least 6" and raked and leveled regularly.

Keeping Slides and Swings Safe

Slides and swings are a common cause of playground-related injuries among children under age 6.

Slides are safer if they meet the following criteria:

- Platforms are large enough to accommodate several children.

- Handrails are positioned to give children support while moving from a standing to a sitting position.

- Slide chutes have sides at least 4" high along their entire length.

- The bottom of the slide is parallel to the ground to reduce speed and facilitate the transition from a sliding to a standing position.

- The exit end of the slide is located in a section of the playground area that is not congested.

- Metal slides are located in a shaded area. (Metal slides can get hot; adults should always check their temperature before children use them.)

For swings, keep the following safety features in mind:

- Swing seats are made of lightweight, flexible materials such as rubber, canvas, or plastic to minimize the severity of any impact incidents.

- Swings for very young children provide equal support on all sides and are free of entrapment or strangulation hazards. (Bucket-style seats are one good option.)

- "S" hooks used to suspend swings are closed tightly so that children's clothes don't get caught in them.

- Structures that support swings are located away from other equipment and activities.

- Tire swings are separated from conventional swings.

- Avoid animal swings, rope swings, trapeze bars, and swinging exercise rings.

Inspecting and Maintaining Playground Equipment

Regular inspection and maintenance can prevent injuries. On a daily basis, ask yourself the following questions:

- Is the area free of litter, broken glass, and debris?

- Is there any damage (such as broken equipment or missing parts) caused either by wear or vandalism?

- Is there any deterioration of equipment, including rust, cracks, or splinters?

- Does all equipment have adequate protective surfacing and ground cover?

- Are there any hazards (e.g., sharp edges, protrusions, pinch points, and clothing entanglement hazards, such as open "S" hooks)?

- Are there obstacles or large rocks or roots that might cause children to trip?

- Is all hardware secure? Are connecting, covering, or fastening devices in good shape? Are moving parts, such as swing hanger mechanisms, worn out?

Use a safety checklist to be sure you cover all aspects of playground safety.

In addition to frequent general inspections, more detailed inspections are also warranted on a regular basis. Use a safety checklist to be sure you cover all aspects of playground safety.

Using Public Parks

If your Outdoor Area does not include playground structures, find out if there are public parks and playgrounds within easy and safe walking distance. Evaluate if the playground is appropriate for your children:

- Is the playground well-maintained? Is equipment in good repair? Is the ground free of litter and debris?

- Is the equipment appropriate for the children's skills?

- Are there enough adults to supervise the children adequately at all times?

- Are there tables at the playground for quiet activities such as reading or drawing?

- Is there a water fountain?

- Does the playground have clearly defined boundaries so children know where they can and cannot play?

The Creative Curriculum for Preschool

Special Considerations

Teachers must keep special considerations in mind when taking children outdoors. One of these is the weather. Another is any special needs, such as allergies or a disability, that may limit children's access to outdoor play.

 Weather Considerations

The outdoor environment is affected by the weather in many locales. While children need to be outside every possible day, they should never be exposed to danger. Dangerous conditions include lightning storms, weather-watch situations, intense heat or cold, and air-quality alerts.

Adjust your schedule to accommodate changes in weather. For example, on the first nice day of spring or after the first snowfall, extend the time outdoors. On a cold, windy day, cut back on outdoor playtime. In making decisions, keep in mind that often it is adults who find weather conditions bothersome—not children. If the weather isn't dangerous, children should have time outdoors.

When the temperature drops below freezing, take precautions if you have metal structures on your playground. Childrens' tongues can freeze to metal structures. Pulling away—a natural reflex—will cause a painful injury. Teach children not to put their tongues on the equipment. Tell them what to do if their tongue does get stuck: don't move, shout for help. Keep some warm water readily available (e.g., in a thermos) to pour on the tongue to loosen it.

In areas of the country where winters are severe, some of the activities we have suggested can't be conducted routinely. You can go out for a short time, however, to give children some fresh air and a place to use their large muscles. Even a brief time to run around outside each day can be invigorating.

In areas where the temperature gets very hot, you need to be sure children are protected from the sun and do not become dehydrated. Children should wear hats, use sunscreen, and drink plenty of water. Check metal equipment like slides when you first get outside to be sure they are not too hot. If shade is not naturally available, you can create shade areas by using large umbrellas and awnings and by scheduling your outdoor time when the sun is not directly overhead (for example, before 10 a.m. and after 3 p.m.).

Dangerous conditions include lightning storms, weather-watch situations, intense heat or cold, and air-quality alerts.

Even a brief time to run around outside each day can be invigorating.

Allergies to Insect Bites

Your program is likely to include children who are highly allergic to bites from bees, wasps, or other insects. These allergies can become life-threatening situations unless you are prepared to respond effectively. Establish and practice procedures for handling this type of emergency. Keep a kit readily available for treating the child, and be sure all adults know how to use it.

Adaptations for Children With Special Needs

Like all children, those with special needs benefit from outdoor time. Even so, the outdoors can be overwhelming and even frightening to a child who is unsure how to get around an open space safely.

The outdoors can be overwhelming to a child who is unsure of how to get around an open space safely.

Look over your outdoor space from a child's point of view. A child with a visual disability, for example, will need to be oriented to the location of different play structures. Allow the child to touch the equipment as you describe its features and guide his first attempts. Stay close by to supervise and teach other children to assist those children with visual impairments. For a child with a hearing problem, point out possible hazards, such as where to watch out for tricycles. Remind the child to look carefully in all directions before running across the yard. For children with physical disabilities, determine what is appropriate by consulting with experts and the child's family to learn about special adaptations to meet the needs of individual children. Here are some examples of outdoor adaptations:

- Use bucket seats with straps on swings.

- Build ramps over uneven surfaces or on inclines for children who use wheelchairs or who have poor balance.

- Place handholds and rails on climbing equipment and structures.

- Offer sand and water play, art, and other activities on a table so children in wheelchairs can participate with others.

- Place straps on the pedals of wheel toys.

To learn more about how to keep children safe, we recommend reading:

- *Caring for Our Children: National Health and Safety Performance Standards: Guidelines for Out-Of-Home Child Care Programs* (2nd ed.) 2002. (AAP, www.aap.org, 847-434-4000; APHA, www.apha.org, 202-777-2742)

- *Handbook for Public Playground Safety.* 1997, 2002. (U.S. Consumer Product Safety Commission, www.cpsc.gov, 800-638-2772)

When children are safe, they are better able to learn.

What Children Learn Outdoors

When you think about children's time outdoors, you don't necessarily focus on its value for teaching academic content. Nevertheless, there are many ways to connect content, teaching, and learning outdoors. As you become knowledgeable about each of the components of literacy, math, science, social studies, the arts, and technology, you will find many ways to promote children's learning outdoors.

Literacy

Expand children's **vocabulary and language** by asking questions and encouraging them to describe what they see. Use a variety of adjectives when you observe with children: slimy, bright, bold, glowing, rough, furry, prickly, and so on.

Promote **understanding of books and other texts** and **literacy as a source of enjoyment** by including resource books such as guides to living things. Children can use them to find pictures of what they discover outdoors. Read stories such as *The Very Busy Spider* and *The Very Hungry Caterpillar* (Eric Carle), *The Carrot Seed* (Ruth Krauss), *Miss Emma's Wild Garden* (Anna Grossnickle Hines), and *Where Once There was a Wood* or *In the Small, Small Pond* (Denise Fleming).

Teach children jump rope rhymes and clapping games to promote **phonological awareness.** Have them tune into the sounds and sights around them: how the horn on a car sounds vs. the horn on a truck or bus; identifying animal sounds—crickets, birds, mosquitoes, frogs, and dogs.

Teach children about **print and letters and words** by providing traffic signs for wheeled toys. Provide clipboards for children to record observations, cardboard to make signs to identify plants in the garden, or paper to leave a message for the custodian.

Mathematics

Promote **problem solving** by guiding children to find solutions to problems they encounter (e.g., What can we do to keep the balls from going over the fence?).

Teach **number concepts** by talking with children about how many seeds to plant, and helping them mark off the days until the seeds sprout. Use numbers and counting in games such as "Hide 'n' Seek," "Hopscotch," or "Mother, May I?" Reinforce one-to-one correspondence by having each child find a partner for an activity or a game such as "Squirrels and Trees."

Encourage children to explore **patterns and relationships** by noting the patterns on caterpillars, flowers, and leaves. Suggest making a design with the leaves or shells a child has collected. Play follow the leader and have children replicate a movement pattern such as jump, jump, clap, jump, jump, clap.

Emphasize concepts about **geometry and spatial relationships** by taking a shape walk, for example to find triangles or rectangles. Provide boxes, tubes, and other containers for children to use in building projects. When children are on the climbing equipment, use words to describe their position in space (e.g., under, over, inside, next to).

Expose children to **data collection, organization, and representation** by having them sort and classify the objects they find outdoors and making a graph where they can organize and compare the items in their collections.

Nurture children's interest in **measurement and graphing** by including string and yardsticks so they can measure the plants in their garden or the distance between structures outdoors.

Science

Guide children's development of **process skills** by posing questions such as: What would happen if . . . ? How can you find out? What did you learn? Encourage children to be good observers by showing them that you too are interested in finding out what is waiting for you each day outdoors.

Expose children to **physical science** concepts by offering them balls, ramps, tubes, water wheels, funnels, and sifters and by taking an interest in how they use these materials. Set up water tables or plastic pools so children can explore the properties of water.

Encourage children to explore **life science** by putting up bird feeders and keeping them stocked all winter; keeping pets outdoors if feasible and teaching children how to care for them; maintaining a worm farm; taking an interest in all forms of life outdoors. Collect caterpillars and study their eating habits and their life cycle. Bring out a stethoscope so children can listen to their heartbeat after running around the yard.

Promote understanding of the **earth and environment** by learning about trees and plants in your outdoor area and planting a garden with children. Explore shadows: what makes them, how they move, how long they are. Encourage children to collect all sorts of rocks and compare them; examine dirt from different locations; measure puddles after a rain and see what happens to them; collect litter and recycle. Study the seasons and the changes that occur in each one.

Social Studies

Encourage learning about **spaces and geography** by talking about distances when you take a walk (e.g., which is further, the neighborhood park or the post office); providing paper and markers so children can draw their playground.

Explore concepts related to **people and how they live** when you take walks. Identify what stores are in your neighborhood and what different kinds of houses, or visit a construction site.

Make children aware of **people and the environment** by taking a trip to a nearby river, lake, or ocean to see how people use water in the environment and to find out about pollution. Plan a project to clean up litter around the school.

The Arts

Promote growth in **dance** and **music** by encouraging children to use their bodies freely outdoors; bringing music outside so children can dance and move to the different beats; encourage children to move like different animals.

Nurture the **visual arts** by bringing paint, crayons, colored chalk, and other art materials outdoors. Encourage children to observe carefully and draw what they see—clouds in the sky, caterpillars, a flower.

Technology

Increase children's **awareness of people and technology** by talking about different tools and machines they see and use outdoors (e.g., trash trucks, pulleys, phone lines, walkie talkies, pipes and elbows, magnifying glasses, camera.

Provide **technology tools** for children to use outdoors such as binoculars, pulleys, microscopes, thermometers, magnifying glasses, cameras, and a digital camera if you have computers in your classroom.

From this sample list, you can see that the outdoor environment really does expand the opportunities for children to learn. We will build on these suggestions in the next section, where we describe in more detail the role of the teacher.

The Teacher's Role

Outdoors, teachers have to supervise children at all times and step in to stop dangerous behavior and prevent injuries. But just as important is the joy of sharing children's discoveries of nature's wonders and the thrill of helping them to achieve new skills that will serve them for a lifetime. So many teachable moments come up during outdoor time, you don't want to miss them. *Creative Curriculum* teachers take full advantage of the time they spend outdoors with children to achieve the goals and objectives for learning. You begin by observing what children do so you can individualize your responses, as you do in all aspects of curriculum implementation.

Observing and Responding to Individual Children

Observing children outdoors enables you to see how they use their skills in this unique environment. You may see skills displayed outdoors that you didn't know about, discover parts of the child's personality you hadn't seen before, and become aware of unexpected fears or surprising courage.

Because so many activities are going on at once outdoors, watching children without really seeing what is going on is easy. It takes extra effort to observe purposefully. It helps if you can focus your observations by knowing what you want to look for when observing children outdoors.

How Children Explore the Outdoors

The four different kinds of play identified by Sara Smilansky and discussed earlier (pp. 11–13) are a useful framework for thinking about how children use the Outdoor Area.

In functional play children use all of their senses to learn about objects and things in the environment—how they feel, smell, look, sound, and sometimes even taste. They take in the sights and sounds around them, manipulate things, and discover their uses. They ask themselves questions: What can I do with this? What will happen? What does it do? These open-ended questions lead in turn to experimenting and trying out all sorts of possibilities. A child might add some water to sand to see what happens or dump a pail of sand upside down to see if it will form a tower. Providing new materials and giving children time to explore can lead them to endless discoveries outdoors.

Constructive play emerges when children know about the materials available to them and begin using them to build or create something new. In the sandbox, they might make a castle with a moat or a tunnel. They might create an obstacle course or a pirate ship using planks and crates.

Dramatic play takes on a whole new feeling outdoors, where children have more freedom, equipment, and an entirely new setting. For example, children may create cakes and hamburgers out of wet sand and pour coffee using dry sand. Prop boxes supporting farm or camping themes also can be brought to the sand area to promote children's pretend play. Even without props, children may pretend to be firefighters or ambulance drivers on trikes, mountain climbers on climbing structures, or house painters using buckets of water and brushes.

Games with rules are ideal for outdoors where there is plenty of room. The space allows teachers to organize and teach games such as "Hide and Seek" and "Red Light/Green Light."

Responding to Each Child

Take note of how differently children approach the outdoors. Some head outdoors with great exuberance and literally throw themselves into active learning. Others are tentative and a little intimidated by the openness and unpredictability of the outdoor environment. Despite their differences, all children benefit from your support and encouragement to take full advantage of the outdoors to learn and to grow. To learn about a child's use of the outdoors, notice if the child

- prefers some play areas and equipment over others

- accepts new challenges and takes risks carefully

- observes events with curiosity and takes an interest in making discoveries

- is becoming more skillful in large muscle activities like climbing, swinging, and ball games

- enjoys participating in group games

Observing children provides the information you need to determine how to respond best and extend learning. The observations you collect over time enable you to assess each child's progress toward the goals and objectives of *The Creative Curriculum*. By tracking a child's progress on the *Developmental Continuum*, you can identify what skills a child has mastered and what skills need strengthening. The chart that follows gives examples of how you might use your observations to respond to each child.

Take note of how differently children approach the outdoors.

Observation	Reflection	Response
Setsuko stands near the teacher watching the other children play.	Setsuko seems interested in what other children are doing. *(Objective 22, Observes objects and events with curiosity)* The play yard may be overwhelming for her. *(Objective 1, Shows ability to adjust to new situations)* How can I get her involved in an activity where she will feel safe?	Talk with her about what she sees going on. Ask, "What do you think looks like the most fun?" Pair her with another child at a "safe" activity, such as water or sand play, painting with water, swinging.
Kate says to Sonya, "Look at this caterpillar I found. It's eating our tomato plant, just like the one we found yesterday."	Kate is observant and interested in the things around her. *(Objective 22, Observes objects and events with curiosity)* She recalls previous experiences and can describe them. *(Objective 26, Applies knowledge or experience to a new context; and 39, Expresses self using words and expanded sentences)* How can I build on her interest in caterpillars?	Ask questions: "How did you discover it was eating the tomato plant? Is it the same kind of caterpillar you saw yesterday? How do you know?" Bring out some books and field guides on caterpillars. Suggest, "Let's see if we can find out the name of this caterpillar and what else it likes to eat."
During a game of kick ball, Leo steps aside whenever the ball comes toward him to get out of the way.	Leo seems willing to join in the game but may not know what to do. *(Objective 18, Demonstrates throwing, kicking, and catching skills)* He may be worried about getting hurt. *(Objective 6, Takes responsibility for own well-being)* Does he know how to kick a ball? Does he understand the rules of the game?	Join in the game and make sure everyone knows the rules. Reassure him: "That ball is soft and won't hurt you." Later, suggest a simple game of kicking the ball against a fence. Show him how to do it, and invite another child to join the game.
Zack crashes his tricycle into other riders and comes dangerously close to children who are playing nearby.	Zack's behavior is dangerous and must be stopped. *(Objective 9, Follows classroom rules)* Is he purposefully crashing the tricycle? *(Objective 32, Shows awareness of position in space; and 3, Recognizes own feelings and manages them appropriately)* Have I explained the rules for using tricycles clearly?	Stop the dangerous behavior: "Hold on! You are driving too fast and I'm afraid someone will get hurt." Ask questions: "What seems to be the problem? Why are you driving so fast?" Give a clear message: "I can let you back on the road if you can drive safely. Otherwise I have to take your driving license away for today."

Interacting With Children Outdoors

You have a vital role to play during outdoor time each day. Your attention to what children are doing gives them the courage to try new things and take pride in their accomplishments. The outdoor environment provides a natural setting for children to learn to appreciate nature and develop a sense of responsibility for taking care of the environment. Even if your space is less than ideal, you can take children on walks and field trips to expand their world. The important messages children need to learn about the environment don't just happen; you need to make them happen.

Encouraging Children to Explore and Take Risks Carefully

Outdoor time can be a little intimidating for some children. They are not quite sure what to do with such open spaces, challenging play structures, and other children, who are happy to be active and noisy outdoors. These children will need your help as well as your encouragement. Some want to feel your hand on their waist as they climb to the top of the slide or to have you stand at the bottom to catch them. Others just want to know you are nearby. You can ask, "What can I do to help you feel safe?" Climbing up one rung of the jungle gym may be as big an accomplishment for one child as climbing to the top is for another.

Outdoor time can be a little intimidating for some children.

Sometimes a situation becomes too challenging for a child. He may get scared suddenly and ask to be helped down or off a piece of equipment. Such an incident can be an opportunity for encouraging the child to problem solve, or for simply offering help. You can use it to problem solve by first acknowledging that the situation is scary, then providing a way for the child to handle it. "It's a little scary being up so high, isn't it? Is there a way you can come down that won't feel so scary?" If you determine that the child is really scared, it is not a good time to problem solve; just help the child down. As you observe children outdoors, you will have a clearer sense of what challenges each child is ready to tackle, and you can determine the appropriate amount of encouragement a child needs to try something new.

As much as possible let children experience a sense of their own competence without relying on a teacher's praise.

Children often seek reinforcement from their teachers. "Look at me!" or "Watch what I can do!" are often heard on the playground. Some children ask for constant acknowledgment. For these children you might try saying, "Wow! You climbed to the top of the slide all by yourself. How does that make you feel?" or "I bet you're pretty proud of yourself right now." As much as possible let children experience a sense of their own competence without relying on a teacher's praise.

The one place you must always intervene is when children's safety is jeopardized. If a child is standing dangerously close to a swing, or if a child is using woodworking tools in a dangerous manner, you need to step in immediately.

Give clear, specific directions for safety purposes.

When intervening for safety purposes, be sure to give clear, specific directions. If you say, "Be careful with the hammer!" you don't tell a child what he is doing incorrectly; you only interrupt his concentration. More to the point, if he is pounding with the wrong end, you might say, "Zack, turn the hammer over and pound with the flat side." If you get no response, you should show him what you mean. Similarly, calling out a child's name if she is standing in front of the slide and another child is about to slide down and hit her may not have much of an effect. She is likely to stand there and look at you, but she will not necessarily move. She will be likely to move, however, if you say, "Sonya, move out of the way. Tyrone is coming down the slide." After the incident is over, you can remind Sonya of the rules for safe play and of what could have happened.

Nurturing Children's Appreciation for the Natural Environment

One of the greatest benefits of taking children outdoors is the opportunity to nurture their appreciation for the natural environment. You don't have to be a naturalist yourself to instill in children an awe of the world and a desire to discover and uncover what is around them. Even the most urban environment offers elements of nature to study and enjoy. Also, as we have noted already, you can bring nature into the environment you are given.

Today, more than ever before, including some form of environmental education in all programs for young children is vital. Children have fewer opportunities to be exposed to nature firsthand. Many children have never experienced the joy of tramping through the woods, rolling down a grassy hill, looking for life in a pond of water, digging their hands into mud, or turning over rocks to discover insects. If we want children to grow up to be people who care about preserving the environment, we have to start early to cultivate an appreciation for nature.

Teachers are models for children, especially when it comes to appreciating nature. You can nurture children's interest in nature simply by demonstrating your own excitement and curiosity. Focus on having fun with children when you go outdoors and share your enthusiasm for making discoveries.

Suppose, for example, that several children uncover some bugs outdoors and become fascinated by watching them. By showing an interest and asking open-ended questions, you can lead children to observe, predict, and to draw conclusions—the process skills that scientists use to make discoveries. Here are some suggestions:

Tell me what you see.

How are they different from one another?

What do you think they are doing?

How do they move?

What do you think they like to eat?

How could we find out what they are?

In so many ways, the outdoors provides emergent curriculum because you never know what might be awaiting you when you are tuned into nature.

Taking Walks and Site Visits

One way to help children build observation skills and increase their knowledge of the outdoors is to take walks and site visits to places where they can observe nature and the world around them. These walks and visits will be more interesting if you focus children's attention on something in particular. Here again you can model your own interest and curiosity about what you find. Or you might call walks and site visits, "Let's Find Out" activities and, each time, have a different focus. For example, let's find out

if there are any signs of spring (or fall)

what kinds of nests birds build

how many different leaves and seeds we can find

what kinds of trucks are being used at the construction site

how much litter is around our neighborhood

where the garbage goes

why shadows change sizes

Take walks and site visits to places where children can observe nature and the world around them.

Planning ahead will make walks more interesting learning experiences. Some supplies you can bring along to enhance the experience are:

- magnifying glasses
- binoculars
- bags, cartons, jars, or other containers to collect things in
- measuring tape and rulers
- a still camera or a video camera
- a tape recorder
- clipboards and paper and pencils
- field guides

Bring objects collected on walks back to the classroom and display them for closer examination.

You can bring many of the objects collected on walks back to the classroom and display them for closer examination. Plan time to talk with children about what they saw, to look in books and on the Internet to identify what they collected, and to draw pictures. Make a class book with photos the children have taken and write down what they say about each one.

Some walks and site visits require more extensive planning but they can be wonderful opportunities to take children to places they never might see otherwise. Visits to outdoor environments where children can explore and learn about nature are especially important for children who live in large cities. Find out if there are parks, community gardens, a botanical garden, bird sanctuary, trails in the woods, and streams where you can safely take your children for visits to learn about and enjoy nature.

Frequently Asked Questions About Outdoor Play

How long should we spend outdoors each day?

The answer to this question depends on the length of the time children are at the program each day, the proximity of your Outdoor Area, and weather conditions. If the outdoor area is located next to your classroom door and is protected, children might go outside whenever they wish if an adult can supervise their play. In full-day programs, you may have two long outdoor times, one in the morning and one in the afternoon. Each outdoor time should be approximately one hour. When the weather is appropriate, you may decide to spend most of the day outdoors, taking indoor activities outdoors and serving food there as well.

Some teachers limit outdoor time when it's too cold. But most often it is the adults who get cold outside, not the children. If children have warm coats, hats, mittens, and boots (on wet days), they will do fine outdoors. Be sure to keep extra layers at school so you can dress warmly too. Alternatively, in very hot weather, you and the children need protection. In each area of the country, teachers have to pay attention to different issues. You can check your local newspapers, weather channel, or the Internet for alerts about air pollution, ultraviolet ratings, pollen counts, and predicted conditions. See also the suggestions we offered earlier in this chapter when we discussed safety considerations.

How can we study nature when we don't have anything but asphalt and metal play structures?

You have to be creative. Throughout this chapter we offered a variety of suggestions—gardens in containers, bird feeders, worm farms in an old aquarium, cages for pets, and bringing indoor materials outdoors. Take advantage of parks and gardens within walking distance of your program and take walks with children to discover what's in the neighborhood. Arrange for site visits to places where children can explore natural settings freely.

What about sharing the playground with older children?

Sharing a playground with other children is workable. You might try to arrange a schedule with older classes so you can use the playground when they are not around. If this arrangement is not possible, perhaps you can work out a system where one group at a time takes turns using the playground equipment. You also can teach children which playground structures are off limits if you feel they are not appropriate for preschool children.

A Letter to Families About Outdoor Play

What We Do and Why

Physical exercise and fresh air are important for your child's health and well being. We take children outdoors every day so they can run, jump, swing, climb, and use all the large muscles in their bodies. They run around, breathe in the fresh air, look at the clouds, or catch a ball or a bug. They lie on the ground and watch clouds and birds, or they climb high and look down. We also talk about the things children see, hear, touch, and feel so they become aware of changes in the weather, the seasons, the growth of plants, and the animals.

Playing outdoors your child can learn
- to notice and appreciate changes in nature
- to discover how water puddles after a rain and disappears when the sun comes out
- to follow shadows around
- to use his or her body in increasingly skillful ways

We encourage children to wonder about what they see by asking questions:

What do you notice?

Where do you think they are going?

How are they different or the same?

What You Can Do at Home

Fresh air and exercise are very important to your child's health, and to yours. Try to spend time with your child outdoors every day except when the weather is dangerous. Take walks in your neighborhood, go to parks together, explore nature with your child. Watch what your child notices and show you too are interested.

Children love to collect things and then play with them, sort them, and make patterns with them. Bring along a container or plastic bag when you go outdoors so your child can collect treasures along the way—seeds, leaves, rocks—and bring them home to examine. You also can plan special activities outdoors. Here are some ideas:
- Bring drawing paper and crayons outside so children can draw what they see.
- Take a pail of water and large brushes so your child can paint the sidewalk or fence.
- Bring colored chalk, which is perfect for sidewalk art.
- Play catch with balls of all sizes.
- Bring bubble-blowing solution and different-shape blowers.

Make time each day to be outdoors with your child, exploring, making discoveries, and appreciating nature.

part 2
references

American Academy of Pediatrics, American Public Health Association, & National Resource Center for Health and Safety in Child Care. (2002). *Caring for our children: National health and safety performance standards: Guidelines for out-of-home child care programs*(2nd ed.). Elk Grove Village, IL; Washington, DC; Aurora, CO: Author.

Bowman, B. T. (1997). Equity and young children as learners. In A. S. Robinson (Ed.), *Proceedings of the families, technology and education conference*, October 30– November 1, 1997. Champaign, IL: ERIC-EECE. Retrieved March 26, 2002, from http://ericeece.org/pubs/books/fte/ftepro.html

Bredekamp, S., & Rosegrant, T. (Eds.). (1992). *Reaching potentials: Appropriate curriculum and assessment for young children* (Vol. 1). Washington, D.C.: National Association for the Education of Young Children.

Clemens, J. B. (1996). Gardening with children. *Young Children, 51*(4), 22-27.

Clements, D. H., & Swaminathan, S. (1995). Technology and school change: New lamps for old? *Childhood Education, 71*, 275–281.

Cordes, C., & Miller, E. (Eds.). (2000). *Fool's gold: A critical look at computers in childhood*. College Park, MD: Alliance for Childhood.

Epstein, A. S. (2001). Thinking about art. Encouraging art appreciation in early childhood settings. *Young Children, 56*(3), 38–43.

Fouts, J. T. (February 2000). *Research on computers and education: Past, present and future*. Seattle, WA: Bill and Melinda Gates Foundation.

Griffin, C. & B. Rinn. (1998). Enhancing outdoor play with an obstacle course. *Young Children, 53*(3), 18–23.

Haugland, S. W. (2000). *Computers and Young Children* (No. EDO-PS-004). Champaign, IL: ERIC Clearinghouse on Elementary and Early Childhood Education. ERIC Document Reproduction Service No. ED438926.

Haugland, S. W., & Wright, J. L. (1997). *Young children and technology: A world of discovery*. Boston: Allyn and Bacon.

Odoy, H.A.D., & Foster, S. H. (1997). Creating play crates for the outdoor classroom. *Young Children, 52*(6), 12–16.

Schickedanz, J. A. (1999). *Much more than the ABCs: The early stages of reading and writing*. Washington, DC: National Association for the Education of Young Children.

Smilansky, S. (1990). Socio-dramatic play: Its relevance to behavior and achievement in school. In E. Klugman & S. Smilansky (Eds.), *Children's play and learning: Perspectives and policy implications* (pp. 18–42). New York: Teachers College Press.

Smilansky, S., Hagan, J., & Lewis, H. (1988). *Clay in the classroom: Helping children develop cognitive and affective skills for learning*. New York: P. Lang.

Smilansky, S. & Shefatya, L. (1990). *Facilitating play: A medium for promoting cognitive, socio-emotional, and academic development in young children.* Gaithersburg, MD: Psychosocial & Educational Publications.

Teachers Resisting Unhealthy Children's Entertainment (TRUCE) Steering Committee. *TRUCE Toy Action Guide 2001–2002.* West Somerville, MA. Retrieved March 26, 2002 from *http://www.truceteachers.org/TRUCE/toyguide01.pdf*

Totter, A. (1999, September 23). Preparing teachers for the digital age. *Education Week,* pp. 37-42.

U.S. Consumer Product Safety Commission (CPSC). (1997, with subsequent updates). *Handbook for public playground safety* (Publication No. 325). Washington, DC: Author. Available from www.cpsc.gov

Whitehurst, G. J. (1992). *How to read to your preschooler.* Retrieved March 26, 2002, from http://www.whitehurst.sbs.sunysb.edu/pubs/ctread.htm

Windsor, C. B. (1996). Blocks as a material for learning through play. In E. S. Hirsch (Ed.), *The block book* (3rd ed.). Washington, DC: National Association for the Education of Young Children.

Appendix

Weekly Planning Form

Planning Changes to the Environment

Study/Project: _____

Week of: _____

Teacher: _____

Assistant: _____

Blocks	Dramatic Play	Toys and Games	"To Do" List:
Art	Library	Discovery	
Sand and Water	Music and Movement	Cooking	
Computers	Outdoors	Family/Community Involvement	

© 2002 Teaching Strategies, Inc.

Planning for Groups

	Monday	Tuesday	Wednesday	Thursday	Friday
Group Time (songs, stories, games, discussions, etc.)					
Story Time					
Small-Group Activities					
Special Activities (site visits, special events, etc.)					

Notes *(reminders, changes, children to observe)*

Weekly Planning Form

Planning Changes to the Environment

Week of: __May 5-9__   Study/Project: __Worms (week 3)__

Teacher: __Ms. Tory__   Assistant: __Mr. Alvarez__

Blocks Add ramps and arches	**Dramatic Play** Offer props (shipping boxes, etc.) children might use to recreate a worm farm	**Toys and Games** Use food and other cards from lotto games to make a new game for the area called, "Can I compost this?"
Art Add wire, wire cutters, pipe cleaners, cardboard, boxes, dirt, clay, playdough and up close photograph of a worm	**Library** Add informational books and storybooks on worms	**Discovery** Have clipboards available for children to record observations of worms Add magnifying glasses
Sand and Water Add variety of sifters and sieves	**Music and Movement** Add sleeping bags for children to crawl around like worms	**Cooking** Make fruit salad; peel carrots (add peelings to compost bin)
Computers Add *One Small Square: Backyard* CD-ROM	**Outdoors** Offer garden tools to begin preparing area to plant vegetables and add worm compost	

"To Do" List:

- Permission slips for field visit
- Check w/ Mr. Fox at worm farm
- Ask librarian to locate books about worms

Family/Community Involvement

Ask parent volunteers to work with children building the worm viewing area outside.

© 2002 Teaching Strategies, Inc.
Permission is granted to duplicate the material on this page for use in programs implementing *The Creative Curriculum for Preschool*.

Planning for Groups

	Monday	Tuesday	Wednesday	Thursday	Friday
Group Time (songs, stories, games, discussions, etc.)	Move like a worm to "Glow Worm" song	Discuss tomorrow's site visit; write down children's questions	Prepare for site visit	Discuss site visit; did we find the answers to our questions	Discuss what we need to do to make our worm farm better
Story Time	*Inch by Inch*	*The Very Hungry Caterpillar*	*Are You My Mother?*	*Wonderful Worms*	*The Empress and the Silkworm*
Small-Group Activities	Animal classification game (Ben's mom will help)	Observe a worm and a caterpillar; record how they are the same and how they are different		Compare samples of dirt children brought from home and compost.	Work with group building outdoor worm viewing area
Special Activities (site visits, special events, etc.)	Have Mrs. Johnson (the science teacher) show how to use and care for the microscope she's lending the class	Teach children how to use disposable cameras	Visit to the worm farm! Take pictures, bring clipboards	Write thank-you letter to Mr. Fox; invite children to draw pictures to include	

Notes *(reminders, changes, children to observe)*

Observe Tasheen, Ben, and Carlos for patterning skills and arranging objects in a series

Observe Juwan, Setsuko, and Tyrone for following directions, hearing and discriminating sounds in words

The Creative Curriculum® Goals and Objectives at a Glance

SOCIAL/EMOTIONAL DEVELOPMENT

Sense of Self

1. Shows ability to adjust to new situations
2. Demonstrates appropriate trust in adults
3. Recognizes own feelings and manages them appropriately
4. Stands up for rights

Responsibility for Self and Others

5. Demonstrates self-direction and independence
6. Takes responsibility for own well-being
7. Respects and cares for classroom environment and materials
8. Follows classroom routines
9. Follows classroom rules

Prosocial Behavior

10. Plays well with other children
11. Recognizes the feelings of others and responds appropriately
12. Shares and respects the rights of others
13. Uses thinking skills to resolve conflicts

PHYSICAL DEVELOPMENT

Gross Motor

14. Demonstrates basic locomotor skills (running, jumping, hopping, galloping)
15. Shows balance while moving
16. Climbs up and down
17. Pedals and steers a tricycle (or other wheeled vehicle)
18. Demonstrates throwing, kicking, and catching skills

Fine Motor

19. Controls small muscles in hands
20. Coordinates eye-hand movement
21. Uses tools for writing and drawing

COGNITIVE DEVELOPMENT

Learning and Problem Solving

22. Observes objects and events with curiosity
23. Approaches problems flexibly
24. Shows persistence in approaching tasks
25. Explores cause and effect
26. Applies knowledge or experience to a new context

Logical Thinking

27. Classifies objects
28. Compares/measures
29. Arranges objects in a series
30. Recognizes patterns and can repeat them
31. Shows awareness of time concepts and sequence
32. Shows awareness of position in space
33. Uses one-to-one correspondence
34. Uses numbers and counting

Representation and Symbolic Thinking

35. Takes on pretend roles and situations
36. Makes believe with objects
37. Makes and interprets representations

LANGUAGE DEVELOPMENT

Listening and Speaking

38. Hears and discriminates the sounds of language
39. Expresses self using words and expanded sentences
40. Understands and follows oral directions
41. Answers questions
42. Asks questions
43. Actively participates in conversations

Reading and Writing

44. Enjoys and values reading
45. Demonstrates understanding of print concepts
46. Demonstrates knowledge of the alphabet
47. Uses emerging reading skills to make meaning from print
48. Comprehends and interprets meaning from books and other texts
49. Understands the purpose of writing
50. Writes letters and words

Index

A

Abstract thinking, 21
Adaptive equipment, 37, 71–72, 181, 375, 481, 510
Afternoon activities, 93
Aggressive behavior, 118, 291. *See also* Challenging behavior
Allergies and health conditions of children, 89, 452, 465, 510
Alphabet, 129, 133, 174, 378. *See also* Letters and words
Arrangement of objects, 8, 24, 26,162. *See also* Mathematics
Art (visual), 154, 155, 317–349
    art appreciation, 345
    classroom area for, 62, 320–333
    connecting with Curriculum objectives, 318–319
    content learning via, 334–335
    frequently asked questions about, 347–348
    interacting with children in art area, 341–346
    Letter to Families, 349
    materials for, 322–331, 332, 347–348
    observing and responding to individual children, 337–340
    safety issues, 341–342
    teacher's role, 336–348
Arts, 152–155
    art area, 154, 155, 317–349. *See also* Art (visual)
    block play, learning opportunities, 254
    computer use, learning opportunities, 483
    connecting arts content, teaching, and learning, 154–155
    content in interest areas, 188–189
    cooking experiences, learning opportunities, 455
    dance, 152, 155. *See also* Music and movement
    discovery area, learning opportunities, 393
    drama, 153–154, 155, 271–293. *See also* Dramatic play
    library area, learning opportunities, 364

    music, 153, 155, 423–441, 429. *See also* Music and movement
    outdoor play, learning opportunities, 513
    sand and water area, learning opportunities, 412
    toys and games, learning opportunities, 305
Assessment, 199–208
Assimilation, 6
Assistive technology, 37, 181, 481
Attendance, taking of, 82–83
Attention
    getting attention of children, 101, 181
    need for, 120
Attention-related disorders, children with, 36, 180, 375, 480
    Attention span, 29
    audio selection and, 359
    book selection and, 355
    boredom factor, 121
Audio materials, 359, 374, 436. *See also* CDs
Auditory learners, 31
Autism, 36, 37–38
Autonomy, 3–4

B

Basic human needs (Maslow), 2–3
Bedding for rest time and naps, 69, 91
Behavior of children. *See* Disruptive behavior; Temperament
Belongingness, 2, 84, 103
Belongings, classroom places for, 70, 77, 219
Bilingual children, 38–41. *See also* English Language Learners
Biting, 118. *See also* Challenging behavior
Block play, 243–269
    classroom area for, 62, 75, 78, 246–252, 267
    connecting with Curriculum objectives, 244–245
    content learning via, 253–254
    family participation, 229
    frequently asked questions about, 267–268
    interacting with children during, 261–267

    Letter to Families, 269
    materials for, 247–250
    observing and responding to individual children, 255–260
    teacher's role, 255–269
Bodily/kinesthetic intelligence, 10
Body movement. *See* Music and movement
Books. *See* Library; Literacy skills
Boys vs. girls. *See* Gender differences
Brain research, 5–6, 20, 32, 40
Bulletin boards, 219
Bullying, 119. *See also* Challenging behavior

C

Calendars, 85. *See also* Structure of day
Calm-down place, 111
Care of the classroom. *See* Clean-up; Maintenance of classroom
Categorization of objects. *See* Arrangement of objects
CDs, 359, 361, 476, 479. *See also* Audio materials
Challenging behavior, 14, 116–122
    biting, 118
    bullying, 119
    causes of, 120–121
    environmental causes and strategies, 80–81
    friendless children and, 105
    physical aggression, 118
    self-control by child to overcome, 121–122
    spanking as punishment, 239
    superhero play, 291
    teacher's problem-solving steps, 117
    temper tantrums, 119
Child development and learning, 17–59
    areas of development, 18–22
    art and, 337–339
    children with disabilities, 36–38
    cognitive development. *See* Cognitive development
    computer usage and, 485
    culture and, 34–35
    Developmental Continuum, 42–58. *See also* Developmental Continuum
    developmental stages, 23–26

English Language Learners, 38–41
five-year-olds, 25–26
four-year-olds, 24–25
gender differences, 27–28
gifted children, 35–36
individual differences, 27–41
language development, 22. *See also* Language development
learning styles, 31–32
life experiences of children, 33
outdoor play and, 514–515
physical development, 20. *See also* Physical development
sand and water play and, 413
social/emotional development, 18–19. *See also* Social/emotional development
temperament of children, 28–30
three-year-olds, 23–24
writing skills, 367–368
Child-initiated learning, 173–174
Children with disabilities, 36–38. *See also* Assistive technology
adapting instruction to include, 180–181
art area difficulties, how to handle, 346
book selection to represent, 357
computer adaptation for, 480–481
forerunner skills and, 44
library area difficulties, how to handle, 374–375
making friendships, 105
outdoor activities, 510
peer buddies for, 180, 375
visual cues for, 180–181
Children's work
collecting for assessment purposes, 199
display of, 68–69, 77, 333, 345
encouraging children to talk about, 75
portfolios of, 200–204
protection of, 74–75, 77
Choice time, 86, 87–88, 93
Classroom community, 9, 102–122
English Language Learners, 182
friendships among children, 105–108
positive relationships, 102–108
rules for, 108–110
social problem solving, 110–115
teacher's relationship with children, 102–105, 122
Classroom jobs and shared responsibility, 73–74, 78
Classroom space, 62–81

adaptation for special needs children, 71–72
attractive and comfortable setting, 70–71, 76, 219, 320, 360
belongings, places for, 70, 77, 219
calm-down place, 111
corners, use of, 64
displays. *See* Displays in classroom
evaluation of effectiveness of, 76–81
floor coverings in, 64, 68, 71
group time area, 67–68
interest areas, 62–67
  art, 62, 320–333
  blocks, 62, 75, 78, 246–252, 267
  computers, 62, 474–481
  cooking, 62, 446–452
  diagram of, 63
  discovery area, 62, 384–390
  displaying and labeling materials, 65–67, 77, 78
  dramatic play, 62, 274–279
  equipment and materials for, 65
  guidelines for setting up, 64
  library, 62, 354–361
  music and movement, 62, 426–427, 440
  outdoor play, 496–510
  popularity of, 79
  sand and water play, 62, 406–410
  toys and games, 62, 75, 298–303
  weekly planning, 98
lighting in, 64, 71
mail/message boxes for families, 219
maintenance of, 73–75, 76
plants and pets in, 65, 71, 76
private spaces in, 71, 77
quiet areas, 78
safety issues, 64, 67, 70
storage space. *See* Storage in classroom
tables. *See* Tables
traffic patterns in, 64, 72, 79
Clay and molding materials, 326–329
Clean up, 65, 66, 88
  art activities, 154
  block play, 252, 268
  cooking activities, 449
  mealtimes, 90–91
  sand and water play, 420
Closing ritual, 85
Cognitive development, 6–9, 21

Developmental Continuum and, 24–26, 51–54
Collage materials, 325–326
Coloring books, 347
Communication with parents. *See* Family communications; Letter to Families
Community environment of classroom. *See* Classroom community
Comprehension. *See* Literacy skills
Computer play, 471–491. *See also* Technology
  accessories for computers, 476
  adaptation for children with special needs, 72, 480–481
  classroom area for, 62, 474–481
  connecting with Curriculum objectives, 472–473
  content learning via, 482–483
  developmental stages, 485
  frequently asked questions about, 489–490
  hardware, 475–477
  interacting with children, 487–488
  materials for, 475–481
  observing and responding to individual children, 484–486
  software, 477–479
  teacher's role, 484–490
  web sites, selection for appropriateness, 479–480
Concreteness and preoperational children, 7–8
Conferences with families, 231–234
Confidence. *See* Self-confidence
Conflict among children. *See* Disagreements among children
Connectedness. *See* Belongingness
Construction sites, as outdoor play, 502
Constructive play, 12, 306, 413, 514
Content of Curriculum, 125–163
  arts, 152–155. *See also* Arts
  family contribution to, 226
  literacy, 126–133. *See also* Literacy skills
  mathematics, 134–141. *See also* Mathematics
  process skills, 161–162
  science, 142–145. *See also* Science
  social studies, 146–151. *See also* Social studies
  technology, 156–160. *See also* Technology
The Continuum. *See* Developmental Continuum
Cooking, 443–469
  classroom area for, 62, 446–452

connecting with Curriculum objectives, 445–446

content learning via, 453–455

display of cooking equipment and tools, 449–450

frequently asked questions about, 468

health and safety issues, 450–452, 465

interacting with children, 459–467

knives, use and storage of, 447, 449, 450, 465

learning basic techniques, 456–457

Letter to Families, 469

materials and equipment for, 447–449, 450

observing and responding to individual children, 456–458

recipes, use of, 456, 460–467

Counting, 134

Creativity and computer activities, 485

Culture

books reflecting different cultures, selection of, 356, 357–358

child development and, 34–35

classroom displays to include diversity, 69, 77, 219

enrollment questions about, 215

family differences, 212–213, 226, 236–238

food and, 89, 467

songs and dances of different cultures, 437, 438

toys and games chosen to convey social values, 301

D

Daily schedule, 92–97. See also Structure of day

Dance, 152, 155, 435. See also Music and movement

Data collection, organization, and representation, 138–139, 141. See also Arrangement of objects

Decentering, 7

Description of objects, 8

Developmental Continuum, 42–58, 530

Assessment System, 199, 205

beyond the Continuum, 45

cognitive development, 51–54. See also Cognitive development

explaining to families, 227, 240

forerunner skills, 44–45

language development. See Language development

observing of children, use in, 169–172

physical development, 49–50. See also Physical development

placing child within, 187, 204–205

planning in relation to, 206–208

social/emotional development, 46–48. See also Social/emotional development

Developmental spelling, 129

Developmental stages. See Child development and learning; Developmental Continuum

Developmentally appropriate practice, 1

art area, 347

software and computers, 477–478, 489

Disabled children. See Children with disabilities

Disagreements among children, 106, 110–115

Disciplining children by spanking, 239

Discovery area, 381–401

classroom area for, 62, 384–390

computers in, 474

connecting with Curriculum objectives, 382–383

content learning via, 391–393

frequently asked questions about, 400

interacting with children in, 397–399

Letter to Families, 401

materials for, 385–390

observing and responding to individual children, 394–396

stages of learning in, 394–395

teacher's role, 394–400

tools in, 384, 385, 501

Dishwashing, 410

Displays in classroom. See also Photographs

children's work, 68–69, 77, 333

asking children to pick art work for, 345

"Classroom Community" display with photos, 69, 77

classroom materials, 65–67, 77, 78

classroom rules, 110

fine art, 345

schedule of events, 77, 96–97

Distractability, 29. See also Attention span

Diversity. See Culture

Doubt, 3–4

Dramatic play, 12, 153–154, 155, 271–293

classroom area for, 62, 274–279

connecting with Curriculum objectives, 272–273

content learning via, 280–281

frequently asked questions about, 291–292

interacting with children during, 283, 284, 287–290

Letter to Families, 293

observing and responding to individual children, 282–286

props, use in, 282, 284, 289–290

selecting and displaying materials, 275–276

study topics and, 276–279

suggestions to stimulate, 287–290

teacher's role, 282–292

E

Earth and the environment, 144, 145. See also Science

Egocentrism, 7, 23, 24

"Eight Stages of Man" (Erikson), 3

Emotions, 3–4, 5

acknowledgment of child's feelings, 117

calming down, 111, 181

intelligence and, 10

social/emotional development, 18–19. See also Social/emotional development

Empathy, development of, 19, 24, 106, 271, 351

English Language Learners, 38–41

adapting instruction to include, 181–183

book selection for, 358

classroom design to help, 78

labels in English and home languages, 66, 78, 182, 303

phonological awareness of, 128

vocabulary and language growth, 127

Enrollment, 214–215, 226

Environment in classroom. See Classroom community; Classroom space

Equipment. See Materials and equipment

Ergonomics, 474

Esteem. See Respect

Ethnic diversity. See Culture

F

Family communications, 223–224. *See also* Letter to Families
> booklet on program for families, 220
> bulletins, 224
> class web site, 224
> on culture, 34, 236–238
> daily exchanges, 223
> differences between families and program, how to address, 239–240
> on disruptive behavior, 92, 118, 122
> e-mail, 224
> at enrollment, 214–215
> formal communications, 224
> on health problems, 120, 452
> home visits. *See* Home visits
> journals, 224
> on life experiences of child, 33
> meetings and conferences, 231–234
> misunderstandings with families, 236–238
> notices, 224
> open house, 220
> prior to start of program, 214–217
> stressful situations, families in, 235–236
> telephone calls, 224
> thank-you notes, 224

Family Science Night, 400

Family's role, 211–241. *See also* Family communications; Letter to Families
> building trust, 221
> classroom participation by families, 228–231
> conferences with families, 231–234
> curriculum suggestions by families, 226–227
> differences among families, 212–213
> differing viewpoints between families and program, 239–240
> at enrollment, 214–215
> English Language Learners, 183
> fathers, involvement of, 222
> grandparents, involvement of, 222
> home visits. *See* Home visits
> introducing program to parents, 220
> making things for program, 226
> misunderstandings with families, 236–238

> partnering with families on children's learning, 225–234
> planning for family/community involvement, 98
> resources available to parents, 219
> sharing culture, job, or talent, 226
> stressful family environment, 235–236
> welcoming family to classroom, 218–219, 223

Fear
> behavior problems due to, 121
> dramatic play and, 271, 292
> irrational fears, 25

Field trips, 99, 277, 519–520

Fine art displays and appreciation, 345

Fine motor skills. *See* Motor skills

Finger-play, songs with, 437

First few days, 100–101

Five-year-olds, 25–26
> small-group time for, 86
> understanding rules, 108

Floor coverings in classroom, 64, 68, 71, 355, 408, 420

Food. *See also* Cooking
> allergies and health conditions of children, 89, 452, 465
> as art material, 348
> mealtimes, 89–91
> as reward or punishment, 91, 468
> toys and games linked to, 302

Forms, Weekly Planning, 98–99, 526–529

Foster Grandparents, 222

Four-year-olds, 24–25
> computer use by, 489
> small group time for, 86
> understanding rules, 108, 307

Frequently asked questions
> about art, 347–348
> about block play, 267–268
> about computers, 489–490
> about cooking, 468
> about discovery area, 400
> about dramatic play, 291–292
> about library area, 376–378
> about music and movement, 440
> about outdoor play, 521
> about sand and water play, 419–420
> about toys and games, 313–314

Friendship-making, teacher's help for children, 105–108

Frustration of child, how to handle, 346

Functional play, 11, 306, 413, 514

G

Games, 295–315. *See also* Toys and games
> outdoor, 502–503, 515
> with rules, 13, 307, 515

Gardening, 499. *See also* Plants

Gender differences, 27–28
> in choice of books, 357
> in play, 79, 267, 292, 301, 302

Geography, 146–147, 150. *See also* Social studies

Geometry and spatial sense, 136–137, 141, 392. *See also* Mathematics

Getting attention of children, 101, 181

Gifted children, 35–36, 45
> adapting instruction to include, 179–180, 377
> reading ability of, 180, 377

Girls vs. boys. *See* Gender differences

Goals and objectives of the Curriculum, 42, 45, 530
> arts content and, 154–155, 318–319
> block play and, 244–245
> computer play and, 472–473
> cooking activities and, 445–446
> discovery area and, 382–383
> dramatic play and, 272–273
> library area and, 352–353
> literacy content and, 132–133
> math content and, 140–141
> music and movement and, 424–425
> outdoor play and, 494–495
> sand and water play and, 404–405
> science content and, 144–145
> social studies content and, 150–151
> technology content and, 159–160
> toys and games and, 296–297

Graduation ceremonies, 240

Grandparents' role, 222

Graphs and graphing, 8, 21, 138–139, 512

Gross motor skills. *See* Motor skills

Group time, 84–86
> classroom area for, 67–68
> cooking activities, 460
> large group, 84–85, 183–185
> planning for, 99, 207–208
> small group, 86, 185–187

Gun-free zone, 268

H

Handwriting. *See* Writing skills
Hardship and resilience, 13–14
Health, 5. *See also* Allergies and health conditions of children
    sand and water area, concerns, 419–420, 498
    screenings, 5
    teaching about, 143–144, 145
Hearing impaired children. *See* Children with disabilities
Helmets for children, 498
Hierarchy of needs (Maslow), 2
History, 149. *See also* Social studies
Holiday art, 348
Home visits, 69, 215–217, 226

I

Imagery. *See* Representations made by children; Symbolic thinking
Independence, development of, 18
    first few days' activities, 101
    five-year-olds, 25
    four-year-olds, 24
Individual Education Programs (IEPs), 36–37
Initiative of children, 4, 18, 24
Intelligence, 9–11, 35. *See also* IQ
Interacting with children, 175–178
    art area, 341–346
    block play, 262–267
    computer activities, 487–488
    cooking activities, 459–467
    discovery area, 397–399
    dramatic play, 287–290
    library area, 370–375
    music and movement, 434–440
    outdoor play, 517–520
    sand and water area, 416–418
    toys and games, 310–312
Interest areas. *See also* specific area (e.g., Blocks; Dramatic play)
    chart for exploring content of, 188–189
    classroom space for, 62–67
    planning boards in, 87–88
    teaching of, 187–189
Interests of children, 30–31
Internet use, 224, 479–480
Interpersonal intelligence, 10
Intrapersonal intelligence, 10
Invented spelling, 129

Investigation stage and computer activities, 485
Involvement stage and computer activities, 485
IQ
    early childhood's experiences and, 5
    limitations of traditional tests, 9
Irrational fears, 25

J

Job chart, 74, 78
Journals, 224, 374

K

Kinesthetic learners, 32
Kitchen area. *See* Cooking

L

Labeling materials and classroom locations, 65–66, 77, 78
Language development, 18, 22, 126–127, 132. *See also* English Language Learners
    Developmental Continuum for ages 3-5, 55–58
    five-year-olds, 26
    four-year-olds, 24, 25
    phonological awareness, 127–128
    three-year-olds, 23, 24
Large-group time, 84–85, 99, 183–185
Learning, approaches to, 173–198
    asking children questions, 177–178
    child-initiated learning, 173–174
    conversation with children about their work, 177
    interacting. *See* Interacting with children
    teacher-directed learning, 174–175
Learning environment, 61–123. *See also* Classroom space
Learning styles, 31–32
Letter to Families, 220
    art, 349
    block play, 269
    computers, 491
    cooking, 469
    discovery area, 401
    dramatic play, 293

    library area, 379
    music and movement, 441
    outdoor play, 522
    sand and water play, 421
    toys and games, 315
Letters and words, 129, 133, 174, 367–368
    books selected to help children learn, 357
    teaching writing of, 377
Library, 351–379
    children with disabilities, addressing special needs of, 374–375
    classroom area for, 62, 354–361
    connecting with Curriculum objectives, 352–353
    content learning via, 362–364
    displaying and caring for materials, 354, 356, 360–361, 371
    frequently asked questions about, 376–378
    interacting with children in, 370–375
    Letter to Families, 379
    observing and responding to individual children, 365–369
    reading books aloud to children, 370–373
    selecting materials for, 355–360
    teacher's role, 365–378
    writing materials, 359–360, 361. *See also* Writing skills
Life experiences
    of children, 33
    of families, 212
    of teacher, 213
Life science, 143–144, 145. *See also* Science
Lighting in classroom, 64, 71
Linguistic/verbal intelligence, 10
Listening and speaking skills, 22, 55–56, 112
Listening to music, 431, 434
Literacy skills, 22. *See also* Language development
    art area, learning opportunities, 344
    block play, learning opportunities, 253
    components of, 126–131
    comprehension, 129–130, 133
    computer use, learning opportunities, 482
    connecting literacy content, teaching, and learning, 132–133
    content in interest areas, 188–189

cooking area, learning opportunities, 453
Developmental Continuum for ages 3-5, 57–58
discovery area, learning opportunities, 391
dramatic play, learning opportunities, 280
letters and words, 129, 133. *See also* Letters and words
library area, learning opportunities, 351, 362
motivation and enjoyment, 131, 133
music and movement, learning opportunities, 428
outdoor play, learning opportunities, 511
phonological awareness, 127–128, 132. *See also* Phonological awareness
print, acquiring knowledge of, 128, 132
sand and water area, learning opportunities, 411
toys and games play, learning opportunities, 304
understanding books and other texts, 130–131, 133
vocabulary, 126–127. *See also* Vocabulary growth
Logical/mathematical intelligence, 10
Logical thinking and reasoning, 6–8, 21
Developmental Continuum for ages 3-5, 52–53

M

Maintenance of classroom, 73–75, 76, 78
repairability of computer, 477
Maintenance of playground equipment, 508
Make-believe, 282. *See also* Dramatic play
Maps, 146
Maslow, Abraham, 2–3
Materials and equipment, 65. *See also* Adaptive equipment
art materials, 322–332, 347–348
blocks, 243, 247–250
clay and molding materials, 326–329
collage materials, 325–326
computer play, 475–481
cooking, 447–449

discovery area, 384, 385–387, 501
displaying and labeling materials, 65–67, 77, 78
dramatic play, 275–276, 289–290
handling of, teacher-directed learning, 174
introduction of, 183–185
library area, 355–360
listening materials, 359, 374
musical instruments, 426–427
outdoor play, 497–508
painting materials, 322–325
playdough, 326–329
playground equipment, 505–508
sand and water play, 407–410
story retelling materials, 358
technology tools. *See* Technology
toys and games, 299–302
walks outdoors, 520
woodworking, 331
writing materials, 359–360, 374
Mathematical intelligence, 10
Mathematics, 134–141
art area, learning opportunities, 334
block play, learning opportunities, 253
comparisons, 135, 137, 141
computer use, learning opportunities, 482
connecting math content, teaching, and learning, 140–141
content in interest areas, 188–189
cooking experiences, learning opportunities, 453
data collection, organization, and representation, 138–139, 141
discovery area, learning opportunities, 391
dramatic play, learning opportunities, 280
geometry and spatial sense, 136–137, 141, 392
library area, learning opportunities, 363
measurement activities, 137–138, 141
music and movement, learning opportunities, 428
number concepts, 134–135, 140
number symbols, 135, 140
one-to-one correspondence, 135
outdoor play, learning opportunities, 511–512
patterns and relationships, 136, 140
sand and water area, learning opportunities, 411

toys and games play, learning opportunities, 304–305
Mealtimes, 5, 89–91, 93, 446. *See also* Food
Measurement activities, 137–138, 141
Meetings with families, 231–234
Misbehavior. *See* Disruptive behavior
Mistakes by children, 103
Misunderstandings with families, 236–238
Modeling behavior, 8, 107
Models or precut patterns, use of, 347
Morning activities, 93
Motor skills, 20. *See also* Physical development
Movement. *See* Music and movement
Multiple intelligences, 9–11
Music and movement, 5, 153, 155, 423–441
classroom area for, 62, 426–427, 440
connecting with Curriculum objectives, 424–425
content learning via, 428–429
cultural diversity, 437, 438
frequently asked questions about, 440
interacting with children in art area, 434–440
Letter to Families, 441
musical instruments, 426–427, 431
musical/rhythmic intelligence, 10
observing and responding to individual children, 430–433
teacher's role, 430–440

N

Names of children and taking attendance, 82–83
Naps, 77, 91–92
National Association for the Education of Young Children (NAEYC), 1, 490
Natural science, 144, 145, 521. *See also* Science
Naturalist intelligence, 11
Negotiation of conflict, 106
Note taking during observation, 166, 167–172, 200, 395
used to place child in Developmental Continuum, 204–205
Notice of transition times, 88, 252
Number concepts, 134–135, 140. *See also* Mathematics

O

Objectives of Curriculum. *See* Goals and objectives of the Curriculum
Observing of children by teacher, 103, 122, 166–172
    art area, 337–340
    for assessment purposes, 199
    block play, 255–260
    computer activities, 484–486
    cooking activities, 456–458
    Developmental Continuum, use in, 169–172
    discovery area, 394–396
    dramatic play, 272–286
    formal observation, 167
    informal observation, 166
    library area, 365–369
    music and movement, 430–433
    note taking during, 166, 167–172, 200, 204–205, 395
    objectivity, 167–168
    outdoor play, 514–516
    sand and water play, 413–415
    toys and games play, 306–309
Occupational therapists, 37
Open-ended questions, 177–178. *See also* Interacting with children
Open house, 220, 226
Opening ritual, 85
Organization of materials and information. *See* Arrangement of objects
Outdoor play, 493–522. *See also* Field trips
    area for, 78, 496–510, 521
    children with special needs, 510
    connecting with Curriculum objectives, 494–495
    content learning via, 511–513
    frequently asked questions about, 521
    interacting with children, 517–520
    Letter to Families, 522
    materials and equipment, 497–508, 520
    observing and responding to individual children, 514–516
    safety concerns. *See* Safety
    stages of, 514–515
    teacher's role, 514–522
    weather considerations, 509, 521

P

Painting. *See* Art (visual)
Pairing children. *See* Peer buddies for children with disabilities
Parents. *See* Family communications; Family's role
Patterns and relationships, 136, 140. *See also* Mathematics
Peace table in classroom, 112
Peer buddies for children with disabilities, 180, 375, 481
People and how they live, 147–148, 150. *See also* Social studies
People and technology, 158–159, 160. *See also* Technology
People and the environment. *See* Social studies
People and the past. *See* Social studies
Personal belongings. *See* Belongings, classroom places for
Pets
    in classroom, 65, 71
    outdoor, 500–501, 512
Phonetic spelling, 129
Phonics, 127
Phonological awareness, 127–128, 132, 366
    books selected to help children with, 357
    reading aloud and, 362
    songs contributing to, 437
Photographs
    of children in classroom, 69, 77, 78, 219, 220
        labeling places for children's belongings with, 70
        permission of parents, 202
        taking during home visits prior to school, 69, 217
        use in taking attendance, 83
    of children's work, 75, 201–202
Physical activity, 5. *See also* Physical development
    bodily/kinesthetic intelligence and, 10
    games with rules involving, 13
Physical aggression, 118. *See also* Challenging behavior
Physical development, 20
    Developmental Continuum for ages 3-5, 49–50
    five-year-olds, 25
    four-year-olds, 24
    three-year-olds, 23

Physical science, 142–143, 145. *See also* Science
Physical therapists, 37
Physiological needs, 2
Piaget, Jean, 6–8
Picture labels, 66, 70, 78, 97
Pictures drawn by children. *See* Art (visual)
Pictures of children. *See* Photographs
Planning boards in interest areas, 87–88
Planning in relation to Developmental Continuum, 206–208. *See also* Developmental Continuum
Plants, 65, 71, 76, 384, 499
Plasticene, 327
Play
    afternoon time for, 93
    block play, 243–269. *See also* Block play
    computer play, 471–491. *See also* Computer play
    dramatic play, 271–293. *See also* Dramatic play
    outdoor play, 493–522. *See also* Outdoor play
    role in learning, 11–13
    sand and water play, 403–421. *See also* Sand and water play
    three-year-olds, 23
    types of, 11–13
Playdough, 326–329
Playground structures and equipment, 505–508, 521. *See also* Outdoor play
Portfolios of children's work, 200–204, 345
Postings in classroom. *See* Displays in classroom
Praise, 104–105, 261, 343–344, 517
Predictable books and stories, 356, 373
Predictions, learning how to make, 351, 488
Preoperational stage (age 2-5), 7–8
Preschool children, 18–26
    ages and stages of, 23–26
    areas of development, 18–22
    preoperational stage, 7–8
Pretend play, 12, 282. *See also* Dramatic play
    outdoor, 502–503
    toys and games used in, 307
Print, acquiring knowledge of, 128, 132. *See also* Literacy skills
Private spaces in classroom, 71, 77
Problem solving, 21, 26
    by auditory learners, 31
    by bilingual children, 39
    classroom rules, to develop, 110

Developmental Continuum for ages 3-5, 51
  in group time, 84, 114
  involving children in, 80, 88
  as process skill, 162
  social problems in classroom, 110–115
Process skills, 161–162, 392
Projects. *See* Studies and projects
Props. *See* Materials and equipment
Prosocial behavior and Developmental Continuum, 48
Public park, use for outdoor play, 508
Punishment of children by spanking, 239
Puzzles, 72, 299, 301. *See also* Toys and games

Q

Questions for children as learning technique, 177–178. See also Interacting with children
Quiet signal, 101
Quiet time, 78, 93

R

Reading aloud, 129, 370–373
Reading skills, 22. *See also* Literacy skills
  of bilingual children, 39
  Developmental Continuum for ages 3-5, 57–58, 376–377
  of gifted children, 180, 377
Recording observations. *See* Note taking during observation
Rejection, 105–108
Relationships in classroom, 102–108
  teacher with children, 102–105, 122
Repetition, 101
Representations made by children, 21, 31, 162
  Developmental Continuum for ages 3-5, 54
Research. *See* Theory and research
Resilience research, 13–14
Respect, 2, 19, 74, 108
  for children's culture. *See* Culture
  teacher's respect for each child, 103, 104
Responsibility and classroom jobs, 73–74, 78

Rest time, 91–92, 93
Retelling stories, 358, 373
Role play, 282
Rules, classroom, 108–110, 341-342, 420
Rules, games with. *See* Games

S

Safety, 2
  art materials, 347–348
  classroom rules to ensure, 108–110
  classroom space arranged for, 64
  cleaning agents, 450
  cooking area, 449, 450–452, 465–466
  dangerous behavior and, 118, 122, 174
  getting attention of children, 101
  helmets for children, 498
  outdoor play, 496, 506–508
    teacher intervention, 517
    weather conditions, 509
  pets, 500
  sand and water area, 419–420
  sharp items, classroom storage of, 67, 70
  toys and games, 301, 498
  woodworking, 341–342
Sand and water play, 403–421
  classroom area for, 62, 406–410
  connecting with Curriculum objectives, 404–405
  content learning via, 411–412
  equipment and materials for, 407–410
  frequently asked questions about, 419–420
  interacting with children in art area, 416–418
  Letter to Families, 421
  observing and responding to individual children, 413–415
  outdoor, 497–498, 512
  safety and health issues, 420, 498
  teacher's role, 413–420
Scaffolding, 9
  interacting with children by scaffolding learning, 175
Schedule. *See* Structure of day
Science, 142–145. *See also* Discovery area
  art area, learning opportunities, 345
  block play, learning opportunities, 254

  computer use, learning opportunities, 483
  connecting science content, teaching, and learning, 144–145
  content in interest areas, 188–189
  cooking experiences, learning opportunities, 454
  discovery area, learning opportunities, 392
  dramatic play, learning opportunities, 281
  earth and the environment, 144, 145
  library area, learning opportunities, 363
  life science, 143–144, 145
  music and movement, learning opportunities, 428–429
  outdoor play, learning opportunities, 512
  physical science, 142–143, 145
  sand and water area, learning opportunities, 412
  toys and games play, learning opportunities, 305
Scribbling, 337, 367
Second Language Learners. *See* English Language Learners
Security, 2, 5
Self-awareness of teachers, 213
Self-confidence, 19, 20, 103, 344
  gifted children, 36
  three-year-olds, 23
Self-control, 18, 24, 121–122, 239, 271
Self-respect, 2, 119
Senior citizen homes, partnering with, 222
Sense of self and Developmental Continuum, 46
Sensorimotor stage (birth to age 2), 7
Shame and doubt, 3–4
Sharing, 23, 24, 106. *See also* Turn taking
  classroom set-up to minimize problems of, 65, 79, 314
Sharp items, 67, 70, 447, 449, 450
Sign-in, 83, 219
Singing, 431, 436–438. *See also* Music and movement
Small-group time, 86, 185–187
  cooking activities, 460
  first few days, 101
  weekly planning for, 99
Smilansky, Sara, 11–13, 271, 282–284, 327
Smocks for children, 78, 325, 406, 408, 419, 449

Snacks, 5, 91. *See also* Cooking; Food
Snow table, 410
Social/emotional development, 5, 8–9, 18–19
    Developmental Continuum for ages 3-5, 46–48
    five-year-olds, 25
    four-year-olds, 24
    gifted children, 180
    interpersonal intelligence and, 10
    prosocial behavior and Developmental Continuum, 48
    responsibility for self and Developmental Continuum, 47
    sense of self and Developmental Continuum, 46
    three-year-olds, 23
Social studies, 146–151
    art area, learning opportunities, 345
    block play, learning opportunities, 254
    computer use, learning opportunities, 483
    connecting social studies content, teaching, and learning, 150–151
    content in interest areas, 188–189
    cooking experiences, learning opportunities, 454
    discovery area, learning opportunities, 392–393
    dramatic play, learning opportunities, 281
    geography and spaces, 146–147, 150
    library area, learning opportunities, 364
    music and movement, learning opportunities, 429
    outdoor play, learning opportunities, 513
    people and how they live, 147–148, 150
    people and the environment, 148, 151
    people and the past, 149, 151
    sand and water area, learning opportunities, 412
    toys and games, learning opportunities, 305
Socialization, 18
Sociodramatic play, 12, 153, 182. *See also* Dramatic play
Software, 477–479
Songs. *See* Music and movement; Singing
Sorting. *See* Arrangement of objects
Sounds. *See* Phonological awareness

Spanking, 239
Spatial sense. *See* Geometry and spatial sense
Spatial/visual intelligence, 10
Speaking skills. *See* Language development; Listening and speaking skills
Special education, 36–38
Special needs children, 35–38. *See also* Children with disabilities
Speech synthesizer, 481
Spelling, 129
Start of day and opening ritual, 85
Start of program year
    family communications prior to, 214–217
    first few days, 100–101
    home visits prior to. *See* Home visits
Stereotyping children and families, 35, 45, 213
Storage in classroom, 69–70
    art materials, 332
    blocks and props, 251
    CDs, 479
    computer software, 479
    cooking equipment, 449, 450
    food, 465
    library area, 361
    musical instruments, 427
    outdoor materials, 504
Story time, 99. *See also* Library
Stress and learning, 5
    families in stressful situations, 235–236
Structure of day, 82–101
    choice time, 87–88
    daily events, 82–92
    daily schedule, 77, 92–97
    first few days, 100–101
    group time, 84–86
    mealtimes, 89–91
    rest time, 91–92
    taking attendance, 82–83
    transition times, 88–89
    weekly planning, 97–100
Studies and projects, 190–198
    choice of topic for, 191
    dramatic play and, 276–279
    family participation in, 226
    planning, 192–193
    sample study of worms, 194–198
Suggestion boxes, 219
Superhero play, 291, 302
Symbolic thinking, 21, 31, 54, 351, 366
Synapse, 5

T
Tables, 64, 72, 389, 407–408, 410, 435
Take-aparts for discovery area, 390
Taking attendance, 82–83
Taking turns. *See* Turn taking
Tapes. *See* Audio materials
Teachable moments, 174–175, 377
Teacher-directed learning, 174–175
Teacher's role, 13, 103, 165–209
    adapting instruction to include all children, 179–183
    approaches to guide learning, 173–178
    art area, 336–348
    assessing children's learning, 199–208
    block play, 255–269
    coaching children on behavior, 106–107, 120
    computer activities, 484–490, 489–490
    cooking experiences, 456–468
    dramatic play, 282–292
    group instruction, 183–187
    helping children make friends, 105–108
    interacting with children. *See* Interacting with children
    interest areas, teaching of, 187–189
    library, 365–378
    music and movement, 430–440
    observing of children, 166–172. *See also* Observing of children by teacher
    outdoor play, 514–522
    praising children. *See* Praise
    relationship with children, 102–105, 122
    sand and water play, 413–420
    self-awareness and family differences, 213
    studies to integrate learning, 190–198
    toys and games, 306–314
Teaching approaches to guide learning, 173–178
Technology, 156–160. *See also* Computer play
    art area, learning opportunities, 335
    awareness of, 157, 160
    basic operations and concepts, 157, 160

block play, learning opportunities, 254

computer use, learning opportunities, 483

connecting technology content, teaching, and learning, 159–160

content in interest areas, 188–189

cooking experiences, learning opportunities, 455

discovery area, learning opportunities, 393

dramatic play, learning opportunities, 281

library area, learning opportunities, 364

music and movement, learning opportunities, 429

outdoor play, learning opportunities, 513

people and, 158–159, 160

sand and water area, learning opportunities, 412

tools, 158, 160, 393

toys and games play, learning opportunities, 305

Temper tantrums, 119. *See also* Challenging behavior

Temperament, 28–30

Testing limits, 117–118. *See also* Disruptive behavior

Theory and research, 1–15

brain research, 5–6, 20, 32

Erikson, Eric, 3–4

Gardner, Howard, 9–11

Maslow, Abraham, 2–3

Piaget, Jean, 6–8

resilience research, 13–14

Smilansky, Sara, 11–13

Vygotsky, Lev, 8–9

Three-year-olds, 23–24

computer use by, 489

small group time for, 86

understanding rules, 108, 307

Time. *See* Structure of day

Tours of classroom, 101, 220

Toys and games, 295–315

classroom area for, 62, 75, 298–303

computers in toy and game area, 474

connecting with Curriculum objectives, 296–297

content learning via, 304–305

displaying and caring for, 303

frequently asked questions about, 313–314

games with rules, 13, 307

interacting with children playing with, 310–312

Letter to Families, 315

observing and responding to individual children, 306–309

open-ended toys, 300, 313

selection of materials for, 299–302

teacher's role, 306–314

violent toys and games, 301, 302

Traffic patterns in classroom, 64, 72, 79

Transition times, 88–89, 101, 180, 371, 440

Trust, 3, 18, 23

building trust with families, 221

Turn taking, 19, 23, 106, 307, 314

U

Unfinished projects, preservation of, 75

V

Verbal intelligence, 10

Violence

gun-free zone, 268

toys and games, avoiding emphasis on violence, 301, 302

Visitors to classroom, 218–219, 223

Visual art. *See* Art (visual)

Visual cues for children with disabilities, 180–181

Visual impairment. *See* Children with disabilities

Visual intelligence, 10

Visual learners, 31

Vocabulary growth, 22, 126–127, 132, 357, 366. *See also* Language development

Vygotsky, Lev, 8–9

W

Walks outdoors, 519–520

Warning of transitions, 88, 252

Weather considerations for outdoor play, 509, 521

Web sites, access by children, 479–480

Wechsler Intelligence Scale for Children, 9. *See also* IQ

Weekly planning, 97–100

Weekly Planning Forms, 98–99, 526–529

Welcoming children to classroom, first few days, 100–101

Welcoming family to classroom, 218–219, 223

Woodworking, 331, 341–342

Work of children. *See* Children's work

Worms, study of, 194–198, 501

Writing skills, 22, 367–368. *See also* Literacy skills

Developmental Continuum for ages 3-5, 57–58

teaching formal handwriting, 377

Z

Zone of Proximal Development (ZPD), 9

About the Authors

Diane Trister Dodge

Diane Trister Dodge, M.S., founder and president of Teaching Strategies, Inc., is a well-known speaker and author of numerous books for teachers, administrators, and parents. She has worked in Head Start, child care, and public school programs as a teacher and trainer and directed national projects on early childhood education. She served on the Governing Board of the National Association for the Education of Young Children (1990-1994), and the Center for the Child Care Workforce. She currently sits on the boards of several other local and national organizations serving young children and families.

Laura J. Colker

Laura J. Colker, Ed.D., is the author or co-author of numerous articles, monographs, and books for teachers, caregivers, administrators, families, and children. She is a guest editor for NAEYC's *Young Children* and is an ongoing consultant to the Department of Defense Education Activity's Sure Start and kindergarten programs and Reading Is Fundamental (RIF). Dr. Colker conducts staff development and teaches courses on child development issues worldwide.

Cate Heroman

Cate Heroman, M.Ed., Director of Preschool/Kindergarten Initiatives at Teaching Strategies, Inc., is the co-author of several books on curriculum and assessment. She helped to develop CreativeCurriculum.net, an interactive web-based assessment system linked to *The Creative Curriculum Developmental Continuum*. In addition to her many years as a preschool and kindergarten teacher, she is an experienced staff developer and served as an administrator in early childhood and elementary education at the Louisiana Department of Education.

Notes

Notes

Order Form

Please type or print clearly.

4 Ways to Order

Order online
www.TeachingStrategies.com

Order by phone
800-637-3652
Washington, DC area
301-634-0818
8:30 a.m.–5:30 p.m. Eastern Time, M–F

Order by fax
301-634-0826
24 hours a day

Order by mail
Teaching Strategies, Inc.
P.O. Box 42243
Washington, DC 20015

Ship to:

NAME

ORGANIZATION

ADDRESS

CITY	STATE	ZIP
PHONE	FAX	

E-MAIL

Bill to:

Your Teaching Strategies Customer Number:
(If known)

NAME

ORGANIZATION

ADDRESS

CITY	STATE	ZIP
PHONE	FAX	

Order:

ITEM #	QTY	DESCRIPTION	UNIT PRICE	TOTAL
			$	$
			$	$
			$	$
			$	$
			$	$
			$	$
			$	$
			$	$
			$	$
			$	$

Please call for information on quantity discounts.

	SUBTOTAL	$
	SALES TAX CA, DC, IL, MD, NC: Add appropriate sales tax.	$
	SHIPPING **United States:** Orders up to $60.00—$5.00; Orders over $60.00—12% of total. **International/U.S. Territories:** $20.00 (first book) + $7.00 for each additional book. **Rush Delivery:** Call for shipping charges. **Method:** ❏ 2-day ❏ 3-day ❏ Next-day ❏ International	$
	TOTAL	$

Method of payment

All orders must be accompanied by payment, P.O. number, or credit card information. Customers with an established credit history are welcome to use P.O. numbers.
First-time customers must enclose pre-payment with order.

❏ Check (payable to Teaching Strategies)   ❏ Money order

❏ Purchase order (must include copy of P.O.)   ❏ Visa   ❏ MasterCard

❏ American Express   ❏ Discover

CREDIT CARD OR PURCHASE ORDER NUMBER   EXPIRATION DATE

SIGNATURE OF CARD HOLDER

❏ Yes, I would like to receive occasional e-mail notifications about new Teaching Strategies products and special offers. I understand that Teaching Strategies will not share or sell my e-mail address with any other individual, company, or organization.

Guarantee: Teaching Strategies guarantees your complete satisfaction. If you are not happy with your order, simply return the item(s) in sellable condition within 30 days for a full refund, excluding shipping and handling fees. However, all video/DVD and software sales are final. Teaching Strategies is not responsible for returned items that are lost or misdirected. Prices subject to change without notice.

Thank you for your order.

Teaching Strategies, Inc. strives to improve the quality of early childhood programs by producing comprehensive and practical curriculum and training materials. Our products and staff development services are making a difference in preschools, elementary schools, Head Start, school-age programs, and child care programs worldwide.

Curriculum

The Creative Curriculum® for Preschool
This fully updated edition keeps its original environmentally-based approach and clearly defines the teacher's vital role in connecting content, teaching, and learning.
#CB0019, $44.95
Also available in Spanish: #CB0155, $44.95

A Trainer's Guide to The Creative Curriculum® for Preschool
Volume 1: Getting Started
This book features workshops on each component and interest area of the Curriculum. It is a strong foundation for starting to use *The Creative Curriculum®*.
#CB0177, $39.95

The Creative Curriculum® for Preschool Implementation Checklist
This tool assesses the degree to which *The Creative Curriculum® for Preschool* is being implemented as intended. Designed for use by teachers, administrators/supervisors, and trainers.
#CB0156, $19.95
Classroom Profile: **#CB0157, $14.95 (set of 10)**
Progress & Planning Form: **#CB0158, $14.95 (set of 20)**

Also available in Spanish: #CB1249, $19.95
Classroom Profile: **#CB1256, $14.95 (set of 10)**
Progress & Planning Form: **#CB1263, $14.95 (set of 20)**

Assessment

The Creative Curriculum® Developmental Continuum Assessment Toolkit for Ages 3–5
An integrated assessment system using a valid and reliable instrument—*The Creative Curriculum® Developmental Continuum for Ages 3–5*. Provides tools to collect data and analyze children's progress. Boxed set contains forms to record progress for a class at three checkpoints each year.
#CB0130, $89.95
Also available in Spanish: #CB0142, $89.95

CreativeCurriculum.net
A complete online version of our assessment and outcomes reporting tools. Includes individual child profiles, group planning reports, parent communication features, and activities for each child. For a free 30-day trial, visit www.CreativeCurriculum.net.

Literacy

Literacy: The Creative Curriculum® Approach
Preschool literacy experiences should be intentionally built into the entire daily schedule and all interest areas in the classroom. This book shows you how to maximize literacy learning opportunities within the context of a comprehensive, integrated curriculum. This book supplements *The Creative Curriculum® for Preschool*.
#CB7877, $39.95

A Trainer's Guide to The Creative Curriculum® for Preschool
Volume 2: Literacy
A companion to Literacy: The Creative Curriculum Approach, this book provides a series of workshops designed to help teachers create literacy-rich environments and maximize literacy learning throughout the day.
#CB7842, $29.95

Mathematics: The Creative Curriculum® Approach
Young children love mathematics and are interested in numbers, shapes, sizes, and patterns. The preschool teacher can use these interests to purposefully build mathematical knowledge and understanding by carefully planning lessons and maximizing learning in interest areas and throughout the day. Children will thus learn math as part of a comprehensive, integrated curriculum. This book supplements *The Creative Curriculum® for Preschool*.
#CB7880, $39.95

Studies

The Creative Curriculum® Study Starters
This science and social studies resource—a set of guides to developing studies that spark children's curiosity—helps you identify children's questions, learn background information, organize the environment, support investigations, include content knowledge, and involve families.

Volume 1: Set of six, *Teacher's Guide,* and binder: #CB108X, $64.95
Volume 2: Set of six, *Teacher's Guide,* and binder: #CB1171, $64.95
Individual topics: $12.95

For complete list of currently available titles visit www.TeachingStrategies.com/studystarters